Research Methods in
Intercultural Communication

Guides to Research Methods in Language and Linguistics

Series Editor: Li Wei, University College London, London, UK

The science of language encompasses a truly interdisciplinary field of research, with a wide range of focuses, approaches, and objectives. While linguistics has its own traditional approaches, a variety of other intellectual disciplines have contributed methodological perspectives that enrich the field as a whole. As a result, linguistics now draws on state-of-the-art work from such fields as psychology, computer science, biology, neuroscience and cognitive science, sociology, music, philosophy, and anthropology.

The interdisciplinary nature of the field presents both challenges and opportunities to students who must understand a variety of evolving research skills and methods. The *Guides to Research Methods in Language and Linguistics* addresses these skills in a systematic way for advanced students and beginning researchers in language science. The books in this series focus especially on the relationships between theory, methods and data- the understanding of which is fundamental to the successful completion of research projects and the advancement of knowledge.

Published

1. *The Blackwell Guide to Research Methods in Bilingualism and Multilingualism*
   Edited by Li Wei and Melissa G. Moyer

2. *Research Methods in Child Language: A Practical Guide*
   Edited by Erika Hoff

3. *Research Methods in Second Language Acquisition: A Practical Guide*
   Edited by Susan M. Gass and Alison Mackey

4. *Research Methods in Clinical Linguistics and Phonetics: A Practical Guide*
   Edited by Nicole Müller and Martin J. Ball

5. *Research Methods in Sociolinguistics: A Practical Guide*
   Edited by Janet Holmes and Kirk Hazen

6. *Research Methods in Sign Language Studies: A Practical Guide*
   Edited by Eleni Orfanidou, Bencie Woll, and Gary Morgan

7. *Research Methods in Language Policy and Planning: A Practical Guide*
   Edited by Francis Hult and David Cassels Johnson

8. *Research Methods in Intercultural Communication: A Practical Guide*
   Edited by Zhu Hua

Research Methods in Intercultural Communication

A Practical Guide

Edited by Zhu Hua

WILEY Blackwell

This edition first published 2016
© 2016 John Wiley & Sons Inc

Registered Office
John Wiley & Sons Ltd, The Atrium, Southern Gate, Chichester, West Sussex, PO19 8SQ, UK

Editorial Offices
350 Main Street, Malden, MA 02148-5020, USA
9600 Garsington Road, Oxford, OX4 2DQ, UK
The Atrium, Southern Gate, Chichester, West Sussex, PO19 8SQ, UK

For details of our global editorial offices, for customer services, and for information about how to apply for permission to reuse the copyright material in this book please see our website at www.wiley.com/wiley-blackwell.

The right of Zhu Hua to be identified as the author of the editorial material in this work has been asserted in accordance with the UK Copyright, Designs and Patents Act 1988.

All rights reserved. No part of this publication may be reproduced, stored in a retrieval system, or transmitted, in any form or by any means, electronic, mechanical, photocopying, recording or otherwise, except as permitted by the UK Copyright, Designs and Patents Act 1988, without the prior permission of the publisher.

Wiley also publishes its books in a variety of electronic formats. Some content that appears in print may not be available in electronic books.

Designations used by companies to distinguish their products are often claimed as trademarks. All brand names and product names used in this book are trade names, service marks, trademarks or registered trademarks of their respective owners. The publisher is not associated with any product or vendor mentioned in this book.

Limit of Liability/Disclaimer of Warranty: While the publisher and authors have used their best efforts in preparing this book, they make no representations or warranties with respect to the accuracy or completeness of the contents of this book and specifically disclaim any implied warranties of merchantability or fitness for a particular purpose. It is sold on the understanding that the publisher is not engaged in rendering professional services and neither the publisher nor the author shall be liable for damages arising herefrom. If professional advice or other expert assistance is required, the services of a competent professional should be sought.

Library of Congress Cataloging-in-Publication Data

Research methods in intercultural communication : a practical guide / edited by Zhu Hua. – First Edition.
    pages cm. – (Guides to research methods in language and linguistics)
  ISBN 978-1-118-83746-7 (hardback) – ISBN 978-1-118-83743-6 (paper)   1. Intercultural communication–Research.   2. Intercultural communication–Methodology.   I. Hua, Zhu, 1970– editor.
  P94.6.R48 2016
  303.48′20721–dc23
                                                                                          2015023712

A catalogue record for this book is available from the British Library.

Cover image: © kaan tanman/Getty

Set in 10/12pt Sabon by Aptara Inc., New Delhi, India

1   2016

Contents

Notes on Contributors		vii
Acknowledgements		xiii
Preface		xv

I   Linking Themes, Paradigms, and Methods

1	Identifying Research Paradigms *Zhu Hua*	3
2	Studying Culture *Adrian Holliday*	23
3	Studying Identity *Jo Angouri*	37
4	Studying Discourse *Leila Monaghan*	53

II   Key Issues and Challenges

5	How to Identify Research Questions *Zhu Hua, Prue Holmes, Tony Young, and Jo Angouri*	73
6	How to Research Multilingually: Possibilities and Complexities *Prue Holmes, Richard Fay, Jane Andrews, and Mariam Attia*	88
7	How to Research Interculturally and Ethically *Jane Woodin*	103
8	How to Assess Intercultural Competence *Darla K. Deardorff*	120
9	How to Work with Research Participants: The Researcher's Role *Fred Dervin*	135
10	How to Develop a Research Proposal *Jane Jackson*	147

III Methods

11	Questionnaires and Surveys *Tony Johnstone Young*	165
12	Interviews *Barbara Gibson and Zhu Hua*	181
13	The Matched-Guise Technique *Ruth Kircher*	196
14	Discourse Completion Tasks *Emma Sweeney and Zhu Hua*	212
15	The Critical Incident Technique *Helen Spencer-Oatey and Claudia Harsch*	223
16	Ethnography *Jane Jackson*	239
17	Virtual Ethnography *Aoife Lenihan and Helen Kelly-Holmes*	255
18	Multimodality *Agnieszka Lyons*	268
19	Critical Discourse Analysis *John P. O'Regan and Anne Betzel*	281
20	Conversation Analysis *Adam Brandt and Kristian Mortensen*	297
21	Corpus Analysis *Michael Handford*	311
22	Narrative Analysis *Anna De Fina*	327

Index   343

Notes on Contributors

Jane Andrews is Senior Lecturer in Education at the University of the West of England, UK. She teaches on education and early childhood studies undergraduate programs, jointly leads the professional doctorate in Education (EdD), and supervises doctoral students in areas of language and education.

Jo Angouri is an Associate Professor at the University of Warwick, UK. Her research expertise is in sociolinguistics, pragmatics, and discourse analysis. She has carried out research in a range of corporate and institutional contexts and her work concerns both online and face to face interaction. She has published work on language and identity as well as teamwork and leadership in medical settings. She has recently edited a special issue on Multilingualism in the Workplace (*Multilingua*, 2014) and co-edited one (with Ruth Wodak) on Euro/Crisis Discourses (*Discourse and Society*, 2014).

Mariam Attia is Research Associate at the School of Education, Durham University, UK, where she combines her commitment to researcher development with her exploration of the processes of researching multilingually. Her research interests cover the areas of reflective practice, teacher development, and non-judgmental discourse in professional interaction.

Anne Betzel is Lecturer in Applied Linguistics at Middlesex University and Kingston University, UK, where she teaches a number of undergraduate and postgraduate modules in English Language and English Language Teaching. Her research interests include language and politics, critical discourse analysis, and the role of language in constructing different types of social practices.

Adam Brandt is a Lecturer in Applied Linguistics at Newcastle University (UK), where he is a Degree Program Director for a range of MAs in Cross-Cultural Communication, and teaches courses on "Methods in Cross-Cultural Communication Research" and "Micro-Analysis of Intercultural Interaction." His research employs CA and MCA, particularly in settings where interculturality and/or second language use is relevant. He has published research in journals such as *Language and Intercultural Communication* and *Discourse Processes*.

Anna De Fina is Professor of Italian Language and Linguistics in the Italian Department and Affiliated Faculty with the Linguistics Department at Georgetown University, USA. Her interests and publications focus on discourse and migration, identity, and narrative. Her books include *Identity in narrative: A study of immigrant discourse* (2003, John Benjamins), *Analyzing narratives* (2012, Cambridge University Press, co-authored with Alexandra Georgakopoulou), and the co-edited volumes *Dislocations, relocations, narratives of migration* (2005, St. Jerome Publishing, with M. Baynham), and *Discourse and identity* (2006, Cambridge University Press, with Deborah Schiffrin and Michael Bamberg).

Darla K. Deardorff is a research scholar at Duke University (Durham, USA) as well as Research Associate at Nelson Mandela Metropolitan University (South Africa) and at Meiji University (Japan). Known for developing the first research-based framework of intercultural competence, she is author of numerous publications including *The Sage handbook of intercultural competence* (Sage, 2009) and *Demystifying outcomes assessment for international educators* (Stylus, 2015). She is a frequently invited speaker around the world and founder of ICC Global.

Fred Dervin is Professor of Multicultural Education at the University of Helsinki (Finland). He also holds several associate professorships around the world. Dervin specializes in language and intercultural education, the sociology of multiculturalism, and linguistics for intercultural communication and education. He has widely published in international journals on identity, the "intercultural," and mobility/migration. His website: http://blogs.helsinki.fi/dervin/.

Richard Fay is a Lecturer in Education (TESOL and Intercultural Communication) at The University of Manchester's Institute of Education (UK). He co-ordinates the PhD in Education (with a particular focus on applied linguistics research), and leads both the MA in Intercultural Communication and the Manchester Global Award. He is currently a Co-Investigator on the AHRC-funded project "Researching Multilingually at the Borders of Language, the Body, Law and the State."

Barbara Gibson is a consultant, researcher and lecturer focused on intercultural communication and global business. With more than 25 years' experience as a corporate communication professional, she has worked with companies worldwide, and is a past international Chair of the International Association of Business Communicators. She currently serves as President of the UK chapter of the Society for Intercultural Education, Training & Research (SIETAR). She lectures at both undergraduate and postgraduate levels for a number of institutions, including Birkbeck, University of London; Syracuse University; Hult International Business School and Oklahoma City University.

Michael Handford is Professor of the Institute for Innovation in International Engineering Education at the University of Tokyo, Japan, where he lectures graduates on professional discourse analysis and intercultural communication. He has published in the areas of ESP, professional and business discourse, intercultural communication, and conflictual communication, is the author of *The language of business meetings*

(Cambridge University Press), and is co-editor, along with James Paul Gee, of *The Routledge handbook of discourse analysis*.

Claudia Harsch is an Associate Professor at The Centre for Applied Linguistics, the University of Warwick, UK. She researches and teaches in the fields of language assessment, educational evaluation and measurement, intercultural communication, the implementation of the Common European Framework, and teacher training. She explores aspects like the conceptualization of intercultural competencies and ways to foster and assess them, the role of assessment across cultures or the development and validation of tools for educational evaluation. Claudia is interested in teacher training and ongoing professional development, specifically in the field of assessment literacy.

Adrian Holliday is Professor of Applied Linguistics at Canterbury Christ Church University, UK, where he directs doctoral research in the critical sociology of TESOL and intercultural communication. He has written about appropriate methodology, native-speakerism, qualitative research methods and intercultural communication. His recent book, *Understanding intercultural communication: Negotiating a grammar of culture*, Routledge 2013, explores the engagement with intercultural issues in everyday life.

Prue Holmes is Reader in the School of Education at Durham University, UK. She leads the MA program on Intercultural Communication and Education, and supervises doctoral students in this area. She is Co-Investigator on the AHRC-funded "Researching Multilingually at the Borders of Language, the Body, Law and the State." (http://researching-multilingually-at-borders.com/) and the EU-funded project "Intercultural resources for Erasmus Students and their Teachers" (IEREST) (http://ierest-project.eu/). Prue publishes in the areas of intercultural communication and education, and student mobility. She chairs the *International Association of Languages and Intercultural Communication* (IALIC).

Jane Jackson is Professor of Applied Linguistics and Intercultural Communication in the English Department at the Chinese University of Hong Kong. Her primary research interests are education abroad, language and intercultural communication, and identity. Recent books include *Introducing language and intercultural communication* (Routledge, 2014), *The Routledge handbook of language and intercultural communication* (Editor) (Routledge, 2012), *Intercultural journeys: From study to residence abroad* (Palgrave MacMillan, 2010), and *Language, identity, and study abroad: sociocultural perspectives* (Equinox, 2008).

Helen Kelly-Holmes is a Senior Lecturer in Sociolinguistics and New Media at the University of Limerick, Ireland. Her research interests focus on the interrelationships between (new) media, markets and languages, and on economic aspects of multilingualism. Her publications include *Advertising as multilingual communication* (Palgrave, 2005), *Language and the market* (edited with Gerlinde Mautner, Palgrave Macmillan, 2010), *Multilingualism and the periphery* (ed. with Sari Pietikäinen, Oxford University Press, 2013) and *Thematising multilingualism in the media* (edited with Tomasso Milani, John Benjamins, 2013).

Ruth Kircher is a lecturer in English Language at Liverpool Hope University in the UK. Her research interests are in the fields of sociolinguistics, the social psychology of language, and second-language learning. In particular, her research focuses on societal multilingualism and related issues such as social identities, language attitudes, and language policy and planning. Ruth is especially interested in contexts in which minority languages co-exist alongside English, including French in Canada and Welsh in the UK.

Aoife Lenihan is an independent researcher having completed her PhD on new media and sociolinguistics. Her main research interests include multilingualism, minority languages, globalization, media discourse and new media. Her work has appeared in *Digital discourse* (Oxford 2011) and *The language of social media* (Palgrave 2014).

Agnieszka Lyons is a Lecturer in Applied Linguistics at Queen Mary University of London, UK. Her research interests include multimodal and mediated discourse analysis, intercultural communication as well as text-based mobile and electronically mediated communication, particularly in the context of establishing reference frame and enacting physicality. She is interested in the notion of evoked multimodality and narrativity in text-based forms of electronically mediated discourse.

Leila Monaghan has a PhD in linguistic anthropology and currently teaches at Southern Illinois University, Carbondale, USA. Her research and teaching crosses the fields of anthropology, communication, history, Deaf studies, disability studies, women's studies and American Indian studies. Co-edited books include *Many ways to be Deaf* and *A cultural approach to interpersonal communication*. Her current research is on Arapaho and Cheyenne women in the Great Plains Wars.

Kristian Mortensen is Associate Professor at the Department of Design and Communication, University of Southern Denmark. His work focuses on social interaction as an embodied and situated practice and the range of resources (in particular verbal and vocal, the human body and material artefacts) that participants draw on in their sense-making practices. His work has appeared in journals such as *Discourse Processes*, *Journal of Pragmatics* and *Journal of Applied Linguistics*.

John P. O'Regan is Senior Lecturer in Applied Linguistics at UCL Institute of Education, University College London, UK, where he is a doctoral supervisor and leads the MA in Applied Linguistics. He specializes in World Englishes, intercultural communication, and critical discourse analysis, and is the author of articles covering a wide range of topics in applied linguistics and cultural studies.

Helen Spencer-Oatey is a Professor and Director of The Centre for Applied Linguistics, the University of Warwick, UK. Her main research interests are in intercultural interaction, face, and interpersonal relations. Her current research projects include the competencies of global leaders and employees, and intercultural integration in educational contexts. Her publications include the following books: *Culturally speaking* (2000/2008, Continuum), the *Handbook of intercultural communication*

(2007/2009, de Gruyter, with Kotthoff), and *Intercultural interaction* (2009, Palgrave Macmillan, with Franklin).

Emma Sweeney is a teacher of English language and Study Skills for Specific Academic Purposes at INTO University of Exeter. Her main research interest is intercultural business communication. She has published articles in the *Journal of Business Communication* and *Intercultural Communication*.

Jane Woodin is Director of MA Studies for the School of Languages and Cultures at the University of Sheffield, UK. She has run a Masters program in Intercultural Communication since 2003, and recently set up an MA Program in Intercultural Communication and International Development. Her research interests include intercultural communication in applied linguistics, discourse and conversation analysis, language teacher education and dialogic approaches to learning. Her work has appeared in journals such as *ReCALL*, *Language and Intercultural Communication*, and the *European Journal of Higher Education*.

Tony Johnstone Young is Senior Lecturer in Language and Communication at Newcastle University, in the north of England. His research and supervision focuses on intergroup communication, particularly between people living with dementia and medical professionals; between "international" students and hosts in higher education contexts; and between teachers and learners in English language classrooms, and he has published extensively in these areas. In 2010 he was awarded the James J Bradac Prize for his contributions to dementia communications research.

Zhu Hua is Professor of Applied Linguistics and Communication at Birkbeck, University of London, UK. Her main research interests are intercultural pragmatics, language and intercultural communication, and child language development. Her most recent book-length publications on Intercultural Communication include *The language and intercultural communication reader* (2011, Routledge) and *Exploring intercultural communication: language in action* (2014, Routledge). She is a joint editor for the book series *Routledge Studies in Language and Intercultural Communication*.

Acknowledgements

This publication is the product of collaborative efforts of many people. When Li Wei set up the series *Guides to Research Methods in Language and Linguistics*, modelled on his successful and award-winning *The Blackwell Guide to Research Methods in Bilingualism and Multilingualism* (co-edited with Melissa Moyer), I was approached by Danielle Descoteaux at Wiley-Blackwell to compile a volume on intercultural communication. I liked the idea, but could not immediately embark on the project, since I was working my way through a research monograph. Thank you, Danielle and Li Wei, for your patience and the gentle nudges at the right times. I am glad that I took on the challenge.

The contributors have been wonderful to work with. Their professionalism and collegiality have made the whole process enjoyable. Thanks also go to Julia Kirk at Wiley-Blackwell whose editorial support has been most effective. I am also grateful to Jennifer Watson, who proofread a selection of this collection. The editing of the book benefitted from a three-month sabbatical leave granted by Birkbeck College, University of London in 2013. Last but not least, I would like to thank Li Wei whose support as my "significant other," colleague, and Series Editor is indispensable as ever.

Preface

As part of the series *Guides to Research Methods in Language and Linguistics*, this volume aims to provide an introduction to the key methodological issues and concerns in the study of Intercultural Communication for students on advanced undergraduate and postgraduate programmes in Intercultural Communication, language and linguistics, applied linguistics, TESOL, education, translation, communication studies, and other related subjects. It can also be used by research students in these subject areas.

As a field of enquiry growing out of a number of disciplines and subdisciplines, Intercultural Communication does not "own" many discipline-specific methods and methodologies, although it has witnessed and contributed to the development of some distinctive research paradigms over the years. Many of the methods used in Intercultural Communication studies are adopted from other disciplines. With many methodology guides available, including previously published edited volumes in this series and many volumes on single methods (e.g. longitudinal study, interviews, questionnaires, conversation analysis, etc.), this volume does not intend to give verbatim guidance on general principles and procedures of methodologies that have been used and written extensively elsewhere. Rather, it aims to contextualize research methods and methodologies in Intercultural Communication studies by examining how research paradigms influence the way Intercultural Communication scholars study culture, identity, and discourse (Part I), what issues are specific to or salient in Intercultural Communication research (Part II); and what type of research questions a methodology is suitable for in the context of Intercultural Communication studies and the new frontiers in Intercultural Communication research (Part III).

The volume does not start with methods. Rather, it opens with two parts that often receive little attention in research training, but have significant bearings on the validity of research questions and the interpretation of results. Part I focuses on linking themes, paradigms and methods. It starts with an overview of research paradigms, followed by chapters dedicated to three key topics in the study of Intercultural Communication: culture, identity, and discourse. Part II discusses the key issues and challenges in research strategies, planning, and implementation, including identifying research questions, researching multilingually, interculturally, and ethically, myths and challenges in measuring intercultural competence, the researcher's role, and a step-by-step guide to developing a research proposal. Part III comprises accounts of twelve research methods or techniques. Each chapter addresses the questions of what the method is about, why this method and why not (strengths and limitations), how to do it, what research themes this method is associated with, how it works with other methods, and what are the new and emerging data-collection and analysis methods and tools.

To illustrate what it is like to apply a method, most chapters feature at least one Case in Point or Case Study, where examples of published studies or projects, sometimes undertaken by the contributors themselves, are summarized and reflected on. Each chapter includes special features – a Summary, Key terms, and Further Reading and Resources – to help the reader to explore each topic further beyond the contents of the chapter.

Part I Linking Themes, Paradigms, and Methods

1 Identifying Research Paradigms

Zhu Hua

> **Summary**
>
> This chapter starts with an overview of the multidisciplinary nature of Intercultural Communication as a field of enquiry. It then discusses what a paradigm is and why it is essential to understand paradigms before embarking on research designs. It introduces five key paradigms in Intercultural Communication studies: positivist, interpretative, critical, constructivist, and realist paradigms, in terms of their main assumptions, research themes, and disciplinary connections. Some general questions regarding paradigms are discussed in the last section.

Introduction

Intercultural Communication as a field of enquiry is concerned with how people from different "cultural" backgrounds interact with each other and negotiate "cultural" or linguistic differences perceived or made relevant through interactions, as well as the impact such interactions have on group relations and on individuals' identities, attitudes and behaviors. Although, historically, terms such as "cross-cultural communication," "inter-ethnic communication," "inter-racial communication," and, more recently, "international communication" have been used, more and more people now use Intercultural Communication as an umbrella term to include studies of interactions between people of different cultures, comparative studies of communication patterns across cultures and studies of discursive construction and negotiation of cultural differences.

The field of Intercultural Communication (abbreviated as IC) has a distinctive, multidisciplinary background. Its main concerns have been researched extensively, and largely separately, across a number of established disciplinary and theoretical perspectives including the following:

- The disciplines that examine linguistic and interactional aspects of communication between different groups, such as interactional sociolinguistics, pragmatics, cross-cultural / intercultural pragmatics, discourse studies, translation studies, ELF (English as Lingua Franca) and bi- / multilingualism studies.
- The disciplines that are concerned with the development and learning of skills to communicate interculturally, such as intercultural education, language learning and teaching.
- The disciplines that study cultural practices or seek to identify cultural variations in communication patterns, such as cultural and linguistic anthropology, ethnicity studies, gender studies.
- The disciplines that regard Intercultural Communication as a special case of communication, such as communication studies and interpersonal communication.
- The disciplines that study human behavior and mental process including both their variability and common trends under diverse cultural conditions, such as cross-cultural psychology.
- The disciplines which critically examine the relationships between culture, communication and power (e.g. global politics of cultural prejudice), such as critical discourse studies and critical cultural studies.
- The (sub)disciplines and models that look at contributions that society makes to individual development through interactions between people and the culture in which they live in, such as sociocultural theory of learning in second language acquisition.

As a consequence of its multidisciplinary nature and the inherent complexity of the phenomenon under study (e.g. debates on what culture is, Holliday, 2011, 2013, Chapter 2, this volume), IC studies encompass many different paradigms. While different paradigms complement each other and potentially bring a rich understanding of the phenomenon under study, they can also be a source of confusion for newcomers to the field. In this chapter, I shall first outline what a paradigm is and then introduce five key paradigms in the field of Intercultural Communication in terms of their main assumptions and research themes and disciplinary connections. Some general questions regarding paradigms are discussed in the last section.

What is a Paradigm?

A paradigm is the overarching constructive framework and meta-thinking behind a piece of research. It is "a way of examining social phenomenon from which particular understandings of these phenomena can be gained and explanations attempted"

(Saunders, Lewis, & Thornhill, 2007, p. 112). It represents "a general philosophical orientation about the world and the nature of research that a researcher brings to a study" (Creswell, 2014, p. 6). Admittedly, the term is difficult to grasp. A paradigm is often presented as a philosophical debate with many big, unfriendly, abstract terms thrown into the mix. People often have their own interpretation of what a paradigm is and what differences there are between research paradigm, approach, design, and method (cf. the figure on the interconnection of worldviews, designs, and research methods in Creswell, 2014, p. 5). In practice, paradigms do not get much attention in research method training: they are often treated as something added on, rather than introduced as an essential consideration. The lack of translation equivalent in many languages also makes it difficult for students to fully embrace the concept.

Putting aside these difficulties, I cannot but stress the essential role of paradigms in research design. Paradigms determine research design and data collection method(s) and analysis and not the other way around. De Vaus (2001) once compared the role and purpose of a research design in a project to knowing what sort of building (such as an office building, a factory for manufacturing machinery, a school, etc.) is being constructed before ordering materials or setting critical dates for completion of the project stages. Following this analogy, paradigms would be equivalent to architectural styles, i.e., whether it is going to be gothic, baroque, modern, postmodern, oriental, etc. In the context of IC studies, the issue of paradigms is even more relevant, given its connections with multiple disciplines, since each discipline has different takes on what culture is, what Intercultural Communication is about, and the role culture plays in everyday life. Awareness of differences or tensions between different paradigms would help researchers find a "path" through the vast amount of literature available in the field and appreciate the different perspectives and insights that are offered by different paradigms.

So, what are the key paradigms out there? You may have come across many terms ending with "-ism," such as positivism, postpositivism, constructivism, interpretivism, pragmatism, etc. They are, indeed, some examples of paradigms often mentioned in the literature. To tell them apart from each other, scholars (e.g. Guba & Lincoln, 1994) often ask the following questions:

1 What are the form and the nature of reality? Does the "reality" under study exist and operate independently? Or is it subject to perceptions and actions of individuals or social actors who inhabit it? These questions are often described as researchers' "ontological" positions.
2 What is the nature of acceptable knowledge and findings and what is the nature of the relationship between the researchers and their findings? What counts as data and findings? Are they regarded as truth or facts waiting to be discovered or are they subject to the researcher's interpretation or mediation? These questions are sometimes referred to as "epistemological" concerns.

Answers to these two sets of questions differentiate each research paradigm. In the following section, I shall introduce five identifiable research paradigms in the field of Intercultural Communication with illustrative examples. The boundaries of paradigms are not set in stone. Scholars may have different interpretations of what has made a paradigm interpretive, critical or constructivist. There are cross-overs in conceptualizations and agendas between different paradigms, in particular, among the last four paradigms.

Amid the literature aiming to compare and explain various research paradigms generically, I find two publications particularly useful. One is Guba & Lincoln's book chapter (1994) which compares the four paradigms – positivism, postpositivism, critical theory, and constructivism – in terms of their positions with regard to the sets of questions discussed above. The other is John Creswell's book (2014) on research design, in which he highlights differences between positivist, constructivist, transformative, and pragmatism paradigms in a less terminology-laden manner. The discussion on the key generic features of each paradigm in IC studies below is largely based on Guba & Lincoln (1994) and Creswell (2014). The discussion on how these features manifest themselves in IC studies is informed by Martin, Nakayama, & Flores' work (2002) and the overview and the scope represented in various published handbooks and readers available in the field.

What are the Significant Paradigms in Intercultural Communication studies?

First of all, what are the key paradigm questions to be asked in IC studies? Translating the general ontological and epistemological questions discussed above to the context of IC research, these are:

- Reality (ontological) questions:
    - What is culture and what is not culture?
    - Is there such a thing as a cultural norm?
    - How does culture influence individuals' communication behaviors or practice? Is there a cause-and-effect relationship between culture and individuals' communication behaviors or practice?
    - What role do individuals, power or ideology play in constructing culture?
- Knowledge and researcher (epistemological) questions:
    - Is it possible to isolate culture or cultural norms for research purposes?
    - What do researchers do with culture or cultural norms? Do researchers seek to discover and describe them; use them as an explanatory factor; use them to predict what is going to happen in Intercultural Communication; interpret them in relation to other factors such as power, ideology; or apply them to inform or improve practice?
    - How do researchers account for problems in Intercultural Communication?

Based on these questions, there are five main paradigms in IC studies. These are positivist, interpretive, critical, constructivist, and realist paradigms. The first three have been discussed in some detail in Martin et al. (2002).

The Positivist Paradigm

Typically, studies following this paradigm set out to identify patterns and the causal effect of culture on communicative behaviors and practices. They treat cultural values, cultural norms, and communicative behaviors as variables and seek to make generalizations based on a set of measurements.

Their main assumptions are:

- Culture is (relatively) stable and fixed and, therefore, can be isolated for research purpose.
- Cultural norms exist and can be identified through measurement.
- Culture values determine communication behaviors.
- Misunderstandings in Intercultural Communication can be accounted for in terms of differences in cultural values.
- Researchers can generalize cultural patterns, compare different cultures and use cultural values as an explanatory variable.

This paradigm has many followers in IC studies, in particular, studies carried out in the traditions of psychology and communication studies. The best known examples in psychology are cultural value studies in the 1970s and 1980s which attempted to categorize national cultures in terms of cultural values and dimensions. For example, the Dutch psychologist Geert Hofstede collected questionnaires from more than 100,000 IBM employees in 40 countries and identified four cultural dimensions, termed individualism vs. collectivism, high vs. low power distance, masculinity vs. femininity, high vs. low uncertainty avoidance (Hoftstede, 1991, 2001). Other scholars following a similar approach include Fons Trompenaars & Charles Hampden-Turner (1998), Shalom Schwartz (1992, 1994), and Kluckhohn & Strodtbeck (1961). Their work is further extended by the cross-cultural psychologist Harry Triandis (1990, 1995) who reconceptualized the dichotomy of individualism vs. collectivism. Over the years, cultural value studies have been criticized for their essentialist and over-generalized view of culture, i.e. members of a cultural group are treated as the same, sharing definable characteristics whatever the context may be (e.g. McSweeney, 2002). Nevertheless, the classification systems proposed by various scholars do act as a convenient, albeit rather simplistic, tool in revealing cultural differences in values and beliefs. Studies following this particular line of enquiry are still widely cited in business and organization management studies and applied in intercultural training.

In communication studies, a group of scholars turned their attention to the process of intercultural communication and brought general communication theories into the study of interactions between people of different cultures. The bulk of this work was done in the 1980s, and the leading researchers included William Gudykunst, Stella Ting-Toomey, Young Yun Kim, and Guo-Ming Chen (see Gudykunst, 2005 for a review of their work), to give a few examples. A number of models and theoretical accounts were proposed, such as cultural adaptation, communicative effectiveness and competence, conflict management, anxiety/uncertainty management, communication accommodation theory, and identity negotiation and management (e.g. Chen & Starosta, 1998; Gudykunst, 2005; Gudykunst & Kim, 2003; Ting-Toomey, 1999).

Within Applied Linguistics, cross-cultural/intercultural pragmatics, the study of speech acts by language users from different linguistic and cultural backgrounds, shares many assumptions of this positivist paradigm. These studies investigate how speech acts of request, apology, greeting, etc., are realized in different languages and to what extent a speaker's choice of linguistic politeness strategies is influenced by factors such as relative power, social distance and degree of imposition in a given culture.

> **Case in Point: An example of the positivist paradigm in action**
>
> Matsumoto et al. (2008). Mapping expressive differences around the world: The relationship between emotional display rules and individualism versus collectivism. *Journal of Cross-cultural Psychology*, 39, 55–74.

The study follows the positivist paradigm and sets out to measure and compare different cultural norms on emotion display rules. It proposes five hypotheses concerning the relationship between display rules and a country's individualism–collectivism scores under the assumption that display rules are culture-specific. It administers a questionnaire called the Display Rule Assessment Inventory with more than 5000 respondents in 32 countries. Some universal and culture-specific patterns which have been identified are:

- There is a relatively small variation between participants from different countries in overall expression endorsement.
- There is a tendency to give greater expression display endorsement towards members of their own groups than towards members of other groups.
- Participants from individualistic cultures have higher scores of expressivity endorsement compared with those from collectivistic cultures.

The Interpretative Paradigm

Studies following this paradigm seek to uncover and interpret culture through the context where it exists, and are very often carried out in the tradition of ethnographic study of culture. A proponent of this paradigm was the American anthropologist Clifford Geertz. He was not interested in analyzing culture as "an experimental science in search of law" (1973, p. 5), but was keen to inspect events through "thick description," i.e. describing and observing behaviors in detail and in their contexts as opposed to the practice of merely recording what happened. The main assumptions shared by these studies are:

- Culture cannot be reduced as abstract entities. It exists and emerges through details, actions, meaning and relationship.
- Culture and cultural norms can be captured through detailed observation and description.
- Communicative behaviors, along with their meaning, constitute culture, while at the same time, are informed by culture.
- The researcher's role is not to identify rules and the causal link between culture and communicative behaviors, but to try to interpret culture in its entirety.

There are many fruitful ethnographic studies of cultures. The earliest well-cited works were Edward Hall's works on time and space (1959/1973, 1966/1990). Hall, widely regarded as the founder of the field of Intercultural Communication, made the strong claim that "culture is communication and communication is culture" (1959/1973, p. 191). Other studies include Carbaugh (2005), which investigates discursive practices in several cultures; Katriel (1986), which examines the Dugri talk, also known as "Israeli directness of style"; and Scollon & Scollon (1990), which identifies differences in language use by Athabaskan (an indigenous language of North America) and English speakers.

Within Applied Linguistics, the line of investigation that is close to this interpretive paradigm is the work on ethnography of speaking (also known as the ethnography of communication) by Dell Hymes (1962, 1964) and his followers. As an analytical framework, ethnography of speaking offers a checklist known as SPEAKING (S for setting, P for participants, E for Ends, A for Act Sequence; K for Key; I for Instrumentalities; N for Norms; and G for Genre) in describing ways of speaking in a speech community. In the example shown in Table 1.1, Scott Kiesling (2012) compares ways of speaking in a gathering between the Kuna community in Panama and a male undergraduate social club in a college in Northern Virginia, USA.

By using the SPEAKING grid, similarities and differences between the events are drawn out. For example, both events have certain routines and expectations of the role of participants. Both endorse a "one speaker at a time" style of turn-taking. However, the Kuna gathering comes through as a staged performance with only chiefs and spokespersons speaking or chanting to each other. For the social club, there is more interaction with ordinary members, who are allowed to challenge previous speakers.

Recently, the interpretive paradigm has been used in studies examining local practices in organizational contexts such as business communication. Below is an example.

Case in Point: An example of the interpretive paradigm in action

Ehrenreich, S. (2009). English as a lingua franca in multinational corporations – exploring business communities of practice. In A. Mauranen, & E. Ranta (Eds.), *English as a lingua franca. Studies and findings* (pp. 126–151). Newcastle upon Tyne: Cambridge Scholars Publishing.

In this article, the author sets out to investigate how English is used as a lingua franca in German multinational corporations, and how English lingua franca users perceive and manage intercultural issues in their daily business communications. Using an ethnographic multimethod and an interpretive paradigm, the author collects interview data and observational and recorded data of business activities, including meetings, phone conferences, and dinners, from two participating companies. She finds a number of salient features of the communicative practices among the company employees. For example, although 70% of communication is carried out in English, communication is very much multilingual in nature, with English used as lingua franca alongside other languages for various functional purposes. Efficiency rather than appropriateness is the key goal and concern of communication. The employees are confident about their language use and there are many instances of creativity in mobilizing linguistic resources. While communicating in

Table 1.1 SPEAKING grid (adapted from Kiesling, 2012, pp. 86–87)

	Kuna	Male undergraduate club
Situation	Evening. Round house with "chiefs" in center, then men, then women.	Sunday evening. Classroom with officers at front and younger men to the left.
Participants	Chiefs (minimum two), spokesmen, policemen, villagers.	Full members of the club.
Ends/purpose	Social connection and cohesion. Build status, settle dispute in favor, teach/learn about culture.	Conduct club business (planning, decision-making); social cohesion and connection; build status, get elected, have certain policies adopted.
Act Sequence	Pre-meeting talk: informal talk or public discussion of important issues Form: the points of chief's chanting are indirect; reformulation/interpretation by "spokesman"; set sequence of acts Content: historical, mythical-cosmological-historical; local history; Kuna versions of the Bible; chief's personal experience, dreams; stories.	Pre-meeting talk: chatting about social events over the weekend Form: direct and often confrontational Content: set sequence of topics: reports, old business, new business.
Key	Usually serious but can be lightened.	Serious but with lots of intermittent joking. Often adversarial and confrontational.
Instrumentalities	Channel: oral Mode: chanting, speaking Forms of speech: chief language (chiefs), ordinary Kuna (spokesmen and others).	Channel: oral Mode: speaking Forms of speech: American English, with varying levels of standardness.
Norms	Interaction: two chiefs, one chanting, the other responding. Spokesperson speaks when chief is finished Interpretation: interpreted as lessons or entertainment (or both), fitting into the cosmology and social structure of Kuna.	Interaction: one speaker at a time determined by the president or other presiding officer. Short unratified responses are OK. Challenges to previous speakers are OK. Interpretation: interpreted as contributions to the club. Many utterances in response to others will be seen as challenges to the first speaker, but are interpreted as part of the debate and an important ideology in the governing.
Genres	Meeting	Meeting

English, employees are aware of the need to negotiate the norms or rules for intercultural interactions and show greater tolerance and preference for cultural hybridity in communication.

The Critical Paradigm

Martin & Nakayama (2000, cited in Halualani & Nakayama, 2010, p. 2) defined the critical paradigm in IC studies as one that addresses issues of macro contexts (historical, social, and political levels), power, and the hidden and destabilizing aspects of culture. Influenced by cultural, critical and feminist studies, critical communication pedagogy, organizational communication, media studies, performance studies, and race and ethnic studies, among others, studies following this paradigm position culture as a part of macro social practice contributing to, and at the same time influenced by, power and ideological struggle. In their interpretation of intercultural contact, they take into account social, political, economic and linguistic power differences between and within groups, with the ultimate goal of bringing in social change. By doing so, they bring a critical perspective to the understanding of cultural differences, which they believe is a product of reification by those in power (i.e. ascribed cultural differences) or subordinate cultural groups themselves (i.e. (re)claimed cultural differences).

The paradigm is not new. According to Halualani & Nakayama (2010), as a response to the positivist and interpretative paradigms dominant in the 1980s and 1990s, a number of scholars (e.g. Collier, 1998; Drzewiecka, 1999; Gonzalez, Houston, & Chen, 1994; Hall, 1992; to give just a few examples cited in Halualani & Nakayama, 2010) have raised questions about the lack of attention to the way larger structures of power impact on intercultural communication. They critically examined the relationship between culture, communication, and politics, in the following aspects (Halualani & Nakayama, 2010, p. 3):

- situated power interests,
- historical contextualization,
- global shifts and economic conditions,
- different politicized identities in terms of race, ethnicity, gender, sexuality, region, socioeconomic class, generation, and diasporic positions.

The publication of *The handbook of critical intercultural communication* edited by Nakayama & Halualani (2010) and *Intercultural communication: A critical introduction* by Ingrid Piller (2011) represents the most recent scholarly attempt to position Critical Intercultural Communication studies as a paradigm that provides new opportunities of understanding the inner workings of intercultural relations and communication. The main assumptions in these critical paradigms include (see Halualani & Nakayama, 2010):

- Culture is an ideological and power struggle.
- Understanding and researching culture differences cannot be achieved without paying attention to macro contexts in which differences are ascribed, reified or glossed over.

- Communication is not just a process of encoding and decoding, but a process of "the creation, constitution, and intertwining of situated meanings, social practices, structures, discourses and the nondiscursive" (p. 7).
- The "inter" component in Intercultural Communication represents an intersecting methodology through which the relationship between culture, identity, and power can be investigated.
- The researcher's role is to unpack the relationship between power, culture and communication and, in doing so, to achieve social justice and equality.

> **Case in Point: An example of the critical paradigm in action**
>
> Thurlow, C. (2010). Speaking of difference: Language inequality and interculturality. In T. Nakayama & R. T. Halualani (Eds.), *The handbook of critical Intercultural Communication* (pp. 227–247). Oxford: Blackwell.

As part of his attempt to unpack the role of language in the production of difference, Crispin Thurlow (2010) examines three areas in which linguistic ideologies (i.e. people's perception and belief about language use) come into play. One such area is tourist discourse, which constitutes a major site of intercultural exchange. Through a detailed analysis of the representation of local, non-English languages in British television shows, Thurlow demonstrates that in these shows, the use of local languages was very much tokenistic. They are reduced to basic formulaic phrases such as "hello" or "thank you" and frequently employed as resources for relating "foreignness" to audiences, sometimes as objects of fun. Therefore, he concluded that these highly staged and stylized exchanges can only serve to reify a "neocolonial vision / spectacle of Other and of intercultural exchange" (p. 235). This type of critical analysis, as Thurlow explains, enables researchers to demonstrate that "even the smallest, quickest, most trivial moments of language use reveal the effects of power" (p. 236).

The Constructivist Paradigm

Whilst the critical paradigm emphasizes the impact of macro structure on intercultural communication, the constructivist paradigm pays attention to the subjective nature of meaning-making and argues that intercultural differences and cultural memberships are socially constructed. A number of clarifications are in order here. In the literature, constructivism sometimes refers to Piagetian learning theory. As a paradigm, however, the term stands for a school of thoughts competing with the positivist paradigm in that it regards the person as actively engaged in the creation of their own world (Burr, 2003). In some works (e.g. Mertens, 1998, cited in Creswell, 2009), constructivism combines with interpretivism into a single paradigm, drawing on their shared position on subjectivity and agency of the person. This usage is echoed by Holliday when he talks about an interpretive constructivist approach in Chapter 2 of this volume. In others (e.g. Silverman, 2006), the term constructionism, instead of constructivism, is used along with other paradigms. Despite sometimes interchangeable use of the two terms in the research method literature, there are differences between constructivism and constructionism: for the former the focus is on internal, cognitive process of individuals, while the latter, often referred to as social constructionism, pays attention to the joint social activities and their impact on meaning construction (Burr, 2003; McNamee, 2004). In this chapter, constructivism is used in a more inclusive sense, taking account of those studies with a strong emphasis on social construction of meaning (cf. constructionism in Angouri, Chapter 3 of this volume).

Many discourse studies that appeared in the late 1980s and 1990s followed this line of approach. An example is a special issue of *Pragmatics* (edited by Michael Meeuwis, 1994a) which includes works by Day (1994), Meeuwis (1994b), Sarangi (1994), Shea (1994) and Shi-xu (1994), on the role of discourse and interaction in constructing a speaker's cultural or ethnic memberships. The main assumptions are:

- Culture and intercultural differences are socially constructed.
- Understanding of culture and intercultural differences is subjective and emerges through discourse and interaction.
- The researcher's role is to understand culture and intercultural differences as discursive and emergent, and contingent on participants' meaning-making. They do not prescribe what culture is or is not, nor attribute problems in intercultural communication to cultural factors.
- The focus is on the process of interaction and what the participants achieve out of the experience in terms of new values, identities and practices.

A line of enquiry that follows the constructivist paradigm in recent years is interculturality studies, in which scholars seek to interpret how participants make aspects of their identities, in particular their cultural identities, relevant or irrelevant to interactions through interactional resources (e.g. Higgins, 2007; Mori, 2003; Nishizaka, 1995; Sercombe & Young, 2010; Zhu Hua, 2014). These studies take intercultural encounters as instances of "talk-in-interaction" and "being intercultural" as a socially constructed phenomenon. They believe that cultural memberships (e.g. Japanese vs. American) are not always relevant to intercultural interactions. Instead, the relevance of identities is contingent on the participants' orientation. It restores speakers or participants' agency to the central role in social construction; a factor which is very often neglected in the earlier studies of Intercultural Communication. In "doing" cultural memberships, Participants employ a range of interactional work and discursive practices. They can, on the one hand, ascribe or cast cultural memberships to others, and, on the other hand, accept, avow, display, ignore, reject, or disavow cultural memberships assigned by others. They can also claim or appropriate memberships of groups to which they do not normally belong. The following is an example of an interculturality study.

Case in Point: An example of the constructivism paradigm in action

Day, D. (1998). Being ascribed, and resisting. Membership of an ethnic group. In C. Antaki, & S. Widdicombe (Eds.), *Identities in talk* (pp. 151–170). London: Sage.

In this article, the author, starting from the view that ethnic identity is a situated accomplishment of conversation participants, examines the "ethnification" processes whereby conversation participants ascribe other participants to a cultural or ethnic group. The following conversation is an example in which a participant resists others' ascription of a cultural identity. The participants in the conversation were workers in a Swedish factory whose workforce has a high percentage of immigrants. They were planning a party.

Example

51 Lars: don't we have something that, one can eat
52 that, China or
53 Rita: Chinese food is really pretty good
54 Xi: haha () it doesn't matter, I'll eat anything
55 Rita: ah (that's [what I that)
56 Lars: [yeah, but this concerns everyone
57 doesn't it?
(Day, 1998, p. 162; transcription conventions: (): unclear speech; [: overlap)

In the conversation, Lars suggested Chinese food for the party they were planning. Rita took the next turn and made a comment about Chinese food. Since it was not clear from the data how the following turn was allocated, we could only speculate that Xi, an ethnic Chinese, felt obliged to take up the floor when her cultural expertise was made relevant. She faced two choices: either dismissing the potential relevance of the category of being a Chinese or continuing the flow of the discussion by commenting on Chinese food as a cultural insider. She opted for the first by suggesting that she was fine with any type of food, thus presenting herself as an individual rather than a cultural expert on Chinese food. Her subtle resistance to making her Chinese background salient in the conversation, however, encountered admonishment from Lars, who was quick to point out that this was not just about Xi herself.

The Realist Paradigm

Contrary to the constructivist paradigm, the realism paradigm calls for a "realist" view of the relationship between structure and agency. Emerging out of dissatisfaction with the "inherent explanatory limitations of constructivism paradigm" (Reed, 2005, p. 1629), the realism paradigm acknowledges both agency of individuals and constraints of social and historical conditions. It accepts that individuals' behavior is constrained by the parameters of broad societal norms and inherited structures of belief, power, opportunity and so on (Holms, Marra, & Vine 2011, p. 13). Specifically, its main assumptions are (based on Holmes et al., 2011; Kumaravadivelu, 2008; Reed, 2005):

- Culture, as one component of underlying deeper macro structures or mechanisms, shapes events and regularities including individuals' behaviors at a surface level.
- There is a reflexive relationship between the underlying structures and mechanisms and human activity. As Lopez and Potter eloquently put it, "social structure is, of course, dependent upon human activity. Without that it would not exist.

However, it does have an independence as well. ... it pre-exists us. We are shaped and affected by social structures. Social forces act on us. Social structures limit our range of possible choices of action ... We do not create social structure. We reproduce and transform it. But it too causally affects us." (Lopez & Potter, 2001, p. 15)

- The underlying structures and mechanism including culture norms do not exist as discrete facts or statistically generalized patterns. They can be inferred through a process described as "retroduction," whereby researchers can reason backwards from the phenomenon under investigation and ask the question "What, if it existed, would account for this phenomenon?" (Reed, 2005, p. 1631).
- The focus of the realist paradigm is, therefore, very much on explanation, rather than seeking to describe and predict using cause-and-effect logic (as in the positivist paradigm), to interpret culture in its entirety (as in the interpretative paradigm), to transform (as in the critical paradigm), or to foreground subjective nature of social behavior (as in the constructivist paradigm).

The realist paradigm is a relatively newly recognized paradigm. There are some book-length publications explaining its main positions as a research paradigm, e.g. Lopez & Potter (2001) and Danermark, Ekstrom, Jakobsen, & Karlsson (2002). While some of its main assumptions and assertions have been articulated in various forms in IC studies, there are still very few empirical works aligned with the realist paradigms. Nevertheless, they have brought interesting insights to two key issues in IC studies. One is the intersectionality of cultural norms with other norms or forces that may be in operation. Arguments are made that cultural norms are enmeshed with norms of different types and at different levels including societal norms, organizational norms, community of practice / team norms, and interactional norms (e.g. Holmes et al., 2011). Therefore, sometimes when things go wrong, it is not "*ethnicity per se*," but other factors such as familiarity with the system, that cause the problem (Roberts, Campbell, & Robinson, 2008). The other is the issue of cultural identities. Scholars following the realist paradigm have made the case that individuals can assert their agency through identity work, but there are limits to it. Such limitations have several sources. One is the constraints of "culturally available, sense-making frameworks or 'discourses'" (Ehrlich, 2008, p. 160) which individuals buy into or use without questioning. Individuals carry important cultural identities and structures with them even when they "cross intercultural lines" (Holliday, 2013, p. 168). There are also competing forces of global, national, social and individual realities in the era of globalization which both unite people by facilitating global flow of culture and interactions and, at the same time, divide people through "an increase in ethnic, racial, religious, and national consciousness" (Kumaravadivelu, 2008, p. 158).

Case in Point: An example of the realist paradigm in action

Holmes, J. (2013). Exploring evidence of socio-cultural norms in face-to-face interaction. Conference presentation in IALIC 2013 Annual Conference (Language and Intercultural Communication in the Workplace: Critical Approaches to Theory and Practice) December 2013, Hong Kong.

Holmes, J., Marra, M., & Vine, B. (2011). *Leadership, discourse and ethnicity*. Oxford: Oxford University Press.

As an example, Holmes et al. (2011) and Holmes (2013) illustrate how a realist paradigm helps with the interpretation of Maori leadership style at work. She demonstrates how Yvonne, a managing director of a Maori organization orients to both Pākehā (the Māori term for a white New-Zealander) and Māori conceptions of leadership in her reports in a monthly staff meeting.

Pākehā leadership style	*Māori* leadership style
What we've what we've done is made a commitment (just) to clients or to director or whoever (you're) doing the work for that this is what we're going to provide we're going to provide a quality product and we're going to provide it on time and within budget	Yesterday I talked, I had to give a presentation I was invited by [name of prestigious person]… I felt the presentation wasn't that good because my briefing was about a two second phone [laughs] call [laughter] and so I had no idea who was going to be at the conference and () what's it about I had no programme beforehand so I was a bit unprepared

According to Holmes et al. (2011), while Māori and Pākehā both value strong, authoritative and decisive leadership styles, Māori leaders place high value on modesty and humility. In the first example, Yvonne has positioned herself as a leader who provides the rationale for working towards a common goal, which is matched in her discourse style. There are no hedges or mitigating devices to modify the force of her statement. The use of the phrase "we're going to provide" reinforces her message. The repeated use of the inclusive pronoun *we* serves as a marker of solidarity. In the second example, Yvonne, the same person, was giving an update about a promotional presentation she has made in a self-deprecating way, conforming to the Māori value of *whakaiti*, i.e. being humble and modest. In doing so, she constructed herself as responding positively to an opportunity to promote the company while at the same time being able to critically evaluate her own performance. Holmes (2013) argued that differences in her leadership discourse are influenced by social-cultural expectations on leadership, the organizational culture and gender norms. The most important message from her study is that one speaker brings different norms into focus in different contexts.

Some General Questions about Paradigms

I have identified five key paradigms in Intercultural Communication studies above. These paradigms represent different kinds of philosophical worldviews and research orientations that researchers may endorse. In this final section, I would like to discuss several general issues regarding these paradigms.

The first one is a question raised in Saunders et al. (2007, p. 116): Which research paradigm is better? This is perhaps the most frequently asked question about paradigms. But as Saunders et al. have eloquently argued, the question in fact misses the point. It is not the question of whether one is better than the others. The question should be which paradigm is more suitable for some types of research questions than others. Some examples of the IC research questions that a paradigm is capable of answering are:

- The positivist paradigm: What are culture-specific patterns? How to account for culture-specific patterns in terms of cultural values?
- The interpretive paradigm: How to describe and interpret communicative behaviors in context? What do these communicative behaviors tell about the culture shared by individuals?
- The critical paradigm: What role do power and ideology play in shaping the reality? How are cultural differences reified by those in power?
- The constructivist paradigm: How are intercultural differences socially or discursively constructed?
- The realist paradigm: To what extent can culture account for problems in interactions? How to acknowledge both individuals' agency and the role of deeper structures and mechanisms, of which culture is one component, in understanding the phenomenon under investigation?

The second question: Do paradigms come and go? Some paradigms may be more dominant than others at certain times and promoted by some research groups to meet their research priorities. In the available accounts of paradigms in IC (e.g. Martin, Nakayama, & Carbaugh, 2014), the links between some particular paradigms and geographical areas and periods of time are established. As an example of diversity in paradigms, Holliday (Chapter 2, this volume) provides an account of an interpretive constructivist paradigm and critical cosmopolitan approach. Some journals prefer certain paradigms than others, because of their disciplinary connections and aims and scopes. For example, *International Journal of Intercultural Relations*, as stated on its website, is primarily interested in topics such as acculturation; Intercultural Communication; intergroup perceptions, contact, and interactions; intercultural training; and cultural diversity in education, organizations and society. It aims to engage with scholars from fields of psychology, communication, education, management, sociology, and related disciplines. Its articles generally adopt a positivist paradigm, as evident in the January issue of 2014, for instance. In contrast, *Multilingua: Journal of Cross-Cultural and Interlanguage Communication* takes a critical stance on issues of language and communication in globalization, transnationalism, migration, and mobility across time and space, and affiliates itself with critical sociolinguistics. A quick browse of the topics covered in the articles published in the journal shows a mixture of constructivist, critical, interpretive and realist paradigms, but the absence of the positivist paradigm is noticeable.

Understanding Your Own Positions

A PhD doctoral student once said to me, "It took me a long time to learn what the terms such as ontological or epistemological really mean, but once I have understood them, I can see how much it would have guided me if I were aware of these issues right from the beginning." Indeed, one's orientation to a particular paradigm makes a significant difference to research approaches, designs, and data collection methods and analysis. The following questions, I hope, are helpful in understanding your own orientation in approaching your research.

1. What is the aim or purpose of your research? Is it primarily finding facts or patterns, identifying the links between variables, seeking an explanation, understanding the process of meaning-making, unpicking the relationship between power structure and human behaviors, or solving a problem?
2. What is the nature of findings in your research? Are they facts, and therefore relatively objective, or opinions / argument, and therefore subjective?
3. What criteria do you use in assessing the quality of your research? Do you use the terms "validity," "reliability," "representativeness," "holistic," "transformative" (i.e. bringing changes), or "situatedness"(i.e. taking account of macro factors such as social, political, cultural, and economic factors, as well as local factors such as location of interactions, participants involved, how something is said to whom, etc.)?
4. Are you encouraged to bring in your "voice" in your research? Do you go about your research as a "natural scientist," one who does not "interfere" with the data and remains extrinsic to the data? Or, is your voice integral to the process of data collection, analysis and interpretation?

Key Terms

Epistemology A term that describes researchers' beliefs about the nature of knowledge and findings as well as the relationship between the researcher and the research in a field of study. Examples of the issues concerned are: what counts as data and findings? Are findings regarded as truth or facts waiting to be discovered or are they subject to researchers' interpretation?

Intercultural Communication As a field of study, it is concerned with how people from different cultural backgrounds interact with each other and negotiate cultural or linguistic differences which may be perceived or made relevant through interactions, as well as what impact such interactions have on group relations and on individuals' identities, attitudes and behaviors. It is abbreviated as IC in this volume.

Ontology A term that describes researchers' beliefs about the form and the nature of reality. Examples of the issues concerned are: does the reality under study exist and operate independently? Is the reality subject to perceptions and actions of individuals or "social actors" who inhabit it?

Paradigm The overarching constructive framework and meta-thinking behind a piece of research. It reflects the researcher's general orientation towards the form and nature of the reality under study, the nature of knowledge and the role of the researcher.

Research approaches Research plans and procedures that "span the steps from broad assumptions to detailed methods of data collection, analysis, and interpretation" (Creswell, 2014, p. 3).

References

Bennett, M. J. (2005). *Paradigmatic assumption of Intercultural Communication*. Hillsboro: IDR Institute www.idrinstitute.org. Retrieved June 10, 2015 from: http://www.idrinstitute.org/allegati/IDRI_t_Pubblicazioni/3/FILE_Documento.pdf

Burr, V. (2003). *Social constructionism*. East Sussex: Psychology Press.

Carbaugh, D. (2005). *Cultures in conversation*. Mahwah, NJ: Lawrence Erlbaum.

Chen, G-M., & Starosta, W. J. (1998). *Foundations of Intercultural Communication*. Needham Height, MA: Allyn & Bacon.

Creswell, J. W. (2009). *Research design. Qualitative, quantitative, and mixed methods approaches* (3rd ed.). Thousand Oaks, CA: Sage.

Creswell, J. W. (2014). *Research design. Qualitative, quantitative, and mixed methods approaches* (4th ed.). Thousand Oaks, CA: Sage.

Danermark, B., Ekstrom, M., Jakobsen, L., & Karlsson, J. (2002). *Explaining society: Critical realism in the social sciences*. London: Routledge.

Day, D. (1994). Tang's dilemma and other problems: Ethnification processes at some multicultural workplaces. *Pragmatics*, 4, 315–336.

Day, D. (1998). Being ascribed, and resisting. Membership of an ethnic group. In C. Antaki, & S. Widdicombe (Eds.), *Identities in talk* (pp. 151–170). London: Sage.

de Vaus, D. (2001). *Research design in social research*. London: Sage.

Ehrenreich, S. (2009). English as a lingua franca in multinational corporations – exploring business communities of practice. In A. Mauranen, & E. Ranta (Eds.), *English as a Lingua Franca. Studies and findings* (pp. 126–151). Newcastle-upon-Tyne: Cambridge Scholars.

Ehrlich, S. (2008). Sexual assault trials, discursive identities and institutional change. In R. Dolon, & J. Todoli (Eds.), *Analysing identities in discourse* (pp. 159–177). Amsterdam: John Benjamins.

Geertz, C. (1973). *The interpretation of cultures*. London: Hutchinson.

Guba, E. G., & Lincoln, Y. S. (1994). Competing paradigms in qualitative research. In N. K. Denzin, & Y. S. Lincoln (Eds.), *Handbook of qualitative research* (pp. 105–117). Thousand Oaks, CA: Sage.

Gudykunst, W. (Ed.) (2005). *Theorizing about Intercultural Communication*. Thousand Oaks, CA: Sage.

Gudykunst, W. B., & Kim, Y. Y. (2003). *Communicating with strangers. An approach to Intercultural Communication* (4th ed.). New York: McGraw-Hill.

Hall, E. T. (1959/1973). *The silent language*. Garden City, NY: Doubleday.

Hall, E. T. (1966/1990). *Hidden dimension*. Garden City, NY: Doubleday.

Halualani, R. T., & Nakayama, T. K. (2010). Critical Intercultural Communication Studies: At a crossroads. In T. K. Nakayama, & R. T. Halualani (Eds.), *The handbook of critical Intercultural Communication* (pp. 1–16). Oxford: Blackwell.

Higgins, C. (Ed.). (2007). *A closer look at cultural difference: "Interculturality" in talk-in-interaction*. A special issue of *Pragmatics*, 17(1).

Hofstede, H. (1991). *Cultures and organizations: Software of the mind*. London: McGraw-Hill.

Hofstede, H. (2001). *Culture's consequences: International differences in work-related values* (2nd ed.). Beverly Hills, CA: Sage.

Holliday, A. (2011). *Intercultural Communication and ideology*. London: Sage.
Holliday, A. (2013). *Understanding Intercultural Communication. Negotiating a grammar of culture*. London: Routledge.
Holmes, J. (2013). Exploring evidence of socio-cultural norms in face-to-face interaction. Conference presentation in IALIC 2013 Annual Conference (Language and Intercultural Communication in the Workplace: Critical Approaches to Theory and Practice) December 2013, Hong Kong.
Holmes, J., Marra, M., & Vine, B. (2011). *Leadership, discourse and ethnicity*. Oxford: Oxford University Press.
Hymes, D. (1962). The ethnography of speaking. In T. Gladwin, & W. C. Sturtevant (Eds.), *Anthropology and human behavior* (pp. 13–53). Washington, DC: Anthropological Society of Washington.
Hymes, D. (Ed.). (1964). *Language in culture and society*. New York: Harper and Row.
Katriel, T. (1986). *Talking straight: Dugri speech in Israeli Sabra culture*. Cambridge: Cambridge University Press. A selection is reprinted in Zhu Hua (Ed.) (2011), *The language and Intercultural Communication reader* (pp. 152–164). London: Routledge.
Kiesling, S. (2012). Ethnography of speaking. In C. B. Paulston, S. F. Kiesling & E. S. Rangel (Eds.), *The handbook of intercultural discourse and communication* (pp. 77–89). Oxford: Blackwell.
Kluckhohn, F., & Strodtbeck, F. (1961). *Variations in value orientations*. New York: Row, Petersen.
Kumaravadivelu, B. (2008). *Cultural globalization and language education*. New Haven, CT: Yale University Press.
Lopez, J., & Potter, G. (Eds.) (2001). *After postmodernism: An introduction to critical realism*. London: Athlone Press.
Martin, J., & Nakayama, T. K. (2000). *Intercultural Communication in contexts* (2nd ed.). Mountain View, CA.: Mayfield.
Martin, J. Nakayama, T. K., & Flores, L. A. (2002). A dialectal approach to Intercultural Communication. In J. Martin, T. K. Nakayama, & L. A. Flores (Eds.), *Readings in Intercultural Communication. Experiences and context* (pp. 3–12). Boston: McGraw Hill.
Martin, J., Nakayama, T. K., & Carbaugh, D. (2014). The history and development of the study of Intercultural Communication and applied linguistics. In J. Jackson (Ed.): *The Routledge handbook of language and Intercultural Communication* (pp. 17–36). London: Routledge.
Matsumoto, D., Yoo, S. H., Fontaine, J., Anguas-Wong, A., Arriola, M., Ataca, B., et al. (2008). Mapping expressive differences around the world: The relationship between emotional display rules and individualism versus collectivism. *Journal of Cross-cultural Psychology*, 39, 55–74.
McNamee, S. (2004). Relational bridges between constructionism and constructivism. In J. D. Raskin, & S. K. Bridges (Eds.), *Studies in meaning 2: Bridging the personal and the social* (pp. 37–50). New York: Pace University Press.
McSweeny, B. (2002). Hofstede's model of national cultural differences and their consequences: A triumph of faith – a failure of analysis. *Human Relations*, 55(1), 89–118.
Meeuwis, M. (Ed.). (1994a). *Critical perspectives on Intercultural Communication*. A special issue of *Pragmatics*, 4(3).
Meeuwis, M. (1994b). Leniency and testiness in Intercultural Communication: Remarks on ideology and context in interactional sociolinguists. *Pragmatics*, 4, 391–408.
Mertens, D. M. (1998). *Research methods in education and psychology: Integrating diversity with quantitative and qualitative approaches*. Thousand Oaks, CA: Sage.
Mori, J. (2003). The construction of interculturality: A study of initial encounters between Japanese and American students. *Research on Language and Social Interaction*, 36(2), 143–184.

Nishizaka, A. (1995). The interactive constitution of interculturality: How to be a Japanese with words. *Human Studies*, 18, 301–326.
Piller, I. (2011). *Intercultural Communication: A Critical Introduction*. Edinburgh: Edinburgh University Press.
Reed, M. (2005). Reflections on the "realist turn" in organization and management studies. *Journal of Management Studies*, 42(8), 1621–1644.
Roberts, C., Campbell, S., & Robinson, Y. (2008). *Talking like a manager: Promotion interviews, language and ethnicity*. Research report for Department of Work and Pensions. Retrieved 11 June, 2015 from: http://webarchive.nationalarchives.gov.uk/20130128102031/http://www.dwp.gov.uk/asd/asd5/rports2007-2008/rrep510.pdf
Sarangi, S. (1994). Intercultural or not? Beyond celebration of cultural differences in miscommunication analysis. *Pragmatics*, 4, 409–427.
Saunders, M., Lewis, P., & Thornhill, A. (2007). *Research methods for business students*. Harlow: Prentice Hall.
Schwartz, S. H. (1992). Universals in the content and structure of values: Theory and empirical tests in 20 countries. In M. Zanna (Ed.), *Advances in experimental social psychology* (Vol. 25) (pp. 1–65). New York: Academic Press.
Schwartz, S. H. (1994). Are there universal aspects in the structure and contents of human values? *Journal of Social Issues*, 50(4), 19–45.
Scollon, R., & Wong-Scollon, S. (1990). Athabaskan–English interethnic communication. In D. Carbaugh (Ed.), *Cultural communication and intercultural contact* (pp. 259–287). Hillsdale, NJ: Lawrence Erlbaum.
Sercombe, P., & Young, T. (Eds.). (2010). *Communication, discourses and interculturality*. A Special issue of *Language and Intercultural Communication*, 11(3), 181–272.
Shea, D. P. (1994). Perspective and production: Structuring conversational participation across cultural boarders. *Pragmatics*, 4, 357–390.
Shi-xu (1994). Discursive attributions and cross-cultural communication. *Pragmatics*, 4, 337–356.
Silverman, D. (2006). *Interpreting qualitative data* (3rd ed.). Thousand lOaks, CA: Sage.
Thurlow, C. (2010). Speaking of difference: Language inequality and interculturality. In T. Nakayama, & R. T. Halualani (Eds.), *The handbook of critical Intercultural Communication* (pp. 227–247). Oxford: Blackwell.
Ting-Toomey, S. (1999). *Communicating across cultures*. New York: Guilford.
Triandis, H. C. (1990). Cross-cultural studies of individualism and collectivism. In J. J. Berman (Ed.), *Nebraska Symposium on Motivation, 1989*, vol. 37 (pp. 41–133). Lincoln: University of Nebraska Press.
Triandis, H. C. (1995). *Individualism and collectivism*. Boulder, CO: Westview Press.
Trompenaars, F., & Hampden-Turner, C. (1998). *Riding the waves of culture: Understanding diversity in global business* (2nd ed.). New York: McGraw-Hill.
Zhu, Hua (ed.) (2011). *The Language and Intercultural Communication Reader*. London: Routledge.
Zhu, Hua (2014). *Exploring Intercultural Communication: Language in action*. London: Routledge.

Further Reading and Resources

On general discussion on paradigms:
Creswell, J. W. (2014). *Research design. Qualitative, quantitative, and mixed methods approaches* (Chapter 1, The selection of a research approach). Thousand Oaks, CA: Sage.

Saunders, M., Lewis, P., & Thornhill, A. (2007). *Research methods for business students* (Chapter 4, Understanding research philosophies and approaches). Harlow: Prentice Hall.

Guba, E. G., & Lincoln, Y. S. (1994). Competing paradigms in qualitative research. In N. K. Denzin, & Y. S. Lincoln (Eds.), *Handbook of qualitative research* (pp. 105–117). Thousand Oaks, CA: Sage.

On discussion on paradigms in IC studies:

Martin, J., Nakayama, T. K., & Flores, L. A. (2002). A dialectal approach to Intercultural Communication. In J. Martin, T. K. Nakayama, & L. A. Flores (Eds.), *Readings in Intercultural Communication. Experiences and context* (pp. 3–12). Boston: McGraw Hill.

Martin, J., Nakayama, T. K., & Carbaugh, D. (2014). The history and development of the study of Intercultural Communication and applied linguistics. In J. Jackson (Ed.), *The Routledge handbook of language and Intercultural Communication* (pp. 17–36). London: Routledge.

2 Studying Culture

Adrian Holliday

> **Summary**
>
> In this chapter I use a social action "grammar" of culture to indicate the different and interconnected forces that act on culture and Intercultural Communication and provide different foci for research. This picture follows a postmodern paradigm in which culture is a socially and politically constructed concept. The study of culture therefore moves away from differences between cultures and towards the question of how people construct and use culture to make sense of each other. Underlying universal cultural processes imply that all of us are equally engaged in the everyday construction of and engagement with culture wherever it is found. The focus of research is therefore on how these processes bring us together but at the same time pull us apart, as global politics, nation, ideology, and discourses of culture create imageries of difference. With the focus on the construction of culture, the research approach is constructivist and uses ethnographic, qualitative methods.

In looking at the way in which culture should be researched within the broader field of intercultural communication it is important to respond to an exciting period of paradigm change in the field. A positivist, modernist paradigm which attempts to measure and define cultures as solid, fixed, separate geographical blocks which confine the behavior of the people who live within them, is giving way to a postmodern paradigm which recognizes that culture is a fluid and socially constructed entity (Crane, 1994) which is politically and ideologically charged (King, 1991). Within

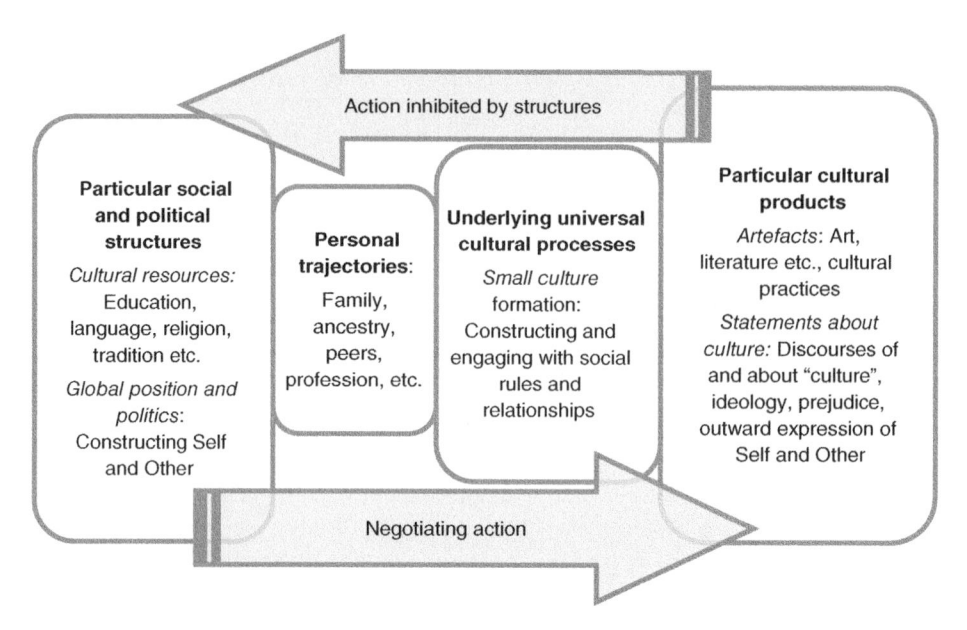

Figure 2.1 Grammar of culture. (Adapted from Holliday, 2011, p. 131; 2013, p. 2.)

Particular social and political structures
Cultural resources: Education, language, religion, tradition etc.
Global position and politics: Constructing Self and Other

Personal trajectories: Family, ancestry, peers, profession, etc.

Underlying universal cultural processes
Small culture formation: Constructing and engaging with social rules and relationships

Particular cultural products
Artefacts: Art, literature etc., cultural practices
Statements about culture: Discourses of and about "culture", ideology, prejudice, outward expression of Self and Other

Action inhibited by structures

Negotiating action

---

the spirit of this postmodern paradigm I therefore follow two broad approaches to culture and to research.

An interpretive constructivist approach appreciates the uncertain, subjective and constructed nature of culture. With specific reference to the relationship between culture and society, I also follow the critical cosmopolitan approach in sociology, which suggests that we are all able to engage creatively with and take ownership of culture wherever we find it (Beck & Sznaider, 2006; Delanty, 2006; Grande, 2006), and the sociology of Max Weber (1964) which recognizes the dialogue between the individual and social structure. While Weber carried out extensive investigation of two major culturally influential systems, Protestantism in Western Europe (Weber, 1950), and Confucianism in China (Bendix, 1966), he always acknowledged the ability of the individual to stand creatively apart from them. This is in sharp contrast to the structural-functionalist picture of an organic social system which contains and defines the behavior and values of the individual, as set out by Emile Durkheim (1933) and later Talcott Parsons (1951), which has influenced so much of what might now be called an essentialist notion of national culture in recent decades of Intercultural Communication studies, which has been very influential in the positivist paradigm.

My interpretation of Weber's social action model is presented in my grammar of culture in Figure 2.1. The grammar is purposefully loose and complex to emphasize an unwillingness to define culture too closely, to mirror its ill-defined nature in everyday reference. It indicates a number of areas that need to be kept in mind when designing and carrying out a research project. I shall therefore use it to signal both what needs to be researched and the methodological issues and disciplines that need to be considered when doing so. I shall therefore first look at the constructivist interpretive approach and then at how each part of the grammar might generate research projects.

An Interpretive Constructivist Approach

The relationships within the grammar broadly indicate an interaction between structures and products, on the left and right, both mediated by politics and ideology, and the way that individuals construct meaning as they build their lives. There is also a complexity and uncertainty in the grammar that implies that explanation can never be complete but must emerge gradually through successive layers of hesitant investigation and interpretation. In contrast to more experimental research approaches, an interpretive constructivist approach invites a richness of variables through which the meanings implicit in this complexity can begin to emerge with a distinctively healthy uncertainty (cf. constructivism, in Zhu Hua, Chapter 1, this volume).

To allow full expression of this delicate relationship between culture and research, the approach is able to take in a wide range of data collection strategies, ranging from full-blown ethnography, where communities are researched in depth for extended periods, to methods that employ an ethnographic approach. The core of ethnography here is that meanings are allowed to emerge from the deep fabric of social life rather than being prescribed by researcher agendas. The balance between emergence and prescription is of course subtle, because research and researchers do have agendas. Also, it was not until the 1980s that ethnography itself seriously engaged with the dangers of prescription (Clifford & Marcus, 1986). The danger of prescription would be where the questions being asked tend positivistically to determine or presume the nature of culture before beginning, and thus lead the research. For example, asking about the defining differences between two cultures presumes that there are two cultures with distinct features; and in interviews this can lead people to also think in these terms just enough to get very different responses than if this framing was not suggested. This is particularly the case when culture itself is such an open and interpretable concept that can mean different things to different people at different times.

The type of data collected is determined both by what is being looked for and what seems appropriate to the particularities of the social setting, which may emerge as important during the process of the research. In the classic ethnographic approach the focus and methods emerge after the researcher has entered the field (Spradley, 1980, p. 32). A range of different types of data could be relevant, such as what people say, write and do, artefacts such as choices of clothing, eating and so on, and the way in which people respond to surroundings and events. Looking at groups of people in specific social settings enables an investigation into how participants construct meaning as a group in response to the setting. Methods of data collection and analysis, whether interviews, focus groups, narrative, spoken interaction, documents, visual media, critical discourse analysis, conversation analysis, or language corpus analysis, must be deployed to allow the richness of social life to emerge and be sufficiently cautious to take the researcher beyond themselves.

The variety of possibilities means that strategic decisions about data and analysis need to be made throughout the whole process. This in turn emphasizes its inevitably subjective nature and the implicatedness of the researcher. The scientific validity of the research depends not on the control of variables and singularity of method, as in more experimental approaches, but on disciplines for approaching and looking at social events, and then making decisions. There needs to be a laying bare of the strategies of the procedure of the research: Who is the researcher? How are they related to the participants? What are their prejudices and beliefs? How may all of this affect the research, and what issues does this raise? And then, in relation to these issues: How is the relationship between the participants and the researcher managed? How are the participants to be approached? How are the research and the researcher to be presented to them? How are questions to be asked? In what events, in what settings, with what sorts of interventions, and why? What sort of space is allowed the participants, and will they have the opportunity to say the unexpected?

Other disciplines derive naturally from an ethnographic approach and are designed to prevent seduction by easy answers – a danger that is particularly evident with the strong academic and popular tradition, coming from the positivist paradigm, of perceiving culture as simplistically solid. Making the familiar strange and bracketing, or recognizing and putting aside our own orientations, are both designed to help researchers look beneath and beyond the traditionally expected. In talking about culture, steps must also be taken to help our participants to be similarly critical. Thick description, where different pieces of data are juxtaposed to build a picture of what is going on (Geertz, 1993, p. 6), also helps to reveal deeper, gradually built and unexpected connections.

Particular Social and Political Structures

On the left of the grammar (Figure 2.1), these are structures that in many ways form us and make us different from each other. They include nation, religion, language and the economic system, and correspond to the popular notion of culture in the national, regional or religious sense, though they will rarely map precisely onto each other. In effect, this domain provides us with cultural resources – the influence on our daily lives of the society where we were born and brought up, the way we were educated, our national institutions, the manner of our government, our media, our economy, and so on, which are different from nation to nation and will undoubtedly impact in the way we are as people. These are resources in the sense that we draw on them, but they do not confine everything we do and think.

Probable topics for research in this domain would be which resources individuals draw upon when they encounter unfamiliar cultural environments, and how they make use of them to make sense of and engage with the new. The critical cosmopolitan approach is particularly interested in cultural travel and valuing the existing cultural experience that travelers bring with them and build upon. Special care would need to be taken here regarding easy answers. Asking people the straightforward question, "What cultural resources have you drawn upon?" might invite references to common stereotypes about their regional or religious culture, whereas the aim would be to go deeper to explore particular life, work or educational experiences. An example of this is John recalling the formalities of visiting grandparents in childhood in Britain when working out how to behave in family parties in Iran which seem very alien (Holliday, 2013, p. 145). Another is a Chinese student applying strategies she had learnt in China to the task of writing at an Australian university (Tran, 2009, p. 280). Wang's (2012) study of a Chinese business delegation in the US reveals a surprising cultural resource that both Chinese and US colleagues share, which brings them together across seemingly huge cultural barriers – that of humor. The data includes observation of meetings and debriefings with Chinese colleagues each evening.

The global position and politics domain concerns how we position ourselves and our society with regard to the rest of the world. This is influenced by how we are all inscribed by long-standing constructions of who we are in relationship to others, in our histories, education, institutions, upbringing and media representations. This attracts research into the representation of Self and Other – the imagination of who we are in relation to others – in a wide range of the texts and images that influence us. These might include advertising, film and television, literature, fine art, travel documents, written history, government and institutional policy documents, textbooks, and so on. There is an established body of research in this area. Some examples are the analysis of Western representations of the non-West in literature and fine art (Said, 1978), in tourism (Urry, 2002), in nationalism (Hahl, et al., 2015), in English language textbooks (Gray, 2010), and in school textbooks generally – prime locations for national narratives (Hahl, et al., 2015).

A major research methodology here is critical discourse analysis, which looks at the ideological content of texts. In terms of intercultural awareness, language students can be invited to carry out critical reading of such texts and images to learn appreciation of their cultural ideologies in their own societies and those of others (e.g. Wallace, 2003). When asking people what cultural resources they draw upon (see above), it is also possible to apply a degree of critical discourse analysis to what they say, because the choice of cultural resources will also be influenced by this Self and Other positioning. For example, when British John draws upon his childhood experience of his grandmother's house to deal with eating with an Iranian family one might ponder on what is behind this association with respect to perceptions of modernity and tradition, and ask him further how he is positioning himself with regard to visiting his grandmother.

Personal Trajectories

Moving into the center of the grammar (Figure 2.1), personal trajectories comprise the individual's personal travel through society, bringing histories from their ancestors and origins. Through these trajectories they are able to step out from and dialogue with the particular social and political structures that surround them and even cross into new and foreign domains. Useful research here would be to invite narrative accounts from individuals who have traveled culturally or lived at cultural interfaces. What is crucial here is to encourage richness of detail and complexity in order to get beyond essentialist accounts of "visiting" different regional or religious "cultures."

Richness, detail and complexity which transcend essentialism can be found in existing narrative accounts. A well-known auto-ethnographic text is Eva Hoffman's (1998) account of living in North America with a Polish background. Another example is Stephanie Vandrick's (1999) personal account of the impact of her childhood as a missionary child in India on her professional life. Good literary fiction also provides excellent examples of the complexities of cultural travel. Excellent here is Chimamanda Ngozi Adichie's (2013) novel, *Americanah*, which recounts the story of a young Nigerian university student's experience of prejudice and identity with relation to culture, race and language as she moves from home to long-term residence in the US. What is significant about this is its being an account from the Periphery. By "from the Periphery" I mean feeling in the position of always being defined by others (Hannerz, 1991). Adichieh's account is very much one of a person being able to use unrecognized cultural capital from Nigeria to stamp her identity creatively and innovatively on being in the US, eventually to the extent that she can return to her native Nigerian English in maintaining her identity.

Seeking understandings of Periphery cultural realities is very much a theme of critical cosmopolitanism as well as critical theory, where non-Western realities have been hidden by a top-down, Western-led globalization (Bhabha, 1994, p. xiv; Delanty, et al., 2008; Kamali, 2007), and "the margins begin to contest, the locals begin to come to representation" (Stuart Hall, 1991, p. 53). The Periphery stamping identity on Center cultural domains therefore becomes a form of bottom-up globalization. This point relates to all the research discussed in this chapter, where in all cases it is important to look beyond traditional views of regional or religious cultural difference. Therefore, one might encourage research which brings de-centered accounts, whether from so-called Western or non-Western participants. By this I mean that they should be bottom-up, starting with the detail of everyday experience, rather than beginning with the grand narratives of cultural difference. Through this process it may well become apparent that the traditional cultural categories of who people are may be found inadequate, and the results of cultural travel itself may not be what is expected. In an interview study of 28 people of diverse national backgrounds I discovered that personal trajectories covered whole life experiences which traced back to ancestry, through professional and friendship groups, as well as travel to, and sojourn in, foreign national locations. Helping participants to develop their narratives can be a far from straightforward process. Researchers need to be prepared to engage in co-construction and to offer their own experience of life history (Merrill & West, 2009, p. 117). This is demonstrated in my own study of a single interview, where I interrogate my own role in helping my interviewee to construct her cultural history (Holliday, 2012).

Seeking de-centered accounts is not the same, in my view, as non-Western accounts which present a polarized "us"-"them" picture of culture conflict by countering Western essentialist pictures of the non-West with equally essentialist accounts of non-Western cultural attributes that are being denied. This is a particular version of the "West versus the rest" discourse which results in self-marginalizing or self-Othering (Kim, 2012; Kumaravadivelu, 2012, p. 22).

Underlying Universal Cultural Processes

So far I have not distinguished between people from different cultural backgrounds in my discussion of research. There will of course be immense variety in cultural practices between different cultural locations, which will provide variety in the cultural resources which individuals can draw upon, variety in cultural practices (see below), and variety in how people in different locations are treated or perceived within the global politics of world cultural positioning. However, the central domain of the grammar (Figure 2.1) indicates that the basic manner in which we engage with culture, wherever we find it, is shared by all of us. These underlying universal cultural processes involve skills and strategies through which everyone, regardless of background, participates in and negotiates their position within the cultural landscapes to which they belong or with which they engage. This is the basis upon which we are able to read culture creatively wherever we find it.

At the core of the underlying universal cultural processes domain is small culture formation. The research which this invites in intercultural communication studies should be the detail of how we form culture on the run, or how we form and perform routines and rules that enable us to make sense and interact in the process of daily construction of culture (Holliday, 2013, p. 56), and how we do this in diverse and new cultural locations. This is at the core of intercultural competence and awareness, and of interculturality. One area of research would be to look at the detail of how people interact through observation of behavior, analysis of talk, or self-reporting of instances of interaction. The latter could be recall of experience through logs, diaries, field notes, personal narratives, reconstructions, and so on.

Here, again, it is important to move away from traditional preoccupations which have often looked at miscommunication as the medium product of intercultural communication, and then sought to solve the problem through increased understanding of foreign practices. Instead, research on this area needs to look at the manner in which misunderstandings are negotiated as a normal part of everyday small culture formation. In terms of developing intercultural skills, the focus here would move to an understanding not so much of difference but of the sorts of processes we all go through to resolve communication issues. Here, going back to the use of cultural resources, we would apply an understanding of how the processes of resolution already work in our past everyday experience – of how we already have the basic mechanisms for engaging with miscommunication – asking questions, making allowances, finding middle ways, negotiating, sorting out face, and managing Self and Other.

This area will also take in all the research related to other sections of the grammar in that all of them relate in different ways to underlying universal cultural processes and small culture formation.

Particular Cultural Products

On the right of the grammar (Figure 2.1), these are the outcome of cultural activity. The first domain, artefacts, includes the "big-C" cultural artefacts such as literature and the arts. This is clearly a traditionally rich area for a wide range of research. These artefacts also include cultural practices, which are the day-to-day things we do which can seem strange to people coming from foreign cultural backgrounds – how we eat, wash, greet, show respect, organize our environment, and so on. These are the things which are most commonly associated with "our culture" or national culture; but they also differ between small groups within a particular society. Within a critical cosmopolitan paradigm, these practices take on a different significance to the more traditional view that they represent deep values that characterize the people who "belong to that culture," who practise them. Instead they represent a set of behaviors which are accessible to outsiders in the same sense that practices in a particular organization are accessible to new employees in that organization given the politics and structures which might include or exclude. In other words, their accessibility depends on politics; and any statements that they are somehow sacred in their rootedness in "blood and soil" are indeed political. This understanding opens the way to the important concept within critical cosmopolitanism of contestation of practices in the public domain (Delanty, 2008, p. 93). Research in this area could therefore look into the us-them politics surrounding cultural practices – how they are formed and protected, how they are rationalized by their adherents in terms of histories and traditions, how they are presented to newcomers, and how inclusion and exclusion operates. Such research could again involve ethnographies comprising observation of behavior, analysis of interactions, and interviews with and accounts from participants.

At the core of this research will be the key set of phenomena in the second part of this domain of the grammar – statements about culture. These are the way that we present ourselves through what we choose to say about our cultural background. These statements can often make claims about regional or religious cultures such as "in my culture we are always on time," "we don't make decisions without consulting the group," "we respect our parents" or "we value the individual." Such statements must not be taken at face value because they can project idealized images of how we see ourselves. Dervin (2011, p. 187) makes an interesting point about stereotypes. Rather than discussing whether or not they are true, we should investigate why people wish to construct them in the way they do. The same would apply to statements about culture.

Useful research could therefore be carried out to investigate what is behind such statements. This could involve exploring the underpinnings of their constructions through interviews and narrative enquiry, but also direct observation of these constructions in interaction and group behavior. Dervin & Machart's (2015) edited collection on how culture is treated as an excuse in a wide range of social settings is an important contribution here in that, by means of interviews and critical discourse analysis, it looks at how culture is used by different groups, from governments, through minorities, to performers and in fine art to promote either political or micropolitical identities. This research would contribute to the understanding of underlying universal cultural processes and small culture formation. It would also help the understanding of processes of inclusion and exclusion in cultural practices. Angouri & Glynos (2009, p. 11) report how, by following up questionnaire data with in depth interviews, it was discovered that European company managers' initial statements about the importance of national culture were by no means what they appeared to be. They conclude that "treating 'culture' as floating signifier in organizational practices means treating it as a window into which subjects feel it possible to project their meanings, aspirations and fantasies" (2009, p. 14). Amadasi (2014) uses focus groups and conversation analysis to explore how the children of immigrant families in Italy construct diverse images of cultural identity in opposition to an expected deficiency through cultural alienation.

Cultural Negotiation

The themes of inclusion and exclusion related to cultural practices relate to the arrows across the top and the bottom of the grammar (Figure 2.1). In Weber's social action theory everyone has the potential to dialogue with structures of their society. However, the degree to which this potential can be realized will depend on other forces of tradition, politics, hierarchy, and prejudice acting against it. Intercultural competence will also be mediated by these forces. When we travel, the degree to which we will be able to engage creatively with the practices we find will also depend not only on the restrictive forces acting against us, but also the restrictions of prejudice, hierarchy and tradition which we carry with us. In this sense, all the research proposed in this chapter needs to address this politics.

At the center of the prejudice which continually inhibits cultural travel and expression are global position and politics on the bottom left, and discourses of and about "culture" on the right of the grammar. The former have already been discussed in the particular social and political structures section. In Holliday (2013, pp. 109–110) I introduce working titles for a number different discourses. I have already referred to the "West versus the rest" discourse above which encourages an us-them polarization. I define discourse as a way of using language which represents ideas about how things are. Discourses can be a powerful means of establishing ideas and forms of behavior. Particularly powerful in this respect is the popular "essentialist culture and language" discourse which maps precisely nation, language, culture, and behavior onto each other. It has been noted by a number of critical sociologists that this discourse, promoted by nineteenth-century nationalism, has had a long-standing influence on social science in the form of a methodological nationalism (e.g. Beck & Sznaider, 2006). This discourse clearly encourages a divisive picture of culture which confines us to images of ourselves and others which keep us apart.

The essentialist culture and language discourse is, however, converted into prejudice by two further discourses. The "cultural relativism" discourse, while claiming equality and mutual respect between cultures, encourages the view that people outside the West, confined by collectivist cultures, should not be expected to participate in the individualist activities which are thought to characterize Western people, such as critical thinking, autonomy, and self-determination. In effect this is a patronizing exclusion of people who are thought not to be able to do what we can. This patronage is deepened by a "West as steward" discourse, in which Western people feel that they are in a position to help the non-West to develop. In a number of places in Holliday (2013, pp. 16, 70, 157) we see people who do well in Western domains being congratulated by Western friends or colleagues for having learnt from the West and a denial that they bring anything of value from their own cultural background. There are also other cases where people are met with deep prejudices based on long-standing yet mistaken narratives about where they come from (Holliday, 2013, pp. 84, 89, 138). The outcome is a particularly hidden form of prejudice which appears on the surface to be well-wishing – a neoracism which hides beneath presumably innocent talk of cultural difference (Spears, 1999; Wodak, 2008, p. 65).

The area of cultural prejudice is a particularly difficult to research because so much remains hidden, not just between the lines of apparently mild statements, but also by the powerful essentialist culture and language discourse that has been promoted by the positivist paradigm for a considerable time, which projects intercultural communication as an entirely neutral matter. Also, there is not just one but a number of discourses which work together to weave a significant smokescreen; and, as has been clear throughout, key concepts such as culture, discourse, and the West are themselves highly contested. Critical discourse analysis of documents, conversations and interactions in which there is comment on performance between residents and newcomers would be important ways forward. Narrative-based studies with long-term sojourners would need to be prepared to dig deeply into how they had been treated. There would need to be a principled shift from the view that "problems" with cultural "competence" are caused by the orientation of the cultures from which people come, to a more positive view that they are caused by the prejudices which they meet.

> ### Case in point
>
> Holliday, A. R. (2013). *Understanding intercultural communication: Negotiating a grammar of culture*. London: Routledge.
> Baumann, G. (1996). *Contesting culture*. Cambridge: Cambridge University Press.
> In this section I will look at two studies. One, my own, which explicitly addresses the exigencies of my grammar of culture, and one which also broadly represents an interpretivist constructivist approach. In each case I will pinpoint a particular method which I believe helps the study to address the issues raised by a postmodern paradigm in looking at culture.

In my 2013 book, *Understanding Intercultural Communication: negotiating a grammar of culture*, I employ what has been described elsewhere as creative non-fiction (Agar, 1990). This involves writing ethnographic reconstructions of composites of observed events, interviews and other circumstantial data. It is designed to address the problem that much of what is witnessed in everyday life is hard to catch in more established qualitative data. The validity is based upon the application of the ethnographic disciplines of making the familiar strange, bracketing, and thick description. This is practised in the writing of the narratives, where:

1. everything can be sourced to real events,
2. there is an adherence to what has been seen and heard with minimal embellishment of adjectives,
3. characters are allowed to take on a life beyond the intentions of the writer,
4. a further character who interrogates the views being expressed is always introduced,
5. statements about culture or discourses of culture always come from the characters and are interrogated by others.

The narratives are always followed by a further interrogation of what they mean and the agendas of the characters. I do also make it clear that I am subscribing to a critical cosmopolitan discourse and therefore do not look for solid culture difference. Therefore, in all cases, the characters in the narratives are not different because of their different cultures, but in the ways in which they align themselves or are faced with different discourses of culture in the different settings in which they reside.

Gerd Baumann, in his 1996 book, *Contesting culture*, reports an ethnographic study of how culture is constructed in everyday life by different individuals and communities in a multicultural London suburb. He observes how individuals construct and use culture to mean different things at different times depending on the topic of conversation, and can have multiple membership of cultural groups and activities. He notes how "culture-making is ... a project of social continuity placed within, and contending with, moments of social change." The people in his study "reify cultures while at the same time making culture" (1996, p. 31). He is able to arrive at these observations, finding ways to get around dominant discourses of culture, by applying the discipline of thinking of his participants as people rather than starting with the view that they belong to specific cultures.

Conclusion

Looking at researching the intercultural from a social action perspective, within a postmodern paradigm, and employing a constructivist and interpretivist perspective has necessarily taken in a wide range of possibilities. On the one hand the options are wide open, with the potential for multiple forms of data, as they relate to almost every aspect of social life. The recognition that subjectivity and creativity in research is viable releases researchers to employ everything they bring with them to make sense of the intercultural world. On the other hand, however, in a world that is shot through with hidden discourses and ideology, and politics and prejudice, there is need for researchers to apply immense rigor as they manage their relationships with these obscure and shifting forces of which they are a part.

Key Terms

Discourse A way of using language which represents ideas about how things are.
Essentialist Explaining people's behavior as the essence their culture, and that all people from that culture will behave in that way.
Neoracism A form of rationalizing the subordination of a defined group of people on the basis of culture even though race is not an explicit agenda in the minds of the people concerned.
Prejudice Images built on prior formulae for Self and Other representation.
Small culture A cultural environment which is located in proximity to the people concerned.

References

Adichie, C. N. (2013). *Americanah*. London: Harper Collins.
Agar, M. (1990). Text and fieldwork: "Exploring the excluded middle." *Journal of Contemporary Ethnography*, 19(1), 73–88.
Amadasi, S. (2014). Beyond belonging. How migrant children actively construct their cultural identities in the interaction. *Interdisciplinary Journal of Family Studies*, 19(1), 136–152.
Angouri, J., & Glynos, J. (2009). *Managing cultural difference and struggle in the context of the multinational corporate workplace: solution or symptom?* Colchester: World Network in Ideology in Discourse Analysis, Working Paper Series, no. 26.
Baumann, G. (1996). *Contesting culture*. Cambridge: Cambridge University Press.
Beck, U., & Sznaider, N. (2006). Unpacking cosmopolitanism for the social sciences: A research agenda. *British Journal of Sociology*, 57(1), 1–23.
Bendix, R. (1966). *Max Weber: An intellectual portrait*. London: Methuen.
Bhabha, H. (1994). *The location of culture*. London: Routledge.
Clifford, J., & Marcus, G. E. (Eds.). (1986). *Writing culture: The poetica of politics of ethnography*. Berkeley: University of California Press.
Crane, D. (1994). Introduction: The challenge of the sociology of culture to sociology as discipline. In D. Crane (Ed.), *The sociology of culture* (pp. 1–19). Oxford: Blackwell.
Delanty, G. (2006). The cosmopolitan imagination: Critical cosmopolitanism and social theory. *British Journal of Sociology*, 57(1), 25–47.
Delanty, G. (2008). Dilemmas of secularism: Europe, religion and the problem of pluralism. In G. Delanty, R. Wodak & P. Jones (Eds.), *Identity, belonging and migration* (pp. 78–97). Liverpool: Liverpool University Press.
Delanty, G., Wodak, R., & Jones, P. (2008). Introduction: migration, discrimination and belonging in Europe. In G. Delanty, R. Wodak, & P. Jones (Eds.), *Identity, belonging and migration* (pp. 1–20). Liverpool: Liverpool University Press.
Dervin, F. (2011). A plea for change in research on intercultural discourses: A "liquid" approach to the study of the acculturation of Chinese students. *Journal of Multicultural Discourses*, 6(1), 37–52. doi: 10.1080/17447143.2010.532218
Dervin, F., & Machart, R. (Eds.). (2015). *Culture as an excuse in Intercultural Communication and education*. London: Palgrave.
Durkheim, E. (1933). *The division of labor in society* (G. Simpson, Trans.). New York: Macmillan.
Geertz, C. (1993). *The interpretation of cultures*. London: Fontana.
Grande, E. (2006). Cosmopolitan political science. *British Journal of Sociology*, 57(1), 87–111.

Gray, J. (2010). The branding of English and the culture of the new capitalism: Representations of the world of work in English language textbooks. *Applied Linguistics*, 31(5), 714–733. doi: 10.1093/applin/amq034

Hahl, K., Niemi, P.-M., Longfor, R. J., & Dervin, F. (Eds.). (2015). *Diversities and interculturality in textbooks: Finland as an example*. Newcastle-upon-Tyne: Cambridge Scholars.

Hall, S. (1991). Old and new identities, old and new ethnicities. In A. D. King (Ed.), *Culture, globalisation and the world-system* (pp. 40–68). Basingstoke: Palgrave.

Hannerz, U. (1991). Scenarios of peripheral cultures. In A. D. King (Ed.), *Culture, globalisation and the world-system* (pp. 107–128). Basingstoke: Palgrave Macmillan.

Hoffman, E. (1998). *Lost in translation*. London: Vintage.

Holliday, A. R. (2011). *Intercultural communication and ideology*. London: Sage.

Holliday, A. R. (2012). Interrogating researcher participation in an interview study of intercultural contribution in the workplace. *Qualitative Inquiry*, 18(6), 504–515. doi: 10.1177/1077800412442811

Holliday, A. R. (2013). *Understanding intercultural communication: Negotiating a grammar of culture*. London: Routledge.

Kamali, M. (2007). Multiple modernities and Islamism in Iran. *Social Compass*, 54(3), 373–387. doi: 10.1177/0037768607080833

Kim, M.-S. (2012). Trends in intercultural communication research – from a research culture of war to a research culture of peace. Paper presented at the BAAL Special Interest Group in Intercultural Communication: intercultural communication in international contexts – training and development, practice and research, Open University, Milton Keynes.

King, A. D. (Ed.). (1991). *Culture, globalisation and the world-system*. Basingstoke: Palgrave.

Kumaravadivelu, B. (2012). Individual identity, cultural globalisation, and teaching English as an international language: the case for an epistemic break. In L. Alsagoff, W. Renandya, G. Hu, & S. McKay (Eds.), *Principles and practices for teaching English as an international language* (pp. 9–27). London: Routledge.

Merrill, B., & West, L. (2009). *Using biographical methods in social research*. London: Sage.

Parsons, T. (1951). *The social system*. New York: Free Press.

Said, E. (1978). *Orientalism*. London: Routledge & Kegan Paul.

Spears, A. K. (1999). Race and ideology: An introduction. In A. K. Spears (Ed.), *Race and ideology: Language, symbolism, and popular culture* (pp. 11–58). Detroit, MI: Wayne State University Press.

Spradley, J. P. (1980). *Participant observation*. New York: Holt, Rinehart & Winston.

Tran, L. T. (2009). Making visible "hidden" intentions and potential choices: International students in intercultural communication. *Language and Intercultural Communication*, 9(4), 271–284.

Urry, J. (2002). *The tourist gaze* (2nd ed.). London: Sage.

Vandrick, S. (1999). ESL and the colonial legacy: A teacher faces her "missionary kid" past. In G. Haroian-Guerin (Ed.), *The personal narrative: Writing ourselves as teachers and scholars* (pp. 63–74). Portland, ME: Calendar Island Publishers.

Wallace, C. (2003). *Critical reading in language education*. Basingstoke: Palgrave Macmillan.

Wang, J. (2012). Chinese professionals' intercultural communication. Paper presented at the BAAL Special Interest Group in Intercultural Communication: intercultural communication in international contexts – training and development, practice and research, Open University, Milton Keynes.

Weber, M. (1950). *The Protestant ethic and the spirit of capitalism* (T. Parsons, Trans. 3rd ed.). London: George Allen & Unwin.

Weber, M. (1964). *The theory of social and economic organization*. New York: Free Press.

Wodak, R. (2008). "Us and them": Inclusion and exclusion. In G. Delanty, R. Wodak, & P. Jones (Eds.), *Identity, belonging and migration* (pp. 54–77). Liverpool: Liverpool University Press.

Further Reading and Resources

Dervin, F. (2011). A plea for change in research on intercultural discourses: A "liquid" approach to the study of the acculturation of Chinese students. *Journal of Multicultural Discourses*, 6(1), 37–52.

Delanty, G., Wodak, R., & Jones, P. (2008). Introduction: migration, discrimination and belonging in Europe. In G. Delanty, R, Wodak, & P. Jones (Eds.), *Identity, belonging and migration* (pp. 1–20). Liverpool: Liverpool University Press.

Holliday, A. R. (2013). *Understanding intercultural communication: Negotiating a grammar of culture*. London: Routledge.

Kumaravadivelu, B. (2007). *Cultural globalization and language education*. New Haven, CT: Yale University Press.

3 Studying Identity

Jo Angouri

> **Summary**
>
> The study of identity occupies a central position in social sciences and humanities, and for many it constitutes a field in its own right. The relationship between language and identity, in particular, is a key area in sociolinguistics, applied linguistics, and Intercultural Communication scholarship. Moving away from a static, universalistic paradigm which understands people as bearers of various identities, there is a growing trend to focus on how identity is constructed in interaction in different professional and everyday contexts. In this chapter I discuss these two positions and pay attention to the notion of cultural identity. I close the chapter with some terminological considerations and areas for further research.

Introduction

The concept of identity is at the core of ongoing debates in social sciences and humanities. Discussing or summarizing what has been written around it would be an impossible task and certainly one that goes beyond the limitations of any one chapter. Here I briefly discuss the notion of categorization and two different approaches to the study of identity emanating from positivism and constructionism (cf. constructivism in Chapter 1, this volume) respectively and will close the chapter by discussing the notion of cultural identity. I draw on some of my recently completed and ongoing work in illustrating the issues raised and also refer to other relevant sociolinguistics, applied linguistics and Intercultural Communication (IC) research.

The relationship between language and identity has been central in the sociolinguistic field since at least the 1960s (See, e.g. Labov's influential 1966 and 1972 studies) and much of the early work attempted to associate linguistic phenomena with distinct social groups (of different nature such as "adolescents" or "middle class" speakers) defined by the researcher. An increasing interest in identity has also been visible in applied linguistics scholarship in the last 15 years (see Norton, 1997, 2000 for a discussion). Research in this area has addressed the relationship between language and identity in relation to language learning, teaching, the learner and the classroom setting. Work on identity, however, goes beyond the linguistics disciplinary boundary and "identity studies" is increasingly seen as an area in social sciences that is becoming a field in its own right (see e.g. Côté, 2006). This involves discussing identity both at the level of the individual and that of the group.

The theoretical underpinning of identity scholarship has always been multidisciplinary, influenced by work in a range of disciplines and areas of study: psychology, social theory, gender theory, and sociology to name but a few. Work by Erikson as early as 1968 on ego-identity (sense of self) or Butler's work on performativity (e.g. 1999), S. Hall (e.g. Hall & Du Gay, 1996) and Giddens (1991) on identity and politics (by no means an exhaustive list) as well as work in linguistics (e.g. audience design by Bell, 1984), and other disciplines, evidently, have influenced the development of current thinking in the area. The work of these theorists has shed light on aspects of human existence and, at the same time, has shown the complexity of other coterminous notions, notably self, group, role. To add to terminological proliferation it is not uncommon for these terms to be used either interchangeably or to be subsumed under the "identity umbrella."

What plays a significant part in designing and carrying out projects that address identity, in one guise or another, and hence influence methodological decisions, is whether identity is understood, by the researcher, as something people "have" or something we all "do." I discuss this in some detail below. In keeping with the spirit of the volume I refrain from analyzing philosophical stances and will instead pay more attention to the implications and the ways in which research projects operationalize these notions. Given the space available, the discussion in the next few pages is necessarily simplified and I illustrate the key issues through relevant examples. I have structured this chapter in four parts; starting from positivism, I then turn to the essentialist approach to the study of identity and also address strategic essentialism. Following this, the discussion moves to social constructionism, and I close the chapter with a short discussion on cultural identity and the implications that can be drawn for the ways in which such terminology is used in relevant work.

Positivism, Essentialism and Strategic Essentialism: Ontology and Epistemology

Understanding individuals as bearers of a set of characteristics or specific attributes (e.g. age, gender, ethnicity, class) which can be predetermined and can serve to both cluster individuals (and groups of individuals) together and to separate, compare, and contrast them was very common in early sociolinguistic and applied linguistic research as well as in the growing field of IC. In this context, identity is often understood as the sum of different characteristics seen as facets or aspects of self and which seem to pre-exist the contexts within which the individuals operate. Identity, then, can be captured and described (just as "culture"). This approach to identity resonates with a positivist paradigm according to which reality pre-exists the social order and can be known by objective means of enquiry. In this school of thought, the rigor of the method is related to the validity of the research and the robustness of the findings. Positivism (according to Comte, see Lenzer, 1975/1998 and also Chapter 1, this volume), attempts to allow for the data to show how the real world, governed by natural laws, works. It rejects anything metaphysical and is in line with an empiricist research tradition. The term as used by Comte (his work mainly took place between 1830 and 1850) denotes scientific enquiry, which is useful in understanding and placing the term in the philosophy of science arena.

Following positivism, postpositivist thinking does not attempt to find the "absolute truth" any more. It does not argue that objective truth does not exist but, rather, that it is very difficult to achieve. Hence, work falling within this paradigm aims to test the theories that can unveil how things (at least partly) work. Both positivism and its successor aim for generalizability and have been associated with quantitative research. Positivism had a profound influence on thinking in social sciences and in identity scholarship. Research taking this point of view aims to measure attributes that are associated with an individual or group, typically through conventional tools such as surveys or questionnaires, in order to generalize the findings to the wider population. In line with the characteristics of quantitative research, large datasets are necessary for claims to be substantiated.

Positivism is widely associated with essentialism in writings on identity. Although the two traditions have different trajectories and points of reference, in so far as identity scholarship is concerned, they meet in attempting to capture the "realities which lie behind the appearances" (Popper, 1963, p. 139). Essentialism has been criticized severely in recent scholarship for reducing a complex reality to a set of characteristics which oversimplify individuals and groups. To go into more detail, Bucholtz (2003, p. 400) provides a useful overview in stating:

> Essentialism is the position that the attributes and behavior of socially defined groups can be determined and explained by reference to cultural and/or biological characteristics believed to be inherent to the group. As an ideology, essentialism rests on two assumptions: 1) that groups can be clearly delimited and 2) that group members are more or less alike.

These two assumptions have been debated vividly in social sciences in the 1970s, 1980s and 1990s. In sociolinguistics and applied linguistics the debate has been less pronounced, compared to other disciplinary areas, until more recently. Without going into much detail here, I would argue that there is consensus that boundaries between groups in society are porous and that the essentialist level of homogeneity is unattainable and ideological. As an illustration, work on the notion of community in sociolinguistics (notably, speech community) has shown the impossibility of setting rigid boundaries between different social assemblages (e.g. Gumperz & Levinson, 1996).

Overall, work under the constructionist stance, whereby reality is understood as subjective and emergent, negotiated in the context of interaction, has had a profound influence on establishing the complexity of identity work speakers do in interaction. This is particularly visible in recent work in sociolinguistic enquiry (e.g. Mendoza-Denton, 2004), where social demographic categories (e.g. age, class, gender) are not preordained but understood as negotiated between the participants and captured, often, in naturally occurring interaction (see discussion on data below). Despite the criticisms, however, essentialism is still dominant. Caveats against oversimplifying labels are very common but this does not mean that essentialism is off the agenda. Accounts of what "women," "young people," or "British people" do or talk like still proliferate and are used to explain away differences, linguistic or other. The use of macro categories to operationalize identity has a long tradition, and there is a clear parallel with the use of the term "culture" in this sense (see Chapter 2, this volume, and the section on cultural identity below). Although research has shown that projecting common characteristics to all individuals in a group is limited and limiting, essentialism also resonates with lay discourses, a point to which I return later.

Essentialism is not, as with any philosophical stance, one single doctrine. Different researchers operationalize it differently. As Spivak notes "essentialism is a loose tongue" (Spivak & Rooney, 1994, p. 159) and the term is used to denote different stances and positions. There are, however, some key tenets that are shared by either strong or moderate essentialism. As an illustration, from the philosophy field, Ereshefsky (2010) summarizes three tenets of traditional essentialism as follows:

> In brief, traditional essentialism holds that essences in kinds have the following three features: (1) they occur in all and only the members of a kind, (2) they play a central role in explaining the properties typically associated with the members of a kind, and (3) they are intrinsic properties (2010, p. 675).

I find this summary very useful in providing the gist of the matter and for clarifying the arguments that have been put forward in the anti-essentialism scholarship, which strongly argues against flat, reductionist accounts of people and phenomena (e.g. Stone, 2004). Anti-essentialism thinking, however, soon came under scrutiny, too, for undercutting political action, particularly in relation to feminist politics, ethnic minorities, or discrimination at work, to name but a few (see Ang, 2001 for a discussion). The key argument from this point of view is that essentialism can be used strategically by researchers who recognize its limitations. In other words, by reducing a complex reality or by focusing on a single attribute or set of attributes, a political goal becomes achievable, and work that often concerns either issues or groups that are marginalized becomes prominent. There is clearly a lot of ideological analytical validity in this proposition, which may at least partly explain why the paradigm is still appealing for novice and senior scholars alike. Anti-essentialism has been clearly articulated in feminist scholarship, where strategic essentialism has been seen as descriptively false but politically useful. Feminist scholars, however, have also shown how essentialism is not a necessary stance for supporting the feminist agenda (see Stone, 2004, for a discussion). One important issue to raise here is that of whose voice is being heard in strategic essentialism and how the researchers' understanding of what the agenda is (or should be) is to be aligned with the participants' perceptions (with all the constraints associated with who the actual participants are, how they have been selected, and so forth, which apply to any line of enquiry). There is space for this discussion to become more prominent in the field and to relate to other debates on the politics of identity (see, e.g. Hall & Du Gay, 1996; Pavlenko & Blackledge, 2004). What is relevant to our discussion here, however, is that research taking an essentialist viewpoint often does not seem mindful of the limitations of the essentialist stance, nor does it make this explicit for the reader. I elaborate further in the next section.

Constructionism

Following a prevailing trend in social sciences, much of the current research in sociolinguistics, applied linguistics, and IC takes a constructionist approach (Burr, 2003). In line with this school of thought, reality is not seen as existing outside the social order and is not objectively determined. It constitutes a construct that is emergent and negotiated between participants in interaction. Language plays a central role in what Burr calls the social constructionist movement as "when people talk to each other, the world gets constructed" (Burr, 2003, p. 8). From this perspective, macro categories such as "age," "gender," or "ethnicity" are not understood in relation to some abstract criteria but according to the work interactants do in positioning self and other in a given context (on positioning theory see Davies & Harré, 1990). Interactants perform, often in subtle ways, "particular acts and display particular kinds of epistemic and affective stances" in doing identity work (Ochs, 1993, p. 289). Hence, speakers negotiate their interpretations of social phenomena by drawing on discourses available to them. Moving from universal claims about identity categories, the focus is now on the ways in which people negotiate, enact, and perform aspects of self in relation to different sociocultural contexts. Accordingly, the detailed analysis of specific cases and qualitative data becomes more prominent. Constructionist research has led to vivid debates in social sciences; the methodological choices researchers make depend on disciplinary traditions and the research question each investigation seeks to address. In Sociolinguistic Discourse Analysis, one of my own areas of expertise, studies have favored the analysis of naturally occurring data in order to unpack how interactants do identity work in a range of everyday or professional settings (e.g. Angouri & Marra, 2011). The relationship between social organization and identity work in everyday contexts has been the focus also of Conversation Analysis (CA, see Chapter 20, this volume). CA, based on work by Sacks (1972/1992/1995), has shed light on the sequential organization of talk, and provides a solid understanding of the way in which identity positionings are performed in interaction. Moving from the microanalysis of talk and everyday conversations, to the macro context, research by narrative researchers has also shown how people make sense of "self" through stories. Stories reflect the teller's idealized views of self and also provide the means to bridge the "here and now" of the storytelling episode to the broader sociopolitical context within which the teller makes sense of self. The "subject positions," which constitute a "conceptual repertoire and a location for persons" (Davies & Harré, 1990, p. 46) available within a particular context, have been addressed by positioning theorists in a variety of contexts ranging from corporate organizations to psychotherapy and newspaper stories. Narrative analysis is, evidently, not one single approach (see Chapter 22, this volume) and the same applies to all the approaches to the study of interaction mentioned in this section. All the traditions and their associated methodologies, however, have attempted to capture and analyze the subjective nature of identity and the dynamic relationship between the agency of the individual and pre-existing societal structures.

Further to this, no process of negotiation can be understood outside the nexus of power relationships within which the speakers operate. The speakers do not "share" equally the same rights to accept or reject identities projected on or claimed by them. I see identity from this point of view, as a *multi-way* process where identities can be assumed, imposed or rejected in the immediate context of the interaction. Discourse histories, interpersonal relationships, the local context, as well as the wider sociocultural order, are all part of "who says what and who is entitled to what" according the participants' perceptions of the encounter. Constructing a student identity in a supervision meeting, for instance, is very different from when negotiating renting a house with a group of friends.

Overall, a constructionist approach does not necessarily claim that the interactants' work always starts afresh. The fact that structures pre-exist the "here and now" of interaction and the relationship between agency and structure has been widely discussed. The spotlight is on how these structures become relevant and are brought to the fore in any given context. Equally important, in my view, is that a social constructionist perspective allows space for the perception of the participants vs. that of the researcher to be brought into interpretation. I have written elsewhere (e.g. Angouri & Bargiela-Chiappini, 2011) on the relevance of the common distinction in politeness theory (e.g. Watts, Ide, & Ehlich, 1992) between first-order (the participants') and second-order (the researchers') perspectives for the understanding of complex phenomena. This distinction can be, usefully, applied to the study of abstract notions such as identity (note however that the two are not a simple dichotomy; see, e.g. Haugh, 2012). Berger and Luckmann, very early in their seminal work, indicate that "the sociological understanding of "reality" and "knowledge" falls somewhere in the middle between that of the man in the street and that of the philosopher" (1966/1991, p. 2); while the first takes both for granted, the latter steps back and theorizes. It seems to me that sociolinguistics, applied linguistics, and IC research are also between the two positions and can usefully develop further theoretical tools that allow the lay views to feedback into our understanding of identity enactment and processes of categorization.

Let us now look at an example of how participants construct identities in a workplace context. The example in the following Case in Point is part of a dataset from a completed project on decision making in small businesses.

Case in Point

A senior management meeting in a growing small business context. The meeting takes place in the headquarters of a growing nonprofit organization. The participants debate the ways in which they could engage their members and create a shared sense of priorities. Tom is chairing the meeting and is the company's director. (Data source: Jo Angouri)

1	Dan	the other thing that am trying to change (.) the behaviour is that it isnt down to
2		[NAME] (.) alright its a little bit at the moment is that there are some members
3		that act like children and they sort of expect [NAME] to do everything
4	Paul	[yes]
5	Dan	for them
6		(.) and be a parent (.) we – and i think toms ((inaudible)) reaction sometimes is
7		he becomes like a frustrated parent (…)
8	Paul	(…)yes but at that particular time when
9		they re already in a position (.) we know some are sleeping (.) well we can
10		forget those probably because recovery rate is probably gonna be rather rather
11		low (…) the lapsed (.) theres more chance of them coming back in again but
12		they might need a bit of parenting at that early stage (.) but its quite important i
13		agree not to say this is the parenting were going to do and by the way we are
14		going to be dad – that might be tom actually (.) you know (…)
15	Tom	it it may well be
16		(.) but i dont believe the membership has ever seen itself as a membership (.)
17		because theres been nothing to belong to so i think weve weve got a bigger
18		problem uh (.) than the one thats being articulated at the moment (.) and i dont
19		believe that there is a feeling of belonging to anything (.) and i think what i hear
20		dan saying is that in order to create that (.) there has to be a responsibility taken
21		by the members

The three participants construct themselves in a position of authority within the organization. Note how all three take responsibility for engaging the members (e.g. line 1 "I") and also explicitly address Tom's reactions towards the members in a somewhat negative light (e.g. line 7). This, however, does not seem to be perceived as inappropriate by any of the participants and is not sanctioned, e.g. there is no reaction by Tom either immediately or later in the meeting. Tom's role as the company's decision-maker is evident in the meeting; he takes the floor after Paul and Dan have developed their thinking, constructs himself to be in the position of articulating what the "bigger problem" (line 18) is and of summarizing Dan's earlier turns (Holmes & Stubbe, 2003). His position as the most senior member is evident throughout the meeting (not discussed here) but at the same time the shared knowledge and norms between the participants are also relevant to the ways in which the history of the topic is shared. Dan and Paul construct a team identity between the senior management (us) and the members (them) and go so far as to draw a clear power distinction by taking the role of the parent and positioning the members to the role of the children who are in need of "parenting" (lines 13–15). The symbolic power of the metaphors is evident and is becoming a common resource for the team to construct their roles (Tom the "Dad," Dan and Paul possibly the "less strict" parent). They also successfully construct a team identity through the joint elaboration of the metaphor as well as the "us" and "them" distinction which is evident throughout the excerpt.

This brief discussion shows the negotiation of roles between the interactants and the process of projecting identity to both those present at the meeting and, also, the "other" (the members in our case here). Overall, through the analysis of discourse data the analyst gains access to what the participants make relevant in a range of different settings, and a conceptualization of the relationship between agency and structure becomes possible. Moving away from generalization, the priority is on developing theoretical and methodological tools that can capture the ways in which participants index self-positioning and other-positioning. Hence, continuing the dialogue on the affordances of the different traditions for the study of discourse can be particularly beneficial for future research on identity.

To sum up, the constructionist approach to the study of identity has allowed for a mosaic of approaches to capturing the complexities of individual experience. Although an anti-essentialist stance is shared by those who self-ascribe to this paradigm, the debate on how "reality" is understood is not, as yet, closed. There is, however, agreement that thinking in binaries (e.g. essence versus construction) is an analytical decision the researcher makes, rather than inherent to the study of identity in our case. Identities do not exist in a vacuum, as individuals do not negotiate "self" or "other" in a vacuum either. This has been clearly shown in all seminal work in this area. Berger and Luckmann's influential work (1966/1991) highlights the unbreakable bond between personal identity and social structure. Further research is needed, however, on the suitability of our current theoretical and methodological tools to capture these complex relationships.

I now turn to the notion of categorization and the relationship with construction processes.

From Identity Theories to Categorization Processes

Categorization has been seen as "a fundamental and universal process because it satisfies a basic human need for cognitive parsimony" (Abrams & Hogg, 2006; Chapter 20, this volume). The relationship between categorization and stereotyping is central to this point of view and has attracted attention in social psychology and in one of the influential theories for the study of identity, namely social identity theory (Tajfel & Turner, 1979). Social identity theory, according to which group membership is directly related to an individual's sense of self and self-image, has influenced profoundly the thinking in applied linguistics, sociolinguistics, and IC research (for example see Joseph, 2004; McNamara, 1997). Work in this area argues that "self" is related to an individual's position within a system of social categories. The process of categorization is inherently a process of simplification where differences tend to be accentuated and the "in group" is seen in a positive light compared to the "out group." Social Identity theory has been, for many years, juxtaposed to Identity Theory. Identity Theory (see Hogg, Terry, & White, 1995) places emphasis on the roles an individual holds and the expected role performance in a given context. Its key tenet is that the role(s) people hold in any encounter is directly related to ways in which people claim or project their different self-identities (note, for example, in the first Case in Point excerpt the role performance expectations users bring to the encounter from prior knowledge or experience). According to Identity Theory, "self" is enacted through role performance. Identity Theory has been compared and contrasted to Social Identity Theory and until recently the two theories have had separate trajectories. Without debating this any further (see Angouri & Marra, 2011), in line with recent work, I see a direct relationship between the two, as individuals do not operate in a societal vacuum and group membership is related to the ways in which roles are enacted and perceived (for a very good discussion see Hogg et al., 1995; Chapter 20, this volume).

Jenkins (2000) drawing on work by Goffman and Giddens refers to the categorization of the social world in three orders: the individual order, the interactional order, and the institutional order. The interactants operate at the interface of these three orders which "overlap completely; each is implicated in each of the others; none makes sense without the others" (Jenkins, 2000, p. 10). Simply put, the first order has to do with the individual and their own reality, the second is negotiated between people, while the third refers to norms and structures already in place. Group membership and role performance have to do with all three orders; hence studying them together provides a more holistic understanding of identity construction processes.

Categorization is an inseparable part of the theoretical and analytical approaches to the study of identity, and to the ways in which macro- and micro-categories are enacted in interaction have been addressed in different linguistic traditions. Focusing on the notion of "doing," work in the conversation analysis school is particularly relevant. The concept of the Membership Categorization Analysis (MCA) draws on early work by Sacks (1972/1992) and has been more recently developed by Antaki & Widdicombe (1998; see also Stokoe & Attenborough, 2014; Chapter 20, this volume). This approach, in line with the ethnomethodological tradition, focuses on the local context and seeks to unveil how membership belonging is made relevant by the participants (see, e.g. work on gender and MCA, Stokoe, 2012) instead of categories predetermined by the analyst. MCA, in line with the broader CA paradigm, seeks to explore through a detailed analysis of discourse practices the ways that categories are invoked and sustained in different everyday (mainly) or professional contexts. A closer look at different categories (be it a mother, a doctor, a squash player and so on), as enacted in talk, can provide the researcher with the analytical tools to access contextual information that the interactants make relevant and to investigate the negotiation of the categories in the immediate context of the interaction. It is through the utterances' indexical properties that people create relationships between the categories and position self and other. Hence MCA, although not widely known in social science research, can provide an alternative to capturing the perceptions of interactants in relation to categorization processes.

Going further into how membership of a group is enacted and indexed in interaction, I discuss an excerpt taken from an ongoing collaborative project which aims to explore the perceived function of an online arthritis community (Angouri & Sanderson, under review) in the following Case in Point. Our project has addressed ways in which members position themselves in relation to co-members.

> **Case in Point**
>
> A posting from an arthritis online community. The excerpt illustrates one newly diagnosed user who claims a member identity and receives a welcome from a more experienced user.
>
> ```
> It's good that you know for sure finally Nicola ☺ A diag-
> nosis none of us want but you can plough on now with
> help of your docs and hopefully feel better in the
> future. I remember last November [...]- it was the last
> thing I expected on that particular day as they'd always
> seemed undecided about me! Anyway, take your time, read
> up even more than you probably have already, and keep
> coming in here to let us know how things are.
>
> Mary x
>
>
> Thanks Mary, it is certainly a day of mixed emotions.
> I'm already ploughing my way through lots of informa-
> tion. I'll certainly be keeping in touch. There's no
> getting rid of me now I'm a member lol x
> ```

Nicola (in an earlier posting) enacts a "newly diagnosed" position and self-confirms her membership of the group – this is taken up in Mary's response. A diagnosis is constructed as an implicit "prerequisite" for the members of this forum, despite the fact that the community is open to carers or medical professionals, and the analysis of our data has not shown any explicit negotiations between the users. The members of the forum construct a community through sharing stories of "sameness" in relation to the trajectory of the illness but also in the coping strategies they have developed. Nicola accepts Mary's position as a senior user by acknowledging the advice provided and concludes by re-claiming a member identity. Most of the users self-identify as living with arthritis; other labels, however, such as that of a "patient," are not always accepted as a category members self-select or relate to the function of the group. This, however, does not contradict the fact that the forum is supported by an arthritis association, most of the members share stories involving the official medial system (for which they are "patients") and negotiate the wider socioeconomic order that influences treatment plans or decisions about work–family responsibilities amongst others. Through datasets such as those discussed briefly here, a case can be made for going beyond binaries (e.g. self/group, on-/offline, micro/macro context) which seem to capture only part of the way in which interactants draw on local and broader categories in positioning self and other.

To conclude this discussion, the question of how research can capture what the participants consider relevant has been debated in the sociolinguistic and applied linguistic literature (see e.g. what is often referred to as the Schegloff, Wetherell, Billig debate in *Discourse and Society, 10 (4), 1999*). Despite the debate, the different traditions, e.g. Conversation Analysis (Chapter 20, this volume), Critical

Discourse Analysis (Chapter 19, this volume), and Interactional Sociolinguistics, still approach these questions from their distinct perspectives. In my view, however, this is not a limitation, as it greatly contributes to the development of better theoretical and methodological tools for the study of categorization – so long as there is dialogue and cross-fertilization between researchers and areas of study. Collectively, this work has foregrounded the significance of the local context and the need to understand categorization not as stable and predetermined but as a process that straddles agency and structure. The more our thinking develops, the more we operationalize the complexity of the subject matter.

Next I am turning to an area particularly relevant to IC scholarship, that of cultural identity.

Cultural, Ethnic, National, Identity/ies?

Projects in sociolinguistics, applied linguistics and IC often tackle the thorny notions of cultural, ethnic, or national identities. What is problematic, though, is when these terms are used interchangeably – and even to denote one another. Definitions proliferate, but what is particularly relevant is that the "national" typically dominates "cultural." More specifically, the notion of cultural identity is typically used to encompass other, seen as related, concepts – ethnicity and race being the most common. To make it even more complicated, cultural identity is also used interchangeably with national identity. The reasons for this terminological fusion can be at least partly explained from the common equation of culture and / or ethnicity with country and / or nation – a problematic position which, however, goes beyond the scope of this chapter (see Angouri & Glynos, 2009). Similarly, understanding cultural identity as a hierarchically higher concept which can be "divided" into "smaller" identities (or subcultures with distinct identities) is also a position that would need to be unpacked in order to be theoretically sustainable. This is because creating hierarchies means that the boundaries between categories are distinct, context-free and can be defined by the researcher. Although voices in the field of Intercultural Communication are becoming louder, for the need to reconceptualize both the "cultural" and the "identity" it is still not uncommon in current discourses to represent culture as one distinct factor in one's self-identity, and the other way around.

Overall, discourses of group homogeneity are deeply rooted in relevant scholarship. As an example, there is a long tradition in anthropology for ethnic identity to be understood as "a sense of common origin, common beliefs and values, common goals, in brief 'common cause'" (Devos, 1972, p. 435). Other disciplinary areas (including applied linguistic, sociolinguistic, and ICC research) also approached ethnic groups as sharing a common culture (and characteristics such as origin and language, to name only two). This position of "difference," however, has been problematized, and seeing ethnicity (and, by extension, cultural identity) as negotiated and constructed in interaction is becoming a common position. As stated by Mendoza, Halualani, & Drzewiecka (2002) "ethnicity is made up and mobilized each time within specific institutionalized discourses and practices that pre-exist individual acts, and produce, constrain, and regulate definitions of the collective ethnic body" (2002, p. 318).

Discourses equating country to culture (and by extension to identity) are common when interactants position self and other. "Culture" is easily appended to names of countries or even more abstract labels (e.g. a search for "Western Cultural Identity" on Google always returns thousands of results). These first-order positions are valuable but need to be understood and interpreted within the local and wider socioeconomic and political context from which they emerge. Let us see one final example (for a discussion of a longer excerpt from this dataset, see Angouri, 2010).

Case in Point

Interview excerpt with a manager in a multinational company

Helen: German people are considered rude in here [referring to the company] but the mistake the English make is they mix up being rude and being direct uhh I mean you ask a German a question you get an answer right? The English will take three times as long to give the answer and then then they will try to make it as if they don't give you the answer but the answer comes from somewhere else.

Helen here produces an almost prototypical example of cultural difference. Having self-claimed a "German identity" earlier in the interview, specific characteristics are related to this "identity," as seen in the excerpt. Helen reflects on why things do not seem to work to the expected standards in her team and this is explained in terms of cultural difference. This excerpt could be analyzed from a range of approaches and stances. For instance, one could approach it from an essentialist perspective (whereby there is a "German-ness" that is distinct to "English-ness") or as a performance of Helen's role and status (see Sarangi, 2010, for a discussion of the two terms) partly enacted through constructing belonging to a particular group under a national label. Each position is associated with distinct methodological traditions, and the rationale and researchers' stance would need to be made explicit in order to contribute to the ongoing debates in the field. Helen's narrative, from a constructionist perspective, shows that "German" is used here as an identifier of both a group of people and a set of linguistic behavior (directness). At the same time, an essentialist approach would draw on normalized behaviors between two abstract groups and could attribute potential for friction or miscommunication. What I believe is significant here is how, through our current theoretical and analytical tools, we can relate Helen's positioning (first order) to theories of culture, ethnicity, and identity (second order). In other words, not taking a broad-brush relationship between German-ness and directness at face value needs to be followed by an analysis of the ways and the reasons why Helen draws into this normative discourses in addressing work-related concerns. Hence a nuanced set of tools is needed to unpack the complexity of work that is done in this context.

To conclude, cultural identity literature relies heavily on the notion of cultural difference. Difference and sameness, however, are rather fluid notions, negotiated by the interactants, and have different meaning for speakers and researchers (who do not operate in the same contexts nor do they have the same agendas). Hence I align here with the following positions:

1   there is a need to move away from the temptation to "quickly" explain away cultural difference based on nationality accounts; and
2   there is a need to reconsider the relationship between culture and identity and the use of relevant terminology.

Conclusions

In this chapter I have attempted to provide a brief overview of some key theoretical issues related to the study of identity in the context of different schools of thought, particularly positivism and constructivism. I also raised the issue of cultural identity, a term that is widely used but for which the analytical power is not straightforward. My intention is not to argue for theoretical and methodological orthodoxies. However, juxtaposing two abstract notions, culture and identity, which then subsume other cognate notions such as ethnicity, race, or religion, can and does lead to "conceptual diffusion," whereby a term does not map to its subsumed components. The plural inflection (cultural identities is more common than cultural identity) and reference to multiple identities and "fuzziness" indicate the theoretical and methodological need to problematize how the terms "cultural" and "identity" are operationalized and what they signify in the context within which they are used. This is something further research can usefully keep on the agenda, and continue to probe the ways in which the terms are used by both researchers and lay users.

To conclude, the term "identity" has become so extended that it can stand for a range of other more or less complex notions, similarly to culture. The issue, then, is how the terms are used and framed. While "identity" has currency and visibility for the lay user, it is less straightforward in terms of its analytical validity for the researcher. As Brubaker and Cooper (2000) argue, "[identity] tends to mean too much… too little… or nothing at all." Although I do not argue against the use of the term, it is important that the field takes stock of how our (the researchers') discourses capture and reflect the phenomena under study. From an analytical and methodological point of view, it is also important to revisit the relationship between discourse and identity and the debated issue of how much and how we can capture what preexists the "here and now" of the interaction. Finally, the well-known nexus of agency, structure, and power is still open for future projects to address. This is relevant to the design of projects in the area, the methodological decisions scholars make and, importantly, to the ways in which data interpretations feedback on the development of future research in the area.

Key Terms

Categorization In social sciences and humanities the term is often used to refer to the process of organizing concepts or entities according to common characteristics. In the applied and socio- linguistic scholarship, categorization processes are typically understood as subconscious and automatic and relate to animate and inanimate entities. However, the boundaries between different groups as well as the homogeneity of members of groups have been questioned. For example, in sociolinguistics, there have been debates in relation to the notion of "community" and "speech community."

Constructionism The term refers to a school of thought which questions given assumptions about the world and focuses on the subjective nature of reality, which is seen as a situated and dynamic construct. As with any epistemological stance, the term does not refer to one single doctrine. The term in applied linguistics and sociolinguistics is typically associated with social identity. Constructionists reject fixed and static characteristics attributed to individuals outside a given context and foreground the agency of the speaker in claiming, rejecting, and projecting identities on "self" and "other." Constructionism is currently influential in applied linguistics and social sciences more generally.

Essentialism In sociolinguistics and applied linguistics, the term has been used in relation to fixed characteristics or traits projected on all the members of a community/group. The term refers to a philosophical stance associated with the work of Plato and Aristotle on the essence of things and ideas. Debates have been prominent in relation to language and identity, and current views emphasize the situated dynamic negation of identity work speakers do in interaction. One of area of research to which the reader can further refer to on this is language and gender.

Identity theories The term refers to the theoretical work of scholars in a range of fields (sociology and psychology occupy a prominent position) attempting to unpack the relationship between "self" and "other" in various contexts. Social Identity Theory focuses on the importance of group membership as a resource for claiming and enacting self-identity while (Role) Identity Theory emphasizes the notion of "roles" one holds or claims. Recent work brings the two approaches together to provide a holistic approach to "self."

Strategic essentialism A term attributed to Chakravorty Spivak in the context of postcolonial theory. Strategic essentialism acknowledges the limitations of essentialism. It argues, however, that oppressed/marginalized groups may strategically use normative characteristics of different identity positions under a political agenda. Recent critics (including Spivak) problematize the application of strategic essentialism as promoting essentialism instead of being an analytical stance that enables the researcher to unpack the complexities of the relationship between identity and power.

References

Abrams, D., & Hogg, M. A. (2006). *Social identifications: A social psychology of intergroup relations and group processes.* London: Routledge.

Ang, I. (2001). *On not speaking Chinese: Living between Asia and the West*. London: Routledge.

Angouri, J., & Bargiela-Chiappini, F. (2011). "So what problems bother you and you are not speeding up your work?" Problem solving talk at work. *Discourse & Communication*, 5(3), 209–229.

Angouri, J., & Glynos, J. (2009). Managing cultural difference and struggle in the context of the multinational corporate workplace: solution or symptom? *Working paper in ideology in discourse analysis*, 26, 1–20. Retrieved June 10, 2015 from: https://www.essex.ac.uk/idaworld/paper261209.pdf.

Angouri, J., & Marra, M. (Eds.). (2011). *Constructing identities at work*. Basingstoke: Palgrave Macmillan.

Angouri, J., & Sanderson, T. in prep. "You'll find lots of help here": Unpacking the function of an online rheumatoid arthritis (RA) forum.

Antaki, C., & Widdicombe, S. (Eds.). (1998). *Identities in talk*. Thousand Oaks, CA: Sage.

Bell, A. (1984). Language style as audience design. *Language in society*, 13(2), 145–204.

Berger, P. L., & Luckmann, T. (1966/1991). *The social construction of reality: A treatise in the sociology of knowledge*. London: Penguin.

Brubaker, R., & Cooper, F. (2000). Beyond "identity." *Theory and society*, 29(1), 1–47.

Bucholtz, M. (2003). Sociolinguistic nostalgia and the authentication of identity. *Journal of sociolinguistics*, 7(3), 398–416.

Burr, V. (2003). *Social constructionism*. East Sussex: Psychology Press.

Butler, J. (1999). *Gender trouble*. London: Routledge.

Côté, J. (2006). Identity studies: How close are we to developing a social science of identity? – An appraisal of the field. *Identity*, 6(1), 3–25.

Davies, B., & Harré, R. (1990). Positioning: The discursive production of selves. *Journal for the theory of social behaviour*, 20(1), 43–63.

Devos, G. (1972). Social stratification and ethnic pluralism: an overview from the perspective of psychological anthropology. *Race and Class*, 13(4), 435–460.

Ereshefsky, M. (2010). What's wrong with the new biological essentialism. *Philosophy of Science*, 77(5), 674–685.

Erikson, E. H. (1968). *Identity: Youth and crisis*. New York: WW Norton & Company.

Giddens, A. (1991). *Modernity and self-identity*. Cambridge: Polity, 109.

Gumperz, J. J., & Levinson, S. C. (Eds.). (1996). *Rethinking linguistic relativity*. Cambridge: Cambridge University Press.

Hall, S., & Du Gay, P. (Eds.). (1996). *Questions of cultural identity*. London: Sage.

Haugh, M. (2012). Epilogue: The first–second order distinction in face and politeness research. *Journal of Politeness Research*, 8(1), 111–134.

Hogg, M. A., Terry, D. J., & White, K. M. (1995). A tale of two theories: A critical comparison of identity theory with social identity theory. *Social psychology quarterly*, 58(4), 255–269.

Holmes, J., & Stubbe, M. (2003). *Power and politeness in the workplace: A sociolinguistic analysis of talk at work*. Harlow: Pearson.

Jenkins, R. (2000). Categorization: identity, social process and epistemology. *Current Sociology*, 48(3), 7–25.

Joseph, J. E. (2004). *Language and identity: National, ethnic, religious*. Basingstoke: Palgrave Macmillan.

Labov, W. (1966). *The social stratification of English in New York City*. Washington, DC: Center for Applied Linguistics.

Labov, W. (1972). *Sociolinguistic patterns*. Philadelphia: University of Pennsylvania Press.

Lenzer, G. (Ed.). (1975/1998). *Auguste Comte and positivism: The essential writings*. New York: Harper.

Mendoza, S. L., Halualani, R. T., & Drzewiecka, J. A. (2002). Moving the discourse on identities in Intercultural Communication: Structure, culture, and resignifications. *Communication Quarterly*, 50(3–4), 312–327.

Mendoza-Denton, N. (2004) Language and Identity. In J. K. Chambers, P. Trudgill, & N. Schilling-Estes (Eds.) *The handbook of language variation and change* (pp. 475–499). Oxford: Blackwell.

McNamara, T. (1997). Theorizing social identity: What do we mean by social identity? Competing frameworks, competing discourses. *TESOL Quarterly*, 31(3), 561–567.

Norton, B. (1997). Language, identity, and the ownership of English. *TESOL Quarterly*, 31(3), 409–429.

Norton, B. (2000). *Identity and language learning: Gender, ethnicity and educational change*. Harlow: Longman Pearson.

Ochs, E. (1993). Constructing social identity: A language socialization perspective. *Research on Language and Social Interaction*, 26(3), 287–306.

Pavlenko, A., & Blackledge, A. (Eds.). (2004). *Negotiation of identities in multilingual contexts*. Bristol: Multilingual Matters.

Popper, K. R. (1963). *Conjectures and refutations*. London: Routledge & Kegan Paul.

Sacks, H. (1972/1992). *Lectures on conversation* (2 vol. ed.), Edited by G. Jefferson, with introduction by E. Schegloff. Oxford: Blackwell. [Combined vols. ed., 1995].

Sarangi, S. (2010). Reconfiguring self / identity / status / role: The case of professional role performance in healthcare encounters. In G. Garzone & J. Archibald (Eds.), *Discourse, identities and roles in specialized communication* (pp. 33–57). Bern: Peter Lang.

Spivak, G. C., & Rooney, E. (1994). In a word. Interview. In N. Schor & E. Weed (Eds.), *The essential difference* (pp. 151–184). Bloomington: Indiana University Press.

Stokoe, E. (2012). Moving forward with membership categorization analysis: Methods for systematic analysis. *Discourse Studies*, 14(3), 277–303.

Stokoe, E., & Attenborough, F. (2014). Gender and categorical systematics. In S. Ehrlich, M. Meyerhoff, & J. Holmes (Eds.), *The handbook of language, gender, and sexuality* (pp. 161–180). Oxford: Wiley-Blackwell.

Stone, A. (2004). Essentialism and anti-essentialism in feminist philosophy. *Journal of Moral Philosophy*, 1(2), 135–153.

Tajfel, H., & Turner, J. C. (1979). An integrative theory of intergroup conflict. In W. G. Austin & S. Worchel (Eds.). *The social psychology of intergroup relations* (pp. 33–47). Pacific Grove, CA: Brooks / Cole.

Watts, R.J., Ide, S., & Ehlich, K. (eds.) (1992). *Politeness in language: Studies in its history, theory and practice*. Berlin: Mouton de Gruyter.

Further Reading and Resources

Angouri, J., & Marra, M. (Eds.). (2011). *Constructing identities at work*. Basingstoke: Palgrave Macmillan.

Benwell, B., & Stokoe, E. (2006). *Discourse and identity*. Edinburgh: Edinburgh University Press.

Bucholtz, M., & Hall, K. (2010). Locating identity in language. In D. Watt, & C. Llamas (Eds.), *Language and identities* (pp. 18–28). Edinburgh: Edinburgh University Press.

Stryker, S., & Burke, P.J. (2000). The past, present, and future of identity theory. *Social Psychology Quarterly*, 63(4), 284–297.

4 Studying Discourse

Leila Monaghan

> **Summary**
>
> When people from distinct cultures come together, they bring with them separate styles of discourse and sociocultural assumptions within complex grids of power relations. This chapter explores the history of the academic fields that focus on analyzing these complex communicative interactions. Looking at the fields of Intercultural Communication, discourse analysis, discourse studies, and linguistic anthropology from 1950 to the present, this chapter connects the rise of the study of intercultural discourse with both the rise of national civil rights movements of the 1960s and 1970s and more recent growing globalization. The second half of the chapter looks at four different methods of discourse analysis: Dell Hymes's SPEAKING model; Labov and Waletzky's Narrative Analysis method; Scollon, Scollon, and Jones's Discourse Systems approach; and Leila Monaghan's HISTORY model. The strengths and limitations of each model are discussed, giving students and researchers insights into how these methods might be used in their own work.

Introduction

A word, a gesture, a pause can pass in an instant. But with each moment, we build the interactions we live within and that help create our worlds. The study of discourse is

Research Methods in Intercultural Communication: A Practical Guide, First Edition. Edited by Zhu Hua.
© 2016 John Wiley & Sons, Inc. Published 2016 by John Wiley & Sons, Inc.

the study of the creation of cultural worlds. Discourse is fractal, with interconnected patterns at every level of organization. When people from distinct cultures come together, they will bring with them separate styles of discourse and sociocultural assumptions within complex grids of power relations. In the first part of this chapter, I will review the history of how discourse, particularly intercultural discourse, has been studied. It is not a singular history but instead draws upon disciplines ranging from intercultural communication to discourse analysis, sociolinguistics and linguistic anthropology. While quite separate in the early years, these fields begin to coalesce in the 1990s, bringing together a variety of styles of analysis.

In the second part, I will apply four styles of discourse analysis to events at a dinner party I was present at in the New Zealand Deaf community as a demonstration of how a range of discourse analyses work. Dell Hymes's SPEAKING model puts language in context and as part of larger speech genres. Labov and Waletzky analyzed patterns within narratives. Scollon, Scollon, and Jones look at discourse as part of larger cultural systems. Finally, my own HISTORY model contextualizes the ongoing intercultural discourse between the New Zealand Deaf community and the larger hearing society. In the third and final section, I draw lessons from these analyses and other work about the general nature of discourse, tying together what I learned in New Zealand with current work in intercultural discourse.

Intercultural Communication and Discourse Analysis: 1950s to 1980s

The study of Intercultural Communication emerged from the process of teaching Americans foreign languages during the post-World War II era. The effort was led by the US Department of State's Foreign Service Institute (FSI), founded in 1946. Edward T. Hall began focusing on "what he termed microcultural analysis: on tone of voice, gestures, time, and spatial relationships as aspects of communication" (Hall, 1956 in Leeds-Hurwitz, 1990, p. 268). He did not focus on the larger aspects of communication looked at by discourse scholars. By 1976, although he was an anthropologist by training, Hall had moved away from anthropology. His book *Beyond culture* (1976) referred to early anthropologists, including Fraz Boas and Edward Sapir, but made no reference to contemporaneous work on discourse by figures such as Dell Hymes, Erving Goffman, and Keith Basso, who were at that point developing an event based approach to understanding the relationships between language and culture.

The intercultural field in general also moved away from natural settings preferred by anthropologists doing ethnographic research in communities and even the field elicitation sessions used by pre-1960s linguists. By the 1970s, many intercultural communication scholars were doing laboratory-based statistical research. L. S. Harms's (1973) introductory intercultural communication text provides a number of quantitative research projects for beginning students to do modeled on other communication research. The 1960s and 1970s were times of great change, and the field saw itself as dealing directly with the most important issues of the day. Harms discussed Black–White relations and, reflecting his position at the University of Hawaii, the use of Hawaiian pidgin. Acknowledgement that Intercultural Communication offered relevant insights to a wide audience led to widespread institutionalization of the field in the late 1960s and in the 1970s. In the 1970s, universities around the country developed intercultural communication programs (Asante, Newmark, & Blake, 1979). Professional institutions also developed. In 1969, the National Society for the Study of Communication changed its name to the International Communication Association. With the change to ICA, the group wanted to reflect the global scope of research and international membership.

While the field of Intercultural Communication began as an interdisciplinary enterprise with multiple theoretical perspectives, approaches began to solidify by the late 1970s. Molefi Kete Asante, Eileen Newmark, and Cecil Blake (1979) identified two basic approaches: first, cultural dialogue which "seeks to illuminate the realm of self presentation" expanding on the work of Erving Goffman (Asante et al., 1979, p. 15); second, cultural criticism which sought "ways to perfect the communication process across cultures by isolating the barriers (p. 20). They also argued that "more description of the intercultural communication process" is needed, that "our scientists need to observe before they theorize. We must also work with those coherent explanations we have in order to stand higher in the asking process" (p. 12).

The related field of discourse analysis focused on the general exploration of the relationship between language and culture. The first use of the term was by Zellig Harris (1952), a linguist known for a rule-oriented approach to grammar and his influence on his student Noam Chomsky (Watt 1993). However, Harris also was influenced by Edward Sapir, and shared with him an interest in the interaction between language and culture, both in "continuing descriptive linguistics beyond the limits of a single sentence at a time" and "correlating 'culture' and language" (Harris 1952, p. 1, see also Sapir, 1921).

Concurrently, a group of scholars, including anthropologists Gregory Bateson and Raymond Birdwhistell, were developing methods to analyze the richness of naturally occurring interaction in visual form in the "Natural history of an interview" project (see Leeds-Hurwitz 1987). The group analyzed a film Bateson had done with a woman in psychotherapy. While the project ultimately resulted in a 1971 manuscript that was available only on microform (McQuown et al., 1971) and illustrated the difficulties of multilayered analysis of a significant chunk of naturally occurring discourse, the project was a foundational moment in the field of discourse analysis.

Among the earliest discourse analysts was the sociologist, Erving Goffman, who used anecdotal data to elaborate a series of concepts including facework (1955), presentation of self (1959), and frame analysis ([1974] 1986). While Goffman was at the University of California-Berkeley, he was part of a group of young faculty members who occasionally met on Saturdays, including linguistic anthropologists Dell Hymes, John Gumperz, and Susan Ervin-Tripp, all instrumental in the development of the ethnography of speaking/ethnography of communication. Others in the group included Ethel Albert, an early advocate of studying intercultural communication within the field of communication, and the philosopher John Searle (Murray, 1998). Important work from this group and that of the next generation include Gumperz & Hymes (1964); Hymes (1974); and Bauman & Sherzer ([1974] 1989).

Discourse analysis also has strong European roots. The philosopher Ludwig Wittgenstein began exploring the nature of language games in the 1930s and 1940s (Wittgenstein, 1953). In the 1950s and 1960s, J.L. Austin and H.P. Grice also explored the uses of language. Austin ([1962] 1975) looked at what he called "performatives" while Grice (1961, 1975) looked at the meanings and implications of conversations. Searle, an occasional original member of the Berkeley Saturday group, emphasized the importance of looking at the rule-governed nature of speech acts. For Searle, studying language without speech acts would be "as if baseball were studied only as a formal system of rules and not as a game" (Searle 1969, p. 17, see also Slembrouck, 2010).

While mainstream linguistics in the United States, first led by Leonard Bloomfield and then Noam Chomsky, moved away from examining the actual examples of speech use, British linguistics was more oriented towards social interaction. Reflecting the society-wide English focus on social class and its relationship to voice, David Crystal and Derek Davy (1969) examined the importance of style in interactions, while M.A.K. Halliday (1978) looked at register. "Critical linguistics" extended Halliday's work and used linguistic features of discourse forms to analyze sociopolitical processes (see Fairclough, 1992 for review). In Holland, Teun van Dijk's *Handbook of discourse analysis* (1985) presented perspectives of different disciplines, linguistic components of discourse, conversation analysis influenced perspectives, and an events-based and political perspective.

A number of American discourse-oriented scholars reflected the growing awareness of black culture, language, and civil rights of the 1960s. William Labov (1969) in "The logic of non-standard English" argued that what he at the time called Black English Vernacular was as rule governed and logical as any standardized form of English. Courtney Cazden (1968) and Shirley Brice Heath (1982) showed how the discourse used by schools put children who were not from the mainstream at a disadvantage. Ron Scollon and Suzanne Wong Scollon, both Berkeley graduates, produced some of the earliest discourse-oriented work on interethnic communication (Scollon & Scollon, 1981). Work on linguistic gender systems also gained importance including Robin Lakoff's *Language and women's place* (Lakoff & Bucholtz, [1975] 2004) and Daniel Maltz and Ruth Borker's ([1980] 2012) application of Gumperz's ideas about intercultural miscommunication to male–female relationships.

The Expanding Worlds of Discourse Studies: 1990s to 2010s

By the 1990s, discourse studies were solidly international and included the formal recognition of the interconnectedness of Intercultural Communication and discourse analysis. Ron Scollon and Suzanne Wong Scollon, following up their 1981 work on interethnic communication – and long-term field work in Alaska, China and the Pacific Rim – published a series of books and articles on intercultural discourse (Pan, Scollon, & Scollon, 2002; Scollon & Scollon, 2003; Scollon, Scollon, & Jones, 2011). Scott Kiesling and Christina Bratt Paulston (2003) collected articles including theoretical work in anthropology and critical and interactional sociolinguistics and specific instances of discourse and identity building in intercultural situations.

The importance of this discourse-oriented work in the field of Intercultural Communication is evident in the Conference on Intercultural Dialogue held in Istanbul in 2009 organized by Wendy Leeds-Hurwitz and Nazan Haydari (Conference on intercultural dialogue, 2009, Leeds-Hurwitz, 2010). *The global Intercultural Communication reader* provides a review of the most recent work in the field (Asante, Miike, & Yin, 2013).

One of the questions raised by the Conference on Intercultural Dialogue is "How do scholars in different contexts define the concept of culture?" Within linguistic anthropology starting in the 1960s, members of the Berkeley group including Hymes and Gumperz began developing an events-based approach to the relationship between language and culture. Some of the most important work in this vein includes Alessandro Duranti and Charles Goodwin's 1992 *Rethinking context*, which featured conversation analysis and other approaches to the social analysis of context approach that focused on how language both reflects and constructs reality, an issue integral to the wider field of discourse analysis. The articles clearly show the power of language to alter reality. For example, Duranti showed that Samoan respect words can be "strategically powerful tools that can force others to assume particular social personae, to wear social masks from behind which it will be very hard to refuse what is requested" (1992, p. 96).

Work in language ideology provides one major way of seeing the influence of the power of language. Scholars have looked at how ideas about language influence interactions within society. Paul Kroskrity (1998) examined the impact of the use of Kiva language amongst the Tewa of Arizona. Elizabeth Mertz (1998) focused on interactions in an American law school while Don Kulick (1998) analyzed the *kros*, a rant usually performed by women among the Gapun of New Guinea. What is notable about these studies is that the focus is again a discourse, in this case discourses about language. A revised edition of Lakoff's *Language and a woman's place* included a wide array of commentaries connecting her work to current work in gender and intercultural communication (Lakoff & Bucholtz, [1975] 2004). Work on Deaf communities and cultures provides some of the broadest perspectives on the relationships between intercultural communication, discourse, and larger social change (e.g. LeMaster & Monaghan, 2004; Monaghan, Schmaling, Nakamura, & Turner, 2003; Senghas & Monaghan, 2002). More recently, colonial intercultural discourses have been the subject of study (e.g. Hanks, 2010; Messing, 2010; Monaghan, 2011).

The most recent work on intercultural and intracultural discourse analysis reflects the theoretical, methodological and topical breadth of the field. Important general texts include work by Deborah Schiffrin, Deborah Tannen and Heidi Hamilton (2003); Barbara Johnstone (2007); Thomas Nakayama and Rona Halualani (2010); Christina Paulston, Scott Kiesling, and Elizabeth Rangel (2012); James Paul Gee (2014) and Gee and Michael Handford (2013). Critical discourse analysis focusing on understanding power and social inequalities continues to be an important part of the field (Fairclough, 2010; Wodak & Meyer, 2009). The articles in *Discourse studies*, edited by Teun van Dijk, show some of the interests of today's scholars. Work on identity remains important: Mary Bucholtz and Kira Hall's 2005 work "Identity and interaction" has become a classic, and Oraib Mango's 2010 work on Arab American women shows how the concept can fruitfully be applied across communities.

One continuing focus of discourse analysis is to look at the use of specific discourse or linguistic forms. For example, Jessica Robles (2012) looked at "Troubles with assessments in gifting occasions." This kind of analysis is also being applied to ever more settings, from children's psychometric interviews (Iversen, 2012), to speed dating (Turowetz & Hollander, 2012), to a wide variety of virtual settings from email (Ho, 2011), to online support groups for teenagers who self-harm (Smithson et al., 2011). The definition of discourse has also expanded and now, in line with the Deaf-oriented studies discussed above, includes an emphasis on bodies and gestures as well as the traditional analysis of speech (e.g. Chui, 2009; Pratt, 2011).

Four Models of Discourse

Another fruitful way to approach discourse analysis is from the perspective of some of the theoretical models that have been developed over time. Different models reflect different understandings of how events are constructed on an ongoing basis. Dell Hymes's 1974 model was foundational to the rethinking of linguistic anthropology as an ethnographic enterprise connecting specific aspects of discourse with larger cultural contexts. It remains a useful way to quickly review the different pieces of any speech event. Labov & Waletzky ([1967] 2003) looked at how stories are constructed, so their model is useful for analyzing particular stretches of individual narrative. Scollon, Scollon, & Jones (2011) look at how discourse is a reflection of socialization and other cultural practices. The model is particularly useful for comparing multiple examples of speech events. My own model (2011) gives a way to understand speech events within not only cultural contexts but also larger historical contexts.

An example from my own work with the New Zealand Deaf community, a 1992 dinner party of old friends, will be used to demonstrate the different kinds of information each of these models can produce. A key part of the dinner party was the retelling of events that originally occurred in the late in 1940s. Examining the general event and these retellings gives us some fundamental insights into how community and intercultural relations are made or broken with discourse (Monaghan, 1996).

Hymes' SPEAKING Model

Hymes's model is a way to quickly analyze a speech event, its setting and how it fits into larger social categories such as norms and genres. One of his aims in developing the model was to show how speech competence involved much more than knowing the linguistic code (Hymes, 1974).

Setting

The setting for this story was a buffet restaurant at a local Auckland hotel. Diners were seated around the outside of a large U-shaped set of tables, so all participants could see each other at all times.

Participants

The dinner included 14 friends – nine women, five men and myself. Eight of the women and three of the men at the dinner had attended school together in Auckland in the 1940s and 1950s. The two other men were husbands of the women present. The other woman was a well-known Deaf community member who had attended a different Deaf school.

Ends

The event seemed to have multiple aims, something I will return to, but the immediate aim of telling the stories at the heart of the event was to entertain the other diners. A key part of these stories, however, is drawing distinctions between the hearing world of school authorities and the Deaf children they had been. The stories often showed how the hearing world was a fallible one. For example, Kate's story, "Funny Miss Beatty," about a matron slipping and flashing her bloomers in front of laughing children, reveals the human side of even overwhelming authority.

Act sequence

The evening had a number of different parts including preliminary chatting in twos and threes during the meal, general storytelling and then a round of picture-taking.

Key

The key is the tone of the event, in this case one of amusement on the part of most of the storytellers, and great laughter among the audience. The stories told were often cherished memories of the entire community.

Instrumentality

The language of the evening was New Zealand Sign Language as it had been developed by the community members at the dinner. As Deaf children at Titirangi and elsewhere in New Zealand were forbidden to sign, they had developed this form behind the teachers' backs, making not only the story subversive but the language that it was told in, too. Signing was considered subversive until the late 1980s.

Norms

Two sets of norms operate here: those of the school, and those of the audience of the telling of this version of the story. At the time of Titirangi, children were required to conform to school rules by a powerful set of school authorities. These norms included children being obliged to speak and lipread at all times. But another set of norms also existed, that of the community of children. They had values quite separate from that of adults. For them, signing was the key way to communicate with each other.

Genre

Hymes established the SPEAKING model as a way to compare examples within and across genres. In addition to the Miss Beatty story, the other stories at the dinner party including one of a boy flashing a mirror up a teacher's skirt and another of a wife describing the hole in her husband's underwear. These tales give a clear sense of the importance of body humor and the breaking of taboos, hearing norms that the school authorities imposed. This genre of stories of taboo-breaking was both a staple at parties, and a significant part of the process of these adults breaking away to set their own norms and genres and make their own community.

Labov and Waletzky's Narrative Analysis

While Hymes's work compared different genres of performances, Labov and Waletzky ([1967] 2003, pp. 93–102) offered a model for analyzing traditional narratives, individual stories with beginnings, middles and ends. One example would be the Funny Miss Beatty story told that evening by Kate.

> Me, you, not you, that one, yes, not you. Remember Miss Beatty? Funny Miss Beatty. We used to play in the dining room, play room, and Miss Beatty used to walk there. One day she slipped, fell flat on her back. She had on long underpants. All the children stared at her long pants. They were all laughing, looking. It was so funny. The pants went down to the knees. They had elastic, bloomers. Loonng bloomers.

Kate A. got a small round of applause as she walked away from where she had been standing at the end of the U, and did a final single sign to recap her story. "She fell flat on her back." (Monaghan, 1996, p. 239).

Labov and Waletzky looked at how narratives built over their course, and the way that structure builds.

Orientation is how participants set their story with "respect to person, place, time, and behavioral situation." There are two linked orientations in this story. The first is the naming of participants, identifying exactly who and who was not there at the event. Kate went around the room pointing at the diners and identifying their status. She clearly connected this story to the shared history of the group, marking it as part of the unique commonalities they hold. The second orientation is the introduction of Miss Beatty in the dining room. All the people she identified were there that day in the dining room with her.

The complication of the story is Miss Beatty slipping, falling and flashing her bloomers. The children's evaluation of the event was that, "It was so funny." All stared and pointed. The resolution for the children was similar, the lingering sense of how out of the ordinary "Loonng bloomers" were. Erving Goffman in *Frame analysis* ([1974] 1986) defined framebreaks as events that threw the assumptions of a setting into question, for example, a waiter spilling peas. He also saw them as temporary. Peas could be picked up after a waiter spilled them and the ordinary restaurant frame could be restored. In my work with Deaf adults from New Zealand, however, I found that framebreaks such as a matron tripping and flashing her long bloomers at school were used by the children present for years after to build a separate frame (Monaghan, 1996, 2003). The stories of these framebreaks were told and retold and became the basis for a new reality quite separate from that offered by the authorities. Seeing the underside of this world, in this case the underpants, gave an opening for the Deaf students to reframe the world from a completely different perspective, one that did not construct them as passive recipients of information from the school authorities. The development of what would later be known as New Zealand Sign Language was a key part of this process.

Labov and Waletzky's final part of the model is the coda, for them, "a functional device for returning the verbal perspective to the present moment." They "note that all codas are separated from the resolution by temporal juncture" ([1967] 2003, pp. 100–101). What is interesting here is that while there is a clearly disjuncture between the story and the coda – Kate signed it briefly only after the applause and laughter that greeted the story had quieted down and she was leaving the place where she told her story – the coda here is just a brief elegant twist of the hand and splaying of two fingers summarizing the story, "She fell flat on her back." The gesture in some ways places the event in the present as much as the past, metaphorically once again creating a common and ongoing space separated from the structures of the authorities. Thinking about intercultural communication as in part the relationship between two groups of people with an unequal power relationship, the stories were in part about the school authorities that insisting on regulating most aspects of the children's lives. The use of sign language in such a situation as the dinner party marked that the common culture forged in opposition to the authorities outlasted those authorities themselves. This is an example where a Goffmanian framebreak was not temporary but permanent.

Scollon, Scollon, and Jones' Lessons about Discourse

Scollon, Scollon, & Jones (2011) looked at "discourse systems" – the way different communities talk. Among the key features they see are:

- Ideology, the "historical/social/ideological characteristics" including beliefs, religion and worldview.
- Socialization, how one learns "legitimate participation/identity."
- Forms of discourse including "rhetorical strategies," "functions of language," and "modes of communication."
- Face systems which reflect community norms such as politeness strategies, deference, solidarity, hierarchy (2011, pp. 175–176).

One of the striking features of the dinner party is how inextricably entwined were all four aspects of discourse systems. Let me begin with socialization. A starting assumption about many of the discourse systems discussed in Scollon et al. (2011) is that they are ongoing, reflecting previously existing communities and patterns. In one illustration, they give the ancient art of Yoga as an example of discourse system, something that an American may participate in on Sundays or a sadhu in India may devote his or her life to. The dinner party reflects a much more recent tradition, one where the people at this party were present for the creation of this discourse system. At the beginning of her story, Kate pointed out who was there the day that Miss Beatty fell, first herself and then at a number of other diners. "Me, you, not you, that one, yes, not you." By doing this, she marked who was at this seminal event where the Deaf community created itself. The key part of socialization that was being discussed at this party was not by adults towards children but instead between the children themselves, something we can see in other Deaf settings such as the Thai school described by Charles Reilly and Nipapon Reilly (2005).

The ideologies, forms of discourse and face systems at the dinner party were all linked to general New Zealand Deaf culture and the children's acts of breaking away and socializing each other. For example, the community ideology that put a high premium on keeping together was inextricably linked to the value of sign language discourses and visually oriented communication strategies. One New Zealand friend explained to me that Deaf people's tables are always round so everybody can see each other. Similarly, the New Zealand Deaf community face system emphasized solidarity over hierarchy with a strong emphasis on inclusion. One of the jokes in the community was how everyone spent massive energy on driving people without cars to places they wanted or needed to visit.

The New Zealand Deaf community discourse system, like all cultural systems, was both inextricably linked to the position of Deaf people in New Zealand and the tool they used to create a new society outside what had been formally allotted to them by school and government officials. Mary Johnson, a diner who in fact went to a different Deaf school, St Dominic's, the Catholic school, provided one example of how all these features worked together. At the end of the evening, she summed up the ideology inherent in the stories that had been told: "Deaf people… keep together. Remember. It's good. We grow together. It's the same for all of us. Older ones taught younger ones. Nuns didn't know anything" (Monaghan, 1996, p. 245).

Monaghan's HISTORY Model

One limitation that I have found with most discourse models is that they focus on the present rather than how things came to be. In order to look at how specific events such as the dinner party are discourses about history and the past, I developed the HISTORY model. HISTORY stands for "general History, Individual histories, all aspects of the Speech event, the Transformations that take place, the social Organizations framed and constructed by these events, the inherent Repetitions of communicative forms, and the Yearnings of the people involved, the ideological aims of the participants" (Monaghan, 2011, p. 229). In terms of using the model to understand the dinner party, it points the way to seeing the dinner party in the larger context of New Zealand Deaf history. The oral teaching methods imposed upon the children reflect that the first school for the Deaf in New Zealand was founded in 1880, the height of international oralism. When this dinner party took place, in May 1992, sign language had been allowed in schools for only 12 years. Acceptance of signing was, in part, made possible by individual people and events, for example dinner participant Mary Johnson started a Deaf club in Dunedin in southern New Zealand. The Dunedin Deaf club and other Deaf organizations across the country provided a space for transformations, a place where Deaf school children broke from the gaze of authorities and built their own communities. Speech events, such as the dinner party are the vehicle by which these transformations take place, where the yearnings, the desires, the ideologies and the intentions of the participants are expressed, often by reiterating shared stories such as the tale about Funny Miss Beatty.

When thinking about Intercultural Communication, the HISTORY model points out the importance of discussions of the historical past such as the impact of slavery on the African American community, or genocide on Native Americans or Jewish people. But it also asks us to look for the moment when things change, when for example, the Civil Rights Movement of the 1950s and 1960s forever changed the legal frameworks connected to race. We all reflect our histories and are part of making our futures.

A Few Final Lessons about Studying Discourse

Discourse is powerful

One way to view the power of discourse to change society is to see discourse as capable of breaking and remaking frames, multilevel assumptions about how interactions operate and the settings they operate within. In Richard Bauman's term, people can create an "emergent" new reality (Bauman, [1977] 2007). The coming together of individuals from two or more cultures creates the opportunity for new frames of understanding, created by assumptions that interact, mingle and rub up against, or even break one another. A New Zealand Deaf example would be how the stark differences between the ideologies of Deaf community members and those of the education system show that the hegemonic assumptions of those in power do not always withstand scrutiny. Something as simple as a matron slipping can show the weakness of a system.

Critics of Eurocentric ideologies and research approaches such as the work in Nakayama & Halualani's (2010) collection show that parallels can be found in all situations of unequal power. Bryant Alexander wrote of seeing himself and his brothers in the African American young men he taught, noting how they too had been "marked, minimized, and marginalized" (Alexander, 2010, p. 364). Just as Mary Johnson called upon the sameness of Deaf people when she founded the Dunedin Deaf club, Alexander used the discourse of cultural brother as a way to connect to his students and to challenge the black male archetypes that they all lived within.

Discourse is fractal

A fractal pattern is one in which "irregularity remains constant over different scales" (Gleick, 1987, p. 98). Perhaps most familiar from the colorful videos of zooming into infinite Mandelbrot sets, fractal patterns occur in discourse as much as they do in other manifestations of nature. Large institutional attempts to control communication, such as a policy that deaf schools will be an oral-only environment or that the legal system is the final arbiter of right or wrong, get replicated at the most minute level in discourse. As Charles Goodwin (1987) showed, even a pause can be significant in understanding how a particular piece of discourse is constructed. These small irregularities mean irregularities at much larger scales as well. Power is often wielded in these irregular cracks, when Matrons slip and flash their bloomers.

One ongoing field of research that provides clear illustrations of the impact of small intercultural differences is the work of conversation analysts on turn-taking (see Tannen, 2012 for a review). Deborah Tannen, for example, showed how different cultures have different expectations of the space between turns. New Yorkers have among the lowest interturn pauses and therefore are often seen as interrupting other speakers. Tannen, who grew up in Brooklyn, described how she would find herself interrupting her friend and colleague Ron Scollon, who was from Detroit. Suzanne Scollon, from Hawaii, in turn perceived Ron as interrupting her but in turn was seen by the members of the Fort Yukon Athabaskan community in Northern Canada that they worked with as interrupting them. A villager from even farther north in Canada, however, wrote in an exam that, "People in Fort Yukon talk so fast, [Tannen would] probably fit right in" (Tannen, 2012, p. 137). In the worst cases, fractions of seconds of reaction time can cascade into misunderstandings or be used to silence others.

Discourse builds the world

Instances of intercultural discourse are not predetermined but dependent on both the changing worlds the parties bring to the discourse and what happens within the discourse. As Wendy Leeds-Hurwitz (2010) has argued, "Reality is socially constructed, and people are active interpreters of their social environment.... Cultures result from the negotiated creation and shared use of symbols and meanings" (p. 21). Again, the New Zealand Deaf community provides a useful example. A friend from New Zealand remembered the first time she ever heard the term New Zealand Sign Language (NZSL) was at the World Games for the Deaf held in 1989 in Christchurch, New Zealand. In this case, seeing other countries claiming associated sign languages like American Sign Language and Italian Sign Language shifted attitudes about the nature of sign language. Three years later, both the discourse and the institutional environment changed and the first ongoing interpreter training course started in New Zealand (Monaghan, 1996).

Discourse studies provide an array of powerful tools to examine how people interact and help us understand the workings of institutions and politics. Too few studies, however, have been done on events that are turning points within history. Those that have been done show the power of these analyses. Charles Goodwin's 1994 work on the first Rodney King trial showed how the discourse of the lawyers for the defense of the four white policeman caught on tape beating King on March 3, 1991 shaped the perceptions of the jurors and influenced the decisions they made.

The King trial provides a vivid example of how the ability to see a meaningful event is not a transparent, psychological process, but is instead a socially situated activity accomplished through the deployment of a range of historically constituted discursive practices. It would however be quite wrong to treat the selective vision that is so salient in the King trial as a special, deviant case, merely a set of lawyers' tricks designed to distort what would otherwise be a clear, neutral vision of objective events unambiguously visible on the tape. All vision is perspectival and lodged within endogenous communities of practice (p. 606). The acquittal of these officers in turn led to the 1992 Los Angeles protests and unrest.

Goodwin worked with videotapes of the trial, but other documents can also be used to do discourse-based historicopolitical analyses. For example, Marouf Hasian's 2010 work looked at the dissent of George Washington Williams and other people of color who critiqued the brutal regime of King Léopold II of Belgium in the Congo Free State in the 1890s in forums including the international press. Hasian examined not only the discourse in the 1890s but how the ideas presented in Williams's writings were taken up by prosecutors of other crimes against humanity and are still relevant today. Such studies as these of the New Zealand Deaf community and by Goodwin and Hasian can be models for analyzing important current events and watershed moments in history, from changing tides in Deaf education to wars and political movements.

Everything is connected but nothing is replicated

While Deaf culture in New Zealand operates separately from the larger hearing culture that surrounds it, aspects of the larger New Zealand culture, such as the high value placed on social clubs, are shared by both Deaf and hearing communities. Other aspects of culture, however, such as the Deaf emphasis on visual communication methods, will not be shared (Monaghan, 1996, 2003). All discourse reflects the historical time period, sociocultural milieu, and social networks of the participants. This is particularly clear in intercultural settings where two or more cultures come into contact. The contributors to Paulston, Kiesling, & Rangel (2012), for example, discussed intercultural interactions including Anglo (English and American) and Arab (from Senegal to Morocco to the Persian Gulf) (Davies & Bentahila, 2012), Anglo-American and Japanese (Brown, Hayashi, & Yamamoto 2012), and Greece and Turkey (Sifianou & Bayraktaroğlu, 2012). The importance of fine-grained, contextually sensitive analyses is apparent, for example, in Davies and Bentahila's critique of a wide range of work on Anglo-Arab discourse. They fault previous studies for not understanding intracultural variation within larger Arab discourse patterns; overreliance on stereotypical representations of Arab discourse patterns such as "Arab culture is often quoted as a typically high-context culture, where meaning is derived largely from contextual clues" (p. 233); lack of understanding the subtleties of contextual variation; and finally for often not understanding the implications of Arabic speakers having to talk to English speakers in English rather than in their native tongue. Their critique points to the layers upon layers of complexity that can come into an intercultural situation from individual variation to complex negotiations within powerful and sometimes oppressive institutions.

Studying discourse takes work

Finally, the history of the study of intercultural discourse shows how trends in what to analyze and how to do analyses have changed over time. What any good approach shares, however, is a respect for people's words and the interactions they have with each other. The two approaches Asante et al. identified in 1979, examining "the realm of self presentation" (p. 15) and identifying cultural barriers, are still powerful. The first approach is closely connected to methodologies such as conversation analysis as well as discourse analysis models such as Hymes's 1974 SPEAKING model and the narrative analysis of Labov & Waletzky (1967). The second looks at intercultural events and the social structures they exist in, as exemplified by a critical approach to discourse including the work of Nakayama and Halualani (2010) and Norman Fairclough (2010) and explicitly intercultural work, as exemplified by Scollon et al. (2011). The power of both approaches, however, can be enhanced by situating specific analyses within a larger historical context, which gives us ways to understand how power structures come into being, are maintained, or are changed. By approaching examples of discourses with respect for the people involved and a sense of the intricacy of communication, you can see how words, gestures, and pauses can pass in an instant but can build whole new worlds.

Acknowledgements

Many thanks to Zhu Hua for the invitation to be in this volume and for helpful suggestions. Part of this essay was adapted from Monaghan (2012). Thanks to Scott Kiesling, Christina Paulston, and Wendy Leeds-Hurwitz for comments on this earlier manuscript. Any mistakes, however, are my own.

Key Terms

Discourse Patterned, culturally situated communication.
Linguistic anthropology The study of the interactions between language and culture
Models of discourse analysis Specific theoretical and methodical approaches to analyzing texts.

References

Alexander, B. (2010). Br(other) in the classroom. In T. Nakayama, & R. Halualani (Eds.), *The handbook of critical Intercultural Communication* (pp. 364–381). Oxford: Blackwell.
Asante, M., Newmark, E., & Blake, C. (1979). *Handbook of intercultural communication*. Beverly Hills: Sage.
Asante, M., Miike, Y. & Yin, J. (Eds.) (2013) *The global Intercultural Communication reader* (2nd ed.). London: Routledge.
Austin, J. L. ([1962] 1975). *How to do things with words* (2nd ed.). Cambridge, MA: Harvard University Press.

Bauman, R. ([1977] 2007). Five principles. In L. Monaghan & J. Goodman (Eds.), *A Cultural approach to interpersonal communication* (pp. 25–26). Oxford: Blackwell.

Bauman, R., & Sherzer, J. ([1974] 1989). *Explorations in the ethnography of speaking*. Cambridge, UK: Cambridge University Press.

Brown, S., Hayashi, B., & Yamamoto, K. (2012). Japan / Anglo-American cross-cultural communication. In C. Paulston, S. Kiesling, & E. Rangel (Eds.), *The handbook of intercultural discourse and communication* (pp. 252–271). Oxford: Wiley-Blackwell.

Bucholtz, M. & Hall, K. (2005). Identity and interaction: a sociocultural linguistic approach. *Discourse Studies* 7(4–5), 585–614. doi: 10.1177/1461445605054407

Cazden, C. (1968). Three sociolinguistic views of the language and speech of lower-class children – with special attention to the work of Basil Bernstein. *Developmental Medicine and Child Neurology*, 10(5), 600–612.

Chui, K. (2009). Conversational coherence and gesture. *Discourse Studies*, 11(6), 661–680.

Conference on Intercultural Dialogue (2009) Summer Conference on Intercultural Dialogue. National Communication Association, http://convention3.allacademic.com/one/nca/summer09/ (February 4, 2011).

Crystal, D., & Davy, D. (1969). *Investigating English style*. London: Longman.

Davies, E. & Bentahila, A. (2012). Anglo-Arab intercultural communication. In C. Paulston, S. Kiesling, & E. Rangel (Eds.), *The handbook of intercultural discourse and communication* (pp. 231–251). Oxford: Wiley-Blackwell.

Duranti, A. (1992). Language in context and language as context. In A. Duranti, & C. Goodwin (Eds.) 1992. *Rethinking context* (pp. 77–100). Cambridge: Cambridge University Press.

Duranti, A., & Goodwin, C. (Eds.) (1992). *Rethinking context*. Cambridge: Cambridge University Press.

Fairclough, N. (1992). *Discourse and social change*. Cambridge: Polity Press.

Fairclough, N. (2010). *Critical discourse analysis*. London: Routledge.

Gee, J. P. (2014). *An introduction to discourse analysis*. London: Routledge.

Gee, J. P., & Handford, M. (Eds.). (2013). *The Routledge handbook of discourse analysis*. London: Routledge.

Gleick, J. (1987). *Chaos: Making a new science*. London: Cardinal.

Goffman, E. (1955). On face-work: An analysis of ritual elements of social interaction. *Psychiatry: Journal for the Study of Interpersonal Processes*, 18(3), 213–231.

Goffman, E. (1959). *Presentation of self in everyday life*. New York: Doubleday, Anchor Books.

Goffman, E. ([1974] 1986). *Frame analysis*. Boston: Northeastern University Press.

Goodwin, C. (1987). Unilateral departure. In G. Button, & J. Lee (Eds.), *Talk and Social Organisation* (pp. 206–216). Clevedon, UK: Multilingual Matters.

Goodwin, C. (1994). Professional vision. *American Anthropologist*, 96(3), 606–633.

Grice, P. (1961). The causal theory of perception. *The Aristotelian Society: Proceedings, Supplementary Volume 35*, 121–152.

Grice, P. (1975). Logic and conversation. In D. Davidson, & G. Harmon (Eds.). *The Logic of Grammar* (pp. 64–75). Encino, CA: Dickenson.

Gumperz, J. J., & Hymes, D. (Eds.) (1964). *The Ethnography of communication*. Special publication of *American Anthropologist*, 66(6) *Part 2*.

Hall, E. T. (1976). *Beyond culture*. Garden City, NY: Doubleday & Company.

Halliday, M.A.K. (1978). *Language as a social semiotic*. Baltimore, MA: University Park Press.

Hanks, W. (2010) *Converting words: Maya in the age of the cross*. Berkeley: University of California Press.

Harms, L.S. (1973). *Intercultural communication*. New York: Harper & Row.

Harris, Z. (1952). Discourse analysis. *Language* 28(1), 1–30.

Hasian, M. (2010). Critical intercultural communication, remembrances of George Washington Williams, and the rediscovery of Léopold II's "crimes against humanity." In

T. Nakayama, & R. Halualani (Eds.), *The handbook of critical intercultural communication* (pp. 311–332). Oxford: Blackwell.

Heath, S. B. (1982). What no bedtime story means. *Language in Society*, 11, 49–76.

Ho, V. C. K. (2011). A discourse-based study of three communities of practice: How members maintain a harmonious relationship while threatening each other's face via email. *Discourse Studies*, 13(3), 299–326.

Hymes, D. (1974). Ways of speaking. In R. Bauman, & J. Sherzer (Eds.), *Explorations in the Ethnography of Speaking* (pp. 433–452). Cambridge: Cambridge University Press.

Iversen, C. (2012). Recordability: Resistance and collusion in psychometric interviews with children. *Discourse Studies*, 14(6), 691–709.

Johnstone, B. (2007). *Discourse analysis*. Oxford: Wiley-Blackwell.

Kiesling, S., & Paulston, C. B. (Eds.) (2003). *Intercultural discourse and communication: The essential readings*. Oxford: Blackwell.

Kroskrity, P. (1998). Arizona Tewa kiva speech as a manifestation of a dominant language ideology. In B. Schieffelin, K. Woolard, & P. Kroskrity (Eds.), *Language Ideologies: Practice and Theory* (pp. 103–122). Oxford: Oxford University Press.

Kulick, D. (1998). Anger, gender, language shift, and the politics of revelation in a Papua New Guinean village. In B. Schieffelin, K. Woolard, & P. Kroskrity (Eds.), *Language ideologies: Practice and theory* (pp. 87–102). Oxford: Oxford University Press.

Labov, W. (1969). The logic of non-standard English. In J. Alatis (Ed.), *Georgetown Monographs on Languages and Linguistics*, 22, 1–44.

Labov, W., & Waletzky, J. ([1967] 2003). Narrative analysis. In C. B. Paulston, & G. R. Tucker (Eds.), *Sociolinguistics: The essential readings* (pp. 74–104). Oxford: Blackwell.

Lakoff, R. & Bucholtz, M. ([1975] 2004). *Language and women's place* (Revised and expanded edition). Oxford: Oxford University Press

Leeds-Hurwitz, W. (1987). The social history of *The Natural History of an Interview*. A multidisciplinary investigation of social communication. *Research on Language and Social Interaction*, 20, 1–51.

Leeds-Hurwitz, W. (1990). Notes in the history of intercultural communication: The foreign service institute and the mandate for intercultural training. *Quarterly Journal of Speech*, 76(3), 262.

Leeds-Hurwitz, W. (2010). Writing the intellectual history of intercultural communication. In T. Nakayama, & R. Halualani (Eds.), *The handbook of critical intercultural communication* (pp. 21–33). Oxford: Blackwell

LeMaster, B., & Monaghan, L. (2004). Variation in sign languages. In A. Duranti (Ed.), *A companion to linguistic anthropology* (pp. 141–166). Oxford: Blackwell.

Maltz, D., & Borker, R. ([1980] 2012). Male–female miscommunication. In L. Monaghan, J. Goodman, & J. Robinson (Eds.), *A cultural approach to interpersonal communication* (pp. 168–175). Oxford: Wiley-Blackwell.

Mango, O. (2010). Enacting solidarity and ambivalence: Positional identities of Arab American women. *Discourse Studies*, 12(5), 649–664.

Mertz, E. (1998). Linguistic ideology and praxis in U.S. law school classrooms. In B. Schieffelin, K. Woolard, & P. Kroskrity (Eds.), *Language ideologies: Practice and theory* (pp. 149–162). Oxford: Oxford University Press.

Messing, J. (2010). Identity, discourse and (ethno)history. Paper presented at the 109th Annual Meeting of the American Anthropological Association, New Orleans, LA, November 20.

Monaghan, L. (1996). Signing, oralism and the development of the New Zealand Deaf community: An ethnography and history of language ideologies. PhD Thesis, UCLA.

Monaghan, L. (2003). The development of the New Zealand Deaf community. *Deaf Worlds: International Journal of Deaf Studies*, 19, 36–63.

Monaghan, L. (2011). The expanding boundaries of linguistic anthropology: 2010 in perspective. *American Anthropologist* 113(2), 222–234.

Monaghan, L. (2012) Perspectives on intercultural communication and discourse. In C. Paulston, S. Kiesling, & E. Rangel (Eds.), *The handbook of intercultural discourse and communication* (pp. 19–36). Oxford: Wiley-Blackwell.

Monaghan, L., Schmaling, C., Nakamura, K., & Turner, G. H. (2003). *Many ways to be Deaf.* Washington, DC: Gallaudet University Press.

Murray, S. (1998). *American sociolinguistics.* Amsterdam: John Benjamins Publishing.

Nakayama, T., & Halualani, R. (2010). *The handbook of critical intercultural communication.* Oxford: Blackwell Publishing.

Pan, Y., Scollon, S. W., & Scollon, R. (2002). *Professional communication in international settings.* Oxford: Blackwell.

Paulston, C., Kiesling, S., & Rangel, E. (Eds.). (2012). *Handbook of intercultural discourse and communication.* Oxford: Wiley-Blackwell.

Pratt, M. L. (2011). The body in the corpus. *Discourse Studies,* 13(5), 589–592.

Reilly, C. & Reilly, N. (2005). *The rising of lotus flowers: Self-education by Deaf children in Thai boarding schools.* Washington, DC: Gallaudet University Press.

Robles, J. (2012). Troubles with assessments in gifting occasions. *Discourse Studies,* 14, 753–777.

Sapir, E. (1921). *Language: An introduction to the study of speech.* New York: Harcourt, Brace & Company. Retrieved June 13, 2015 from: http://www.gutenberg.org/ebooks/12629.

Schiffrin, D., Tannen, D., & Hamilton, H. (2003). *Handbook of discourse analysis.* Oxford: Blackwell.

Scollon, R., & Scollon, S. W. (1981). *Narrative, literacy and face in interethnic communication. Advances in Discourse Processes.* Norwood, NJ: Ablex.

Scollon, R., & Scollon, S. W. (2003). Discourse and intercultural communication. In D. Schiffrin, D. Tannen, & H. Hamilton (Eds.), *Handbook of discourse analysis* (pp. 538–547). Oxford: Blackwell.

Scollon, R., Scollon, S. W., & Jones, R. (2011). *Intercultural communication: A discourse approach.* Oxford: Wiley-Blackwell.

Searle, J. (1969). *Speech acts: An essay in the philosophy of language.* Cambridge: Cambridge University Press.

Senghas, R. (2003). New ways to be Deaf in Nicaragua. In L. Monaghan, C. Schmaling, K. Nakamura, & G. H. Turner (Eds.), *Many ways to be Deaf.* (pp. 260–282). Washington, DC: Gallaudet University Press.

Senghas, R., & Monaghan, L. (2002) Signs of their times: Deaf communities and the culture of language. *Annual Review of Anthropology,* 31, 69–97.

Sifianou, M., & Bayraktaroğlu, A. (2012). "Face," stereotyping, and claims of power: The Greeks and Turks in interaction. In C. Paulston, S. Kiesling, & E. Rangel (Eds.), *The handbook of intercultural discourse and communication* (pp. 292–312). Oxford: Wiley-Blackwell.

Slembrouck, S. (2010). The "Natural Language School" in analytical philosophy, University of Ghent. Retrieved June 13, 2015 from: http://www.english.ugent.be/da/analyticalphilosophy#sa.

Smithson, J., Sharkey, S., Hewis, E., Jones, R., Emmens, T., Ford, T., & Owens, C. (2011). Problem presentation and responses on an online forum for young people who self-harm. *Discourse Studies,* 13(4), 487–501.

Tannen, D. (2012). Turn-taking and intercultural discourse and communication. In C. Paulston, S. Kiesling, & E. Rangel (Eds.), *The handbook of intercultural discourse and communication* (pp. 135–157). Oxford: Wiley-Blackwell.

Turowetz, J., & Hollander, M. (2012). Assessing the experience of speed dating. *Discourse Studies,* 14(5), 635–658.

van Dijk, T. (Ed.). (1985). *Handbook of discourse analysis* (4 vols.) London: Academic Press.

Watt, W.C. ([2004] 1993). Zellig Sabbatai Harris, 1909–1992. *National Academy of Sciences Biographical Memoirs* 87. Retrieved June 13, 2015 from: http://www.nasonline.org/publications/biographical-memoirs/memoir-pdfs/harris-zellig.pdf.
Wittgenstein, L. (1953). Philosophical investigations. Edited by G. E. M. Anscombe, & R. Rhees; G.E.M. Anscombe (trans.). Oxford: Blackwell.
Wodak, R., & Meyer, M. (2009). *Methods of critical discourse analysis*. Thousand Oaks, CA: Sage.

Further Reading and Resources

Asante, M., Miike, Y., & Yin, J. (2013). *The global Intercultural Communication reader*, (2nd ed.). London: Routledge.
Gee, J. P., & Handford, M. (2013). *The Routledge handbook of discourse analysis*. London: Routledge.
Goffman, E. ([1974] 1986). *Frame analysis*. Boston: Northeastern University Press.
Leeds-Hurwitz, W. (1987). The social history of *The Natural History of an Interview*: A multidisciplinary investigation of social communication. *Research on Language and Social Interaction*, 20, 1–51.
Monaghan, L., Schmaling, C., Nakamura, K., & Turner, G. H. (2003). *Many ways to be Deaf*. Washington, DC: Gallaudet University Press.

Part II   Key Issues and Challenges

5 How to Identify Research Questions

Zhu Hua, Prue Holmes, Tony Young, and Jo Angouri

> **Summary**
>
> In this chapter, we take a practical and case-based approach to discuss the key issues, strategies and practices in identifying research questions. The nine scenarios identified in the chapter range from "not knowing where to start" to "having too many ideas"; from "questions first," where one starts with a research question to "data first, theory or method first," where one knows what data, theory, or a data collection method they would like to work with prior to a research question. The discussion is meant to reflect what we consider as examples of "good practice" and to demonstrate that identifying a research question is a process and requires a series of actions and steps.

Introduction

Identifying your own research questions is perhaps the most personalized part of doing research. It is driven by your individual interests and concerns, draws upon your understanding of the field and your skills, and needs to be tailored around your resources. It is precisely because of its individual nature that the issue of how to identify research questions is rarely talked about in research method textbooks and training workshops, with only a few exceptions (e.g. Boudah, 2011; Gorard, 2013; Saunders, Lewis, & Thornbill, 2007), despite its pivotal role in a research process. Many students find the task of identifying research questions similar to that of finding one's way out of a jungle. In this chapter, we discuss strategies and practices in identifying research questions, using examples from our experience as research student supervisors.

What is a research question? To put it simply, a research question is the question one is trying to address through research. It is where a research project starts and signals how and where it ends. It is the thread of the research design, and decides the method of data collection and analysis. It differs from a research idea, topic, or hypothesis. A research idea can be an inkling or a grounded concern and is allowed to be vague, intuitive, or bold. It is a precursor to research questions and often indicates where the researcher's broad interests lie. A research hypothesis, on the other hand, is a possible answer to your question, based on one's understanding of the topic under study prior to the analysis of data. It is an informed reasoning and articulation of predictions of research outcomes and leads the direction of data analysis. There seems to be certain degree of ambiguity as to the use of the term "hypothesis" in the literature: some use the term to indicate that the research will quantitatively "test" a hypothesis while for others the term stands for "assumptions." It is important to stress, as Boudah (2011) has helpfully pointed out, that although the term "hypothesis" is mentioned very often in research method textbooks, it does not need to be presented as such in all types of research. Qualitative researchers do not typically articulate their predictions of research outcomes as hypotheses because the outcomes are intended to be exploratory or emergent.

What counts as a good research question then? The list varies to some extent depending on the requirements and circumstances of the research project (whether an undergraduate or Masters dissertation, PhD thesis, research project commissioned by an organization, or project proposal seeking funding, etc.). A well-formulated research question contains all of the following characteristics:

- specific in focus and scope
- formulated clearly
- theoretically motivated and informed
- empirically answerable
- feasible within one's resources and allowable timeframe
- appropriate to requirement and expectation
- original enough for the scope of the project
- inviting fresh insights
- ethical.

From the list, you can see that one of the most important aspects of a good research question is that it has to be answerable or researchable, which in practical terms means that it can be done within the time and resources available to you and you know the relevant methods and techniques well enough to carry out the research.

Identifying a good researchable question is a process, and in order to develop it, a series of actions and steps is required. You may be asked to refine, narrow down, sharpen, or revise your research questions – these are all natural steps in developing research questions and should not be taken as indications of a "bad" question. The final questions can emerge through this iterative process. Things we would like to stress here is that it is important to choose a research question that aligns with your research interests –don't forget this is your project. It is also important to consider the expertise and methodological positions of your supervisor/ research groups you are part of so that you can make the best use of resources around you. As discussed in Part I of this volume, Intercultural Communication is a vast, multidisciplinary and developing field, and naturally, intercultural scholars differ in their methodological affinity and conceptualizations. Below, as contributors of this chapter, we take turns to discuss our backgrounds and practice in supervision.

> **Zhu Hua**: I usually introduce myself as an applied linguist rather than an Intercultural Communication specialist. I'm most interested in the interplay between language and Intercultural Communication. While I am amenable to both quantitative and qualitative methods, thanks to my training, most of my works in Intercultural Communication use applied conversation analysis, interactional analysis, and, recently, linguistic ethnography, which I believe give me opportunities to investigate how participants make use of linguistic resources to achieve their goals in various contexts.
>
> **Prue**: I consider myself a researcher of Intercultural Communication. Some people might say this is not a discipline. In a sense they are right in that Intercultural Communication is a developing area of investigation which draws on social science, and interpretive / critical approaches from multiple disciplines in the humanities and social sciences. I always take an interpretive, and, increasingly, a critical approach to understanding intercultural encounters. I like to inform my research with overarching grand theories like social constructionism – how people construct or make sense of their everyday communicative encounters, or phenomenology – how people perceive and interpret their intercultural communication with others. Methodologically, such approaches favor qualitative methods like open-ended interviews, focus groups, (participant) observation, and (written) reflection.
>
> **Tony**: This is actually a difficult question for me to answer briefly, but here goes… I'm an applied linguist by training but was heavily influenced during both my Masters and PhD research by work related to the social psychology of intergroup communication. A lot of my subsequent research has combined quantitative and qualitative techniques in exploring intergroup and intercultural communication. I now work from an "empirical realist" position (Hammersley, 1992) which broadly accepts some external social realities but which also allows for a more critical, constructivist perspective, and so tend to used mixed methods to address research questions. I am usually comfortable supervising projects at a Masters level employing a range of techniques across the spectrum of Intercultural Communication from quantitative / positivistic (psychometrics, for example) to qualitative / interpretive (critical discourse analysis, for example). At PhD level, as the mutual commitment and expectations between supervisor and supervisee are so much higher, I'd expect to supervise projects in thematic areas that I'm interested and have expertise in, but am again quite open in terms of methodological approaches.

(Continued)

> **Jo:** The answer to this greatly depends on where I am and when / by whom I am asked to position myself. I am interested in the relationship between language, culture and identity and my areas of research expertise are in sociolinguistics, pragmatics and discourse analysis. My work is particularly concerned with the analysis of interaction, and I take a critical stance. Although much of my work falls within the scope of the area I understand and define as "Intercultural Communication," I rarely introduce myself as an Intercultural Communication scholar or expert. One of the reasons for this is the importance I attribute to foregrounding my own specific interest in the analysis of interaction. I typically take a mixed-methods perspective, and I'm interested in going beyond epistemological and methodological binaries that are still very common in social sciences and humanities. I work with spoken and written discourse data and I often analyze them from an interactional sociolinguistic perspective. I enjoy supervising projects at all levels and I like those that fall directly in my areas of interest as well as those that take a very different perspective or challenge "orthodoxies" and throw new questions (and possibly some answers into the mix).

The Question of How: Nine Scenarios

Guidelines on research designs and proposals often adopt a linear model, starting with a research question, followed by methods of data collection, analysis, results, discussion, conclusion, and implications. Such a linear approach does not always represent the actual research process. Not all researchers start with a specific and researchable question. Some find their way in through their interest in a particular research design and some have accumulated or have access to data before knowing the formulation of research questions. For them, the challenge is to know how to work their way back and find a research question that is suitable for their design or data. For those who follow the conventional route of starting with research questions, there is a continuum: at one end, some have a more or less worked-out idea – from their professional or personal experiences, the literature, something that was discussed in the class, or as agreed with a supervisor, group or sponsor. This may or may not be sound, but it does give you something to start with. At the other end of the continuum is a student with little idea of what they want to do even after a semester or two of study. In what follows, we will look into nine typical scenarios and discuss strategies and practices we have used in working along with our students in shaping their research questions. In other words, the "talk" below is what we consider as our own "good practice," not as an exhaustive "how to" list.

I Do Not Know Where to Start

Jo Angouri
When the time comes for our MA or PhD students to fill in a proposal form, there is usually some "panic in the air." Tackling this is never a one size fits all model and

I only discuss below some possible "routes" (cf. chapters 1–3 in Litosseliti, 2010). I will use as examples two MA students of mine, named here as Mary and Jay.

Mary came to my office feeling a bit "stuck." She did not know how to find a topic or questions, and hence decided to come and ask me to provide her with "some." You may find, as Mary did, that this could be a simple solution to the problem – it is pretty common in natural sciences but rather unusual in social sciences and humanities. I will not discuss the philosophical underpinnings of disciplinary areas or research traditions here (Alvesson & Sköldberg, 2009). The main issue, in my view, is that if you do not decide yourself on your research questions, you risk working on something that you will not be too enthusiastic about. This of course does not mean to say that you and your supervisor cannot work on the same topic/questions or project, but it is very important to find what you are really interested in. So Mary and I discussed in detail the topics Mary had enjoyed reading about and we started writing down "words." These included a whole range of terms, settings and groups and were of different conceptual level such as "identity," "international students," or "interpreters and ethics." By the end of the meeting Mary had some possibilities to start with. The next task I asked Mary to work on was to write down, in order of priority, what she liked the most and to be pragmatic (see above the qualities of "good" research questions). This led to further meetings and discussion in the supervision context but also in a research group Mary decided to join.

A couple of tips here: as students on PG programs you have already covered a lot of literature. Go back to your modules and remind yourself about the key topics you covered in your essays, presentations, mini-projects. Note down what comes to mind. If you are starting your PhD, refresh your memory on the key issues that made you decide to continue studying. The second and very important point – do engage with research groups and other postgraduate students from your institution or in other universities near you (and there are many on social media, too). As you are reading these lines you may be thinking that you cannot see your supervisor as often or for as long as you would have liked for a range of different reasons. This is something you can (and indeed should) discuss with your supervisor but do not forget to network with others too and benefit from peer feedback.

Moving on to my second case, Jay: Jay knew she was interested in unpacking some of the core notions in the field. She came to my office knowing she wanted to theorize around "culture shock" but did not know where to begin. Jay had already figured out that reading on the topic was a necessary step but soon felt "confused." Although the different viewpoints attracted her to this area and she wanted to "find for herself," it soon became a difficult situation to handle. As you may have already figured out, by the very authors' profiles and Chapter 1 in this volume, work in the IC field takes different, and, not unusually, contradictory, views. Further to this, disciplinary areas (e.g. education or linguistics to name but two) have developed distinct foci and priority areas. Hence Jay felt "lost" in different voices. Most MA and MSc programs cover key notions in IC and provide opportunities to review "state-of the art" work which discusses the different points of view. Hence, going back to the module handbooks to refresh your memory, check the reading list for that part of the course and talking to your lecturers with any specific questions could all help you organize your thinking. If you are starting a PhD, it is important to cover this ground yourself in order to have an understanding of where the field currently stands. It is necessary to know the different views, and to refer to them in your work but you also need to think where you feel more comfortable in terms of your own stance. A tip here is to keep a log of studies / researchers you seem to go back to for reference.

These two cases are not exhaustive, and you may relate to some aspects of them; not knowing where to start is a very common stage and should not panic you. It does not indicate that you have no ideas but is a sign that you need to step back and organize your thinking.

I Have Too Many Ideas. How to Choose One?

Jo Angouri

When you find yourself in a position where you cannot choose, a good place to start is to try to think through your ideas, translate them to possible questions, and prioritize what seems to be more interesting to you. The second pertinent issue is to be pragmatic: Can you study what you are interested in? As an example, you are interested in the role of interpreters in the legal system, but you need to consider access issues. I have touched upon some of that in the previous section, so I am assuming here that you have done this background work already. Pragmatic concerns are very important at this stage: if one of your possible ideas requires significant preparation and planning, this may affect how much time you have for the rest of your project and may be a reason for you to reconsider. Equally, if you have a clear career plan and you have good reasons to believe that researching further in one particular topic may make you more attractive to possible future employers, this may be an important factor to take into account – this is also very relevant if you have a sponsor. Having too many ideas and/or topics is often perceived as a "good" position to be by peers. However, it may lead to feeling "lost" and not knowing "how to choose." I will address the issue again through the eyes of one of my students, named here Carla, currently a PhD student. Carla had developed a strong interest in different areas during the course of her MA and found it challenging to commit to one for her dissertation. So she came to me with a list of possible ideas, which reflected her interest in both translation in multilingual workplaces and ethnic identity representation. These were a) disparate, and b) broad.

Despite some good preparatory work, Carla was still caught between two very different ideas. She decided to focus on ethnic identity construction in the end as she felt she had identified a clearer gap where her research could make a contribution. Identifying an area where further research is needed is an excellent starting point. For postgraduate students interested in a career in research this can also lead to future projects in the chosen area. In Carla's case, the MA dissertation formed the basis for a successful PhD proposal. Her PhD research questions emerged from the analysis of her MA dissertation data, an aspect that shows how research questions can also emerge from your own earlier work.

To sum up, the process of translating the ideas to research topics and questions, bringing in pragmatic considerations, and identifying gaps in the literature and your own personal interest are all good ways to prioritize and organize your options. Support from your supervisor, peers and research groups is, again, paramount in this. So do not forget to involve them in your thinking. If you like visualizing your thinking process, you can do the following exercise: draw a table/boxes with the following headings: Research topic, Research questions, Access (Yes / No), Data collection tools needed, Possible barriers, Relevant studies already identified. This, evidently, is not exhaustive but will provide you with a good summary and allow you to step back and see what your best choice(s) are through a process of elimination.

I Have some Research Questions, But I'm Not Sure if They Are the Right Ones

Prue Holmes
Finding the right research question rarely emerges immediately. It involves a process of ongoing researcher questioning: What does the researcher know about the topic, about the people involved, about the context? What assumptions does the researcher have about the nature of the proposed research? And what is the researcher's relationship and positioning vis-à-vis who and what is being researched? Further, initial research questions may need to be modified as circumstances change. Confidence in and clarity of your research questions may not materialize until later in the study, e.g. at post-pilot or even post-data analysis. Changing policies and practices in the research site may also necessitate further changes.

To illustrate the processes researchers undergo in deciding if they have the right research questions, I draw on a dialogue with one of my doctoral supervisees, Caroline. Caroline was interested in how children (aged 10–11 years) in the International Baccalaureate Primary Years Programme (IB PYP) understood the illusive concept of international-mindedness (IM). As a teacher in the international school of the proposed study, and having a curriculum leadership role, Caroline is deeply interested in the students' learning about and understanding of IM. She felt she knew what questions she wanted to ask and why.

Yet as she developed her study, from writing the initial proposal, to addressing the emergent issues in her literature review, to devising the methodology (and tested in a pilot), she started to question the focus of her research questions. Did they address the problem in the right way? Were they sufficiently focused? How could she access students' understanding of this complex concept through her research questions? Were they answerable? How might she operationalize them through her methodology and methods?

Caroline began to reflect on her own standpoint in the study. She was a researcher, but also an educator; in this role she needed to understand and articulate her beliefs and values (her ontological position) which informed her research topic and field (her knowledge of the IB PYP curriculum, the school and classroom context, and the experiences of her pupils). In other words, there was a meaningful and important interrelationship between the research topic and her interest in it which sustained her interest in the study, enabled her to invest her time and effort, and gave authenticity and meaningfulness to the research. In her words, her interest and engagement came from "an honesty of the heart," enabling her to establish appropriate and meaningful questions in the first place. Further, her second supervisor observed that she was taking a practitioner stance in the research. This standpoint became important to Caroline in clarifying her methodology. It was in a sense a "eureka" moment for Caroline as the process of the entire study unfolded.

So the starting point for deciding whether you have the "right" research questions is to clarify your reasons for undertaking the research, and your standpoint and positioning in relation to the research.

Stage two, for Caroline, involved refining those research questions to fit with what she wanted to find out and how she would get the answers, i.e., what methodology she would employ to answer her research questions. Two things were critical in this refinement.

The first concerned the role of her supervisors, whom she regarded as "critical friends" and coaches. They would question her reasoning in constructing the research questions, unpick and probe, listen and step back, not imposing their own preferred approaches. Could the research questions be answered using the proposed methods? Could her primary schoolchildren come up with explanations for the questions she had posed? Were the research questions too theoretical/conceptual, and thus unanswerable, using the methods she proposed? Did the research methods enable her to answer those research questions? What changes would she need to make to her methods, or to her research questions, to address her research purposes? Caroline likened this to a game of darts: "you're throwing darts, but you need to be able to throw them into the bull's eye." In other words, you need to be realistic about whether your proposed methods allow you to achieve your expected outcomes, and if not, what should be changed or reshaped, either in the research questions and/or in the data collection methods.

In conclusion, identifying the right research questions is an ongoing iterative process concerning a) your (researcher) positioning in relation to the topic, participants, and context of the research; b) the choice of methodology and methods you adopt to operationalize those questions; and c) the evolving and dynamic relationship you have with your supervisors, who, as "objective" and "critical friends," guide you towards settling on those final questions.

My Supervisor said that my Research Question is Too Broad. How Can I Narrow It Down?

Prue Holmes

Another issue, often related to the preceding question, concerns moving from breadth to depth. Caroline began with a broad, overarching research question which reflected her general interest in exploring how her pupils understood the concept of International-mindedness (IM). However, she needed to formulate some subquestions to tackle this broader issue, and thus sharpen the focus of her investigation. She devised three further research questions that probed children's understanding of the concept, how they articulated it, and what it meant to their identity.

These questions called for a qualitative methodology; Caroline chose visual methods and focus groups. However, after conducting her pilot, testing her visual methods, and analyzing her data, she realized that her chosen methods did not enable her to directly answer the research questions; further, the research questions did not enable her to explore sufficiently the concept of IM.

Again, through supervisor–supervisee dialogue she teased out her assumptions and beliefs about the study and her participants (children), and discussed ways of fine tuning the research instruments, and tailoring and focusing the research questions.

Caroline then felt prepared to undertake the main data collection. With a vision of how the research questions would serve as a guide, she felt more confident that, from the analysis of the forthcoming data, she would be able to ascertain whether her research questions were suitably refined or if there was still more work to do.

My Supervisor said that my Research Question is Too Practical

Tony Young

Trying to answer practical, real-world questions is of course an entirely justifiable aim for a social researcher. However, given the nature of academic enquiry, it should never be the *only* aim. All reputable university programs set learning objectives for student research which will make a "contribution to knowledge." Informing these objectives is an implicit or explicit understanding that "knowledge" encompasses both explanations of observed regularities *and* statement of what these regularities are. So research project aims, certainly at Masters level or above, have to encompass both theory and social reality.

There are many cases of students who "arrive" on a program of study with a very firm idea of a practical research outcome which they need to achieve, and who often frame their proposal as "action research." A proposal like this might seek to investigate a work-related problem which a sponsor has been involved in identifying prior to the program of study.

A recent (real-life, but anonymized) case-in-point illustrates how an action research project can incorporate both practical and theoretical contributions. Ahmed was a teacher and teacher educator sponsored by his home government to undertake PhD research. His research idea was to investigate what a study of Intercultural Communication could do to improve English-language students' speaking abilities. Ahmed wanted to take the "intercultural elements" in European language learning and teaching frameworks of reference and relate these to the existing local speaking skills development materials and curricula. He then proposed to teach a subgroup from an "intercultural" perspective. This subgroup would be tested before and after the intervention, with any difference in attainment attributable to this new "intercultural" speaking curriculum. He also proposed to interview teachers and students after the intervention to see if they liked and would support the wider application of the adapted curriculum.

Ahmed's proposed research question was "What effect studying Intercultural Communication can have on students' speaking abilities in Country X?" with a subquestion asking "What are the views of teachers and learners about a speaking skills curriculum influenced by Intercultural Communication?" There were clearly problems in Ahmed's research design. Among these was the key question of whether all changes in the students' performance could really be attributed to the curriculum change he proposed. He was also making his project extremely high-risk in the sense that if no real difference emerged, he would be unlikely to be able to answer his research question meaningfully. Crucially, his research question also had a very limited and specific outcome-related focus, which didn't seek to establish any real relationship to theory, and which didn't in any way address the key question of "why" an observed effect might (or might not) happen.

After negotiation, Ahmed and I agreed that a better project would be one that made both practical and theoretical contributions, in this case one which addressed the question of "what..." but also the question of "why... ." His revised proposal described a project that investigated the nature of Intercultural Communication in language learning, in particular how this theory had been taken from its "Western" origins and applied elsewhere. This involved looking at the body of theory itself, and at the growing number of empirical investigations of its applications outside Europe and North America, so taking a perspective that combined both intercultural language education theory and the empirical data that explored it. This "looking" was done in collaboration with focus groups of teachers in Ahmed's country of origin.

The project resulted in an agreed speaking-skills development curriculum that took account of other work done, but which also showed something of the local negotiations and adaptations needed for an "imported" broad curricular framework to be successfully taken up. This formed the basis for a teaching intervention which was associated with a small, positive difference to student speaking performance. Interviews with teachers and learners exposed to the new curriculum reported higher motivation to learn, and willingness to communicate in English. Ahmed attributed these effects to the greater interest generated by "real-life" materials which encouraged intercultural exploration, and by the practitioner-involvement in the innovation.

So Ahmed was also able, at the end of his project, to add something to our knowledge about how intercultural language educational communication theory might need to be adapted to account for the types of specific local conditions he had observed. His work was therefore able to say something about the theory which underlined his project, and his contribution to knowledge was so much more substantial.

So, to sum up, if a supervisor says a research project is "too practical", they are most likely referring to a project which is focused on too narrow an outcome. A project can, and often should, address real-life questions: it should also address, and be able to say something about, the thought that has informed approaches to answering the same or similar questions.

I've Changed my Mind and Want to Do Something Else

Tony Young
It is actually quite common for students to change their mind about a research question during their project. Whether this is a problem or not usually depends on when they change it, and on the reason for the change.

The "when" can be pretty crucial. In cases where a student has no clear idea of what they are going to research in advance of starting their project, it is part of the normal cut and thrust of working out a project to formulate, discuss, reject, reformulate, discuss, and reformulate again, possible research questions with a supervisor. This is a healthy and reasonable expectation, and should help to formulate a good question. So basically, in the early stages of a project, or during project planning, mind-changing should be OK.

Problems with mind-changing usually occur if it happens later in a project. If a question has been agreed with a supervisor which is specific, clearly formulated, related to theory and to other work in the field, testable, feasible given resources, appropriate, ethical, and likely to bring proportionate, original insights, and *then* a student changes their mind, this can be a worry. During a research project, most students experience major or minor psychological "wobbles" where they doubt themselves, their research question, their project (even their supervisor...), but these are usually surmountable so long as a project is sound. It is tough doing research, especially if you are new to it, and some doubting is only to be expected.

If, on the other hand, the mind-change is as a result of real, emergent, practical difficulties – perhaps in accessing data – then a question may need to be adapted or reformulated to suit the new circumstances. Examples of this include cases where a study based on planned interviews with small numbers of participants have had to be reformulated because interviewees were not available, or where the context for a proposed participant-observer study has changed, or where the participant-observer can no longer access the context of study. In the latter instance a Masters student of mine proposed to carry out ethnographic research in the fast food restaurant she had a part time job in, but then the restaurant closed down. No context, no insider-observation. Similar problems might occur where the time needed to gain appropriately informed consent prove to be too long for the timeframe of a project, as can occur when researching in medical, social care, or educational contexts involving children.

In cases such as these, where unanticipated things happen, reformulation is, I'd suggest, fine, and contingencies can usually be put in place ahead of problems occurring. In all other cases, I tend to quiz student pretty closely (but nicely) on the likely results of a change to what has been agreed as a "good question." Is their project still do-able in the (usually very tight) timeframes available to them if they change their research question? If not, then it is usually best to carry on as planned. If so, then provided the new question fits all the criteria for being a "good" one, we can talk. And if it's just a wobble, we can talk about that too.

I Have Got the Data. Is It Possible to Choose a Research Question that Utilizes the Data?

Jo Angouri
A lot depends here on what data you have, how this was collected, who owns the data, whether you have access to consent forms and the participants for follow on if necessary and needed. Let's see this in some more detail. Starting from your data and feeling your way into your specific research questions is by no means new in research in general and in qualitative research in particular. Ethnographic research (and ethnographically informed work) aims to get an emic (insider's) understanding of the phenomenon under study. Projects start with broad aims and objectives and research questions then emerge in the process. If you are interested in ethnographic work it is very important to prepare yourself for the data collection and to keep detailed logs. The observations you made during your fieldwork need to be carefully noted as they and you become part of your dataset (e.g. Giampapa & Lamoureux, 2011). Hence, if you have good-quality data which you have collected following the appropriate procedures for your research you can certainly use them to guide you towards both an exact topic and subsequently research questions.

If your data were collected for a different purpose (even if that is a different project you carried out) you need to carefully consider the ethics and whether your participants have given you consent for new research on these data. Let's assume that the answer to this is positive and that you have some good-quality data which you have analyzed in some detail before. Your original work will have provided you a good overview of what is going in on in that dataset, hence you may decide to go back and do a meta-analysis of this work. In some recent work we carried out a meta-analysis of data that were collected originally for a different project. Discussions between the two authors led to the conception of the work which we report in a paper (see Sanderson & Angouri, 2014). The first author, who had collected the data, knew from her previous work that the existing dataset was ideal for what we wanted to problematize. Hence we decided to work on this dataset for our project. Although the paper drew on the same dataset we carried out a different analysis which involved going back and re-coding the data in order to address our research questions. As this was a very rich dataset, the first author's earlier work gave us a good underpinning and starting point.

I'm Interested in a Particular Data Collection Method or Technique. How Can I Turn It Into a Research Question?

Zhu Hua

From time to time, students come up to me after a specific research method training session and declare that the method is so interesting that they are going to DO it. In theory it should be research questions that determine research methods, not the other way around. However, given the range and different nature of data-collection methods available nowadays, knowing which method you are most confident with or interested in at the starting point of a research project can help you to narrow down research questions. So, if you have set your heart on a particular research method, where do you go from there?

First of all, ask yourself why you are interested in this method. This question will help you to understand where your preference comes from: is it for a practical reason or does the method appeal to your analytical skills or investigative mind? One student who is interested in questionnaires said that it is convenient for her; another who is interested in corpus analysis said that he found the way patterns are extracted from a large sample very "scientific."

Secondly, ask what is special about this method. If the previous question is more about your intuition about the method you are interested in, this question is one step further and seeks an overall assessment of this method. You may like to check the notes you have taken from research methods training workshops or read a couple of the key references on the method. Questions you may like to think include: what are the strengths and limitations of the method? Is the limitation going to be a problem for you?

Thirdly, having understood the strengths and weakness of the method, you need to ask what kind of research questions the method is mostly suitable for. All research methods are better suited to a certain type of research questions than others. For example, as a research method that is capable of getting information from a large sample of people and makes quantitative analysis feasible, questionnaires are suitable for research questions that are intended for finding out how representative a practice or an opinion is, i.e. how many people said A vs. how many people said B. In contrast, interviews, which are sensitive to individual differences and allow in-depth discussion, are suitable for research questions that focus on differences in opinions and "why."

Fourthly, do a literature survey using a combination of the research areas and the method you are interested in and see what kind of research questions have been studied in your chosen area. You could cast your net wide and use key words in various database and on-line resources (such as JSTOR, Linguistics and Language Behavior Abstracts, etc.). As an example, after I key in Intercultural Communication and questionnaires in the International Bibliography of the Social Sciences (IBSS) at the time of writing this chapter, 34 results came up. In addition to searching databases and on-line resources, you can also have a look at the list of topics of past dissertations in your institution, if they are available.

Fifthly, having gained some ideas about the range and type of specific research questions your chosen method is capable of answering through literature review, it is time for you to make a list of three research topics/areas you are most interested in. You can ask yourself the following questions: Is your chosen research method suitable for your research question? Is your research question best answered through your chosen research method? If not, why? If you still find it difficult to decide which one you will go for, it is time to make an appointment to see your supervisor.

I'm Interested in Testing a Theory. How can I turn it into a Research Question?

Zhu Hua

If you are interested in a theory or model, you can design a research project that either evaluates the theory or applies the theory to interpret a phenomenon. The following examples are selected from Masters-level dissertation projects which I have supervised. The first one validates a model, while the second one adopts a model in its attempt to understand community practice.

Simon is interested in an organizational psychology model called "cultural intelligence," known as CQ, which refers to one's capability to function effectively in culturally diverse settings. He has been reading around the topic and has come across a journal article with a title *"Cultural intelligence: its measurement and effects on cultural judgment and decision making, cultural adaptation and task performance"* by Ang Soon et al. (2007) published in *Management and Organization Review 3(3)*, 335–371. The article investigated the link between components of CQ and intercultural effectiveness through empirical studies carried out in the USA and Singapore. Noticing that the model has been validated on two cultures only, Simon decided to carry out a project to test the strength of the relationship between CQ components and intercultural effectiveness in multicultural teams in the UK. He contacted the authors and sought their permission in using the same set of questionnaires to measure participants' cultural intelligences and their performance levels.

Lenin is interested in interculturality approach, a line of investigation which seeks to interpret how participants make aspects of cultural identities relevant or irrelevant to interactions. He decided to use this approach to understand how both first and second generation Colombian migrants access and gain membership into Latin American diasporic working communities in London. Specifically he would like to look at how the Colombian community members use culturally driven in-group discourse to negotiate their acceptance into more established Latin American community in London. To do this, he used ethnography to observe their communication practice and with the participants' permission, recorded some conservation between members of two communities.

Conclusion

Research questions guide the entire study and provide the focus for the writing up of each chapter. They require refining and reshaping as the study progresses, especially in the developing, piloting, and data-collection phases. This is even more so for those adopting a bottom up approach and aiming to derive a holistic picture through focusing on specific and local information first. Finalizing research questions is important, especially when analysis begins and writing up takes place. Students also need to differentiate refining and revising research questions from getting lost on their way - always return to the central research question if you are not sure that a subquestion you are looking at is relevant. Is what you are doing helping you get to grips with the central research question? If not, reconsider.

Key Terms

Hypothesis An informed reasoning and articulation of predictions of research outcomes which leads the direction of data analysis. However, there is certain degree of ambiguity as to the use of the term hypothesis in the literature: some use the term to indicate that the research will quantitatively "test" a hypothesis while for others the term stands for "assumptions".

Research idea An inkling or a grounded concern which is allowed to be vague, intuitive, or bold. It is a precursor to research questions and often indicates where the researcher's broad interests lie.

Research question A research question is the question one is trying to address through research. A well-formulated research question contains all of the following characteristics: specific in focus and scope, formulated clearly, theoretically motivated and informed, empirically answerable, feasible within one's resources and allowable timeframe, appropriate to requirement and expectation, original enough for the scope of the project, inviting fresh insights, and ethical.

References

Alvesson, M., & Sköldberg, K. (2009). *Reflexive methodology: New vistas for qualitative Research*. Thousand Oaks, CA: Sage.

Boudah, D. J. (2011). *Conducting educational research: Guide to completing a major project.* Thousand Oaks, CA: Sage.

Creswell, J. W. (2014). *Research design: Qualitative, quantitative and mixed methods Approaches.* Thousand Oaks, CA: Sage.

Giampapa, F., & Lamoureux, S. A. (2011). Voices from the field: Identity, language, and power in multilingual research settings. *Journal of Language, Identity & Education,* 10(3), 127–131.

Gorard, S. (2013) *Research design: Creating robust approaches for the social sciences.* Thousand Oaks, CA: Sage.

Hammersley, M. (1992). *What's wrong with ethnography.* London: Routledge.

Litosseliti, L. (Ed.). (2010). *Research methods in linguistics.* London: Bloomsbury.

Parsons, R. D., & Kimberlee S. B. (2002). *Teacher as reflective practitioner and action researcher.* Belmont, CA: Wadsworth / Thomson Learning.

Sanderson, T., & Angouri, J. (2014). "I'm an expert in me and I know what I can cope with": Patient expertise in rheumatoid arthritis. *Communication & Medicine,* 10(3), 249–261.

Saunders, M., Lewis, P., & Thornbill, A. (2007). *Research methods for business students* (4th ed.). London: Prentice Hall.

Further Reading and Resources

Litosseliti, L. (Ed.). (2010). *Research methods in linguistics.* London: Bloomsbury.

Saunders, M., Lewis, P., & Thornbill, A. (2007). *Research methods for business students* (4th ed.). London: Prentice Hall.

6 How to Research Multilingually: Possibilities and Complexities

Prue Holmes, Richard Fay, Jane Andrews and Mariam Attia

Summary

This chapter aims to develop researchers' awareness and understanding of the process of researching multilingually – where they must use, or account for the use of, more than one language in the research process. We provide a conceptual framework that guides researchers in: 1) realizing that using more than one language is possible; 2) considering the interconnecting possibilities and complexities of researching multilingually, e.g. being reflexive and reflective, considering the spaces of the research, and the relationships entailed in the research context; and 3) becoming purposeful about the decisions they make in all phases of the research process, e.g. from the initial design of the project, to engaging with different literatures, to developing the methodology and considering all possible ethical issues, to generating and analyzing the data, to issues of representation and reflexivity when writing up and publishing. The chapter draws on examples from the authors' AHRC-funded Researching Multilingually network project (AHJ005037/1).

Introduction

In our increasingly interconnected world, there are many, often underdiscussed, possibilities for using more than one language in a research project, and there are also many, often underexplored, complexities in doing so. Although the use of more than one language is a common practice in some linguistically-oriented fields (e.g. Foreign Language Education, Area Studies, Translation Studies, Intercultural Communication, Cross-cultural Pragmatics, and Multilingualism Studies), such possibilities may exist, we would argue, in any and all fields of research. These wider possibilities pose a challenge to the increasing, but often inequitable, use of English as the dominant language of much international dissemination of research.

Multilingual research possibilities commonly arise in the work of multicultural and multilingual research teams (see Woodin, Chapter 7, this volume), but for the single researcher, too, more than one language might be used in all and any of the stages of a research project – from designing the project, to addressing ethical responsibilities, to engaging with existing scholarship and writing literature reviews, to developing the methodology and the tools and instruments used in collecting/generating data and then analyzing it, to writing up and representing the research (and those involved in it) to wider audiences, to maintaining a reflective and reflexive stance throughout the project, and so on.

All of these possibilities are invoked by our terms "researching multilingually" (RM-ly) and "RM-ly practice" (Holmes, Fay, Andrews, & Attia, 2013). Further, as we speak of the "possibilities for" and the "complexities of" RM-ly, we are suggesting that there is more than one way of researching multilingually. Accordingly, researchers need to consider all these possibilities and complexities. Having done so, they can make informed decisions and demonstrate what we term "researcher purposefulness" (or more technically, "researcher intentionality," see Stelma & Fay, 2014; Stelma, Fay, & Zhou, 2013) in their RM-ly practice.

Insights on RM-ly

To date, little guidance on RM-ly practice is available (whether in English or in other languages) in the research manuals. Nor does it seem to feature much, if at all, in research(er) training programs. Furthermore, the conventions of research texts (e.g. journal articles, doctoral theses) do not often provide researchers with space and encouragement to make transparent their RM-ly practice and the purposeful choices underpinning it.

However, some published studies do discuss issues of direct relevance for our RM-ly concern. For example, Magyar & Robinson-Pant (2011) note how research supervisors in UK contexts may discourage the use of literature published in other languages, and can be critical of writing styles that do not conform to Anglocentric academic conventions. Insights are also emerging on power negotiations in research, and the acknowledgement of the roles of differing perspectives, histories and contexts among interviewers, interpreters, and translators, for example, on their linguistic choices in research projects (Chen, 2011; Kitchen, 2013; Pant-Robinson & Wolf, 2014; Pavlenko, 2005; Temple, 2008; Temple & Edwards, 2002).

This chapter is informed by insights arising from the Researching Multilingually network project (http://researchingmultilingually.com; see Holmes, et al., 2013) in which researchers from a range of disciplines reported how they became aware of the RM-ly possibilities and reflected on the issues arising in their RM-ly practice. We conceptualize their processes of developing researcher competence vis-à-vis RM-ly practice in three parts (realization, consideration, and informed and purposeful decision-making). First, we report on various ways in which researchers have reflected on the trigger through which they became aware of RM-ly possibilities (*Realization*). Then, we present aspects of RM-ly practice which we find helpful when considering what the RM-ly possibilities and complexities might look like – namely: reflective and reflexive; spatial; and relational aspects (*Consideration*). Finally, we present three case studies in which researchers reflect on their RM-ly practice and issues arising in it (*Informed and purposeful decision-making*).

Developing Researcher Competence (vis-à-vis RM-ly Practice)

Our model for this process has three parts, as shown in Figure 6.1.

The three-part conceptualization could easily suggest that researcher development (vis-à-vis RM-ly practice) is essentially a step-by-step, linear process. However, the researcher-development process is more organic, varied and complex than that. To exemplify this process we draw on the researcher-development profiles recorded for the Researching Multilingually network project. Unless indicated otherwise, all quotations and paraphrases in the discussions below are taken, with the consent of the researchers concerned, from the Researching Multilingually network project website researcher profiles and/or presentations.

---

1   **Realization**–often triggered by a particular conversation in the research process (e.g. during supervision)–that multilingual possibilities and complexities merit attention ...

prompting ...

2   **Consideration**–bearing in mind the reflexive and reflective, spatial, and relational aspects of the research–of the possibilities for, and the complexities of, RM-ly practice in research activities ...

leading to ...

3   **Informed and purposeful decision-making**, e.g. by researchers, about, for example:

a)   research design–planning, designing, implementing, monitoring and fine-tuning (e.g. responding to unexpected contingencies) their research and its multilingual dimensions; and

b)   (re)presentation–the production of research texts (e.g. theses, articles) which are also shaped by purposeful decisions regarding multilingual possibilities; and e.g. by supervisors, by:

c)   purposefully questioning the researcher's research design and representation decisions.

Figure 6.1   The three-part process of developing researcher competence vis-à-vis researching multilingually practice.

(1) Realization – becoming aware of RM-ly possibilities

For some researchers, their own linguistic abilities felt valuable from the outset of their research: "I knew all the way that being fluent in a number of languages could broaden my research horizon" (Victor). For others, that value became more apparent when they moved abroad to undertake postgraduate research studies and the linguistic aspects of their experience became more marked (Fenia). But for some researchers, the "study abroad" research space might not seem so open to this valued multilingual dimension: "It was not until my doctoral studies… that I realised how hard I had been trying to develop my academic self monolingually in another language [English] while ignoring the value of my mother tongue and its enriching implications for me as a researcher" (Xiaowei). Similarly:

> I first realised that I could, in the sense of having the permission to, conduct my doctoral research multilingually when [my supervisor] explained the way in which I could handle my multilingual data. Being permitted to present the data in its original language within the thesis surprised me to the extent of not believing it at first. [Parneet]

In the above quotations, the trigger for raised awareness of RM-ly possibilities is the doctoral supervision process, and in the Researching Multilingually network project it became clear that this doctoral site provided awareness-raising potential for supervisors as well as students. Within the doctoral experience, the researchers in our project reported particular triggers for becoming more aware of the RM-ly potential. Fieldwork experiences provide one such trigger. Thus, for Ayesha, it was when she "struggled with [a] huge amount of data… some of which was in English, some in Urdu and some in [a] mixture of both" that she became aware of RM-ly complexities and greatly concerned with "how to present the data so that the meaning of what is being said is not lost."

Reflective Prompts

Are you aware of the RM-ly possibilities of your research project? If so, how did you become aware?
What triggered your interest in this area of research practice?

---

(2) Consideration – of RM-ly Possibilities and Complexities

For this part of the process, researchers need, first, to consider a range of general RM-ly issues, and second, to thoroughly think through the RM-ly possibilities and complexities of their own research attributes, preferences, project, and context. In the discussion below, we expand on the general issues by summarizing the many insights we gained through the Researching Multilingually network project (see a fuller discussion of these in Holmes et al., 2013, pp. 292–295). Then, we turn to the more specific area of consideration, where we suggest that researchers can – as managed through reflective and reflexive habits – consider the interconnecting multilingual possibilities in the spaces in which their research happens (i.e. the *spatial*) and in the relationships their research involves (i.e. the *relational*).

(a) Some general considerations

From the Researching Multilingually network project we became aware of many possibilities for and complexities of RM-ly practice. These insights included:

- working cross-culturally with ethical guidelines and other institutional documentation (see Olga's case study below);
- engaging with literature in more than one language, and in languages other than English;
- studying within often monolingually oriented universities such as English-medium universities in the United Kingdom;
- deciding where to present data which is not in the language used to report the study (e.g. in the main body of the text? In footnotes? In the appendices?);
- negotiating how to perform appropriate academic and researcher identities (e.g. whether to use 'I') when researching across languages and cultures;
- being transparent about the multilingual research processes used throughout the study;
- deciding which language(s) to use when building rapport with researcher colleagues and participants;
- deciding which language(s) to use when generating data;
- deciding which language(s) to use when analyzing data;
- working with translators and interpreters;
- negotiating the geopolitics of particular languages in particular research contexts and of English as the dominant language of international research dissemination; and
- deciding which languages to use in representing the research in theses, journal articles, reports and other forms of dissemination.

Underlying the above issues is a clear indication that RM-ly possibilities and complexities exist in each and every stage of the research process.

(b) The reflective and reflexive aspect

Engaging in constant reflection is central to understanding and improving practice and to supporting researcher continuous development (Schön, 1991). As researchers make multilingual decisions, they are invited to critically reflect on their research undertaking and deeply analyze their conceptual and methodological stances. Reflective accounts, in the form of journals for example, are often used to complement other sources of data such as interviews or observations, thereby enriching the entire research process (Borg 2001; Burgess, 1981). In addition to engaging in careful observation and examination of their practice, researchers are in constant interaction with their work. So, as they reach out to shape their research, the experience of that reaches back to shape them. Reflexivity can therefore be understood as this mutually shaping interaction between the researcher and the research (Edge, 2011; Dervin, Chapter 9, this volume).

Earlier literature (e.g. Magyar & Robinson-Pant, 2011; Temple & Edwards, 2002) has emphasized the key role of reflection and reflexivity in research studies where more than one language is involved. In this chapter, we have noted the triggering role of doctoral supervision discussions. However, for that trigger to lead the researcher towards a systematic exploration of the RM-ly possibilities and complexities, the researcher needs to be in the habit of reflecting (on the process and progress of their research) and being reflexive (considering their shaping influence on the research and its influence on them). Thus, as was her habit, Parneet's reflections record how, only after a further tutorial confirming RM-ly possibilities, she "set foot on beginning to understand [her] experience of engaging in multilingual research." She also explained that while investigating her context, she was open to what she could learn from the stories her participants offered her, and thereby engage in bidirectional reflexive interactions.

Thus, an off-the-cuff comment from Parneet's supervisor regarding language issues only became a trigger because Parneet was in the habit of keeping a reflective journal of her doctoral supervisions; through her reflection on her supervisor's comment, a moment of realization dawned. A similar point could be made about Xiaowei's reflections on her supervisor's questioning. For Xiaowei, the questions asked by her supervisor may have provided the push, but it was only through her reflective and reflexive writing that she articulated how these questions had pushed her to notice "so many things to which [she] had been blind, such as relevant literature written in Mandarin, similar research studies undertaken in Mandarin with unique methodological insights and the potential of richer interpretations of the data when drawing on different linguistic resources."

Reflective Prompts

Are you in the habit of maintaining reflective records about the (e.g. linguistic aspects of the) progress and process of your research and the triggers for further thinking that occur along the way? How do you do this?

Are you in the habit of considering your shaping influence (e.g. regarding language choices) on the research, and its influence on your thinking also? How do you manage this?

(c) The spatial aspect

Leah Davcheva and Richard Fay (2012) mapped the multilingual possibilities and complexities of their research project – which involved researching one language (Ladino) through fieldwork in another (Bulgarian) and analysis and presentation in a third (English) – in terms of four "spaces." We draw on these four spaces from Davcheva and Fay's research to give examples of how participants in our

Researching Multilingually network project presentation use these spaces in their own research:

1. The *researched* phenomenon, i.e. what is being researched (the "what"), e.g. for Ayesha (mentioned above), the focus was on the classroom practices of English language teachers in Pakistan.
2. The *research* context (the "where"), e.g. for Xiaowei (mentioned above), her research "home" was the English-medium UK university where her doctorate was being supervised.
3. The *researcher's* linguistic resources (the "who"), e.g. for Parneet (mentioned above), her multilingualism in languages spoken in both northern and southern India enabled her to be flexible about which languages to use when interviewing street-connected children from different parts of the country.
4. The *representational* possibilities, i.e. dissemination in English only and/or (an)other language(s) (the "for where" and/or "for whom"), e.g. to date, Leah and Richard's work has been presented and published in Bulgarian, English, German, and Spanish.

> **Reflective Prompt**
>
> What RM-ly possibilities and complexities can you map out using these four "spaces" as a frame of reference?

(d) The relational aspect

Researchers rarely work alone. In carrying out their research projects they work with a range of people in various roles. In doing so they must establish multiple relationships with, for example, supervisors, participants, translators, interpreters, transcribers, editors, and funders. Research processes and outcomes are shaped importantly by the ways in which these relationships are managed interpersonally and linguistically, and by decisions about which languages are privileged within and across these relationships, and for what purposes. So, our second aspect concerns *relationality*, i.e. who is involved in the research, what are the relationships between them, what functions and/or purposes do these relationships have, and how are these relationships negotiated and managed.

Jane Andrews' (2013) research exemplifies this relational aspect. When Jane began collaborating with a community interpreter (in order to engage in conversations about children's learning with parents from linguistically diverse backgrounds), she realized that "the specific challenges [arose] from engaging in research where shared language(s) and cultural understandings cannot be taken for granted." This realization raised for her "many interesting questions … in terms of the relationship between research participants and researcher and between interpreter and researcher." These included areas such as the extent to which an interpreter should be considered an additional researcher in the research encounter. This then raises questions regarding the need to brief interpreters about the wider goals of the research, including them in processes of analysis and writing, and the potential costs such involvements entail.

The importance of relationship building and developing trust between researcher and participants is also evidenced in Prue's research (in English) with Chinese international students who had English as an additional language (Holmes, 2014). As one of the participants reflected in the final interview after 18 months of fieldwork, "Initial data might not be very accurate… we were getting the right answers for you." The participants used complex cognitive and affective processes to describe their intercultural communication experiences in English: e.g. perceptions and emotional experiences; the researcher–researched relationship, which included deference to the researcher in some instances and participant agency in others; presentational strategies of the self; and face strategies. They were also negotiating the meaning of the interview questions vis-à-vis the research topic and aims, and the importance and significance of their own narratives and responses in meeting these aims. To facilitate participants' responses in the interview context, Prue allowed them to preview the open-ended interview questions a few days before the interview.

> **Reflective Prompts**
>
> Who is involved in your research (i.e., in all stages and aspects of it)? What are their linguistic resources? What are yours? Which languages might be used for which parts of your research? Who decides? What difference does this make?

(3) Informed and Purposeful Decision-Making – Three Case Studies

To exemplify the third aspect of RM-ly practice – informed and purposeful decision-making – we draw on three case studies. In each we exemplify aspects of developing researcher awareness and purposefulness of RM-ly concerning research design (the planning, designing, implementing, monitoring and fine-tuning of the multilingual dimensions of the research) and (re)presentation (the writing up of research). The first case study (Sara) deals with issues of data generation as the researcher engages with multilingual datasets in the analysis and writing up stages. The second (Olga) discusses the negotiation of ethical norms associated with gaining access to research sites and eliciting informed consent. The third (Ana) explores complexities arising when both the researcher and participants are fluent in the languages of the research, and the implications for data representation.

> **Case Study 1: Sara and Colleagues RM-ly Focus – Data Generation**

Sara is a United Kingdom (UK)-based doctoral researcher who feels she is always translating herself from her first language (Italian). Her RM-ly development was a result of "making a virtue out of necessity." Her research foregrounds the complexities of generating data when researchers and participants speak multiple languages, and, in most cases, do not have English (the language of the research project) as their first language.

Sara was a (paid) researcher in a project which sought to understand the cultural participation and attitudes to diversity and foreignness among 68 immigrant/refugee/asylum-seeking women in a city in the northeast of England (see Ganassin & Holmes, 2013, for further details of the RM-ly aspects of this project). The study was designed in English by native-speaker UK researchers, but the data generation was conducted by 17 researchers, largely volunteers, who were mostly multilingual. Among the participants and researchers more than 25 languages were spoken.

Through their planning for the data generation processes, the researchers shared an ethical concern about representing all voices in order to avoid cultural and linguistic domination by themselves or any particular participants. Thus, acknowledging the multiple languages at play was important in addressing questions of representation, and of who speaks for whom. They also planned to conduct the focus groups in cultural spaces where the participants felt a sense of belonging.

However, the linguistic diversity and asymmetry among the participants made planning the focus groups difficult and also seemed to affect the confidence of some women in participating. To engage participants, the researchers tried to use simple but meaningful language in designing and asking questions, and rephrased sentences when participants appeared not to understand. They drew on the multilingual resources present in the group and the women's relationships with one another to provide peer support. They joined in the interpretation as the women spoke for one another in multiple languages. Some participants "whispered" words/phrases in one language to another participant who would translate. However, some conversations (e.g. those in Dari and Farsi) were not translated for several reasons: the focus group recordings were inaudible due to the multiple languages and speakers present, the researchers lacked knowledge of some of the languages, and the project did not have resources to pay for translators or interpreters. Such conversations were thus absent in the data. These linguistic asymmetries raised important concerns about the authenticity of the emergent data. Furthermore, the researchers questioned the extent to which they were constructing the data themselves through their language support to participants.

The focus group discussions were translated and transcribed into English. Sara translated into English the words and phrases that the participants had translated into French during the focus groups. As Sara was involved in the analysis, she did not believe it was necessary to include French words in the transcription. In her postresearch reflection, Sara noted that the multilingual complexity of the data was an unrecognized aspect of the data generation, transcription, translation, and analysis. She also realized the importance of "flexible multilingualism," (as illustrated in the researchers' and participants' data generation strategies described above) in the project design and its operationalization. Flexible multilingualism draws upon, or makes strategic use of, the multilingual skills naturally present in the research context, and in doing so, accommodates participants', and researchers', asymmetric multilingual practices (Ganassin & Holmes, 2013). Although the research team were aware of, and had discussed the implications of, the multilingual nature of the research, they had not foreseen the degree of complexity, or the consequences for the authenticity and trustworthiness of the research outcomes, so crucial among this marginalized, vulnerable, and disadvantaged group of women.

> **Reflective Prompts**
>
> How do you deal with the multiple languages at play when you are generating, and analyzing, the data for your project? Who speaks for whom, when, where, and why and in what language(s)? How do you use the multiple languages in the writing up ((re)presentation) of your data?

> **Case Study 2: Olga RM-ly Focus – Negotiating Access and Informed Consent**

In her doctoral research, Olga sought to use multiple sources and informants to investigate her area of study into the processes of national identity construction experienced by children in schools in northern Cyprus, a self-declared state also known as the Turkish Republic of Northern Cyprus (TRNC). As a multilingual researcher with some knowledge of Turkish, Olga gathered paper-based sources such as documents relating to the curriculum, textbooks, and materials portraying images relevant to analysis of the construction of identity. The study also made use of observations of teaching, interviews and focus groups with children and adults in education settings. Throughout the study, data sources were in either of the two languages of the study: Turkish or English. In this brief account of Olga's research processes, two issues are highlighted for consideration:

1 negotiating differing norms relating to ethical processes such as gaining access to research sites and informed consent; and
2 engaging with multilingual datasets both in the analysis stage and in the writing stage.

Doctoral students in any given context will have their studies governed by their institution's academic regulations and by discipline specific guidelines e.g. the British Educational Research Association Ethical Guidelines for Educational Research (2011). Such regulations and guidelines inevitably reflect norms and expectations of that institution regarding the conduct of research. By conducting her research in a national and institutional setting that differed from the context in which she was registered as a student for her studies, Olga encountered some distinctive challenges relating to research norms and approaches to multilingual data which are discussed here.

Gaining access to research settings (in this case, schools) and then requesting informed consent from groups and individuals is explored in detail in the research methods literature, and potential clashes between norms surrounding these processes are also explored (e.g. Honana, Hamida, Alhamdana, Phommalangsya, & Lingard, 2013). Holliday's (1999) work delineating "small" cultures and "large" cultures is valuable here in helping researchers to understand the differences between ways of embarking on a process of gaining access and informed consent in one context as opposed to another (the one used for educational researchers in northern Cyprus and the one used in the UK higher education institution where Olga was registered as a doctoral student). Ways of conducting educational research in one UK higher education institution and in schools in northern Cyprus were governed by different regulations, and consequently, the linguistic and other resources used to enact access and consent processes were noted by Olga as being quite different. This meant that Olga needed to keep in mind the expectations of these two "small cultures" to ensure that she conformed to the spirit of gaining access and informed consent in an ethical manner, and also, that she obtained the documentation needed to demonstrate she had done this, so that her doctoral study evidenced her ethical practice.

The mediating role played by Olga in negotiating consent in keeping with the expectations of two different small cultural contexts is mirrored by her role in considering how to handle her bilingual dataset. The dataset needed to be explored by Olga with support from her supervisory team, so questions were raised here about how and when the team would see the data from a language they did not share (Turkish). In addition, Olga was concerned to provide readers of the completed thesis with access to the full dataset (not just a version translated into English) to ensure they could appreciate the nature of this data. An example of this concern is seen in the nature of the Turkish language letter granting access to schools which included both text and an official stamp confirming access.

By reflecting at each stage of the research process on the choices to be made and implications that might ensue (i.e. illustrating the "consideration" part of the process of developing researcher competence in RM-ly practice in Figure 6.1 above), Olga reached some principled decisions on how to progress with her research project (i.e. the "informed, purposeful decision-making" in Figure 6.1). Her approach involved continued dialogues with her supervisors about her data and keeping the needs of new readers in mind by making use of the space in a thesis to ensure data in all languages was available. Although this approach was not straightforward, in the words of Olga, the goal was reached: that, as a researcher, she was doing justice to her data and her participants in representing their experiences in their full richness.

> **Reflective Prompts**
>
> How might you ensure that readers of your research get a full sense of the research encounter? Will you provide multilingual datasets to readers?

> **Case Study 3: Ana RM-ly Focus – Data Representation**

It could be assumed that considering RM-ly issues might only be a concern for researchers who do not share the languages of their research participants. Ana's doctoral study illustrates the point that while multilingual researchers may be able to engage with their participants in shared languages and analyze their data in the language in which it was generated, the processes of consideration and informed, purposeful decision-making are still significant.

Ana's doctoral study highlights the challenges faced by multilingual researchers who are fluent in the languages used in the study and in the language required by the academic institution awarding the doctorate. Ana's research participants were British students of Italian and Italian students of English, and the context was that of language-learning experiences during university study abroad trips. Particular attention is given here to the choices Ana faced in relation to her dual role as both researcher and translator of her data, her sense of responsibility towards her participants when representing their interactions as data in English and Italian, and the way in which she was drawn into a process of defining her conceptualization of translation in the context of her study.

Ana's study looked at cross-cultural adaptation as documented through students' participation in online communication on social networks such as Facebook, using what has been named a "lifestream" approach (see Eric Freeman & David Gelernter (n.d.)). The study involved an analysis of data from social network posts in two languages. The participants' online interactions moved rapidly between English and Italian, and Ana found that the way that she represented this data required careful consideration. She noted that she needed skills beyond being a mere "technical" translator of her own data: she needed to consider how to convey the nuances within students' lexical choices as they expressed their feelings about adapting to a new culture. Ana explained her desire as a researcher to return to her translations of her data to ensure they were "polished."

Ana's sustained work on achieving a faithful representation of her participants' meanings came from her awareness of the needs of readers of her thesis who could not be assumed to be fluent readers of Italian. An outcome of this process was the decision she made to present her data in English translation (where necessary, i.e. where participants code-switched between English and Italian) in the main text of her thesis, but to make use of footnotes for the "original" or bilingual text. In different academic contexts such a decision may be constrained or permitted by regulations associated with the context of writing. UK higher education institutions tend to require doctoral theses to fall within a specified word limit and as such the inclusion of datasets in the original language and the language of assessment (Italian and English, respectively, in this case) may have implications for the extent to which this approach can be used systematically. However Ana's intention to show the original versions of her dataset fit well into a thorough and transparent research process which readers can gain access to.

Ana's reflections provide insight into the following areas:

1 the complexities involved in researching multilingually in terms of the roles required of the researcher as both researcher and data translator (*realization, consideration*);
2 the attention needed to be paid to the potential readers of the research so they can gain access to the nuances available to the researcher-translator (*informed, purposeful decision-making*); and
3 the need for the researcher to engage in understanding their translation processes as being part of the analysis and not merely a technical stage of the research (*realization*).

> **Reflective Prompts**
>
> How will you represent the nuances of translated multilingual data in your writing? How will you reflect data which move between languages?

Conclusion

Given that researching is inevitably a multilingual endeavor, and that researchers are faced with political considerations about which language(s) to (re)present and/or publish their work in, developing an RM-ly dimension to research is both inevitable and imperative. In this chapter we have presented a framework for researching multilingually that attempts to address this complex situation. We offer a three-part process of realization, consideration, and informed and purposeful decision-making – organic, varied, and complex – that is illustrative of RM-ly practice. By drawing on examples from our Researching Multilingually network project, and through three illustrative case studies of RM-ly in the field, we have, we hope, opened up your thinking about the multilingual aspects of your research project. Finally, we hope that the prompts may trigger you to reflect on the possibilities and complexities of your own RM-ly practice. In turn, these realizations will build your confidence in making informed choices about RM-ly practice and enable you to make your RM-ly practice transparent in the writing up of your own research project.

Acknowledgements

We thank the Arts and Humanities Research Council (AHRC) for their funding of the research grant (AH/J005037/1) which made this research possible. We are also grateful to the case study researchers who have given us their permission to reflect on their experiences of researching multilingually.

Key Terms

Developing researcher competence The ongoing process of becoming more confident and assured when making research(er) decisions as appropriate for particular studies and contexts and for those involved in them.

Researching multilingually (RM-ly) The process and practice of using, or accounting for the use of, more than one language in the research process, e.g. from the initial design of the project, to engaging with different literatures, to developing the methodology and considering all possible ethical issues, to generating and analyzing the data, to issues of representation and reflexivity when writing up and publishing.

Researcher purposefulness The informed and intentional research(er) thinking and decision-making which results from an awareness and thorough consideration of the possibilities for and complexities of all aspects of the research process (including RM-ly).

Research relationships Who are the people in the whole research project, e.g. researcher(s), supervisors, participants, translators, interpreters, transcribers, editors, and funders, and how do their relationships influence language choices within all phases of the project (from design to (re)presentation and publication)?

Research spaces The multilingual aspects of the project, e.g. the research phenomenon (the "what"), the context of the research (the "where"), the linguistic resources of the researcher (the "who"), the representational possibilities (the language(s) of dissemination, the "for where" or "for whom").

References

Andrews, J. (2013). "It's a very difficult question, isn't it?" Researcher, interpreter and research participant negotiating meanings in an education research interview. *International Journal of Applied Linguistics*, 23(3), 316–328.

Borg, S. (2001). The research journal: A tool for promoting and understanding researcher development. *Language Teaching Research*, 5(2), 156–177.

Burgess, R. (1981). Keeping a research diary. *Cambridge Journal of Education*, 11(1), 75–83.

Chen, S.-H. (2011). Power relations between the researcher and the researched: An analysis of native and nonnative ethnographic interviews. *Field Methods*, 23(1), 119–135.

Davcheva, L., & Fay, R. (2012). An examination of the research and researcher aspects of multilingually researching one language (Ladino) through fieldwork in another (Bulgarian) and analysis and presentation in a third (English). Paper presented at the 1st AHRC Researching Multilingually seminar, hosted by Durham University, March 28–29, 2012.

Edge, J. (2011). *The reflexive teacher educator in TESOL*. London: Routledge.

Freeman, E., & Gelernter, D. (n.d.). Lifestreams: Organizing your electronic life. Retrieved June 14, 2015 from: http://cs-www.cs.yale.edu/homes/freeman/lifestreams.html.

Ganassin, S., & Holmes, P. (2013). Multilingual research practices in community research: The case of migrant / refugee women in north-east England. *International Journal of Applied Linguistics*, 23(3), 342–356.

Holliday, A.R. (1999). Small cultures. *Applied Linguistics*, 20(2), 237–264.

Holmes, P. (2014). Researching Chinese students' intercultural communication experiences in higher education: Researcher and participant reflexivity. In J. Byrd-Clarke & F. Dervin (Eds.), *Reflexivity and multimodality in language education: Rethinking multilingualism and interculturality in accelerating complex and transnational spaces* (pp. 100–118). London: Routledge.

Holmes, P., Fay, R., Andrews, J., & Attia, M. (2013). Researching multilingually: New theoretical and methodological directions. *International Journal of Applied Linguistics*, 23(3), 285–299.

Honana, E., Hamida, M. O., Alhamdana, B., Phommalangsya, P., & Lingard B. (2013). Ethical issues in cross-cultural research. *International Journal of Research & Method in Education*, 36(4), 386–399.

Kitchen, M. C. (2013). Methods in focus group interviews in cross-cultural settings. *Qualitative Research Journal*, 13(3), 265–277.

Magyar, A., & Robinson-Pant, A. (2011). Special issue on university internationalisation – towards transformative change in higher education. Internationalising doctoral research: Developing theoretical perspectives on practice. *Teachers and Teaching*, 17(6), 663–76.

Pant-Robinson, A., & Wolf, A. (2014). *Researching across languages and cultures*. Centre for Applied Research in Education Working Paper, No 1, May.

Pavlenko, A. (2005). *Emotions and multilingualism*. Cambridge: Cambridge University Press.

Schön, D. (1991). *The reflective practitioner*. Aldershot: Ashgate.

Stelma, J., & Fay, R. (2014). Intentionality and developing researcher competence on a UK master's course: an ecological perspective on research education. *Studies in Higher Education*, 39(4), 517–533.

Stelma, J., Fay, R. & Zhou, X. (2013). Developing intentionality and researching multilingually: An ecological and methodological perspective. *International Journal of Applied Linguistics*, 23(3), 300–315.

Temple, B. (2008). Narrative analysis of written texts: Reflexivity in cross language research. *Qualitative Research*, 8(3), 355–365.

Temple, B., & Edwards, R. (2002). Interpreters / translators and cross-language research: Reflexivity and border crossings. *International Journal of Qualitative Methods*, 1(1), 1–12.

Further Reading and Resources

The following special issue showcases six selected case studies from the AHRC-funded "Researching Multilingually" project:

Andrews, J., Holmes, P., & Fay, R. (Eds.) (2013). Researching Multilingually (Special Issue). *International Journal of Applied Linguistics*, 23(3).

The "Researching Multilingually" website, http://researchingmultilingually.com/, offers a comprehensive resource for researchers, including 35 presentations and more than 50 profiles in which researchers from diverse disciplines report how they became aware of RM-ly possibilities, outline their RM-ly practice and reflect on RM-ly issues arising in their projects.

The AHRC large-grant project, "Researching Multilingually at the Borders of Language, the Body, Law, and the State" http://researching-multilingually-at-borders.com/ (AH/L006936/1) led by Alison Phipps (University of Glasgow) is underpinned by our own RM-ly research. Further examples of (developing) RM-ly work can be found there and in the case studies associated with this project.

7 How to Research Interculturally and Ethically

Jane Woodin

> **Summary**
>
> Intercultural Communication research involves a wide range of approaches and activities, incorporating culture as a construct in a variety of ways. This chapter discusses the implications for your research project of taking what might be considered a cross-cultural as opposed to an intercultural approach; the first of these involving a more concrete approach to culture as behavior which can be identified and described, and the second involving an understanding of culture as created within interaction. Issues relating to researching one's own culture as insider, and others' culture as outsider are discussed, as is the increasingly common activity of working alongside participants and collaborators from different cultural backgrounds. Theoretical and practical perspectives are addressed, together with some questions for consideration in relation to ethics in Intercultural Communication research.

Introduction

The terms *cross-cultural* and *intercultural* themselves can imply a certain approach to intercultural communication. Gudykunst (2000) and Spencer-Oatey (2000) understand the term cross-cultural research as comparing behavior among two or more cultural groups when they interact with others of that same group (e.g. comparing

Research Methods in Intercultural Communication: A Practical Guide, First Edition. Edited by Zhu Hua.
© 2016 John Wiley & Sons, Inc. Published 2016 by John Wiley & Sons, Inc.

request strategies in Spain and China), and intercultural research as examining patterns of behavior when two or more cultural groups interact (e.g. request strategies when Chinese and Spanish people interact). Some would argue that this intercultural research approach is problematic, as it can assume that Chinese and English are categories which are relevant to an interaction. To many, the term cross-cultural assumes a particular paradigm of work whose research approach is likely to focus on cultural difference as central in the research design. Other research, which is often termed "intercultural" might focus upon how culture is drawn upon, referred to or made relevant by interlocutors in interaction. This second research approach is more closely related to Gudykunst and Spencer-Oatey's use of *intercultural*, in that it recognizes the relevance of culture in the focus of study, but does not necessarily seek to pre-define how culture might be conceptualized in the field under study. For example, there might be many approaches to researching cultural practices of the use of song at intercultural weddings. A cross-cultural approach might consider the use of song in both of the cultural groups involved, as separate practices and comparing those practices; an intercultural approach might consider the instances of the use of song in the wedding itself, and try to uncover the cultural meaning of the song – this might or might not include references to cultural practices of each of the groups represented.

Research which is categorized under the umbrella term of "Intercultural Communication" can therefore vary enormously in its methodology, focus, and conceptual basis. Indeed it has been said that there is no inherent theoretical difference between communication and intercultural communication (Verschueren, 2008), so we might raise the question of whether we need to focus on Intercultural Communication research as an area distinct from communication research in general. However, the burgeoning interest in Intercultural Communication as a field of study would suggest the opposite, and many of us who research in the Intercultural Communication field have first-hand lived experiences of the intercultural. There are examples of racism and/or marginalization on the grounds of difference (e.g. Lippi-Green, 1997), of communication difficulties in intercultural couples (e.g. McFadden, 2001), which may lead us to experience difference, whether it can be justified theoretically or not. Our lived reality may tell us differently. This lived reality can often affect encounters as we may, for example, find ourselves prejudging a person or a group based on how they look or on what they say, or indeed find that others do so with us. It is unlikely that any intercultural encounter is entirely devoid of assumptions.

In relation to identity, Baynham makes a useful distinction between identity as *brought along* and identity as *brought about*:

> "Identity brought along" thus captures the accumulation and sedimentation of identity positions in habitus not as some essentialist pre-existing category but as discursively constituted, enabled and constrained by the limits of language. "Identity brought about" captures the performativity by which identity is contingently made and re-made in discourse, either with or against the grain of dominant discourses. (Baynham, 2015)

This distinction could also apply to the discussion on culture; while a "brought-along" concept of culture could be understood as familiar cultural references or practices which we may draw upon in interaction or which perhaps may influence our thinking or behavior, a "brought-about" concept of culture will focus more upon how meaning is made between interlocutors in an interaction.

A consideration of how you are researching interculturally in your own research project will help you to be aware of your perspective on your research project; it is highly likely that your project will benefit from making your position explicit.

This chapter will consider both cross-cultural and intercultural approaches, as they are interdependent in a number of ways. It is also of importance to consider cross/intercultural issues relating to the research topic itself, such as:

- the researcher researching another culture as an outsider– i.e. researcher as a cultural outsider;
- the researcher researching his/her own culture as an insider;
- the researcher researching the process of becoming part of another culture as an insider/outsider (most usually through participant observation)
- the researcher researching in a research team which is cross-/intercultural in nature.

Cross-Cultural Approaches

If our main focus is on culture as brought along, we are likely to have pre-defined groups described in cultural terms. Such an approach was considered novel in the late 1980s or early 1990s in Europe, with the increase in recognition that there were cultural differences in the way in which people, communicated, thought and felt. The Cross-Cultural Speech Act Project (CCSARP), for example, undertook a cross-cultural comparison of a number of speech acts (e.g. asking to borrow a car from a neighbor), and asked speakers of some languages (e.g. Spanish-speaking Argentinians, English-speaking Australians) how they would make such requests (Blum-Kulka, House, & Kasper, 1989). This research project received much attention at the time, as it described and showed how things might be said and done differently in different languages, revealing how language can play a part in speech acts and contribute to cross-cultural misunderstanding. The authors themselves recognized critiques of this approach (e.g. in relation to methodology of written discourse completion tasks to ascertain what someone "would say" in speech, or the assumption that a more direct request would carry the same illocutionary force in languages); nonetheless this work was seminal in highlighting the fact that all languages cannot be assumed to work in the same way as US or UK English. In some cases the speech acts were shown to differ in structure, for example through the level of directness or indirectness. The design of the research took as its starting point an *a priori* definition of culture relating to the linguistic practice of language-speaking communities. Another example of cross-cultural research is the work of Wierzbicka and colleagues, who undertook in-depth studies of the differences in key words, or emotions (such as *anger* or *freedom*) across cultures and languages (Wierzbicka, 1997, 1999). Her work warns of the dangers of assuming that an English language term, for example, can be assumed to carry the same meaning in other languages. Such understanding could be vital in a cross-cultural counseling situation (see for example Lago, 2011). In a very different area, if you are researching the practice of website localization for different language users, or those from different cultural backgrounds, there will be considerations which you will need to address in relation to positioning of text or icons (for example depending on those who read from right to left or left to right) or on which colors or combination of colors are culturally appropriate (see for example Madden, Hewett, & Roth, 2000).

A cross-cultural approach can be highly informative, revealing, and even equalizing. On the other hand, the following issues can be problematic:

- the assumption that any cultural group described is homogenous (at least for the purposes of the research);
- the identification of culture; as a predefined category by which behavior can be described or understood to the detriment of other factors (e.g. gender, access, power, being an individual);
- a danger of assuming a static nature to any cultural description, forgetting that it is time- and context-bound and limited.

An Intercultural Approach

A research project whose main concept of culture is in relation to meaning-making in interaction will consider how culture is identified as salient by participants or groups in an interaction, whether it be one-to-one, one-to-group or group-to-group. For example, Hinnenkamp (1987) identified how, in a street encounter between two people, the category "Turkish" was made relevant in conversation between a German (native German-language speaker) and a Turk (non-native German-speaker). Through considering what happened in the conversation at the moment of identification of "culture" (in this case ethnic identification), Hinnenkamp was able to identify a change in positioning between the two interlocutors, and a move at the point of ethnic distinction from the cooperative nature of the conversation into a "non-cooperative" one, where the native German speaker began to use non-native-like language and addressing his interlocutor in the informal address "du."

Such an approach will be heavily reliant on discourse analysis in some form (e.g. critical discourse analysis, conversation analysis; Chapter 19 and Chapter 20 respectively in this volume) thereby giving centrality to the role of language. Researching culture as brought about could be said to be focusing largely on the "how" of culture in intercultural communication. Scollon & Scollon (2001) propose what they call a "mediated discourse approach" to analysis of intercultural encounters, focusing on social action. Arguing that the central question should be: "[W]hat is the social action in which you are interested and how does this analysis promise to focus on some aspect of social life that is worth understanding?" (2001, p. 545), they suggest that we ask how the concept of culture arises in the social actions: "Who has introduced culture as a relevant category, for what purposes and with what consequences?" (p. 545).

From the above, it can be seen that these two approaches are not mutually exclusive. For example, what is considered as culture in the Scollons' approach still needs to be defined by the researcher. In Hinnenkamp's example, Turkish ethnicity has not only been identified as relevant in the conversation, but also the conversation itself has already been deemed relevant by the researcher. The nature of the conversation might also have induced the researcher to identify income-related categories or pension-related categories as evidence of raising of culture in interaction, both of which are evident in Hinnenkamp's example. Categorization of exactly what is seen in research terms as cultural is clearly still in the hands of the researcher, even in an intercultural focus.

Researching with culture as meaning-making in interaction brings with it other aspects which can be problematic, such as:

- the complexity of trying to understand/single out elements from the context which can be clearly identified as relevant to advancing the Intercultural Communication field;
- how to manage change, flexibility and variability in any redefinition of culture, categories of culture, intercultural communication, etc.

However, this approach is highly significant in understanding real and situated interactional practice as opposed to potential interactional practice. Without considering the role of culture in interaction, it is hard to understand how any cross-cultural "brought along" approach would have real-world value.

All projects have a specific focus, however, and decisions need to be made by the researcher as to how the project will be identified, positioned in the field and the key terms defined. Exactly how we define culture will depend upon our research focus, approach and assumptions (Holliday, Chapter 2, this volume); what matters is that these issues are made explicit in terms of the decisions made, and justified in terms of the project.

The Researcher as Cultural Outsider

In the example of tandem learning given in the Case in Point below, the researcher was to some extent a cultural outsider. She was not a student, she was not participating in the conversations, and her role was not part of the research focus. She was a member of staff who had considerable experience of tandem learning in an educational context, and with a knowledge of both English (native language) and Spanish (degree level), and a background in education. In other ways, she was a cultural insider. She was familiar with the educational context, an English speaker, learner of Spanish and had herself participated in tandem learning; she also had the advantage of not needing to rely on others' linguistic interpretations in her research (Holmes et al., Chapter 6, this volume).

There are some advantages to being a cultural outsider. You may be able to see a research scene without an insider bias – you may, for example identify patterns in communication which an insider may not be aware of. You may find it easier to identify themes and issues. As an informed outsider, you may have a well-researched understanding of a situation which may not be known to your participants. However, there are also limitations to being a cultural outsider. The privilege of information and knowledge in relation to your project may make it difficult to understand the reality of your informants from their perspective. In addition, if there are questions of power, for example, if you are from a dominant cultural community (e.g. white middle class researching a group of asylum seekers), your position as an outsider, an informed researcher and as a member of a dominant group can distance you from your participants and affect the contributions of your participants. There may be a danger of "othering" your participants (Holliday, 2006; Said, 1978), that is, of reducing their complex identities and experiences to a set of information which you perceive as important or salient, often described in cultural terms.

There are a number of issues you may need to consider if researching culture as an outsider. In a brought-along view of culture, you need to consider whether the culture you are focusing on is relevant/meaningful also to the group you are studying. For example, you may have identified differences in conceptualizations of emotions in Arabic and English, but this might not be relevant to your research on communication between speakers of English and Arabic during a joint project. Your categories of groups may also need to be different, so in the research design, you will need to consider whether the category of "cultural group" you have chosen is in fact categorized/identified in the same way by participants themselves. The use of outsider categories can be offensive; Braun and Clarke (2006) state that the term "homosexual" is often related to deviance or mental illness, and that it may be more important to use terms which people use for themselves such as "gay man" or "lesbian" (see ethics section below). Cultural categories also carry different meanings in different parts of the world. For example, ethnic terms such as "European" may mean something very different in Europe than in New Zealand where "New Zealand European" means "White European" (Braun & Clarke, 2006, p. 300). The term "Asian" might mean something very different even in different UK contexts. For example, in a university context it might refer to students or staff from India, Pakistan, China, Malaysia and a host of other countries in the geographical continent of Asia, whereas in a local newspaper it might refer to peoples of Pakistani or Indian ethnic origin, as these are the groups which have traditionally made up the majority of ethnic backgrounds from Asia, in the UK. Braun and Clarke recommend that the researcher is as specific as possible when making ethnic references; certainly the references need to be in line with your research approach and research questions.

If your focus is more on meaning-making in interaction, you are probably interested in cultural practice – i.e. how culture is created in interaction. You may be able to identify cultural references, but what they mean to informants may be limited by your own perspective. While you may be able to understand how culture is drawn upon, without some insider knowledge you may find it hard to understand the complexities of your participants' experiences. This may be enough for the purposes of your research, such as in the example given from Hinnenkamp (see earlier), but it is important to recognize the assumptions on which your project is based and the ensuing limitations of interpretation from an outsider approach.

The Researcher as Cultural Insider

If the researcher sees themselves as or is seen by others as a cultural insider, there is perhaps less danger of othering one's own culture/cultural practices. There may, however, be an assumption that you know the group very well, and you may find that you rely on your own experience and assume that you know well the perspectives of others. Your confidence in believing that you know your group well may cloud your open-mindedness, and you may find that you jump to conclusions faster than you should, thus missing out important opportunities for seeing more than your own perspective allows for. You may also find that you feel a right to "speak for all" as you have first-hand experience of the group. For example, if you are researching students' experiences of group work in higher education, you might find yourself influenced by your own experiences of group work, and this may cloud your view of others' experiences.

Being a cultural insider may also mean that you can feel that you "know" intuitively what is going on in a certain situation, and find it hard to evidence this for outsiders. For example, Arafat (2013) was working on research into transcultural mental health, while she was a transcultural mental health worker herself. Her research spanned working with different Black and Minority Ethnic (BME) groups. Her experience with Arabic-speaking patients was that the patients were able to empathize with her in a way which did not necessarily happen with other language-speaking groups. By virtue of being a cultural insider, she was accepted immediately in her role. When writing up her research, however, she needed to step outside of the role of insider and provide evidence to support her insider understanding of patients' experiences.

From Insider/Outsider to Participant Observation

One MA student, Carrie, undertook research into a rock society of which she was a long-standing member. She initially felt that there was "nothing of interest" in the group: "all they do is drink, eat, and talk about rock music, as well as a bit of air guitar or headbanging" (personal communication). However, when she began to ask questions, for example in this case, she asked herself which members talked about what to whom, she began to notice hierarchies within the society, and was able to focus on finer details and complexities of the communication in the club. One might have the same feeling entering an English pub, particularly if you are used to going there (as I am): that there is nothing unusual that happens there. However, reading Kate Fox's (2005) example of ordering in the pub, reminds us about the unspoken rules of who has the right to call out their order "Mine's a pint!" or who is able to keep an unpaid bill at the bar, or sit at the bar. It might be difficult for an outsider to have identified the fine nuanced behavior as described in Fox's work. This is not to say that you have to be an insider in order to understand the detail of meaning which we attach to behavior in any given social situation; it is likely to require some insider understanding, however.

It is clear from the examples given above that there are advantages to both an insider's and an outsider's perspective, and disadvantages too. Crucial to research approaches used in anthropology is the concept of *participant observation*, researching as both an insider and an outsider. This is understood as an ethnographic approach. Only a brief description is given here, as the chapter by Jackson

(Chapter 16, this volume) covers the subject fully. Traditionally, an ethnographer would live for a period of time in an unfamiliar cultural environment and, through the process of participant observation, would become familiar with the insider's perspective. Ethnographic approaches to researching culture are on the rise for good reason, as they can help to overcome the limitations described above. The researcher in an ethnographic approach is required to observe as an outsider, through scratch notes of events, field notes and discovering themes as they arise from data. Reflexivity is a key element in ethnography; the researcher develops a strong recognition of their own assumptions including scrutiny of their own notes for evidence of possible assumptions. Another technique is "making strange," whereby the researcher will step back from a cultural scene and try to see it with fresh eyes. Alternatively, if you are an outsider to your research scene or group, you can use techniques such as recording verbatim key phrases or folk terms, use nonverbal communication, and talk with members of the group, as well as sharing experiences, in order to help you to acquire, albeit partially, an insider's view.

Interestingly, an ethnographic approach also positions the researcher her- or himself interculturally, through the need for the researcher to move between their perspective and those of others; skills which are important for mediators (Dervin, Chapter 9, this volume). Much work was undertaken introducing ethnography into the field of language learning and teaching in the 1990s (see for example Barro, Jordan, & Roberts, 1998).

An ethnographic approach in your research project can, therefore, bring a complexity which might be missed in an insider or outsider approach alone. Ethnographies can often be long-term, require patience, open-mindedness and an ability to manage large amounts of complex data.

In all of the above approaches discussed, it can be seen that the role of the researcher is all-important and ever present. Some students starting out on their projects find it hard to recognize their role in their project, and will seek to minimize it or try to neutralize it through an attempt at "objectivity." It is recommended that a more honest and ethical approach is to consider all the way through your project what influence you and the decisions you are making are having on the project itself, and to make this explicit in the research (see ethical considerations, below).

Case in Point

Woodin, J. (2010a). Tandem learning as an intercultural activity. University of Sheffield: unpublished PhD Thesis.
Woodin, J. (2010b). Cultural categorisation: what can we learn from practice? An example from tandem learning. *Language and Intercultural Communication, 10(3)*, 225–242. doi: /10.1080/14708470903348556

Woodin (2010a, b) undertook a study of tandem learners' conversations. Her central research question was: "How do tandem learners talk about word meaning?" and in order to understand this, she adopted the approach described in Scollon & Scollon (2001), as discussed earlier: "Who has introduced culture as a relevant activity, for what purposes and with what consequences?" A particular interest of the research was to understand how the intercultural aspect of the tandem relationship might play out in a bilingual conversation.

Research design: The research involved a cross-cultural element through a focus on tandem learners who are native speakers of one language and learners of their partners' mother tongue. This is identified in the research plan, so there was already this restriction on the research. The cross-cultural element was within the frame of the NS/NNS framework, and a mixed approach was taken to data collection.

Twenty participants were recruited from existing tandem partnerships. Partners therefore already knew each other, and all had completed their assessments. Interlocutors were given a word to discuss in one language for 10 minutes (a different word in each language) and offered an optional help sheet to give them ideas for talking about the word meaning if they wished. A comparative pre-test of word associations (following Szalay & D'Andrade, 1972) was undertaken for a representative group of self-identified native Spanish speakers and English speakers, both also from the student population, and compared across languages. Following Gudykunst's distinction (see earlier), this could be classed as a cross-cultural approach (with "culture" understood as the meaning of the words as identified through the association task). This provided some indication that there might be differences in how the key words were understood in each language-speaking group. To address the main research question, however, further approaches were needed as the comparison did not offer any explanation as to what might happen in interaction between the Spanish and English speakers. The conversations themselves were transcribed and analyzed according to the question "Who has raised culture, for what purposes and with what consequences?" (See earlier); through this process, the raising of "culture" was analyzed in a number of ways, including (for greater detail, see Woodin, 2010b):

- country/language categorization (e.g. if a participant said "Spain," or "English");
- individual identity distinction (e.g. points at which the partners used "I");
- marking difference in the word meaning directly;
- showing relativity in relation to the word meaning.

The identification of these categories as salient for this particular research was not an entirely straightforward process, but was developed in a dialogue with the data. For example the researcher identified some obvious cultural references, such as *English* or *Spanish*; more in-depth analysis revealed other interesting aspects such as, for example, the recognition of the relativity of meaning of a word. These categories were developed through the data analysis; they also formed part of the results, as they allowed the researcher to understand how interlocutors were positioning themselves in relation to the word meaning and their partner.

Results: The results revealed a range of issues, one of which was the nonalignment of language with word meaning. It was relatively common for interlocutors to position themselves as native or non-native speakers in relation to language-related questions (e.g. as relevant verb endings or a request for vocabulary), but they did not appear so ready to defer to their native speaker partner over questions relating to the meaning of the word itself. For example, a native English student would insist that the word *cooperar* had an element of coercion in it even in the face of her native Spanish partner disagreeing with her. A brief viewing of dictionary definitions comparing *cooperar* and *cooperate* will show a stronger propensity of obligation in the English word, whereas the Spanish word is more closely related to a sense of help or solidarity.

It needs to be remembered that all of the above was in the context of word-meaning, as this was the focus of the study. A different research project with a different focus would be designed differently; what is important is that the research method, approach, and design can be justified in terms of the project. In this example, both cross-cultural and intercultural elements can be seen in the research design.

The role of the researcher in relation to the researched is of paramount importance in intercultural communication, as there clearly are intercultural issues involved here too. The researcher was in some ways a cultural insider, in that she worked in the university where the students studied; she was a native English speaker but also a teacher of Spanish; this made her in some ways a linguistic insider in that she could understand both languages, but more of an insider to the English-speaking students. She had also participated in tandem learning herself, which gave her some participant-observer skills, but she was also a tutor, and so could be considered an outsider to the student experience. This illustrates how complex the insider–outsider relationship can be, and certain decisions were made in order to try to keep the relationship between the Spanish and English groups as equal as possible (e.g. speaking with the Spanish participants in Spanish).

Researching in a Research Team that is Cross-/Intercultural in Nature

Researching in a cross-/intercultural team can bring its own challenges, some of which are relevant to any multicultural team in the workplace in general, given that working in diverse teams is becoming an everyday issue. In some fields, such as science and engineering, there are long established international, intercultural, and multilingual collaborations. Virtual working is also far more common than it used to be, and so it may be that you are researching with a group of researchers who are all based in very different environments, or you may be a group working in the same location. As has been discussed earlier in this chapter and elsewhere in this volume, the interpersonal and intercultural issues are not always indistinguishable. As Glaser puts it:

> [M]ulticultural teams may comprise individuals who like to work by trial and error or members who prefer looking for the best solution before engaging in a specific task. They may be composed of members to tend to harmonize or members who tend to polarize. They may be either conflict averse or ready to address controversial issues openly; they may be seeking equality among team members or accept a high degree of power distance; they may strive for continuity or for change; they may they may either have a strong preference for certainty and clarity or they may be open to face ambiguity. (Glaser, 2010, pp. 187–8).

Glaser continues by stating that while literature on the subject can proclaim that diversity is the key to success in teams, there are also many examples of failure in multicultural teams as well. Hoecklin (1994) reports on research which points to an accentuation of national differences in international teams, but reminds us that anthropological research shows how groups can have extraordinary resilience in adapting to change. Given that monocultural groups do not necessarily fare any better (for example, all male, mono-national teams have also recently reported to make bad business decisions (*The Economist*, 2014), it remains the case that working, researching and studying interculturally is imperative for most of us in our lives.

Within a wide-ranging or highly diverse team, it may take some time to clarify assumptions and develop joint understanding. Intercultural competence models speak of open-mindedness, articulation of positions, and ability to read documents, skills of interpreting and relating, and working interculturally could benefit from such information. Guilherme, Keating, and Hoppe propose a model for intercultural working which involves the concept of intercultural responsibility, which they define as: "a conscious and reciprocally respectful, both professional and personal, relationship among the team group members, assuming that they have different ethnic backgrounds, whether national or sub-national" (Guilherme, Keating, & Hoppe, 2010, p. 79). They argue that *coherence* is a key term in developing and supporting intercultural responsibility.

For intercultural research teams, much can be learnt from the experiences of working in multicultural teams. There is, in addition, the element of the research process itself. There may be different perspectives on developing research questions, on the role of the researcher, and on methodology. It is clearly a complex business, which is well-illustrated by the following example from Fay & Dacheva (2014), which deals with a highly creative way of researching interculturally while undertaking a joint narrative research project with the Ladino speaking Jewish Bulgarian community:

> To some extent, we both bring complementary insider and outsider perspectives to the study – we say "to some extent" mindful of the limitations of insider–outsider terminology but appreciative of the differing perspectives we were both able to bring to the research. Leah is from the Sephardic community in Bulgaria but is, to some extent, an outsider to UK-based English-medium research communities; and Richard is part of the UK-based English-medium academic world but has no direct heritage connection with the Sephardic community or with Bulgaria. Thus, we brought varied insights, interests, and preoccupations to the analytical processes, including our differing: cultural and linguistic backgrounds; exposure to literatures relevant to the topic; experiences of narrative research; levels of involvement in the data generation and restorying processes; and relationships with the storytellers. (Fay & Dacheva, 2014, p. 28)

It is clear from the above example that there may be different points in the research process where one or another of the research team has insider understanding, an opportunity to use different languages, or cultural knowledge (either lived or learnt through research) which can contribute in its own way to the research. Fay and Dacheva developed a process of "reciprocal researcher reflexivity" which involved documenting the research process itself as well, and offers an example for research teams to understand more deeply the intercultural research process.

Case in Point

Castro, P., Lundgren, U., and Woodin, J. (2013). *Conceptualizing and assessing International Mindedness (IM): An exploratory study*. Geneva: International Baccalaureate.

> Castro, Lundgren, and Woodin conducted a joint research project for the International Baccalaureate which involved jointly agreeing a methodology for researching the International Baccalaureate's (IB) use of the term *internationalmindedness*.

The team already knew each other, having been long-standing members of an intercultural research group. They worked on this project largely through skype conversations, with one face-to-face meeting at a crucial moment. Differing working practices in each of the universities in Spain, Sweden, and the UK meant that the funding for the project had to be presented in different ways to each university for the financing of the project. This resulted in long delays in operationalizing certain aspects of the project. Staff availability to work on the project did not always overlap because of their workloads in the different universities; streamlining the timing of the project, while an inherently practical issue, became very important. Each member brought to the group their own idiosyncrasies, cultural experiences, and influences, interests, and habitual ways of working. Considerable time was taken up with clarifying each of our approaches, trying to understand each other's view, and deciding on next steps. It helped enormously that the team had already met face to face a number of times at conferences and seminars, and had published a paper together. Nevertheless, the need for clarification of what we meant by certain phrases or activities was all-important, as was accepting all ideas as valid and working through them to reach a consensus. At times any one of us could become wedded to a particular approach or perspective; this would be eased through questioning our and each other's reasons, loyalties, and perspectives. It was not an easy process, and probably required more time, discussion, and compromise than we had realized, but the compensation for this was deeper understanding of the research project, ourselves and each other, as well as an end-product which was better and more interculturally relevant than one which could have been produced independently.

Ethical Considerations

How ethical questions are discussed, understood, and carried out may well vary across groups. Schwartz, drawing on others, defines ethics as human values, "desirable goals, varying in importance, that serves as guiding principles in people's lives" (1994, p. 88). While international efforts such as the Universal Declaration of Human Rights may be an excellent attempt at defining universal human values, it is recognizably difficult to identify universality where language and culture are concerned. For example the British Psychological Association (BPA, 2009) has four main ethical principles: respect, competence, responsibility, and integrity, and the Canadian Psychological Society (2001) cites their ethical principles as: respect for the dignity of persons; responsible caring, integrity in relationships; and responsibility to society, stating that where conflict of ethical principles takes place, the principles carry different weight (first to last). The British code, however, calls on what the BPA call the "British eclectic tradition," whereby ethical decision-making relies on using the principles as a guide, but other factors such as context also need to be taken into account.

Ethics are particularly important when researching interculturally, then, as we may be working with different value systems. While some of these will be individual and others national-, group-, or practice-bound, the issues are the same. For example, child labor may be seen as unethical in one country and there may be legislation against it; in another it may be generally accepted. Such a problem is discussed by Ting-Toomey (1999), drawing on the work of Pederson. Ting-Toomey distinguishes between ethical absolutism and ethical relativism. In the first approach, there are assumed standards of good and bad behavior which can be applied to all cultural groups, and the importance of cultural context is minimized. The effect of this is that mainstream culture can dominate, with little regard for cultural or ethnic differences. Such an approach can be seen as ethnocentric, marginalizing nondominant group voices. Ethical relativism, on the other hand, takes the role of culture seriously, through focusing on understanding each cultural group in its own terms, determining right and wrong largely by the culture of the individual, and not using outside criteria to explaining actions of a group. Ting-Toomey proposes a combined approach for intercultural contexts, whereby judgments about ethical behavior require a recognition of both underlying fundamental similarities across cultures and idiosyncratic/unique features of a cultural group. Human respect is valued as an end in itself as opposed to a means to another end, involving collaborative dialogue, attitudinal openness, and much hard work from all concerned. An ethical absolutist approach might state that child labor is morally wrong; a relativist approach might not adopt a position apart from that it is up to each cultural group or country to decide for themselves, and accept that there will be cultural reasons for this. A derived ethical approach would involve deriving universal ethical guidelines while still placing ethical evaluations in their cultural and historical context. One would try to understand the reasons behind the practice, and then evaluate the questions from a humanistic standpoint; for example:

- Who or which group perpetuates this practice in this culture?
- Who or which group resists this practice and with what reasons?
- Who is benefiting?
- Who is suffering (voluntarily or involuntarily)?
- Does it cause unjustifiable suffering to an individual or a selected group of individuals at the pleasure of another group?
- What is my role & my voice in this dilemma?
- Should I condemn, go along with it, reject the practice, withdraw from the cultural scene, or act as a change agent?
(Adapted from Ting-Toomey, 1999, p. 273)

Such an approach to the question of child labor would then recognize that context needs to be taken into account; if for example, a child works in order for his/her family to be able to survive or to be able to go to school, then the situation is very different ethically from a child working for the benefit of a large multinational corporation wishing to sell goods cheaply to the European market. Ting-Toomey argues that for too long, universal ethics have been dominated by Eurocentric perspectives, driven by Western cultural values, to the detriment of other approaches from marginalized groups. This perspective is touched on by Phipps, who questions UK higher education ethics practices, which, for example, require a date for destruction of recorded material, an action which does not work for all research projects:

> I have been working with refugees and we have been sharing common stories of home. These stories are precious to us. It would be wrong and harmful for me to enact a second destruction of home, for the sake of a tick on a box on a form. The idea, for example, of using an interview schedule or a questionnaire, of plonking a tape recorder on a table, explaining the place of a consent form and asking for a signature, whilst also asking for photographs, enacts bureaucratic procedures well documented by scholars of colonialism. (Phipps, 2013, p. 19)

There may be certain expectations in relation to recruiting participants which could raise ethical issues. For example, as Zhu (2014) noted:

> I heard recently from a researcher who collected speech data on a language facing extinction: When she went to approach one of the few speakers of the language in the world, the participant started bargaining for the fee and made it very plain that other teams paid more!

Such a request could cause problems for a researcher who has already had their ethics proposal approved, having stated that they were not going to offer payment or rewards for their participants. The influence of decisions from other research teams in this case are outside the control of the researcher, and it may well not be possible to find out beforehand what other groups are doing. The example also raises two further ethical questions. The researcher will need to address whether they consider that their data are in some way influenced by the fact that payment has been made. The researcher may also wish to consider the perspective of their participants, whose socioeconomic position may well differ greatly from the privileges afforded to the institutions and their students who carry out such research. From their perspective, people are taking advantage of their stories. In either case, it is important to document the processes of coming to decisions, in the same way that it is considered standard practice nowadays to reflect on the role of the researcher in the production of data (e.g. the role of the interviewer in eliciting certain responses in interviews).

Conclusion

This chapter has considered how researching cross-culturally or interculturally can be understood, and offered some suggestions for consideration. To summarize, it is impossible to provide a checklist of all of the issues involved in this area, but here are some starting points, in no particular order (the research process is, after all, often circular):

- Consider your research question: ask yourself how your concept of culture/Intercultural Communication is both limiting and driving your research, and recognize the limitations which accompany that approach.

- Consider in which ways you consider yourself to be an insider or outsider and how this influences the approach to your research.
- Recognize and articulate your position – this allows it to be coherent to others (see Guilherme et al., 2010).
- Take an interculturally responsible position to working in a team: commit to dialogue, respect and reciprocity (including questioning how these terms might be construed across cultures and contexts).
- Consider the ethical decisions taken; document them and question your decisions.
- Keep an open mind.

Researching interculturally inevitably involves personal investment and the ability to adopt perspectives of others, understand multiple perspectives, take a position and seek mutual understanding. It's a complex business, but highly rewarding.

Key Terms

Culture as "brought along" The concept of culture as a repeated set of practices which become familiar to us over time as things we have/do and which we may bring with us to an interaction.
Culture as "brought-about" Culture as made/ created during the process of interaction.
Cultural insider The researcher when they are researching a cultural group they consider themselves to be part of.
Cultural outsider The researcher when they are researching a group they consider themselves not to be part of.
Intercultural ethics A consideration of ethical issues in research which may be specific or of particular relevance to Intercultural Communication research.

References

Arafat, N. (2013). Language, culture and mental health: Exploration of the transcultural mental health worker role. University of Sheffield: unpublished MA dissertation.
Barro, A., Jordan, S., & Roberts, C. (1998). Cultural practices in everyday life: the language learner as ethnographer. In M. Byram & M. Fleming (Eds.), *Language Learning in intercultural perspective: Approaches through drama and ethnography* (pp. 76–97). Cambridge: Cambridge University Press.
Baynham, M. (2015). Identity: Brought about or brought along? Narrative as a privileged site for researching intercultural identities. In F. Dervin & K. Risager (Eds.), *Researching identity and interculturality* (pp. 67–85). London: Routledge.
Blum-Kulka, S., House, J., & Kasper, G. (eds.). (1989). *Cross-cultural pragmatics, requests and apologies*. Norwood: Ablex Publishing Corporation.
Braun, V., & Clarke, V. (2006). Using thematic analysis in psychology, *Qualitative Research in Psychology*, 3(2), 77–101.

British Psychological Society (2009). *Code of ethics.* Retrieved June 15, 2015 from: http://www.bps.org.uk/sites/default/files/documents/code_of_ethics_and_conduct.pdf.

Canadian Psychological Association (2001). *Code of ethics.* Retrieved June 15, 2015 fromhttp://www.cpa.ca/docs/File/Ethics/cpa_code_2000_eng_jp_jan2014.pdf

Castro, P., Lundgren, U., and Woodin, J. (2013). *Conceptualizing and assessing International Mindedness (IM): An exploratory study.* Geneva: International Baccalaureate.

The Economist (2014). Women managers in Asia: Untapped talent. Retrieved June 15, 2015 from: http://www.economist.com/node/21558321?fsrc=scn/fb/wl/ar/untappedtalent.

Fay, R., & Dacheva, L. (2014). Zones of interculturality and linguistic identity: Tales of Ladino by Sephardic Jews in Bulgaria. *Language and Intercultural Communication,* 14(1), 24–40.

Fox, K. (2005). *Watching the English.* London: Hodder.

Glaser, E. (2010). Working in multicultural teams. In M. Guilherme, E. Glaser, & M. Mendez-Garcia (Eds.), *The intercultural dynamics of multicultural working* (pp. 186–206). Clevedon: Multilingual Matters.

Gudykunst, W. (2000). Methodological issues in conducting theory-based cross-cultural research. In H. Spencer-Oatey (Ed.), *Culturally speaking: Managing rapport through talk across cultures* (pp. 293–315). London: Continuum.

Guilherme, M., Keating, C., & Hoppe, D. (2010). Intercultural responsibility: Power and ethics in intercultural dialogue and interaction. In M. Guilherme, E. Glaser, E. & M. Mendez-Garcia (Eds.), *The intercultural dynamics of multicultural working* (pp. 75–94). Clevedon: Multilingual Matters.

Hinnenkamp, V. (1987). Talking a person into interethnic distinction: A discourse analytic case study. In J. Blommaert, & J. Verschueren (Eds.), *The pragmatics of international and Intercultural Communication* (pp. 91–110) Amsterdam: John Benjamins.

Hoecklin, L. (1994). *Managing cultural difference: Strategies for competitive advantage.* London: The Economist Intelligence Unit.

Holliday, A. (2006). Native Speakerism. *ELT Journal,* 60(4), 385–387.

Lago, C. (ed.) (2011). *The handbook of transcultural counselling and psychotherapy.* Milton Keynes: Open University Press.

Lippi-Green, R. (1997). *English with an accent: Languages, ideology and discrimination in the United States.* London: Routledge.

Madden, T.J., Hewett, K., & Roth, M.S. (2000). Managing images in different cultures: A cross-national study of color meanings and preferences. *Journal of International Marketing,* 8(4), 90–107.

McFadden, J. (2001). Intercultural marriage and family: Beyond the racial divide *The Family Journal,* 9, 39–42.

Phipps, A. (2013). Intercultural ethics: questions of methods in language and Intercultural Communication in *Language and Intercultural Communication,* 13(1), 10–26.

Pan, Y., Scollon, S-W., & Scollon, R. (2002). *Professional communication in international settings.* Oxford: Blackwell.

Said, E. (1978). *Orientalism.* London: Routledge.

Scollon, R. & Scollon S. W. (2001). Discourse and Intercultural Communication. In D. Schiffrin., D. Tannen, & H. Hamilton (Eds.), *The handbook of discourse analysis* (pp. 538–547). Oxford: Blackwell.

Spencer-Oatey, H. (ed.) (2000). *Culturally speaking: Managing rapport through talk across cultures.* London: Continuum.

Szalay, L., & D'Andrade, R. G., (1972). Scaling versus content analysis: Interpreting Word Association Data from Americans and Koreans. *South Western Journal of Anthropology,* 28, 50–68.

Ting-Toomey, S. (1999). *Communicating across cultures.* New York: Guilford Press.

Verschueren, J. (2008). Intercultural communication and the challenges of migration. *Language and Intercultural Communication,* 8(1), 21–35.

Wieirzbicka, A., (1997). *Understanding cultures through their key words*. Oxford: Oxford University Press.
Wierzbicka, A. (1999). *Emotions across languages and cultures: Diversity and universals*. Cambridge: Cambridge University Press.
Woodin, J. (2010a). Tandem learning as an intercultural activity. University of Sheffield: unpublished PhD Thesis.
Woodin, J. (2010b). Cultural categorisation: what can we learn from practice? An example from tandem learning. *Language and Intercultural Communication*, 10(3), 225–242. doi: /10.1080/14708470903348556
Zhu, H. (2014). Personal communication.

Further Reading and Resources

Byrd Clark, J., & Dervin, F. (Eds.) (2014). *Reflexivity in language and intercultural education: Rethinking multiculturalism and interculturality*. London: Routledge.
Deardorff, D.K. (Ed). (2009). *The Sage handbook of intercultural competence*. London: Sage.
Guilherme, M., Glaser, E., & Mendez-Garcia, M. (2010). *The intercultural dynamics of multicultural working*. Clevedon: Multilingual Matters.

8 How to Assess Intercultural Competence

Darla K. Deardorff

> **Summary**
>
> This chapter explores guiding principles in using measures to assess intercultural competence, in particular, the clear articulation of goals and objectives and the rationale for a multimeasure, multiperspective approach. It also discusses other key issues in assessment of intercultural competence including the lifelong process of developing intercultural competence, the need to assess behavior, and using collected assessment information for further intercultural development.

Assessment of Intercultural Competence – Myths, Themes and Implications

A prevailing myth in assessment of intercultural competence is that it is possible to assess intercultural learning/competence by using one tool. Research (e.g. Deardorff, 2009, 2012) indicates that, given the complexity of intercultural development, a multimeasure/multiperspective approach must be used, because no single tool is sufficient to adequately assess intercultural learning.

Another prevailing myth is that the first question to ask is "What tool should we use to assess intercultural learning?" The starting point should not be to select a measurement tool. Rather, it should be to clarify what specifically is to be assessed by defining terminology based on research and existing literature, and then developing specific goals and measurable objectives based on those definitions.

Over the past half-century, a considerable volume of literature has been produced on the concept of intercultural competence and its varying terms. In fact more than 20 different definitions and frameworks are discussed in Spitzberg & Changnon (2009). In 2006, the first research-based definition of intercultural competence appeared (Deardorff, 2006) followed by a synthesis of work published in the Sage handbook of intercultural competence (Deardorff, 2009) and, subsequently, a growing list of publications on this topic, not only in the United States but also in many other countries around the world. From the literature, several themes emerge:

1   Intercultural competence can be assessed, as illustrated by the over 100 existing assessments.
2   Intercultural competence is a complex, broad, learning goal and must be broken down into more discrete, measurable, learning objectives representing specific knowledge, attitude or skill areas.
3   The attainment of intercultural competence is a lifelong developmental **process** which means there is no point at which one becomes fully interculturally competent.
4   Language fluency is a necessary component, but in itself insufficient to achieving intercultural competence.
5   Intercultural competence should be intentionally addressed throughout the curriculum and through experiential learning (such as study abroad, service learning, and so on).
6   Faculty need a clearer understanding of intercultural competence in order to more adequately address this in their courses (regardless of discipline) and in order to guide students in developing intercultural competence.

These emerging themes point to the specific implications for assessment of intercultural competence outlined here:

First, intercultural competence must be defined. In order to assess, it is important to know *what* exactly is being assessed using existing literature to define the concept. Intercultural competence is, broadly speaking, about communication and behavior that is both **effective** and **appropriate** in intercultural interactions, with *effectiveness* referring to the degree to which the individual's goals were achieved while *appropriateness* refers to the manner and context in which those goals were achieved. Influential definitions of intercultural competence include Byram (1997), Deardorff (2009), and Bennett (1993), among others (see Spitzberg & Changnon, 2009, for a more thorough discussion on this). Many of the existing definitions are from Western perspectives. So one must ask the question "Intercultural competence according to whom and to what degree?" Perspectives from Asian viewpoints, for example, may focus more on a relational definition of intercultural competence (See UNESCO, 2013 for more on this).

Second, research results indicate that intercultural competence can, indeed, be assessed (Deardorff, 2011; Fantini, 2009; Stuart, 2009). However, the 100+ existing assessment tools are predominantly self-report instruments, which means only "half of the picture" is measured. What is often missing in assessment of intercultural competence (at least in education and the humanities) is the other half of the picture – the **appropriateness** of communication and behavior, which, according to research studies, can only be measured through **others'** perspectives, beyond self-report. This can be done through observation of behavior in real-life situations or through surveys completed by other persons engaged in the interactions.

Third, most assessments of intercultural competence focus on **results** rather than **process** (i.e., how one **approaches** others, reflects critically and thinks interculturally), relying on indirect evidence only (often a survey instrument) which provides an incomplete picture of the development of an individual's intercultural competence. The Association of American Colleges and Universities provides a sample rubric (based on the intercultural competence framework from my research, as well as Bennett's Developmental Model of Intercultural Sensitivity, 1993) for measuring direct evidence of intercultural learning. However, it is important to note that even this rubric does not capture the full complexity of intercultural competence, and thus rubrics must be developed in alignment with specific learning objectives within the development of intercultural competence.

Fourth, assessment of intercultural competence should adopt a multimethod, multiperspective approach that is focused more on the process of intercultural competence development than on an end-result (Deardorff, 2012; Deardorff & Edwards, 2012; Gordon & Deardorff, 2013). Examples of how intercultural competence is currently assessed include embedded course assessment, self-report instruments, reflection papers, critical incident analysis, interviews, observations of behavior in specific contexts (by professors, internship supervisors, host families, group members, etc.), simulations and longitudinal studies. While it is encouraging that more institutions, programs and courses are assessing intercultural competence outcomes, there is more work that still needs to be done on improving assessment of intercultural competence and, thus, there are currently very few examples of "best" practices.

Fifth, it is essential to determine whether students can **think and act interculturally** (Bok, 2006). Intercultural competence goes far beyond cultural knowledge and facts. One of the implications of this is that it requires assessment to go beyond verbal measures. For example, are students living an intercultural lifestyle? Are students successful in their intercultural actions and interactions with others? We need to consider evidence of successful interactions (i.e. behaviors in real-life situations) as a key part of assessing intercultural competence.

Getting Started

Both Fantini (2009) and Deardorff (2009, 2011, 2015) discuss the need to base any definition of intercultural competence in existing literature and associated work prior to considering its assessment. (Note that there is a research-based consensus definition and framework that can be used as a starting point for defining intercultural competence, see Figure 8.1). Most definitions and models tend to be somewhat general in terminology. Therefore, once a definition, ideally derived from current literature, has been determined, it is important to develop a process that generates very specific measurable outcomes and indicators appropriate to the context to be assessed. To begin that process, it is best to prioritize specific aspects of intercultural

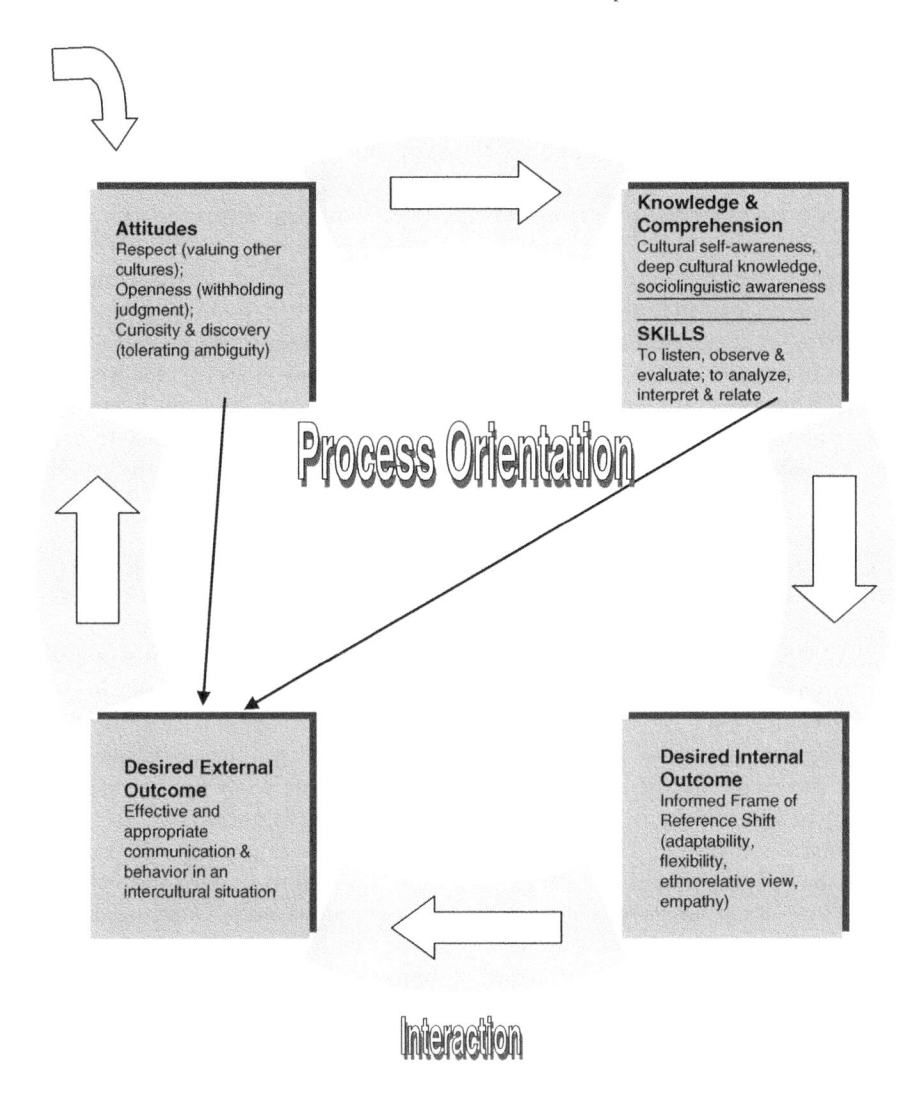

Figure 8.1 Research-based Intercultural Competence definition and framework. (Copyright Deardorff, 2006, 2009.)

Notes:
- Begin with attitudes. Move from individual level (attitudes) to interaction level (outcomes)
- Degree of intercultural competence depends on acquired degree of attitudes, knowledge/comprehension, and skills.

competence, based on the overall mission, goals and purpose of the course, program or organization. The definition that is used for intercultural competence will determine both the aspects to be assessed and the focus of assessment (i.e., individual, program, organization). In the case of learning outcomes, the focus is usually that of the individual and the learning that occurs for each individual. For example, based on the overall purpose of a course or program, "understanding others' perspectives" may be an essential aspect of intercultural competence to be assessed and thus becomes a stated goal. One would engage other key persons in dialogue about the best ways to achieve this goal and to translate this and other goals into specified objectives.

The process of prioritizing various aspects of intercultural competence is an important one and should not be carried out too quickly or taken lightly. Often the process itself involves dialogue and discussion with key stakeholders to determine which specific elements of intercultural competence should be the focus of programmatic efforts and assessment endeavors. It is important that prioritization is not a one-time discussion but rather an ongoing process, since the priorities may change from course to course, from program to program or from year to year. Generally, it is advisable to choose just two or three specific elements of intercultural competence to assess at any given time, due to the time, effort and resources that are needed in the assessment process.

Stating Goals and Measurable Objectives

Once the specific aspects of intercultural competence have been prioritized, the next step is to write goals and measurable objectives related to each of the prioritized intercultural elements. In stating goals, it is important to define success in that particular program or course. What will success look like for the participant in this course or program? By the end of the program or course, what will the participant know and be able to do as a result of the learning that occurred? In other words, what changes will occur? These become the measurable objectives. For example, a goal may be broadly stated as "Participants will be able to understand others' perspectives," or "Learners will demonstrate the awareness, understanding, and skills necessary to live and work in a diverse world," or "Learners will become more interculturally competent." Specific, measurable, objectives must then be articulated that state the learning expectations in achieving these goals. What will the learner need to be able to do to demonstrate achievement of the goal? The objectives become the "roadmap" for reaching the destination – the markers, or "stepping stones" of the important learning that ensures achievement of the goal.

What do measurable objectives, or outcomes look like? In the assessment arena, a common way of thinking about measurable objectives is through the acronym SMART: Specific (what, why, how), Measurable, Action-oriented, Realistic, and Time-delineated. A key part of this statement is that the objective is realistic – it needs to fit what can realistically be accomplished with the parameters of the course or program. For example, it would not be realistic for a participant at a beginning language level to speak another language fluently after only two or three weeks in another country. For short-term study abroad programs in postsecondary institutions, outcomes must realistically match the program length. For example, if the program exposes participants to another culture for six weeks, what can participants, realistically, be expected to achieve regarding intercultural competence development within that six week period, given the level and quality of cultural preparation, the program parameters and the way in which the intercultural experience has been set up? This in turn relates back to the overall priorities and the aspects of intercultural competence that are deemed to be most important to the particular program or course.

In writing an assessment objective, usually only one action verb is used per outcome statement. Outcome statements (objectives) are focused on learning itself, not on infrastructure, instructor or activity. Examples of measurable outcomes under the general goal of "Understanding others' perspectives" might be: "By the end of the program, learners can articulate two different cultural perspectives on global warming," or "By the end of this class, learners can define what a worldview is and three ways in which it impacts one's behavior." Writing specific outcome statements (learning objectives) and developing indicators of the degree to which the statements can be assessed remains an area in need of further research and work.

It is important to spend sufficient time on defining intercultural competence and developing clear, realistic, and measurable learning outcome statements based on the goals, since these outcome statements determine the assessment methods and tools to be used. Given the complexity of intercultural competence, a multimethod, multiperspective, assessment plan is desired. Advocating the use of multiple measures in assessing competence, Pottinger (1979) stresses that "how one defines the domain of competence will greatly affect one's choice of measurement procedures" (p. 30) and notes that pen and paper assessment tests have been widely criticized, due in part to the effect of the test format and also in part to the limits a paper test places on the complex phenomena being measured (pp. 33–34). Since competence varies by setting, context, and by individual, using a variety of assessments ensures more accurate results.

Terms Frequently Used in Assessment

To more fully understand assessment, it is necessary to be clear on the various terms used. Some frequent terms along with their definitions and clarification are given below and are applicable in any assessment context.

What is assessment? *Assessment*, simply put, is the systematic collection, review, and use of information about student learning (Banta & Palomba, 2014; Driscoll & Wood, 2007). According to the assessment expert Thorndike (2005), outcomes-based assessment is about expectations, and it is important for stakeholders to identify desired results. Note that assessment in the context of this chapter does not refer to grading or assigning a grade, although for some educators this may come to mind as a definition.

The starting point of intercultural competence assessment is its goals and objectives, which in turn determine assessment measures and methods. *Goals* are broad statements (expectations) about what students will know and be able to do upon completion of a course or program. Goals are generally too broad to be measurable. *Objectives* are a set of concrete, specific statements (expectations) about student learning and performance that lead to the achievement of a stated goal. Objectives are measureable. Both goals and objectives can be considered *outcomes,* and the terms *objectives* and *outcomes* are often used interchangeably.

Assessment data can be categorized into *formative* and *summative* data, *quantitative* and *qualitative* data, and *direct* and *indirect* evidence. These are key terms to know, understand, and use when assessing intercultural learning. The terms are outlined here:

- *Formative Assessment* refers to ongoing assessment efforts over time and throughout a course, program or experience. The collected information is used to *improve* student learning. Formative assessment, which may take the form of learning assignments throughout an experience or course, often provides more opportunities to give direct feedback to students, such as understanding where students are in the learning process, correcting misperceptions, and identifying gaps in student learning that can still be addressed.
- *Summative Assessment* refers to assessment information collected at the end of a course, program or experience, often used *to prove* what has been learned (results). Summative assessment is often in the form of a final test or demonstration and can be considered more "high stakes" by students. Often, there is little opportunity to provide direct feedback to students; the purpose is more to see how much students have learned at the end of a course or experience and to answer the question: What difference was made? Student achievement can be categorized as summative assessment.

Both formative and summative assessments are important since they serve different purposes. Too often, however, there is an over-reliance on summative assessment, with little attention given to formative assessment.

Quantitative and qualitative assessments are often thought to be mutually exclusive. However, there are ways to quantify qualitative information through coding and categorizing verbal responses. The merits of each type of assessment can also be achieved in a mixed-method approach.

- *Quantitative Assessment* refers to information that can have a numerical value attached to it. Quantitative information is often considered to provide insights into the *breadth* of the assessment context.
- *Qualitative Assessment* refers to information that involves verbal descriptions, either oral or written. Qualitative information often provides richer insights into the *depth* of the assessment context.

Assessment measures can often be categorized as direct or indirect assessment. In intercultural competence assessment, there is a heavy reliance on indirect assessment, particularly through the use of surveys and inventories.

- *Direct assessment* refers to actual evidence of student learning. This is usually collected through student work and performance in a course or learning experience. It can include papers, projects, tests, and observations. Direct assessment is often qualitative or observational in nature.
- *Indirect assessment* refers to *perceptions* of student learning. What do students think they learned as a result of their participation in a course or experience? Indirect assessment is most often collected through self-report surveys, interviews,

and focus groups. Indirect evidence can be either quantitative (survey scores) or qualitative.

When using assessment measures, it is very important to understand and pay attention to the reliability and validity of the instrument. These two terms, reliability and validity, are crucial to assessment as their level can impact the quality of the results.

- *Reliability* is, in short, about consistency. A tool or method is reliable if it yields similar results each time it is administered.
- *Validity* is, in short, about being "on target." A tool is valid if it measures what it says it measures and aligns with the intended use of the results. There are different kinds of validity.

Assessment of Intercultural Competence: Approaches/Methods/Tools

To achieve solid, valid results, approaches to assessment of intercultural competence need to go beyond using one measure, to utilizing a multimeasure approach incorporating both direct evidence and indirect evidence. In fact, by using both direct and indirect evidence, a more complete picture emerges, which can help to explain why surveys, for example, may show regression when, in actuality, the direct evidence may show progress. Below are some examples of methods that can be used in combination.

Learning contracts

When appropriate, it is often helpful to work with learners to have them develop their own learning objectives related to the overall intercultural competence goals. This not only ensures a more effective and relevant learning process, but allows the learner to indicate the evidence needed in order to demonstrate successful learning. Learning contracts consist of the learner negotiating with the educator on the following:

- What specifically will be learned?
- How it will be learned?
- Timeline for learning to occur.
- Evidence of learning.
- Action taken as a result of the learning.

(See the work of Malcolm Knowles (1986) for further details on learning contracts.)

> **Knowledge: Cultural self-awareness**
>
> *Capstone*: Articulates insights into own cultural rules and biases (e.g. seeking complexity; aware of how her / his experiences have shaped these rules, and how to recognize and respond to cultural biases, resulting in a shift in self-description.)
>
> *Milestone*: Recognizes new perspectives about own cultural rules and biases (e.g. not looking for sameness; comfortable with the complexities that new perspectives offer.)
>
> *Milestone*: Identifies own cultural rules and biases (e.g. with a strong preference for those rules shared with own cultural group and seeks the same in others.)
>
> *Benchmark*: Shows minimal awareness of own cultural rules and biases (even those shared with own cultural group(s)) (e.g. uncomfortable with identifying possible cultural differences with others.)

Figure 8.2 Excerpt from Intercultural Knowledge and Competence VALUE rubric, Association of American Colleges and Universities (www.aacu.org).

E-portfolios

Many institutions are turning to e-portfolios as a means by which to collect direct evidence of students' intercultural or global learning. Artefacts placed in the portfolios by students include reflection papers, term papers, photographs, and other documentation of student learning. Software programs exist to support e-portfolio development and track specific learning outcomes. Rubrics become a key way of evaluating these portfolios. To that end, the Association of American Colleges and Universities (AAC&U) worked with faculty members across the United States over an 18-month period to develop rubrics in specific areas, including intercultural learning. An excerpt of the rubric can be found in Figure 8.2 (for the full rubric go to www.aacu.org) This rubric should be adapted to specific contexts and not necessarily used as is (for instance, this rubric highlights two elements each under knowledge, skills, and attitudes essential to intercultural competence, but these may not be the elements prioritized in every context.)

Critical reflection

Reflection is the key to developing learners' intercultural competence (Deardorff, 2006). Journaling, blogging, and reflection papers are useful tools to collect data on student learning. One strategy for pushing students to go beyond descriptive reflection is to use the following "what" questions: What? So What? Now What? Alternatively, simply ask students the question: "As a result of this learning, what will you do now?" (Kneffelcamp, 1989). Writing prompts can also be used, such as "I learned that… This is important because… As a result of this learning, I will…" (Clayton, 2010). Reflection should be thought of as a critical and legitimate process for promoting and assessing learning. Well-designed reflection goes beyond journal writing; it is an "intentional, structured, and directed process that facilitates exploration for deeper, contextualized meaning linked to learning outcomes" (Rice & Pollack, 2000, p. 124). Through effective reflection, students can engage in an examination of their personal opinions, identity, and attitudes, their relation to others, and their day-to-day interactions within society (O'Grady, 2000; Rice & Pollack, 2000). Such reflection, when combined with other data sources/methods, can not only provide insights into the process of honing one's intercultural competence but might also provide a more complete picture of the development of intercultural competence.

Performance

Increasingly, observation of students' performance in intercultural situations is becoming a way of obtaining others' perspectives regarding the appropriateness of students' behavior and communication, more clearly than can be ascertained solely from a verbal survey or through journal self-reflection. For example, host families may be asked to complete a reflection on students' homestays. Supervising teachers may be asked to complete an observation of student teachers' interactions in the classroom. Educators can observe student interactions in the classroom and/or on intercultural teams. Supervisors may be asked to do the same for interns and so on. Such performance assessment provides the opportunity for students to apply intercultural knowledge and skills in relevant contexts and provides more opportunities for authentic assessment in real-life settings.

Indirect evidence

Indirect evidence of student learning around intercultural competence is collected primarily through surveys or inventories from the learner-perspective. There are over 100 such instruments currently available, some more reliable and valid than others. (For a list of such measures, see Fantini, 2009.) In using these instruments, it is critical that users understand exactly what the instrument measures and how it aligns with the stated learning outcome. *If there is misalignment between stated goals/objectives and the purpose of the measure, then the results will be invalid.* It is also very important that use of any of these indirect measures is coupled with direct measures of student learning, as discussed earlier. In selecting intercultural competence assessment tools, some key questions to aid in selecting the most appropriate tool(s) are:

- What are the goals and objectives to be assessed?
- What evidence is needed to indicate success at achieving these objectives?
- What does the tool measure?
- How well does the tool align with the stated objectives?
- What are the limitations and cultural biases of the tool?
- Is the tool valid (accurate) and reliable (consistent)?
- Is there a theoretical foundation for the tool?
- Does the tool measure human development relevant to intercultural competence?
- Are administrative and logistical issues involved manageable?
- How will the data be used to provide feedback to students on their own intercultural competence development?

These questions are important to consider when selecting intercultural surveys and inventories.

> **Case in Point: An Example of Assessment of Intercultural Competence**
>
> One example that incorporates some of what has been discussed above is the tool developed through the INCA (Intercultural Competence Assessment) project called the *Autobiography of Intercultural Encounters* (Council of Europe, 2009).

This tool is designed to help in the analysis of a specific intercultural encounter through a series of questions. The focus is on one's encounter with another from a different cultural background. The first question starts with self-definition. Other questions address the basics of the experience – what happened, when, where, and so on. The questions then go into some of the following issues:

- Why did you choose this experience?
- What were your feelings during this encounter?
- How would you describe the other's feelings during this encounter?
- What could you have done differently in this situation?
- How were your actions influenced by an idea you had about the other? What puzzled you?
- How did you adjust? How did the other person adjust?
- What did you understand only after reflecting on the experience?

This type of reflective tool can be used to address the process of intercultural competence development rather than just the end results. Further, to gauge the appropriateness of the encounter, the other person could also be given some of these questions (if appropriate) such as: What were your feelings during this encounter? What could the other person have done differently in this situation? How do you feel you adjusted to the other person? How appropriate was the other person in this interaction? Responses could be triangulated to determine the accuracy of the initial autobiography.

A set of materials for *Autobiography of Intercultural Encounters* can be found free online, in English, Italian, and French, at the URL in the listed reference. For more research involving INCA tools, see Prechtl & Lund (2009).

Assessment Issues

Other issues and questions with regard to assessment of intercultural competence are:

Lifelong process

One issue is the time factor: given that intercultural competence is a lifelong process, how do assessments address *longitudinal* factors and move beyond a "one point in time" assessment? Furthermore, most assessments of intercultural competence focus on *results* rather than *process* (i.e., how one *approaches* others, reflects critically and thinks interculturally), relying on indirect evidence only (often a survey instrument) which provides an incomplete picture of an individual's intercultural competence development.

Beyond traditional assessments

Most indirect assessments (and even some direct assessment such as self-reflection) are more traditional in nature. They typically assess students' self-perspective or knowledge through the means of a verbal survey, and therefore cannot fully assess Intercultural competence, which comprises not only knowledge, but also, ultimately, communication and behavior in real-life settings.

Developmental

Intercultural competence is a developmental *process,* so to what extent do assessments address the process itself? As a developmental process, individuals will vary in their degree of competence, which leads to the issue of how to address varying levels of competence.

Defining intercultural competence

Given the many definitions that exist, it is important to ask: "intercultural competence according to whom and based on what cultural perspective?"

Appropriateness

Given that intercultural competence is about *effective* and *appropriate* communication and behavior, how will appropriateness be assessed, especially when it is only the other who is the best judge of appropriateness? What is often missing in assessment of intercultural competence is the other half of the picture – the *appropriateness* of communication and behavior, which, according to research studies, can only be measured through *others'* perspectives, going beyond self-report inventories and surveys.

Assessing behavior

Given that most definitions of intercultural competence include communication and behavior as ultimate outcomes, how do assessments measure actual behavior and communication in intercultural contexts? This suggests the need for authentic means of assessment, such as observation of performance/behavior in real-life interactions.

Assessment and Research

Assessment of intercultural competence is undergoing a shift away from sole use of self-report measures to a performance-based, learner-centered paradigm that is relevant, collaborative, integrated, and more meaningful to the learner. There are numerous implications within this changing assessment paradigm. Educators need to change their thinking about assessment from something that is "done to" learners (that ultimately benefits the educators and administrators more than the learners) to assessment as a powerful tool for continuing students' learning and development, and ultimately to view assessment as a transformational tool. Research questions are numerous, and include the following:

- How do learners view these assessments as relevant in their contexts?
- How can assessment of intercultural competence be more collaborative?
- What are effective strategies for assessing the intercultural *process*?
- What are other ways of assessing intercultural competence if the focus is more on the interaction and relationship? How do learners benefit from these assessment efforts?
- If self-perspective instruments continue to be used, *is it always about obtaining the higher score*?

Given the complexities of international education outcomes, though, perhaps a lower score is desired on post-program surveys, which may indicate more of a willingness to learn, a sense of cultural humility, and an awareness of the scope of personal development still needed (depending on the parameters of the actual tool used). How will assessment approaches encourage and recognize lifelong learning in a more holistic manner?

Ultimately, the goal of assessment is to collect **evidence** of development of intercultural competence and to use that information to guide students in their intercultural journey as well as for course/program improvement. In this sense, assessing intercultural competence is about much more than assessing a complex learning outcome: it is about developing an essential lifelong competence.

Acknowledgments

Parts of this chapter are adapted from the following publications:

Darla K. Deardorff (2014). Some thoughts on assessing intercultural competence, *Viewpoints*. Retrieved August, 11 2015 from: https://illinois.edu/blog/view/915/113048.
Darla K. Deardorff (2015). *Demystifying outcomes assessment for international educators*. Virgina: Stylus Publishing.

The chapter was edited by Zhu Hua and Jennifer Watson.

Key Terms

Assessment The systematic collection, review, and use of information about and for student learning.

Intercultural competence A lifelong process involving the development of skills, knowledge, and attitudes needed for effective and appropriate communication and behavior in interactions with those from different backgrounds.

Learning outcomes/objectives A set of concrete, specific statements (expectations) about student learning and performance that lead to the achievement of a stated goal.

Reliability Reliability is an indicator of consistency. A tool or method is reliable if it yields similar results each time it is administered.

Validity Validity is about being on target. A tool is valid if it measures what it is designed to measure and aligns with the intended use of the results.

References

Banta, T., & Palomba, C. (2014). *Assessment essentials: Planning, implementing, and improving assessment in higher education* (2nd ed.). San Francisco: Jossey-Bass.

Bennett, M. J. (1993). Towards ethnorelativism: A developmental model of intercultural sensitivity. In R. Paige (Ed.), *Education for the intercultural experience* (2nd ed., pp. 21–71). Yarmouth, ME: Intercultural Press.

Bok, D. (2006). *Our underachieving colleges: A candid look at how much students learn and why they should be learning more.* Princeton, NJ: Princeton University Press.

Byram, M. (1997). *Teaching and assessing intercultural communicative competence.* Clevedon: Multilingual Matters.

Clayton, P. (2010). Generating, deepening, and documenting learning in experiential education: The power of critical reflection. (Presentation.) Ryerson University, Toronto, Ontario, March, 2010.

Council of Europe. (2009). *Autobiography of intercultural encounters.* Strasbourg: Council of Europe Publishing. Retrieved June 16, 2015 from: http://ecep.ecml.at/Portals/26/training-kit/files/1_AIE_autobiography_en.pdf

Deardorff, D.K. (2006). Identification and assessment of Intercultural Competence as a student outcome of internationalization. *Journal of Studies in International Education*, 10(3), 241–266. Retrieved June 16, 2015 from: http://jsi.sagepub.com/content/10/3/241.full.pdf+html

Deardorff, D.K. (Ed.). (2009). *The Sage handbook of intercultural competence.* Thousand Oaks, CA: Sage

Deardorff, D.K. (2011). Assessing Intercultural Competence. *New Directions for Institutional Research*, 149. Retrieved June 16, 2015 from: http://onlinelibrary.wiley.com/doi/10.1002/ir.381/pdf

Deardorff, D.K. (2012). Intercultural competence in the 21st century: Perspectives, issues, application. In B. Breninger & T. Kaltenbacher (Eds.), *Creating cultural synergies: Multidisciplinary Perspectives on Interculturality and Interreligiosity* (pp. 7–23). Newcastle upon Tyne: Cambridge Scholars.

Deardorff, D.K. (2015). *Demystifying outcomes assessment for international educators: A practical approach.* Sterling, VA: Stylus.

Deardorff, D.K., & van Gaalen, A. (2012). Outcomes assessment in the internationalization of higher education. In D. Deardorff, H. de Wit, J. Heyl, & T. Adams (Eds.), *The Sage handbook of international higher education* (pp. 167–191). Thousand Oaks, CA: Sage.

Driscoll, A., & Wood, S. (2007). *Developing outcomes-based assessment for learner-centered education a faculty introduction.* Sterling, VA: Stylus.

Council of Europe. (2009). *Autobiography of intercultural encounters.* Strasbourg: Council of Europe Publishing. Retrieved June 16, 2015 from: http://ecep.ecml.at/Portals/26/training-kit/files/1_AIE_autobiography_en.pdf

Fantini, A. (2009). Assessing intercultural competence: Issues and tools. In D. K. Deardorff (Ed.), *The Sage handbook of intercultural competence* (pp. 456–476). Thousand Oaks, CA: Sage.

Gordon, J., & Deardorff, D.K. (2013). Demystifying assessment: A critical component in student success. In W. Nolting, D. Donohue, C. Matherly, & M. Tillman (Eds.), *Internships, service learning and volunteering abroad: Successful models and best practices* (pp. 74–81). Washington, DC: NAFSA.

Kneffelcamp, L. (1989). Assessment as transformation. Speech to the American Association for Higher Education Fourth National Conference on Assessment in Higher Education, June 21–24, 1989, Atlanta

Knowles, M. (1986) *Using learning contracts.* San Francisco: Jossey-Bass.

O'Grady, C. (2000). *Integrating service learning and multicultural education in colleges and universities.* Mahwah, NJ: Lawrence Erlbaum Associates.

Pottinger, P. S. (1979). Competence Assessment: Comments on Current Practices. In P. S. Pottinger & J. Goldsmith (Eds.), *Defining and Measuring Competence* (pp. 25–40). San Francisco: Jossey-Bass.

Prechtl, E., & Lund, A. D. (2009). Intercultural competence and assessment: perspectives from the INCA project. In H. Kotthoff & H. Spencer-Oatey (eds.) *Handbook of intercultural communication* (pp. 467–490). Berlin: Mouton de Gruyter.

Rice, K., & Pollack, S. (2000). Developing a critical pedagogy of service learning: preparing self-reflective, culturally aware, and responsive community participants. In C. O'Grady (Ed.), *Integrating service learning and multicultural education in colleges and universities* (pp. 115–134). Mahwah, NJ: Lawrence Erlbaum Associates.

Spitzberg, B. H., & Changnon, G. (2009). Conceptualizing multicultural competence. In D.K. Deardorff (Ed.), *Handbook of intercultural competence* (pp. 2–52). Thousand Oaks, CA: Sage.

Stuart, D. K. (2009). Assessment instruments for the global workforce. In M. Moodian (Ed.), *Contemporary leadership and Intercultural Competence: Exploring the cross-cultural dynamics within organizations* (pp. 175–190). Thousand Oaks, CA: Sage.

Thorndike, R. M. (2005) *Measurement and evaluation in psychology and education* (7th ed.) New Jersey: Prentice Hall.

UNESCO (2013). *Intercultural competences.* Paris: UNESCO.

Further Reading and Resources

Byram, M. (1997). *Teaching and assessing intercultural communicative competence.* Clevedon, England: Multilingual Matters.

Della Chiesa, B., Scott, J., & Hinton, C. (2012). *Languages in a global world: Learning for better cultural understanding.* Paris: OECD.

Deardorff, D.K. (Ed.). (2009). *The Sage handbook of intercultural competence.* Thousand Oaks, CA: Sage.

Deardorff, D.K. (2015). *Demystifying outcomes assessment for international educators: A practical approach.* Sterling, VA: Stylus

Stuart, D. K. (2009). Assessment instruments for the global workforce. In M. Moodian (Ed.), *Contemporary leadership and intercultural competence: Exploring the cross-cultural dynamics within organizations* (pp. 175–190). Thousand Oaks, CA: Sage.

9 How to Work with Research Participants: The Researcher's Role

Fred Dervin

> **Summary**
>
> This chapter proposes to "reeducate" the researcher of interculturality. In order to do so, the author argues that critical reflexivity is essential in all aspects of research (theoretical principles, core hypotheses, research designs, and modes of interpretation and analysis). Most importantly the chapter calls for renewed relationships between the researcher and her informants, i.e. to "work the hyphen" between them in order to render research on the intercultural more ethical, fair but also political. The idea of discomfort in doing research in this field is also problematized through interdisciplinary discussions. Finally, the author advocates moving beyond "repressed reflexivity" by empowering researchers to position themselves while constantly questioning their work and ideologies.

Introduction

I would like to start this chapter by tackling a very basic issue that relates to the role of the researcher of interculturality (note that the term sometimes refers to an approach to Intercultural Communication, see Brandt & Mortensen, Chapter 20, this volume) in today's societies: *Why do we do research on the topic?*

In order to answer this question, I am inspired by two sociologists (Haag & Lemieux, 2012) and the French anthropologist François Laplantine (2013, p. 30). For

Haag and Lemieux, researchers should aim at "thinking otherwise" and not merely reproduce what "commonsense," or decision-makers such as supranational institutions like the European Union, think about intercultural encounters. The latter, for example, tend to "pollute" researchers' discourses with polysemic or often empty yet politically laden keywords that spread through policies and calls for research proposals in Europe, and increasingly worldwide. These discourses can have a negative impact on how powerless individuals are talked about and treated.

Haag and Lemieux also suggest that researchers aim at identifying "mistakes" and inconsistencies that lead to social injustice in what they do and in others' work, clarifying their critiques and, most importantly, provoking public debates to be useful to society.

I believe that this first set of objectives should be central to research on the intercultural, especially in its processual and critical format (we'll discuss the idea of *process interculturality* in this chapter). A lot of research and practice on interculturality has contributed to the building up of stereotypes and prejudice against certain groups, bereaving them of opportunities to be treated in a fair way (Holliday, 2010). It is now time to assume our responsibilities, to unlearn the way interculturality used to be dealt with, and to be ready for real changes.

François Laplantine's proposal (2013, p. 30) is also relevant to what we are trying to achieve in the multifaceted field of interculturality. For the anthropologist, research should consist in (but also lead to) permanent criticality, confusion, perplexity, and complexity to reflect our contemporary worlds. In other words, to paraphrase the philosopher Henri Bergson (1904), disengage from "terra firma" and get used to and allow sharing the "rolling and pitching" of the human experience. These visions of research on interculturality seem to correspond to current critical work and discussions around the topic (Byrd-Clark & Dervin, 2014; Dervin & Risager, 2014; Holliday, 2010, 2013; Piller, 2010; Zhu Hua, 2011).

Some weeks ago I challenged my adherence to these "values" while surfing on the website "I, too, am Oxford" (http://itooamoxford.tumblr.com/). The website contains pictures of "minority" students holding a sign with controversial messages to demand that "a discussion on race be taken seriously and that real institutional change occur" (website). Many of the pictures have very strong messages but I was very much startled by the following one. Held by a Black female student, it read: "All the post-colonial and other critical theories you study do not entitle you to speak for me or over me... ."

Feelings of guilt and "hyper-reflexivity" (Byrd-Clark & Dervin, 2014) overtook me: As a "critical" theorist and researcher, following the aforementioned principles, had I ever done this to anyone, i.e. "spoken for them or over them"? Had I ever in my work "inadvertently (contributed to) the violence of low politics" (Sen, 2007: xvi) to which interculturality can lead under the guise of racism, xenophobia/xenophilia, etc.? Had I ever damaged anyone by, for instance, trying to flatten out the omnipresent discourses on culture in research on the intercultural that I find to be so problematic – having even called for the intercultural without culture (Dervin, 2013)? In my work I have demonstrated that discourses of culture can lead to explicit and implicit moralistic judgments; better and worse, more civilized people; hierarchies (politics of the closed door; insiders and outsiders); unjustified ethnocentrism ("racism without races"); etc. Yet, culture seems to matter to people involved in intercultural encounters. However, as a critical scholar, am I entitled to criticize them for that and to say explicitly or implicitly that they are potentially "wrong" to do so, or that they are fooling themselves? In a similar vein, is it right to fight for everyone's *diverse diversities* in research instead of the usual *essentialist selective diversity* which is often limited to the images of the Other, the one who has crossed a national border or simply the "immigrant" (Wood, 2003)? In our omniscient digital societies, where discourses circulate so quickly, and where researchers increasingly have to find outlets for their voices to be heard, shouldn't we pay more attention to what we have to say about the intercultural, to how we say it and to whom? Make efforts not to hurt anyone's feelings and to treat everyone involved as fairly as possible?

Let me illustrate these questions. In 2013 I experienced some discomfort with messages that I received from immigrants living in Finland after an interview I had given to Finnish national television. A journalist had gone undercover to see how different groups were treated by "Finns" in the areas of work and housing. The results showed that Russian and Somali people were discriminated against. There had been a persistent, obsessive societal discussion around the idea that Finns are racist. To me, as a researcher working from a postmodern paradigm, this assertion does not make sense, since racism is such a polysemic concept, and generalizing for 5 million people seems ridiculous. Of course I do not deny that racism does exist in Finnish society – as in all societies in the West, East, South and North. But I believe that by reiterating these ideas over and over, we are not going anywhere. When the journalist asked me if I thought that Finnish people were racist, I said exactly that. He wrote: "According to Helsinki University's Professor Fred Dervin, the results are hardly surprising. He pointed out that similar tests had been conducted in other parts of Europe with similar outcomes. Dervin, whose work centers on multiculturalism, cautioned against drawing the conclusion that Finns are racist." The messages that I received were both positive and negative but they all seemed to misunderstand what I had tried to say. I felt sorry for some of the people who contacted me because they felt that I had betrayed them by "defending Finns" – being myself an immigrant in this country. In a sense, they felt that I had misrepresented them while "speaking for them." That was of course not what I was trying to achieve: I was not defending anyone, just positioning my views on these issues.

Talking to our readers, be they scholars, decision-makers, journalists, or people on the street is very challenging, especially when time is limited to explain the complexity of our messages. Few people beyond the academy are acquainted with our work, and we need to phrase things in such ways that do not distort our central message. The main problem is that most of the time we do not speak the same language, use the same words, or the same definitions. If I google my name, one of the first websites that pops up is that of the extremist "Tundra Tabloids," a website about "Keeping tabs on the most outrageous happenings in the Middle East, Islamist extremism and Islamist hegemony in Scandinavia and on the political correctness that allows them to flourish." The article, entitled "University of Helsinki Professor Fred Dervin, Multicultural Genius and Mastermind," criticizes me for another interview that I gave to a national Finnish television channel about multicultural education. My views had been distorted by the journalist, who had had me say that "all cultures are equal and people should have the right to their culture in Finland." The article was published without me having the opportunity to proof-read it. Any reader who knows my work would be well aware that I would have never claimed such a meaningless thing... The article from Tundra Tabloids picked up on this erroneous view and argued that I ("another multi-culti 'genius'") was trying to "inflict (my) version of utopia upon society"... .

So, as researchers we face the issues of interacting "properly" and respectfully with our research participants and disseminating our work in such a way that our main messages are not too distorted and can be useful to society. But how do we make sure we respect our participants' voices? Or should we? What would that entail? Furthermore how do we transmit controversial ideas to the general public, which may not be shared by the people we interacted with during our study? In this chapter I would like to discuss working *with* researching participants – instead of *on*.

Critical Reflexivity and Process Interculturality

I would like to start by tackling the issue of reflexivity, especially critical reflexivity, which should be essential to our work (Byrd-Clark & Dervin, 2014). In all aspects of research on the intercultural, be they "formal," such as theoretical principles, core hypotheses, research designs, and modes of interpretation and analysis, or "informal," such as interaction with participants and society at large through, for instance, dissemination and mediatization, the researcher who works from an open approach to the intercultural – "process interculturality" – has to reflect and act constantly upon what s/he feels is acceptable and coherent with the principles presented in the introduction.

For Wimmer and Glick Schiller (2002, p. 326) this corresponds to what they call *methodological fluidity*, or "where there were fixed boundaries, everything is now equally and immediately interconnected. Structures are replaced with fluidity." Reality is not static "but (it) affirms itself dynamically, as continuity and variation. What was immobile and frozen in our perception is warmed and set in motion" (Bergson, 1911 [1998]). In other words, we researchers or our research participants are not static but dynamic, and influenced in our actions and discourses by an uncountable number of elements such as context, social position, emotions, intertextuality, etc. For Amselle (2010, p. 79), this means that we should hear our participants rather than merely listen *to* them. It also means that we should avoid "identity taxidermy," or imposing solid identities, cultures, and even strong identity markers such as the contested idea of "mother tongue" on our research participants, throughout the research process and beyond (in our publications or in paratexts such as discussions with media). These elements need to be negotiated with them. This also requires back and forth movements between the discourses we (co-)create and how we behave and interact with our informants.

Another important aspect of reflexivity is constant criticality towards our theoretical and methodological positions. I feel that the tools that we have developed or borrowed to analyze data from a process interculturality perspective are not adequate to grasp its complexity. Methodologically, there are some issues, as an example, concerning certain substitutes that we use to replace the contested idea of methodological nationalism (or the nation-state as a way of explaining solely intercultural encounters). This paradigm used to be central in research on the intercultural. Many substitutes seem to have been smuggled to do the same thing today:

methodological cosmopolitanism (which appears to be elitist and create new hierarchies), neighborhood nationalism (choosing one neighborhood/district for a study and generalizing from this context), methodological ethnicity, but also such labels as East vs. West, global vs. local, Whiteness vs. the rest, etc. By using these substitutes for a demonstration uncritically we do not seem to be treating our research participants fairly. New categories and hierarchies are created to "box" them. They do not represent the realities of our worlds but they construct a very limited and contestable reality… .

Let me reflect further on the East and West dichotomy, or Europe and the rest of the world, as these have taken on increasing importance over the last years in research on the intercultural. For the last 200 years the West has caused much pain in the world by colonizing parts of it, or by imposing some of its worldviews. As a consequence the West is widely criticized within and outside its boundaries for its wrongdoings. Fair enough. Yet many critical scholars or thinkers seem to have a selective and shortsighted vision of history, which allows them to draw quick conclusions such as "Westerners are bad but the rest of the world is good." If one looks at the world well beyond the previous 200 years it becomes obvious that no one has acted without fighting against, invading, and even destroying the Other. Phenomena such as power relations between places, tribal chiefs, within families, between neighbors, etc. and various forms of colonization (which are not named as such) have always occurred. Of course this is not to excuse what Europeans did. But it does demand a wider and even more critical dialogue on these issues. Many scholars make an attempt at de-essentializing their research, but by using this dichotomy they tend to fall back into the trap.

Another issue relates to the current critiques addressed to the West and/or Europe in terms of how ignorant or biased towards others "they" are – read Africans and Asians. Ignorance about the other is a universal sin because it depends on the individual's interests, her/his geopolitical and historical relations with others, etc. In an interesting novel called *Messages from Finland* (Sesay, 1996, pp. 22–23), an African student in Finland talks about his pre-arrival ideas about the country. It is interesting to see how he makes fun of his own ignorance: "I still recalled one of the books we used for Geography entitled, *Regions and peoples of the world* by Charles McIntyre. It was through this book that I first learnt about Scandinavia and of Finland. … If this place were really so cold, with so harsh winters, then, the immediate reasoning was that life must be primitive indeed. This is true, because our geography teachers had always focused more or less on explaining about the climatic conditions up here. They wasted no time talking about whether there was electricity or skidoos or whether even airplanes dared to come here."

However the most problematic issue in the not-so-new dichotomy of East and West is that of frontiers. Amartya Sen (2007, p. 19) rightly explains that: "given the cultural and intellectual interconnections in world history, the question of what is "Western" and what is not would be hard to decide." This is an important message for critics within the West who criticize Western countries for being this or that. Adrian Holliday notes for example the ideological nonsense represented by the notions of collectivism and individualism and how they are used by both the East and the West to oppose each other. He writes (2010, p. 9): "despite the claim to neutrality, it seems clear that individualism represents imagined positive characteristics, and collectivism represents imagined negative characteristics."

Researchers – even so-called critical ones – should thus be careful about categorizing people in such groups. There are often differences within groups that need to be taken into account. For Gillespie, Howarth, and Cornish (2012, p. 392), social categories should be considered as being perspectival, historical, disrupted by the movement of people and reconstitutive of the phenomena they seek to describe. Such categories are perspectival in the sense that no category is "natural" but is always based on someone's vision (the researcher, the participants, decision-makers who fund research, etc.). It is thus important in our work to clarify this aspect in order to reduce the othering effect (p. 393) but also contradictions. In relation to the historicality of social categories, Gillespie et al. (2012, p. 394) criticize the fact that a lot of work on the other seems to be "stuck in the past." This seems to be the case, for example, in relation to the way that China and the Chinese are treated in research today. An overemphasis on the importance of the philosopher Confucius (551–479 BCE) – whose ideas are being ideologized again in this context after decades of neglect – to explain how and why the Chinese behave or think in such or such ways is problematic. This leads us to Gillespie et al.'s third point: social categories are disrupted by people's movements in and out of contexts, social classes, genders, places, etc. but also moods and illnesses (p. 394). All of these impact on their status as others and should thus be taken into account to avoid, which is Gillespie et al.'s last point, "an unreflective use" which can result in the "same risks as those evidenced in lay thinking" (p. 395).

Co-constructing Research: Beyond "Repressed Reflexivity"?

Though the idea is not novel, our times are those of the recognition of multiple identities. For Amartya Sen (2007, p. 350), "Each of us involves identities of various kinds in disparate contexts." Each of these identities, or an intersection of these identities, can have relevance depending on the interlocutor, the context and the situation. For Gillespie et al. (2012, p. 394), "People move between places, social roles, life stages, genders, abilities, social classes and even cultures – and in so doing, they move between many social categories." The solid approach to culture that used to characterize work on the intercultural did not allow everyone to move between social categories in the same manner and to accumulate, co-construct, and negotiate roles and identities. The more of those, the easier it was to find one's place in a society, and the more chances of succeeding like the others. However, success in relation to e.g. "immigrant" pupils still seems to be explained by their "cultural background" and rarely by other elements (e.g. "this child is not so good at mathematics because of his culture"). We need to look beyond this alibi to analyze contexts, power relations, language (e.g. how teachers talk to the children), discriminatory practices, "boxing," etc., to propose some hypotheses as to why a child is not succeeding. When some of our pupils are "boxed" and sometimes segregated because of their culture (explicitly or not), the array of social categories they are allowed to navigate between is very limited. This is why researchers should rely on an understanding of interculturality "which shows that social categories come and go … . Once the social categories are seen as temporal, they are destabilized, becoming peculiar, something to be interested in, but not something to taken too seriously" (Gillespie et al., 2012, p. 399).

As a consequence researchers need to beware of how they categorize their research participants. In his criticism of Samuel Huntington's *Clash of Civilizations*, Sen (2007, p. 54) explains that he misplaces India in the category of "the Hindu civilization," as it

> downplays the fact that India has many more Muslims (more than 140 million – larger than the entire British and French populations put together) than any other country in the world with the exception of Indonesia and, marginally Pakistan, and that nearly every country in Huntington's definition of the 'Islamic civilization' has fewer Muslims that India has.

The more power people have to determine and construct their own identities (and movements between identities), the better it is for social justice, development and "integration."

Michel Maffesoli (2013) adds to this argument by asserting that current sociological research shows that "The spirit of the times is no longer of subjectivism, but an *outflow* of self, a loss in the other." This is an important argument for research on the intercultural: we should do away with methodological individualism, or the idea that our analyses and interpretation of data depend on what research participants claim, express and construct during our studies. First of all, for Brubaker (2004), research participants "have a performative character" (Brubaker, 2004), so it is difficult to take what they say for granted, since they most certainly play with their multiple identities with us researchers and for us. Secondly, interaction of any sort is about the entanglement of self-in-the-other and other-in-the-self (Gallagher, 2011). This means that in any research context what participants construct is always related to the presence of the researcher. Going back to process interculturality, what happens during research can be summarized as acts of co-construction of identities, discourses and actions. As R.D. Laing wrote: "No one acts or experiences in a vacuum" (Laing, 1961, pp. 81–82).

If researchers do indeed contribute to politics of identity, it means that we need to look into the concept of power. As such if we are not careful enough, we might contribute to othering our participants. It is thus increasingly important for researchers themselves to be critical towards their own potential othering of the research participants they work with. This is often related to some of the intellectual simplifiers that we use in research (culture, gender, ethnicity, etc.) but also to methodologies. For example, in the fields of Intercultural Communication and education the way participants are selected is often biased: either they are selected based on their nationality or on the neighborhood where they live, leading to different forms of "methodological nationalism" (see above). Drawing general conclusions about a people if researchers have not looked into other populations can result in othering. One of my students wanted to work on the problems faced by immigrant learners of mathematics in Finland, claiming that they have specific issues because of their different culture. I asked him to consider "comparing" the sort of problems that Finnish students face when learning mathematics so as not to draw unfair othering conclusions on immigrant children.

One interesting contribution for the field of the intercultural is that of Michelle Fine, who proposed to "work the hyphen" in research:

> By working the hyphen, I mean to suggest that researchers probe how we are in relation with the context we study and with our informant, understanding that we are all multiple in those relations. I mean to invite researchers to see how these "relations" between get us "better" data, limit what we feel free to say, expand our minds and constrict our mouths, engage us in intimacy and seduce us into complicity, make us quick to interpret an hesitant to write" (Fine, 1998, p. 72).

She also suggests that by doing so researchers are able to discuss with the research participants "what is, and is not, 'happening between,' within the negotiated relations of whose story is being told, why, to whom, with what interpretation, and whose story is being shadowed, why, for whom, and with what consequence" (p. 72).

Dialogue around the act of researching within research is, therefore, essential. I believe that it would help us to go beyond mere "ventriloquation" of our participants' discourses (Valsiner, 2002). As such, many intercultural studies create narratives, and do storytelling based on what the participants asserted during the interviews. This is very problematic as such approaches tend to objectivize interaction and the impact of context, situation, and interlocutors but also of contradictions, "lies," power-led discourses, co-constructed utterances, etc. The participants' words then become the "truth," even though, because of, for example, power differentials, it may not be their "truth." For Gillespie, Cornish, Aveling, and Zittoun (2007, p. 38) "the individual will internalize the voices of many different, even conflicting, communities." If we take these words for granted without problematizing the many and varied voices, then are we doing a service to our participants and the "groups" they represent?

The form of reflexivity that should be advocated in research on the intercultural should go beyond this repressed form. Going back to my reaction to the comment from "I, too, am Oxford" mentioned in the introduction, "All the post-colonial and other critical theories you study do not entitle you to speak for me or over me...," maybe I felt uncomfortable because I interpreted it as repressing the researcher's voice. Of course, the researcher is not a superior being, a God-like figure, but I am convinced that through our engagement with permanent criticality, confusion, perplexity, and complexity, we can contribute to changes in the way some issues related to interculturality are dealt with in our societies without having to repress our voices, but by questioning throughout the research process.

An example

In my 2014 article entitled "Towards post-intercultural teacher education: analyzing 'extreme' intercultural dialogue to reconstruct interculturality," I explore the impact of a course on "process interculturality" given to a cohort of local and international student teachers studying to become newly qualified teachers in Finland. Through the use of a documentary set in Israel on extreme intercultural dialogue that the students discussed at the end of the course, I examine how they problematize such a case of intercultural dialogue through what they have learnt and relate it to their future practice and research. The data are derived from a focus group between the student teachers that took place as a final activity in the course. The focus group was recorded straight after watching the documentary on a multicultural class in Israel. The analysis of the students' discussions derives from a linguistic and dialogic approach to discourse. In terms of results, the student teachers were able to discuss the central aspects of, for instance, marginalization in multicultural classrooms in a specific context (Israel) as well as the many and varied confused and confusing identity games taking place in the class. They were able to bring into their discussions some of the notions and concepts introduced during the course: the dangers of categorizations, their historical and perspectival dimensions, othering, multiple identities, etc. There is also some evidence of their relating what they had seen in the documentary to analyzing the power relations in the documentary. Sometimes the approach might push the students towards over-interpretation or one-sided analyses, especially in relation to marginalization and injustice – as if they were activists. I argue that further work on reflexivity is needed for the student teachers who are considered in the Finnish context as apprentice researchers. This means that even more critical reflexivity is needed in training students to do research on such issues in order to make sure that the principles of process interculturality that were proposed to them are coherently and consistently applied in all aspects of researching, for example, the documentary under scrutiny (see the idea of methodological fluidity mentioned earlier).

Conclusion

To conclude this chapter let us listen to Nietzsche's views on education (1874/1983): "real education is liberation. It removes the weeds and rubbish and vermin that attack the delicate shoots of the plant." In this chapter I have tried to propose a reeducation for researchers of interculturality, which consists mostly in unlearning certain ways of doing research and thus becoming "liberated." This means, amongst other things, that researchers should move away from God-like positions (pseudo-objectivity), take responsibility for their actions, and question and criticize systematically what they say and do. It also means that we should accept and put into practice the idea that research situations also consist in becoming aware of, recognizing, pushing through, and presenting and defending one's diverse diversities, and those of our interlocutor. In some cases, our research participants or media partners may not agree with this approach and feel that, by being reflexive – for example, not giving full answers to their questions about what we do – we researchers do not fulfill our roles as explainers of the world.

    A student of mine was once faced with a difficult situation: she had gathered Finnish women who had converted to Islam for a focus group discussion, but had decided not to take part in the discussion, rather, she resolved to let them talk together without her. To her surprise many of the participants disapproved of her way of collecting data, arguing that "that's not the way research is done. We want you to be our spokesperson." The student then spent some time explaining why her vision of research had urged her not to take part in the discussion to lead the discussion, and thus take part in othering them. The participants seemed to have understood her point but were still very disappointed... and my student rather frustrated. Paraphrasing bell hooks (1994, p. 39) when she talks about introducing new ways of questioning in education, we could say that there should be "some degree of pain in giving up old ways of thinking and knowing and learning new approaches." This pain is a constant feeling of discomfort, which should be faced directly by the researcher and the actors involved in her/his work. Sharing the feeling of discomfort with research participants can help to diminish the usual power differentials between Us and Them. It could also help us to "give back to them." This is something that is often ignored in research on the intercultural: research participants tend to be considered as what could be labeled as "discourse valves." How ready are we to give them something back in return? This is where research on interculturality needs to be more involved, more political in a sense.

Key Terms

Diverse diversities The idea of *diverse diversities* is counter to that of mere *diversity*. The latter tends to refer to the Other – the one who has crossed a national border – especially in relation to her (national) culture and ethnicity. *Diverse diversities*, on the other hand, open up the notion by including the intersection of many and varied identities (gender, religion, social class, etc.). Unlike *diversity*, they thus refer to any individual and avoid a politically correct hierarchy between the diverse and the rest.

Methodological nationalism The use of the nation-state as the only identity marker and criterion for selecting research participants and/or explaining and interpreting research results. This perspective is increasingly criticized for ignoring the intersection of many and varied identity markers such as gender, age, social class, etc. as explanatory forces.

Othering The act of othering is a basic component of sociality. When meeting a person, one needs to compare self to other. In this comparative work, differences and similarities are considered. In the context of intercultural encounters these elements tend to be primarily related to people's national identities and can easily lead to stereotyping and feelings of superiority.

Process Interculturality Process interculturality is in a sense a tautology (the same thing is repeated), as the root -ality in intercultur*ality* is used here to translate a processual approach to encounters between self and other. Process interculturality opposes a canonical understanding of the intercultural. It involves taking into account each individual's multiple identities, the importance of contexts, the influence of power relations of interlocutors, etc.

Repressed reflexivity Repressed reflexivity occurs when researchers feel pressured not to be reflexive about what they are analyzing for fear of being accused of not respecting their participants' subjectivity or agency. If identity is co-constructed by researchers and participants, participants' discourses on who they are, what they think and what they do are related to the presence of the researcher and the research context. Thus, repressing reflexivity about what a participant asserts or does in a study is counterproductive.

References

Amselle, J.-L. (2010). *Rétrovolutions: Essai sur les primitivismes contemporains*. Paris: Stock.
Bergson, H. (1911 [1998]). *Creative evolution*. New York: Dover.
Brubaker, R. (2004). *Ethnicity without groups*. Cambridge, MA: Harvard University Press.
Byrd-Clark, J., & Dervin, F. (Eds.). (2014). *Reflexivity in language and intercultural education*. London: Routledge.
Dervin, F. (2013). Do intercultural couples "see culture everywhere"? Case studies from couples who share a lingua franca in Finland and Hong Kong. *Civilisations*, 62, 131–148.
Dervin, F., & Risager, K. (2014). *Researching identity and interculturality*. London: Routledge.
Dervin, F. (2014). Towards post-intercultural teacher education: Analyzing "extreme" intercultural dialogue to reconstruct interculturality. *European Journal of Teacher Education*, DOI: 10.1080/02619768.2014.902441
Fine, M. (1998). Working the hyphens: reinventing self and other in qualitative research. In N. K. Denzin, & Y. S. Lincoln (Eds.), *The landscape of qualitative research: Theories and issues* (pp. 130–155). Thousand Oaks, CA: Sage.
Gallagher, S. (2011). A philosophical epilogue on the question of autonomy. In H. Hermans, & T. Gieser (Eds.), *Handbook of the dialogical self theory* (pp. 488–496). Cambridge: Cambridge University Press.
Gillespie, A., Cornish, F., Aveling, E.-L., & Zittoun, T. (2007). Conflicting community commitments: a dialogical analysis of a British woman's World War II diaries. *Journal of Community Psychology*, 36(1), 35–52. DOI: 10.1002/jcop.20215
Gillespie, A., Howarth, C. S., & Cornish, F. (2012). Four problems for researchers using social categories. *Culture & Psychology*, 18(3), 391–402.
Haag, P., & Lemieux, C. (2012). *Faire des sciences sociales: Critiquer*. Paris: Les Éditions de l'EHESS.
Holliday, A. (2010). *Intercultural communication*. Thousand Oaks. CA: Sage.
Holliday, A. (2013). *Understanding intercultural communication: Negotiating a grammar of culture*. London: Routledge.
hooks, b. (1994). *Teaching to transgress: Education as the practice of freedom*. London : Routledge.
Laing, R. D. (1961). *The divided self: An existential study in sanity and madness*. Harmondsworth: Penguin.
Laplantine, F. (2013). *Quand le moi devient autre: Connaître, partager, transformer*. Paris: CNRS Éditions.
Maffesoli, M. (2013). To each his tribes: From contract to pact. *Secessio*, 2(1). Retrieved June 16, 2015 from: http://secessio.com/vol-2-no-1/to-each-his-tribes-from-contract-to-pact/
Nietzsche, F. (1874/1983). *Untimely meditations*. Cambridge: Cambridge University Press.
Piller, I. (2010). *Intercultural Communication*. Edinburgh: Edinburgh University Press.
Sen, A. (2007). *Identity and violence: The illusion of destiny*. New Delhi: Penguin.
Sesay, L. S. (1996). *Messages from Finland: The exciting book about the experiences of a foreign student*. Turku: Reindeer Books.
Valsiner, J. (2002). Forms of dialogical relations and semiotic autoregulation within the self. *Theory & Psychology*, 12(2), 251–265.
Wimmer, A., & Glick Schiller, N. (2002). Methodological nationalism and beyond: nation-state building, migration and the social sciences. *Global Networks*, 2(4), 301–334.

Wood, P. (2003). *Diversity. The invention of a concept*. San Francisco: Encounters Books.
Zhu Hua (Ed.). (2011). *The language and Intercultural Communication reader*. London: Routledge.

Further Reading and Resources

Dervin, F., & Layne, H. (2013). A guide to interculturality for international and exchange students: An example of *Hostipitality*? *Journal of Multicultural Discourses*, 8(1), 1–19.
Gillespie, A. (2006). *Becoming Other: From social interaction to self-reflection*. Greenwich, CT: Information Age Publishing.
Jovchelovitch, S. (2007). *Knowledge in context: Representation, community and culture*. London: Routledge.
Midgley, W., Davies, A., Oliver, M. E., & Danaher, P. A. (Eds.). (2013). *Echoes. Ethics and issues of voice in education research*. London: Sense Publishers.
Wimmer, A. (2013). *Ethnic boundary making*. Oxford: Oxford University Press.

10 How to Develop a Research Proposal

Jane Jackson

> **Summary**
>
> Careful planning is necessary to conduct a worthwhile research project in intercultural communication, as in other disciplines. This chapter begins by exploring ways to identify and shape a research idea or problem into a proposal for a project that can contribute to knowledge in this field of study. In the sections that follow, I guide you step-by-step through the development of a project proposal. As this process touches on all of the elements in a project, this chapter draws on Parts I and II, and also introduces many of the topics and issues that are discussed in later chapters.

Getting Started

A good project in language and Intercultural Communication begins with a good idea. This may come from an article or book you have read, a YouTube clip, a lecture, online posts, a film with an intercultural theme, study abroad experience, an intercultural conflict situation that you have witnessed, a second-language classroom that you have observed, a multicultural/multilingual scene in your everyday life, discriminatory language you noticed in a website, a confusing encounter with someone who has a different linguistic and cultural background, a list of topics provided in an Intercultural Communication course, etc. Look through the dissertations of previous students in our field to see what topics they have explored. Research articles often conclude with suggestions for future research, and these can also be a source of inspiration. Consider your own interests. If you are genuinely interested in the topic (e.g. a particular issue, problem, theory, methodology), you are more likely to have the motivation and energy necessary to follow through and carry out a successful study.

To shape your idea into a strong project proposal, you first need to enhance your familiarity with the topic. Throughout this groundwork phase, keep track of how your ideas are developing and changing. On your laptop you could maintain a file with your observations and notes about your preferred readings, or you might choose to jot down your thoughts in a notebook, or record audio notes on your iPad. Discover what works best for you and stick to it. Being organized and purposeful at this early stage will pay off later!

Read the titles of publications and skim the abstracts of readings that are most related to your idea so that you can quickly build up more awareness of what has already been done. This can also help you to gain a better sense of what you would like to explore and why. You don't need to wait until you have a fully formed research question before discussing your ideas and interests with others. Talk with your professors and peers about your topic and note their suggestions and observations. Their ideas can help you to refine your focus and select the most relevant readings.

Become mindful of gaps in your knowledge about the topic and figure out how you will learn more. For example, identify the online databases or other resources that are apt to be the most useful (e.g. the journals that publish many articles related to your topic). At this stage it can be very helpful to consult an edited volume that synthesizes the most significant research on your topic. As you select the research articles and other publications that are most closely related to what you would like to do, pay close attention to the type of research design and methodologies employed.

After conducting this preliminary literature review and thinking more deeply about your topic, begin to draft rough outlines for possible projects. Expect to prepare several, with different possible routes of exploration. Next, choose the option that is most likely to work best given your interests, knowledge, research skills, time, expected access to the cultural site/participants, and available resources. Of course, you must also carefully consider any guidelines or requirements set by your instructor, institution, or funding agency. All of the above steps can help you to organize and reshape your ideas before you actually sit down to construct a formal research proposal.

The Research Proposal

When designing a research project, you are usually required to develop a formal written proposal that will be reviewed and evaluated by experienced researchers (e.g. the instructor in your Intercultural Communication course, your thesis supervisor, a research review board, a funding agency). For a course project, your instructor will likely require you to submit a brief proposal or research plan before you begin to collect any data. If you undertake a major project, such as a postgraduate dissertation, your thesis supervisor (and thesis committee) will require you to prepare a more detailed proposal to be sure that your work is well-conceived and feasible. Later in your career, you may seek funding for research in Intercultural Communication. An application form with specific guidelines will likely be provided by the organization or funding body.

Essentially, a formal research proposal indicates what you plan to study, why the project is worthwhile, how you aim to accomplish your research objectives (e.g. address your research questions), and what you expect will result. A well thought-out, written proposal that stems from careful groundwork can provide a solid basis for your project, whereas one that is vague and weak is unlikely to be accepted by your reviewers. Even if the project does go ahead, the outcomes may be far from satisfactory. The time you spend on the refinement of your proposal will be well worth it. Although you may expect some changes after a project gets underway, having a clear plan to guide your work is invaluable.

While the specific requirements for the format and sequencing of contents may vary, there are basic elements that tend to feature in most research proposals, no matter what research design is employed. When planning your project, you will likely need to include most of the elements shown in Table 10.1 in your proposal.

Title Page

On the first page, provide your proposal with a title that indicates the focus and scope of your proposed study. Noun phrase headings are common. While concise, titles should be comprehensive enough to indicate the nature of the project. Sample titles are:

- A case study of the intercultural sensitivity development of a bilingual Iranian immigrant in London
- Language and the negotiation of identities in intercultural interactions: A narrative approach
- A mixed-method study of the impact of a semester abroad on the second language learning and intercultural competence of Taiwanese exchange students
- Language and culture learning in an online ESL course: Insights from learner diaries

Other information that should be included in the cover page will depend on the requirements of the course instructor, thesis supervisor, or agency. When applying for funding, a research proposal form may be provided.

Introduction/Purpose of Study

Following the title page, a clearly written introduction should capture the reader's interest and provide a clear overview of the proposed study. Once the general topic has been established, indicate more specifically what the project is about and how it fits into the interdisciplinary field of intercultural communication.

Table 10.1 Outline of proposal for research project

1. Title page
2. Introduction/purpose of study
   - General introduction to research subject
   - Outline of problem and need for study
   - Statement of purpose
   - Brief overview of project and theoretical framework
   - An indication of the importance and timeliness of the project
   - Definitions of key terms
3. Research questions, hypotheses, or objectives
   - Selection of form to indicate the research purpose of your project (e.g. hypotheses, research questions, guiding questions)
   - Identification of the questions, hypotheses, or objectives
4. Background and review of related literature
   - Describe your background in this research area (e.g. previous studies)
   - Provide information on existing knowledge related to the topic
   - Identify previous studies/publications most relevant to proposed study
5. Research design
   - Type of research design
   - Internal validity and external validity (generalizability) issues
6. Research methods
   Participants/sampling
   - Attributes of the population or phenomenon that you aim to investigate
   - Procedures for selecting a sample or cases that represent the population
   - Sample size and subgroups

   Variables and instrumentation
   - Identification of variables and how you plan to measure them
   - Description of instruments
   - Measurement concerns regarding validity and reliability

   Data collection procedures
   - Description of how you plan to collect and organize data to accomplish your objectives within a given time frame
7. Data analysis
   - Qualitative analysis techniques, if applicable
   - Descriptive and inferential statistical techniques (quantitative studies)
   - Identification of computer software programs
8. Anticipated problems
   - Possible difficulties that may arise
   - An indication of how you plan to deal with these difficulties
9. Significance of the study/Dissemination of results
   - Emphasizes the theoretical or practical benefits and implications of the outcomes of the study
   - Describes how the results would be communicated to professionals, researchers, and/or the public
10. Ethics and human relations
    - Possible threats that your project poses to participants and the action you would take to reduce them
    - Procedures for gaining the trust and cooperation of participants/access to the research site
    - Informed consent procedures
11. Timeline
    - List of the major steps of your project and the date by which each step would be completed
12. Budget (if required)
    - Items and justification
13. References
14. Appendices (optional)

The purpose statement

The purpose statement should be concise and clearly indicate what issue your work would address. You may include a statement like this: "The purpose of this study is to... ." The following are some examples of statements of purpose in Intercultural Communication research proposals:

- This study aims to track the language and intercultural learning of Hong Kong undergraduates who participate in a service-learning project in Mainland China.
- The purpose of this project is to determine the impact of a French-language immersion program on the oral French skills and intercultural awareness of secondary school students.

Justification/Description of study/Expected contribution

In the introduction, researchers need to clearly explain why the selected topic or issue is worthy of investigation. For example, you might point to a gap in the literature or emphasize the need for a replication study in your context. Provide a succinct description of your proposed study; briefly indicate the research design, methodology, and theoretical framework that would underpin your work. Indicate if you plan to extend the work of another researcher, or implement a similar study in a new context with a different population. Explain how your proposed research would build on previous studies and contribute to our knowledge in intercultural communication. If relevant, identify who would benefit from the findings, e.g. pedagogical implications for Intercultural Communication instructors, suggestions for faculty to enhance the intercultural sensitivity of student sojourners. Consider these questions: How would your findings advance Intercultural Communication practice, research, and/or theory? Why would your topic be worth studying? Would the study contribute to the development of a theory or model? Would the findings have practical or theoretical significance?

Definition of key terms

All key terms (e.g. specialized concepts) should be clearly defined in the proposal. This often involves direct quotes of definitions cited in previous studies. Sometimes, researchers modify existing definitions or devise new terms for their proposed study. The following are some definitions of terms extracted from studies in intercultural communication:

- "Intercultural learning is defined in this setting as learning which involves reciprocal knowledge and critical reflection across cultures, involving an understanding of learners' own languages and cultures in relation to the additional target language and culture" (Liddicoat, Papademetre, Scarino, & Kohler, 2003, cited in Moloney, 2013, p. 401).
- "... attitudes to language can be either positive or negative. Therefore, in the event that they are strongly negative, we refer to them as 'language prejudices,' meaning

a 'diversion of rationality that normally renders a value judgement on a language (or any of its features), or on the speakers of a language"' (Tusón, 1997, p. 27, cited in González-Riaño, Hevia-Artime, & Fernández-Costales, 2013, p. 451).

Research Questions, Hypotheses, or Objectives

After presenting an argument for the value of the project, the researcher then states the research questions, hypotheses, or objectives that would guide the study. The form used depends, in part, on the nature of the proposed project.

A research question is "a theoretical question that indicates a clear direction and scope for a research project" (Walliman, 2011, p. 177). In quantitative studies, in particular, these statements should be clearly articulated and identify the proposed variables of interest (e.g. independent, intervening, dependent, control) (Creswell, 2014). Whereas research questions ask what relationships exist between the different variables in the project, a hypothesis predicts the relationship between variables. A hypothesis is "a theoretical statement that has not yet been tested against data collected in a concrete situation, but which is possible to test by providing clear evidence for support or rejection" (Walliman, 2011, p. 172). Hypotheses should be stated clearly and as concisely as possible. In some qualitative or exploratory studies, instead of asking very specific research questions or stating hypotheses, the researcher may indicate the objectives, aims, or broad questions that will guide the study.

In your proposal, decide which form is most appropriate for your study. If your proposed project draws on existing theoretical frameworks, briefly explain how your research questions, hypotheses, or objectives relate to them. (Chapter 5 in this volume, by Zhù Huá, Holmes, Johnstone Young, and Angouri, discusses strategies and practices that are commonly used to identify research questions in intercultural communication. Examples of research questions are also provided.)

Background and Review of Related Literature

This section has three main aims:

1 to illustrate the current state of knowledge and major trends in this research area;
2 to situate the proposed project within the context of what is already known about the topic or issue; and
3 to describe any related experience that you have (e.g. previous studies that you have conducted, if any).

Aim to convince the reader that you have located, read, and synthesized the most significant works related to the hypothesis or focus of your study. It should be clear why each item has been selected. The literature review, which need not be exhaustive, often moves from the general to the more focused studies (e.g. moving from publications about related theories to articles about specific research projects conducted in your context). You may include a discussion of related theories, closely related studies, and publications that provide additional perspectives on the research questions. When summarizing research articles, include core details, such as the studies' hypotheses, theoretical framework, participants, methodology, and most significant/relevant findings. In your review, draw attention to pertinent theoretical models or frameworks that have implications for your study.

The literature review should not simply consist of a list of publications related to your proposed study. Instead of doing a catalogue style of review, make explicit connections between publications, and draw attention to their relevance, limitations, and implications for your proposed study. As well as citing strengths, this section should highlight gaps or deficiencies in research conducted to date (e.g. limitations in instrumentation or data analysis, few studies on the topic in your context). As you summarize the existing state of research on the problem and situate your proposed study with work that has already been done, remember that you are trying to show how your proposed study will fit in and make a contribution to the field (e.g. fill a gap in the literature, build on or improve on previous studies, including earlier work that you have conducted). For more guidance on how to carry out and present a literature review, see Fink (2014) or Machi & McEvoy (2009).

Research Design

Part I of this volume introduced the major research themes and paradigms in the field of Intercultural Communication and discussed some of the options available to researchers when designing projects. Research design refers to the "logic and coherence of your research study – the components of your research and the ways in which these relate to one another" (Maxwell, 2013, p. xii). For Hittleman & Simon (2006, p. 309), it is "the overall strategy or plan used by researchers for answering their research questions." As noted by Vogt, Gardner, & Haeffele (2012, p. 3), "[d]esign is fundamental because everything ultimately flows from the design choice, and because this choice is the one most closely tied to the investigator's research questions and theories."

Intercultural Communication researchers draw on a wide variety of approaches or designs to answer their research questions and test their hypotheses. There are many ways to classify research designs (e.g. quantitative vs. qualitative, single vs. mixed methods, experimental vs. non-experimental, longitudinal vs. non-longitudinal, case study vs. cross-sectional). Some research designs draw on primary data (the collection of original data by the researcher for a particular study), while others rely on secondary data (existing sources of information, such as historical archives, published reports, documentaries) (Vanderstoep & Johnston, 2009; Walliman, 2011).

Two of the most common broad categories of research designs are quantitative research and qualitative research. The former refers to "any study using numerical data with emphasis on statistics to answer the questions," whereas qualitative research "is done in a natural setting, involving intensive holistic data collection through observation at a very close personal level without the influence of prior theory and contains mostly verbal analysis" (Perry, 2011, p. 257). Mixed methods design studies combine methods used with quantitative and qualitative data (Creswell, 2013). For example, a study may combine the quantitative coding and analysis of survey questions with the qualitative coding and analysis of language and culture learning diaries and interviews with the same participants.

Replication design studies are another option and they can be particularly useful for novice researchers. As well as providing a model to follow, the findings of replication studies can help to check the external and internal validity of the original study or bring about new understandings of the subject in one's own context. Replications can take several forms, including: exact or literal replication (exact repetition of an earlier investigation), replication with extension (similar research questions are asked but something new is added), and conceptual replication (the same basic questions are asked but approached from a different perspective) (Abbuhl, 2012; Beins, 2013; Porte, 2012).

In your proposal, identify and describe the research design you would use in your study and explain why you have selected it. As noted above and in Part I of this volume, the design you select depends on the research questions, hypotheses, or objectives that you have proposed. If your study is to be qualitative in nature, explain the criteria you would use to determine the credibility and trustworthiness of the findings that would be generated. If your study is to be quantitative (e.g. experimental designs, causal-comparative designs, correlational designs), identify the threats to the internal validity of your research design and explain the action you would take to reduce or avoid these threats. Also discuss the external validity, that is, indicate the extent to which the study would be generalizable to other samples, populations, or settings (Vanderstoep & Johnston 2009). If your study is to include both quantitative and qualitative elements, explain how you would make use of both types of data (e.g. how you will triangulate data types and sources). (For more discussion on research designs see Creswell, 2013; 2014; Maxwell, 2013; Vogt *et al.,* 2012).

Research Methods

Research methods are the activities researchers use within their research design (e.g. surveys, interviews, tests, direct observations). In this section, describe the participants, sampling techniques, variables, instrumentation, and data collection procedures. (See Part III of this volume for an in-depth discussion of various methodologies (e.g. ethnography, narrative analysis, critical discourse analysis) and types of instruments (e.g. questionnaires and surveys, interviews) that are widely used in Intercultural Communication research.)

Participants/Sampling

In the proposal, it is necessary to provide specific details about the population that would be investigated as well as the research setting (the place where the data would be collected). In this section, clearly indicate how and where you would obtain participants for your study and explain the sampling method that you would use. A sample refers to "the subset of people from the population who will participate in the current study" (Vanderstoep & Johnston, 2009, p. 312).

A study's credibility partly relies on the quality of the procedures used to select the sample. In your proposal describe these procedures in detail and include the following:

1   The type of sampling to be used, e.g. probability sampling (cluster, random, systematic, stratified) or non-probability sampling (expert, purposive) in quantitative studies.
2   The number of participants to be selected and their setting (site of access).
3   The rationale for choosing a particular number of participants and the unit of analysis (e.g. an individual, a specific cultural group, a second language class in a primary school). (Explain why the sample size would be sufficient to accomplish the aims of your study.)
4   The selection criteria, that is, the rationale for choosing individuals for the study that have particular characteristics or attributes (e.g. gender, fluency in a particular language, willingness to disclose, years of residence in the host culture, degree of intercultural competence). If the sample is to be divided into subgroups, describe the characteristics of the members of the subgroups.
5   A detailed account of how you plan to select the sample.

In the following excerpt, for example, Collier (2011, p. 7) describes the sampling procedures she employed in her investigation of the intercultural interactions of bilingual/ multilingual female workers:

> In order to understand how bilingual or multilingual women use their languages within their businesses and to negotiate relationships with workers and culturally different clients, a convenience sample of 50 ($n = 50$) immigrant women entrepreneurs in the Los Angeles and Philadelphia area were surveyed regarding the language practices in their businesses. The surveys were used to screen the participants in order to identify potential candidates for observations. Twenty of these women were interviewed. The primary criteria used to select the participants were the length of time that the woman had operated a business and the self-description of her businesses as successful.

As well as describing your sampling plan and the relevant characteristics of your sample and research site, if appropriate, identify the population to which the results of your study may legitimately be generalized.

Variables and instrumentation

Define the key constructs or variables in your study and indicate how you would measure each variable that you plan to investigate (e.g. interviews and surveys, observation and rubrics, tests and/or self-report measures). For each variable in a quantitative study, identify the types of validity and reliability that need to be considered and explain how you would verify them. If your proposed study is qualitative in nature, indicate how you would draw on both emic (insider) and etic (outsider/researcher) observations (Pike, 1954). As noted by Spencer-Oatey and Franklin (2009, p. 33), "culture can be studied from two perspectives: an etic perspective which entails comparisons across cultures, and from an emic perspective which entails culture-internal research." These observations should be viewed as "complementary rather than contradictory" (Spencer-Oatey & Franklin, 2009, p. 16.)

Provide specific details about any instruments you would use (e.g. survey questionnaires, interview, or focus group protocols) and, when appropriate, include them in the appendices of your proposal. Whenever possible, make use of existing instruments that have a proven track record (e.g. surveys used in previous studies and indicate when and why modifications have been made).

(See Chapter 11 by Young and Chapter 12 by Gibson & Zhù Huá in this volume for more discussion about the design of questionnaires and interviews. Other chapters in Part III focus on other instruments used in Intercultural Communication studies.)

Data collection procedures

It is also necessary to provide information about data-collection procedures, Describe survey, interview, or observation procedures in detail and identify any incentives that would be provided for participants (e.g. money, book coupons). Explain how the letter of consent would be administered and collected.

If you have pilot-tested any of the materials, describe what you have done and indicate the implications for your proposed study. If you plan to do a pilot study, describe the data-collection procedures.

Data Analysis

Explain in some detail how you would analyze the collected data. The mode of analysis should evolve naturally from the design of your study, and be in sync with your specific research questions, hypotheses, and/or objectives. For example, when surveys are used to gather numerical data in a quantitative or mixed-method study, it is logical to use a computer program, such as the Statistical Package for the Social Sciences (SPSS) or the Statistical Analysis System (SAS) to perform the statistical analysis. The specific procedures to be performed depend on the research questions (Antonius, 2013; Beins, 2013; Vanderstoep, & Johnston, 2009). If statistical data would be processed in your study, identify the statistical package or analytical tools that you would use, and explain the purpose and logic of the statistical techniques (e.g. descriptive, inferential).

If your study includes qualitative data, describe how the key themes and categories emerging from oral or written narratives (e.g. diaries, intercultural reflection journals, field notes, interviews) would be coded and analyzed (Boeije, 2009; Gibbs, 2012; Grbich, 2012; Richards and Morse, 2012). For this purpose, specialized computer software packages such as NVivo, Nud*ist, or Ethnograph (Bazeley & Jackson, 2013; Flick, 2013; Paulus, Lester & Dempster, 2013) may be very helpful, especially if you have a large amount of data.

In this section, it is also important to describe how you would triangulate data. Triangulation is "the use of several research methods or kinds of data to examine the same phenomenon" (Vogt *et al.*, 2012, p. 354). In mixed-methods research, for example, quantitative and qualitative data related to the same participants may be brought together to develop a richer understanding of the phenomenon under study.

Anticipated Problems

In some project proposals, researchers describe the difficulties that they anticipate may occur and explain how they intend to solve them if they arise. This section can help convince the reader that the study has been carefully thought out. For your project, consider potential problems scenarios and identify contingency plans. For example, you may not gain access to your preferred site, or individuals you wish to interview may not be available or may not be willing to disclose the information you need. Some of your participants may withdraw midway through your study. What strategies do you have in mind to deal with these common problems? Will you start off with more participants than needed to ensure that you will have a sufficient number for your study?

Significance of the Study/Dissemination of Results

This section emphasizes the implications and benefits of the proposed project, such as how the findings would enhance our understanding of a theory, method, policy, practical approach, etc. You should also identify any weaknesses in your study and explain why they have not been addressed. If appropriate, internal and external validity issues may be expanded on here.

Dissemination refers to the way the outcomes of your research project would be shared with others (e.g. the academic community, the general public, Intercultural Communication specialists), such as through research reports, publications in scholarly journals, conference presentations, the production of practical materials, and websites. For funded projects, this last step is usually compulsory; however, for course projects or theses, the preparation of a detailed research project report or dissertation, and class presentations may suffice.

Ethics and Human Relations

Any research project that will involve the participation of humans should be reviewed by an institutional review board to ensure that the participants' rights to confidentiality and freedom from harm are protected. Most institutions of higher education now require this. Typically, faculty and student researchers submit a form designated for this purpose, which calls for an abstract for the proposed study, details about the research aims, design, and methods, an informed consent form, and any protocols (e.g. survey, interview, focus group) that would be used.

In this section, describe what efforts you would make to safeguard the participants in your study. Explain how you would make clear that their participation is voluntary and they would be free to withdraw at any time. Describe how their confidentiality would be protected and indicate if they would receive a copy of your research report when finished.

If relevant, you may also need to describe how you would gain entry into your proposed research setting. Do you need permission from an authority figure? If yes, how would you obtain it? Also, explain the steps you would take to gain the trust and cooperation of your participants.

If your proposed study would involve vulnerable populations (e.g. young children) or pose significant risks to participants, the review board will likely want to review the full proposal, not just the completed form. To ensure adequate protection for the participants, the reviewers may then recommend changes in the way the study has been planned. Most studies in intercultural communication, however, qualify for an expedited review. In this case, the completed ethics review form is sufficient.

See Woodin, Chapter 7 in this volume, for more discussion of research ethics in Intercultural Communication research. Comstock, 2013 and Shamoo & Resnik, 2009 are also helpful resources on research ethics.

Timeline

As a research project involves many steps, it is important to work out a plan that is both logical and feasible. It is not unusual for novice researchers to try to accomplish too much in too short a time. Devising a timeline forces you to identify specific blocks of time for each step. Depending on the length of your project, you may provide a biweekly or monthly chart or table indicating the sequencing and time allotted for such elements as: pilot-testing, the fine-tuning of instruments, data collection, data analysis, and the writing of your project report. Preparing the timeline as you draft the proposal can alert you to problems and constraints so that adjustments can be made before the formal proposal is submitted for review. Whenever possible, time should be allotted for a pilot study to allow for a trial run of the steps to be implemented in the main study.

Budget (If Required)

If a research proposal is to be submitted to an organization that offers financial support, there is usually a section in the proposal form for a tentative budget. Budgets include such items as salaries for research assistants, equipment, transportation, and general expenses (e.g. photocopying, postage, office supplies, memory sticks), as well as a set amount of money for overhead (a fee for operating expenses in one's institution). You would also likely be required to provide justification for the line items in the budget (e.g. explain why an MP3 player is needed, give the rationale for travel expenses). Even if no funding would be available for your project, you should consider what items would be needed and what costs you would likely incur.

References

Using APA format (or another format required by your reviewers), provide a list of the references cited in your proposal.

Appendices (Optional)

Additional material that supports and enhances your proposal may be included in the appendix, such as questionnaire or interview protocols, informed consent forms, or theoretical models. Each separate appendix should be lettered (e.g. Appendix A,

Appendix B, etc.). The order they are presented in is dictated by the order they are mentioned in the text of the report. You must refer to each appendix within the proposal.

Conclusion

Even if a formal proposal is not required for your research project, I hope this chapter has convinced you that it is well worth the effort. Preparing a well-organized, detailed research proposal will force you to think more deeply about what you are going to do and why. It can identify areas that you still need to work on to ensure a successful study. A detailed description of your project, along with a sensible timeline, can help you to stay on track as you carry out your research. Also, bear in mind that it is natural for a project to change as it takes shape, especially if you are doing an exploratory study and/or working with qualitative data instead of conducting a strictly controlled study (e.g. experimental design). Whatever topic you explore, I wish you much success as you embark on your Intercultural Communication project!

Key Terms

External validity The degree to which the results of a research study can be generalized to individuals and situations beyond those involved in the project.

Internal validity In an experiment, the degree to which extraneous variables have been controlled by the researcher such that any observed effects can be attributed to the treatment.

Research design The overall plan for collecting data in order to answer the research question. It outlines the specific data analysis techniques or methods that the researcher plans to use.

Research proposal A detailed description of a proposed study or project designed to investigate a given problem.

Sampling The process of selecting a number of individuals (a sample) from a population, preferably in such a way that the individuals are representative of the larger group from which they were selected.

References

Abbuhl, R. (2012). Why, when, and how to replicate research. In A. Mackey, & S. M. Gass (Eds.), *Research methods in second language acquisition: A practical guide* (pp. 296–312). Oxford: Wiley-Blackwell.

Antonius, R. (2013). *Interpreting quantitative data with IBM SPSS statistics.* (2nd ed.). Thousand Oaks, CA: Sage.

Bazeley, P., & Jackson, K. (2013). *Qualitative data analysis with NVivo*. (2nd ed.). Thousand Oaks, CA: Sage.
Beins, B. C. (2013). *Research methods: A tool for life* (3rd ed.). Boston: Pearson.
Boeije, H. R. (2009). *Analysis in qualitative research*. Thousand Oaks, CA: Sage.
Collier, S. (2011). Negotiating business, negotiating self: Crossing cultural borders in bilingual entrepreneurial contexts. *Journal of Language, Identity, and Education*, 10(1), 1–21.
Comstock, G. (2013). *Research ethics: A philosophical guide to the responsible conduct of research*. Cambridge: Cambridge University Press.
Creswell, J. W. (2013). *Qualitative inquiry and research design: Choosing among five approaches*. Thousand Oaks, CA: Sage.
Creswell, J. W. (2014). *Research design: Qualitative, quantitative, and mixed methods approaches* (4th ed.). Thousand Oaks, CA: Sage.
Fink, (2014). *Conducting research literature reviews: From the internet to paper* (4th ed.). Thousand Oaks, CA: Sage.
Flick, U. (2013). *The Sage handbook of qualitative data analysis*. Thousand Oaks, CA: Sage.
Gibbs, G. (2012). *Analyzing qualitative data*. Thousand Oaks, CA: Sage.
Grbich, C. (2012). *Qualitative data analysis*. (2nd ed.). Thousand Oaks, CA: Sage.
González-Riaño, X., Hevia-Artime, I., & Fernández-Costales, A. (2013). Language attitudes of Asturian students in the area of Navia-Eo. *Language and Intercultural Communication*, 13(4), 450–469.
Hittleman, D. R., & Simon, A. J. (2006). *Interpreting educational research: An introduction for consumers of research*. Upper Saddle River, NJ: Pearson Merrill Prentice Hall.
Machi, L. A., & McEvoy, B. T. (2009). *The literature review*. Thousand Oaks, CA: Corwin.
Maxwell, J. A. (2013) *Qualitative research design: An interactive approach*. Thousand Oaks, CA: Sage.
Moloney, R. (2013). The role of teacher communication in online collaborative language learning between a Chinese and an Australian school: a cautionary tale. *Language and Intercultural Communication*, 13(4), 400–415.
Paulus, T., Lester, J., & Dempster, P. (2013). *Digital tools for qualitative research*. Thousand Oaks, CA: Sage.
Perry, F. L. (2011). *Research in applied linguistics: Becoming a discerning consumer*. (2nd ed.). London: Routledge.
Pike, K. L. (1954). *Language in relation to a unified theory of the structure of human behavior, Part I*. Glendale, CA: Summer Institute of Linguistics.
Porte, G. (2012). *Replication studies in applied linguistics*. Cambridge: Cambridge University Press.
Richards, L., & Morse, J. M. (2012). *Read me first for a user's guide to qualitative methods*. Thousand Oaks, CA: Sage.
Shamoo, A. E., & Resnik, D. B. (2009). *Responsible conduct of research* (2nd ed.). Oxford: Oxford University Press.
Spencer-Oatey, H., & Franklin, P. (2009). *Intercultural interaction: A multidisciplinary approach to intercultural communication*, Basingstoke: Palgrave Macmillan.
Vanderstoep, S. W., & Johnston, D. D. (2009). *Research methods for everyday life: Blending qualitative and quantitative approaches*. San Francisco: Jossey-Bass.
Vogt, W. P., Gardner, D. C., & Haeffele, L. M. (2012). *When to use what research design*. New York; Guilford Press.
Walliman, N. (2011). *Research methods: The basics*. London: Routledge.

Further Reading and Resources

Beins, B. C. (2014). *Successful research projects: A step-by-step guide*. Thousand Oaks, CA: Sage.

Creswell, J. (2014). *Research design: Qualitative, quantitative, and mixed methods Approaches* (4th ed.). Thousand Oaks, CA: Sage.

Leedy, P. D., & Ormrod, J. E. (2014). *Practical research: Planning and design* (10th ed.) Harlow: Pearson Education.

O'Leary, Z. (2010). *The essential guide to doing your research project.* Thousand Oaks, CA: Sage.

Walliman, N. (2014) *Your research project: A step-by-step guide for the first-time researcher*, Thousand Oaks, CA: Sage.

Part III Methods

11 Questionnaires and Surveys

Tony Johnstone Young

> **Summary**
>
> Survey methodologies, usually using questionnaires, are among the most popular in the social sciences, but they are also among the most misused. Their popularity in small-scale intercultural research is associated with perceived ease of use, and the access they can give to large amounts of data which are analyzable by even very inexperienced researchers. Problems can derive from mismatches between paradigms, research questions and instruments. They can also arise for reasons relating to sampling, instrument design, low response rates, and over-claims for what data from a small sample can really say about a population. This chapter details these potential pitfalls but also shows how the application of relatively simple, tried-and-trusted techniques can avoid them. It also gives a brief overview of approaches to data analysis, and discusses the purposes that questionnaire-based research can serve as part of a mixed-methods design.

What this Method is About

A survey aims to make inferences about a population by examining a sample from that population. This contrasts with a census, which aims to make observations drawn from an entire population. A population here is the group of objects in the world in which the researcher is interested, where objects may include individuals, families, students in a university class, and people sharing a nationality, ethnicity, or cultural background (Groves *et al*, 2009). In terms of their social ontology – their disposition in relation to social entities like "cultures" – social science researchers employing survey methodologies tend more towards an objectivist position, i.e. one that assumes that social phenomena and their meanings have an existence that is separate from social actors, although this position has been softening somewhat over recent years. This shift has particularly been the case in recent intercultural research derived from or influenced by applied linguistics, especially where a general change towards a more constructivist position has taken place (see Part 1 of this volume, and Young & Woodin, 2010). Social phenomena used in everyday discourse from the position of objectivism are seen as having an existence which is in some way "real" and so definable and categorizable: they have an existence independent of social actors (Bryman, 2004). A key example of this is, of course, the idea of a culture (see Holliday, Chapter 2, this volume).

Related to an objectivist stance is a particular view of what counts as knowledge, a particular epistemology (discussed in Zhu Hua, Chapter 1, this volume). Survey-based methodologies in the social sciences have traditionally tended to take a positivist epistemological position, derived from and related to those employed in the natural sciences such as physics or chemistry. Positivism has been variously defined, but can be summarized as a belief that facts are real and discernible (see Chapters 1, 2 & 3, this volume). Social research starting from this position is usually conducted like this:

- Theory is used to try to explain observed realities – why different groups of people see the same behavior as polite or impolite, for example.
- Hypotheses should then be drawn which are explicit and related to this theory – that groups X and Y have the same broad understandings of what politeness is, but different ideas about how it should be manifested, for example.
- Research questions are then formulated to test the hypotheses.
- Valid and reliable data are gathered using a carefully constructed instrument, perhaps a questionnaire. The data are either quantitative or qualitative. Validity refers to whether data "are what the researcher says they are" – so, for example, whether participants answering questionnaire items about their views on what politeness is have given their honest and informed opinions, and not just what they think the researcher wants to hear. Reliability refers to the stability and consistency of data – for example, whether similar data would be got if the same questionnaire was used with a different sample from the same population – if different people also belonging to group X gave the same responses to those group X members sampled in my "perceptions of politeness" project, for instance.
- These data are analyzed using explicit and appropriate techniques – statistical for quantitative data, or through coding (for example) for qualitative data. If I have numeric responses to my questionnaire I might test these to see if group X gave a statistically significantly different response to an item from that given by members of group Y. If I have more discursive data – perhaps in response to an open question (see below), I might analyze this to see if people from the different groups describe the same behavior using different adjectives, for example.

- Conclusions and inferences are drawn which generalize what has been found in the sample surveyed to a wider population. These can be related back to the theory and might tend to confirm, problematize, add nuance or detail to, or refute the theory, or aspects of it.

Anyone deciding to undertake survey-based research needs to be sure that their own ontological and epistemological stances are compatible with this methodology. They should also be aware of the practical considerations related to sampling, design and administration as detailed below.

Why this Method and Why Not

Surveys are most commonly conducted using some form of questionnaire. These are also variously known as "inventories," "tests," "batteries," "checklists," "scales," "surveys," "schedules," "indexes," or "indicators" (Dörnyei, 2007). Questionnaires are defined as any text-based instrument that give survey participants a series of questions to answer or statements to respond to, either by indicating a response – by marking a page, writing a number or checking a box on paper or online, for example, Brown, 2001. It is possible, if more time-consuming and probably expensive, to conduct a survey using structured individual interviews, but questionnaires remain the single most common means of conducting surveys and are indeed probably one of, if not *the*, most commonly used research tools in the social sciences (Fife-Schaw, 2006). Questionnaires seem particularly appealing to less experienced researchers such as students doing dissertation projects, and this may be for the following reasons.

- They are easy to construct, or at least can appear to be so.
- There are many extant questionnaires which can be used or adapted for use, and which are often freely available to researchers.
- They are portable or can be made available online.
- They can be used to gather large datasets relatively easily, either through direct contact, by mail, or online via the web or email.
- The data they gather can be processed and analyzed relatively easily compared to spoken data, which has to be recorded and transcribed before analysis.

It is certainly true that a well-designed questionnaire, appropriately administered, will tick many of these boxes. Questionnaires are very frequently used for things like:

- reporting participants' background and demographic information (age, biological sex, nationality, income);
- reporting behaviors (what people did, or would do, in response to certain cues or stimuli, for example);
- expressing attitudes (towards a cultural group other than their own, for example);

- reporting opinions (about the desirability of multiculturalism or other social phenomena);
- determining their factual knowledge about something (what proportion of a country's population are immigrants, for example);
- determining psychometric properties (such as the degree of extroversion a person exhibits);
- determining their future intentions or aspiration (about whether they will, or would like to, have contact with particular groups of people, for example).

Questionnaire-based studies have, however, been critiqued for a number of reasons, and researchers considering using them should be fully aware of their potential negative side. In this regard, the predominant ontological and epistemological positioning of the theory informing most surveys has been a major target of criticism. Here, a reliance on broad-brush, *a-priori* categorization has been identified which is particularly pertinent to research into matters intercultural (Young & Sercombe, 2010; Part 1, this volume). Additionally, questionnaires have been criticized for superficiality and providing a relatively "thin" description of target phenomena (Dörnyei, 2007). To a certain extent, if this is a concern it can be mitigated by the use of other data, which can be related to questionnaire-derived data in order to get a more nuanced, explanatorily complex picture (for example, semi-structured interviews – see Gibson & Zhu Hua, Chapter 12 of this volume). This is a benefit frequently claimed for mixed-methods studies, discussed below.

Issues of validity related to the translation of questionnaires, and to a bias towards socially desirable responses are also particularly pertinent to intercultural research. Translation issues can be addressed by back-translation, where a researcher has their questionnaire translated into the target language, then has this version translated back into the first language by someone else. If the final version is close enough in meaning (if not word-for-word identical, which is very rarely the case), then the translation is taken to be reliable (see Holmes, Fay, Andrews, & Attia, Chapter 6 of this volume, for a more detailed treatment of researching multilingually). Issues of socially desirable responding are subtler and in many ways more difficult to mitigate. Different groups in different parts of the world have differing degrees of exposure to "being surveyed." Among some groups, questionnaires may only be encountered when administered by universities, governments, or other authorities, and by people who are not used to ideas like research or scientific enquiry. In such cases a certain bias of response might be expected (Fife-Schaw, 2006). More subtly, some researchers have identified phenomena related to acquisition bias – a perceived tendency for some people, and groups of people, to place greater value on moderate, middle-of-the-road responses, or on affirmative responses (Hui & Triandis, 1989). Strategies for correction for acquisition bias include not having mid items on scales. More generally, while validity can never be fully assured, it can be promulgated if questionnaires clearly but respectfully state their expectations of respondents, and if anonymity and/or confidentiality are both assured and maintained (see also Deardorff, chapter 8 of this volume for a discussion of the ethics of researching cross-culturally, and below for issues of validity of responses and questionnaire format and design).

How to Do It

Sampling

Probability sampling

Given sufficient resources, probability sampling tends to be employed by researchers undertaking questionnaire-based research. A probability sample is one that has been selected randomly in some way, so that each unit in a population has a known chance of being selected (Bryman, 2004). So, for example, if one in a hundred students at a university are chosen randomly to participate in a project, and no further selection criteria are employed – for example, gender, nationality, or age – then it can be assumed that what this sample tells you should be closely representative of the views of all of the students, regardless of individuals' gender, nationality, or age. Probability sampling increases the chance of a representative sample being obtained, and decreases the chance of a sampling error, where the sample does not represent the population as a whole.

It is very difficult, however, to select a truly representative sample. Given the very small-scale nature of most intercultural student research, probability sampling is beyond most intercultural researchers as it is simply too painstaking and costly to undertake (Dörnyei, 2007).

Non-probability sampling

A much more realistic aspiration for most intercultural researchers is non-probability sampling, and the vast majority of student questionnaire research undertaken at undergraduate, postgraduate taught, and postgraduate research levels employs this approach. Two broad forms of non-probability sampling are particularly common and useful: these are convenience and snowball sampling. Less common, but still conforming to a non-probability model, is quota sampling.

Convenience sampling is self-explanatory. It involves the researcher choosing participants simply for reasons of ease of access, in terms of physical proximity, accessibility, the timing of the administration of the survey, or the willingness of people to participate, for example. For these reasons a student researcher's peer group at university, or a friendship group, may form the pool from which a convenience sample can be drawn. Convenience sampling is slightly frowned upon by many in social science research as it can make any claims of generalizability particularly difficult. It can also be influenced by the nature of the sample – people who voluntarily respond to surveys may be more interested in the subject matter under investigation than a general population. It is good practice, therefore, to highlight when writing up research the characteristics that a convenience sample shares with the wider population, but also to clearly delineate the limitations imposed on conclusions by the nature of the sample.

Snowball sampling is where a researcher contacts a small number of people who are in the interest group for the project in the first instance. As well as surveying this initial group, the researcher also uses them as a source for other participants, by, perhaps, asking these respondents to supply the researcher with friends' contact details, or asking them to encourage their friends to complete the survey. Snowball sampling is particularly useful where the researcher might find it hard to identify members of a group, perhaps because they are clandestine (drug users or gang members), or because the researcher only knows or has good access to a very few members of the target population, as is often the case where a sojourning "international" student researcher, say, wishes to get access to a large sample from the host community. Snowball sampling shares many of the framing problems inherent in convenience sampling – the sample cannot be said to be random as its relationship to the general population is not clearly discernible. It does, however, share the advantage of being a quick, cheap and convenient way of accessing participants, and given the nature of most student research in particular, this is of vital importance.

Quota sampling, sometimes known as dimensional sampling, starts with a sampling frame which is then divided, proportionally, into subgroups, with the proportions being determined by the overall parameters of the group and subgroups. If a researcher is interested in comparing the intercultural competence of people who have travelled abroad with those who haven't, she might recruit 50 participants from each group, if other data are available that indicate that about 50% of the population have been abroad. If only 30% of the population have been abroad she would recruit 30 who have been abroad and 70 who haven't: the sample is simply framed by the "abroad/not abroad" division. This means that data derived from a quota can be presented as more representative of a larger population than data derived from convenience or snowball samples, but the researcher has to be careful not to push claims of generalizability too far. Quota sampling still conforms to a non-probability model, although it is often presented as fully generalizable in its use in market research or political opinion polling, where it is the predominant model. Here the polling companies can be fairly secure in their knowledge of larger population data – through sophisticated analysis of data from a national census, for example. This means they are able to extrapolate subgroup findings pretty securely, and so can make predictions of voting patterns across a country (for example) with a high degree of accuracy. People conducting small-scale research will find it difficult to convincingly argue that their framing of subgroups reflects such wide patterns, and so, as ever, need to be modest in their claims.

Sample Size

Most student researchers interested in conducting survey-based research ask (aloud, or otherwise) one main question before they begin to get data – "how many questionnaires do I need to get completed?" (or a variant to the same effect). This is also the case with other research methods which involve actively recruiting participants. ("How many interviews do I need to conduct…?"). To the student this is a perfectly reasonable, pragmatic, and important question, getting to the very heart of the practicalities of doing a dissertation project as well and as efficiently as possible. For a project adviser or supervisor, however, it is usually a very knotty question, and one which can only properly be answered with "it depends."

What does survey sample size depend on, above and beyond the practical problems of accessibility, time constraints and cost issues identified above? The other main issues to consider are related to the statistics garnered in quantitative research. Dörnyei (2007, p. 99) gives the following "magic" fractions for the number of participants relative to the size of the population being surveyed, for a study aiming only to *describe* features of a population. Here he recommends that between 1% and 10% of the population should be sampled, with a minimum of 100 participants as a rule of thumb. Features surveyed with this kind of design may include average responses to a question (expressed as means, medians or modes); the range of responses given (from minimum to maximum) and the average disparity of scores (standard deviation, SD), where a high SD indicates considerable disparity in responses, and a low SD, logically enough, indicating more uniformity around mean responses. My experience as both a researcher and as a research supervisor is that small-scale research projects which do not aim for generalizability beyond the sample, or whose findings can be triangulated with other data (in mixed method studies, for example, as discussed below), can be considerably smaller: good projects can survey as few as 20–30 participants provided the researcher is very careful not to make over-statements about findings (see the treatment of the open response questionnaire data in Young & Schartner, 2014, for an example of how this might be done). Essentially, sound basic principles are to know (and state, in your write-up) the limits of what your sample allows you to deduce, and to be careful not to over-claim about the generalizability or significance of your findings.

For inferential research designs, it is generally recognized that samples may be smaller, although given the nature of the statistical analyses employed, bigger is usually better. Inferential research includes statistically valid procedures which allow the researcher to talk about findings in relation to their statistical significance, as discussed above. Dörnyei (2007) recommends the following rough estimates: correlational research – at least 30 participants; comparative and experimental research – at least 15 participants in each group; factor analysis and multivariate procedures – at least 100 participants. He also suggests that researchers might adopt a "reverse approach" (see also Bryman's 1988, p. 28 "reverse operationalism"). Here, because tests of statistical significance take account of sample size, researchers begin at the end, as it were, by approximating the magnitude of power of the expected results of the tests. They then determine the sample size that is needed to reveal this effect, if it is actually there. So, for example, at a $p < .05$ level of significance an expected correlation of .40 would require at least 25 participants. Most statistical texts contain correlational tables which can be referred to for help with this, and free web versions are available.

Format Design

Overall Presentation

It is absolutely vital to get the overall "look" of a questionnaire right. Any questionnaire, even a very long one extending over a number of pages, is much more likely to be completed if it has as uncluttered a layout as possible. If the questionnaire is in too small a font (below 10 points, perhaps), has tiny margins or is single-spaced, it can be awkward to complete and this too will deter people. So a design which balances overall length with clear presentation is optimal. The overall length of a questionnaire is determined by the nature of the enquiry being undertaken, but another sound basic principle is to make it as short as possible, with no redundancies such as questions about demographic information which the researcher isn't actually interested in.

An example of a pen-and-paper questionnaire with a clear, accessible design is the "Learning style survey" produced by Rebecca Oxford and colleagues http://www.carla.umn.edu/maxsa/documents/LearningStyleSurvey_MAXSA_IG.pdf. Most free or low-cost online surveys which researchers can use come ready-built with a clear overall look, and ease of navigation. See, for example, Zoho.com http://www.zoho.com/survey/, or "Free online surveys" at http://freeonlinesurveys.com/.

Component Parts

It is helpful if a questionnaire is formatted in a standard way. Most respondents are likely to have completed questionnaires before, and it is useful if the researcher can conform to their expectations, as this should increase response rate. Most questionnaires consist of a title, some general information about the research project; instructions or guidance for completion, with examples; and final, additional information.

- The *title* identifies the general subject matter of the questionnaire, and gives respondents clear orientation towards its topic area.
- The *general information* section, in most questionnaires states the purpose of the research, and indicates its subject matter. It is, however, advisable to describe the purpose of the study without being "leading" – so tell people you are interested in their experiences as travelers, don't tell them that you are interested in whether women are better travelers than men. Emphasize (and ensure) that responses are completely anonymous or confidential, and that respondents should be as sincere as possible, to help ensure the validity of responses. It is now widely recognized as good practice to ask people to sign something to indicate that they understand and consent to take part. Any signatures might identify a respondent, so you should consider having these on a separate page which can be discarded and destroyed (or deleted) once you have checked that consent has been given (see Woodin, Chapter 7, this volume, for a consideration of research ethics). Consider thanking people for their participation both here *and* at the end of the survey. This is one situation where you really can't thank people enough – your project depends on their willing participation, so hyperpoliteness is appropriate.
- *Instructions or guidance* should be as clear and simple as possible. It is a good idea to both tell and to show people what you want them to do, so give examples formatted exactly like the items they relate to. If item styles change from section to section – from a ranking exercise to a multiple choice, for example – always give the instructions for the new section at the top of that section, and

not as part of the general information. When asking closed questions, a common mistake made by less experienced researchers is not to indicate whether more than one answer is acceptable. In these cases, instructions can be framed like this:
- *Please tick/check only ONE box per item.*
- *Please tick/check ALL the answers that you think are right.*
  If participants tick more than one box and they aren't supposed to, this will invalidate the relevant data.
- *Questionnaire items* themselves should be clearly separated from instructions. Their format is considered below.
- *Additional information* may include a researcher's contact name and email, if these aren't included in the introduction, and "thanks" (again). If you want to get in touch with participants, to take part in follow-up research or to let them have a summary of findings or a link to the research when published – they can indicate their willingness here too, perhaps by giving you their email address. Be very careful to ensure confidentiality if this happens, and let people know that you will only use contact details for these purposes, and won't divulge them to any third parties or use them for any other purpose without permission.

Item Sequence

It can be off-putting to present respondents with requests for demographic information at the beginning of a questionnaire, so there's a growing trend across the social sciences to put this at the end (Fife-Schaw, 2006). Dörnyei (2007, p. 111) recommends that opening items in a questionnaire should be "interesting, relatively simple, yet at the same time focussed on important and salient aspects." Most questionnaires employing both closed and open-ended items (discussed below) have the latter at the end, as they usually require more of participants, with the idea of encouraging a balance of effort across completion. This can, however, have the negative consequence of reducing the response rate to these questions. So, if responses to open-ended questions are the main dataset of interest to the researcher, these should be put at or near the beginning.

Item Types and their Design

"Closed" items give a clear and overt range of possible responses and ask people to choose one or more of these. "Open" or "open-ended" items simply invite a response without giving any particular options, and are often framed as either "Wh-" or "How…?" questions, or as requests – "Please tell us more about your opinions related to…," or simply "Please explain" (perhaps after they have indicated "other" among as range of possibilities). Sometimes they might involve sentence completion – "What I find most difficult about communicating with people who don't speak my language(s) is… ." Closed questions have the perceived advantage of producing quantitative data which is easier to numerically code, and so statistically analyze. Open-ended data can be analyzed quantitatively (through word-frequency counts, for example), but is more usually treated qualitatively.

Dörnyei (2003) lists the main types of closed questions used in questionnaire research in applied linguistics, and his list is also pertinent to research involving language and intercultural communication. He identifies three main types of graduated responses items – Likert scales, semantic differential scales, and numerical ratings scales – and also lists true–false items, multiple-choice items, and rank-order items.

Likert scales: These consist of a stimulus statement which people respond to by indicating how much (or little) they agree with it.

An example Likert scale item:

I found the intercultural effectiveness program intellectually stimulating					
Strongly agree	Agree	Neither agree nor disagree	Disagree	Strongly disagree
	X			

To analyze responses, each response option is given a numerical value (Strongly agree = 5, strongly disagree = 1) and the average response (usually a mean) determined.

Semantic differential scales also give a graduated response. Here, people are asked to indicate where on a continuum between opposite adjectives or adverbs their own response belongs. For example:

I found the content of the intercultural effectiveness training program:

boring __ : __ : __ : __ : _ _ : __ : _X_ : __ : __ *interesting*

I agreed to do the intercultural effectiveness program:

willingly __ : __ : __ : __ : _ _ : __ : _X_ : __ : __ *unwillingly*

Again, for analytical purposes, a numerical value is assigned to responses – the response to the first example above would be recorded as 7 (out of 9 on a scale of "how interesting"). The response to the second example would probably, however, be recorded as 3 out of 9, on a scale of "how willingly," as it is a negatively framed item. In graduated response, closed question surveys of all types, negatively framed items are often mixed in with a large number of positively framed items – for example where more positive or affirmative response are generally on the right, for a couple of items out of ten these may be on the left instead. This is to encourage respondents to really engage with items, and not simply put their ticks or checks in the same places down the page. For analytical purposes, researchers have to remember to "reverse code" such items, so that the example relating to "willingness" above would be coded as 3 (out of 9).

Numerical ratings scales do more or less the same thing, but explicitly ask people to give "a mark out of *x*" to a feature of the target, like a star rating on a review site.

What did you think of the content of the intercultural effectiveness training program?		
Very good	5	
Good	4	X
Fair	3	
Poor	2	
Very poor	1	

The Wording of Items

Getting the wording right in items is essential. Badly worded items produce either no response or a response which is invalid. All questionnaires should be rigorously piloted before they are used in a research project proper. During piloting, ask a subgroup of participants to both complete your draft questionnaire, and to reflect on its design, with a particular emphasis on the wording of items, to determine if any were ambiguous or badly phrased. If any were, reformulate them and pilot them again.

The following general guidance should help with item design:

- Keep language as simple as possible – avoid jargon or complex vocabulary.
- Avoid "double-loading" items. Don't use items like "I enjoyed the course and found it useful." People might agree with "enjoyed" but not with "useful."
- Avoid vague adjectives or adverbials – "The course was fine" or "I hardly ever go abroad" are hard to respond to accurately with a true or false, for example.

See also Bryman, 2004 Chapter 6 for advice on questionnaire design for application to research in the social sciences in general, and Dörnyei, 2007 section 5.2.4 for more detailed discussions and examples related to item design in language-based research. Harkness et al. (2010) is a useful and highly detailed chapter on questionnaire design for comparative research involving multilingual, international and intercultural populations.

Administration

There is little point in designing your own – or finding and adapting – an excellent questionnaire if no one completes it. A major headache which confronts many inexperienced researchers especially is a low, or lower than expected, response rate. Whole projects have foundered on this. You therefore should do as much as possible to try to ensure as high a response rate as is reasonably possible, given constraints of time and other resources.

A first consideration in administering your questionnaire is its mode of delivery. Options here are:

1. Pencil-and-paper, sent via the post, by email or administered in person. Administration in person can be done individually, or to a group. The latter is usually a more efficient and effective means of getting a high number of responses if the researcher can access a large enough group – a class at a school or university, for example, if appropriate permissions have been given. If informed consent can be obtained from participants, and they do have the option of opting out if they wish to, this often works well as a source for data for small-scale projects. Email questionnaires that have to be downloaded and perhaps printed before completion are more fiddly for participants and so can lead to a much lower response rate. Completion online and return as an attachment is better, but if you have gone to the trouble of designing an e-questionnaire, you may as well make it fully accessible and compliable online, as this makes things easier both for your respondents and for you to collect and analyze the data, so long as you and they have ready access to the internet.
2. Online design, collection, and analysis of questionnaire data is becoming increasingly cheap, sophisticated, and widespread. The free sites named above, or sites such as Survey Monkey, allow for both free and paid use: paid use gives users more sophisticated functionality, including data analysis, allows for larger sample sizes and more options on how findings can be presented. Such sites are now readily accessible to most researchers, and are very easy to use both as design tools and for participants (see https://www.surveymonkey.com/). Most researchers email a link to their questionnaire to their sample, or let people know about it via social media, and use follow-up prompts and reminders to encourage participation.
3. A combination of both pencil-and-paper and online also usually helps to increase response rate. Both online and pencil-and-paper versions of your questionnaire should be as near identical in format as possible, to foster reliability. If you combine the two modes of delivery you should state in your methodology section or chapter that you used these two modes in combination, and also consider, in your presentation of findings or in your conclusions, whether the different modes might have affected findings in any way – if group X completed things entirely in-person and group Y entirely online, for example, were response rates different between the two groups, and what effect might this have on generalizability or comparison between the two groups? If there's any possibility of an effect from the different modes of delivery, you should state this as a limitation in your conclusions.

Data Analysis

Space does not allow for a detailed treatment of data analysis here. Enough to say that quantitative survey data can be analyzed by transferring raw data into an application such as Microsoft Excel or IBM's SPSS, either manually or automatically, depending on the mode of administration. SPSS especially allows the full range of complex inferential statistical tests to be run, other applications are generally less general in their functionality, often limited to descriptive statistics such as measures of central tendency. SPSS is rather expensive for individual researchers to access, but most university libraries, in Europe and North America at least, hold licenses which allow use for researchers associated with their institutions. Qualitative questionnaire data, such as responses to open-ended prompts or questions, can be analyzed using qualitative techniques such as thematic content analysis (Boyatzis, 1998). This can be facilitated by applications such as *Nvivo*, again an expensive option for the lone researcher, but often available to users of university libraries.

A good general introduction to statistical analysis is Lowie & Seton (2013). See Bryman, 2004 Chapter 11 for a general overview of quantitative data analysis, and Gibson & Zhu Hua (Chapter 12, this volume) for details of how to use SPSS. Bryman, 2004, Chapter 20 also gives a clear and useful introduction to the use of *Nvivo*.

Mixed-methods Research Using Surveys

There is a growing consensus that mixed-methods research offers a way forward for social research (e.g. Hammersley, 1992; Johnson & Onwuegbuzie, 2004). From this ecumenical position, worth is seen in both the positivist and the constructivist perspectives (see Zhu Hua, Chapter 1, this volume). Well-designed research should be able to combine the quantitative and the qualitative into a single design, provided this is done in a clear and purposeful manner.

Hammersley (1996) proposes three broad purposes for mixed-methods social research.

1 **Triangulation,** which refers to the use of quantitative research to corroborate qualitative findings, or vice versa. Data are validated if they converge with data derived from another source, or problematized if they seem to diverge. Triangulation is particularly useful to many small-scale researchers as it might be difficult to draw inferences from a data from a small number of interviews without a larger sample of quantitative questionnaire data to confirm suppositions, for example.
2 **Facilitation,** which is when one research strategy is used to make using another possible, or more effective. So, for example qualitative data derived from interviews may be used to formulate, or to sharpen, a hypothesis that will inform the research questions underlying a quantitative questionnaire. Another aspect of facilitation is the use of qualitative data to give a more fine-grained, detailed picture of what informs people's attitudes and opinions than a simple statement of these attitudes and opinions allows – qualitative data's "why" combines well with quantitative data's "what."
3 **Complimentarity,** which refers to two different research strategies being used so that different aspects of an investigation can be made to "speak" to each other. An example of this is the study described in Young & Schartner (2014) where longitudinal, qualitative data from semi-structured interviews was used in conjunction with a survey of summative academic achievement data to examine, respectively, the adjustment and the adaptation of students of cross-cultural communication at

a UK university, and so enable the researchers to get a picture of both the processes involved over time, and "bottom line" outcomes of a program of cross-cultural communication education.

Mixed-methods research involving a survey methodology is increasing in popularity in intercultural research, particularly among small-scale researchers, as it can combine the advantages of, and mitigate the disadvantages of, research which operates solely under a quantitative or a qualitative paradigm.

Case in Point

Young, T. J., Sercombe, P. G., Sachdev, I., Naeb, R. & Schartner, A. (2013). Success factors for international postgraduate students' adjustment: exploring the roles of intercultural competence, language proficiency, social contact and social support. *European Journal of Higher Education, 3(2)*, 151–171.

Research questions:
1 How do the intercultural competence, English language proficiency, social contact, and social support of "international" postgraduate students at a UK university relate to different aspects of academic achievement measured over their whole program?
2 How do these contributory factors relate to students' psychological wellbeing, experienced during the program of study?
3 How do they relate to students' satisfaction with life in the new environment during the program of study?

Research design: A mixed-methods study using a questionnaire comprised of demographic information, various psychometric instruments and an open response question, triangulated with data from semi-structured interviews conducted over the program of study.
Participants: Questionnaire participants were 108 non-UK Masters students doing a program in the humanities or social sciences. Interviewees were a subsample of six of these students.
Analysis: Quantitative survey data was analyzed both for descriptive information (percentages of responses and measures of central tendency) and inferentially, for the relationships between the contributory factors and each outcome. Thematic Content Analysis was employed on both the interview transcripts, and on responses to the final open survey question. The thematic focus in the analysis of both sets of qualitative data was students' comments on their own broadly successful and unsuccessful adjustment to the social and academic demands of their sojourn. Subthemes also emerged from analysis relating to each of these broad areas. Qualitative and quantitative datasets were cross-analyzed with the qualitative data being examined to both corroborate and add explanatory detail to the findings of the quantitative data.
Findings: Findings from all datasets indicated strong associations between participants' academic achievement, satisfaction with life in the new environment

and psychological wellbeing, and aspects of their intercultural competence, contact with non-conationals, including hosts, and with their language proficiency. Generalizability was limited to the postgraduate taught population of non-UK students studying in that country, although it was suggested future research using the same research design might extend enquiries beyond that group.

Key Terms

Generalizability Whether data from a sample are really representative of the population.
Population The group of people or objects that the survey is investigating.
Reliability Whether data derived from one sample of a population would also be derived from another sample of the same population, if the same techniques and instruments were employed again.
Sample A representative subgroup of the population that can be surveyed to draw appropriate about the population as a whole.
Validity Whether data are what a researcher says they are, measure what the researcher says they measure, or show what the researcher says they show.

References

Boyatzis, R. E. (1998). *Transforming qualitative information: Thematic analysis and code development* (2nd ed.). London: Sage.
Brown, J. D. (2001). *Using surveys in language programs*. Cambridge: Cambridge University Press.
Bryman, A. (1988). *Quantity and quality in social research*. London: Routledge.
Bryman, A. (2004). *Social research methods* (2nd ed.). Oxford: Oxford University Press.
Dörnyei, Z. (2003). Attitudes, orientations and motivation in language learning: Advances in theory, research and applications. *Language Learning*, 53, 3–32.
Dörnyei, Z. (2007). *Research methods in applied linguistics*. Oxford: Oxford University Press.
Fife-Schaw, C. (2006). Questionnaire design. In G. Breakwell, J.A. Smith & D.B. Wright (Eds.), *Research methods in psychology* (3rd ed.). London: Sage.
Groves, R.M., Fowler, F.J., Couper, M.P., Lepkowski, J.M., Singer, E. & Tourangeau, R. (2009). *Survey methodology* (2nd ed.). New York: Wiley.
Harkness, J.A., Edwards, B., Hansen, S.E., Miller, D.R. & Villar, A. (2010). Designing questionnaires for multipopulation research. In A. Harkness, M. Braun, B. Edwards, T. P. Johnson, L.E. Lyberg, P. Mohler et al. (Eds.), *Survey methods in multicultural, multinational, and multiregional contexts* (2nd ed., pp. 33–58). New York: Wiley.
Hammersley, M. (1992). Deconstructing the qualitative-quantitative divide. In M. Hammersley (Ed.), *What's wrong with ethnography* (pp. 159–182). London: Routledge.
Hammersley, M. (1996). The relationship between qualitative and quantitative research: Paradigm loyalty versus methodological eclecticism. In J.T.E. Richardson (Ed.), *Handbook of research methods for psychology and the social sciences* (pp. 159–174). Leicester: BPS Books.

Hui, C.H. & Triandis, H.C. (1989). Effects of culture and response format on extreme response style. *Journal of Cross-Cultural Psychology*, 29, 296–309.

Johnson, R.B. & Onwuegbuzie, A. J. (2004). Mixed research methods: A research paradigm whose time has come. *Educational Researcher*, 33(7), 14–26.

Lowie, W. & Seton, B. (2013). *Essential statistics for Applied Linguistics*. Basingstoke: Palgrave McMillan.

Young, T. J. & Sercombe, P.G. (2010). Communication, discourses and interculturality. *Language and Intercultural Communication*, 10(3), 181–188.

Young, T. J. & Schartner, A. (2014). The effects of cross-cultural communication education on international students' adjustment and adaptation. *Journal of Multilingual and Multicultural Development*, 35(6), 547–562.

Young, T.J., Sercombe P.G., Sachdev, I., Naeb R. & Schartner, A. (2013). Success factors for international postgraduate students' adjustment: exploring the roles of intercultural competence, language proficiency, social contact and social support. *European Journal of Higher Education*, 3(2), 151–171.

Young, T.J. & Woodin, J.A. (2010). Applied linguistics in Intercultural Communication: Current perspectives and approaches. Paper given at 43rd Annual Meeting of the British Association for Applied Linguistics, University of Aberdeen, UK.

Further Reading and Resources

For cross-national, cross-cultural survey research:

Harkness, J.A., Braun, M., Edwards, B., Johnson, T.P., Lyberg, L.E., Mohler, P. et al. (Eds.). (2010). *Survey methods in multicultural, multinational, and multiregional contexts*. New York: Wiley.

Groves, R.M., Fowler, F.J., Lepkowski, J.M., Singer, E. & Tourangeau, R. (2009). *Survey methodology* (2nd ed.). New York: Wiley.

The work of Jan-Pieter van Oudenhoven, Karen van der Zee and colleagues on and with the *Multicultural Personality Questionnaire* (MPQ) is well worth a look for how a survey instrument can be developed and applied. The MPQ gauges the abilities and predispositions contributing to an individual's adjustment to a new cultural environment, and so gives interesting insights into psychometrics and their application to intercultural research.

For discussion of the MPQ's development and evaluation:

Van der Zee, K.I. & Van Oudenhoven, J. P. (2001). The Multicultural Personality Questionnaire: Reliability and validity of self- and other ratings of multicultural effectiveness. *Journal of Research in Personality*, 35(3), 278–288.

For an example of the MPQ's application:

Van Oudenhoven, J.P. & Van der Zee, K. I. (2002). Predicting multicultural effectiveness of international students: The Multicultural Personality Questionnaire. *International Journal of Intercultural Relations*, 26(6), 679–694.

The questionnaire-based work of Geert Hofstede and colleagues is among the most referenced (and critiqued) in intercultural research. For a detailed treatment of his work, see http://geert-hofstede.com/cultural-survey.html for his "Cultural Compass," and Hofstede, G., Hofstede, G.J. & Minkov, M. (2010). *Cultures and organizations: Software of the mind* (3rd ed.). New York: McGraw-Hill.

12 Interviews

Barbara Gibson and Zhu Hua

> **Summary**
>
> This chapter discusses the use of interviews as a data collection method. Different types of interview are defined, along with consideration of the types of research for which interviews may be best used. Challenges and limitations and other considerations are presented, and practical advice is provided for planning and carrying out interviews and handling data. The chapter includes a Case In Point featuring a research project utilizing interviews to explore intercultural competencies needed by chief executive officers of global companies.

An interview involves two or more people having a discussion for a specific purpose (Kahn & Cannell, 1957, cited in Saunders, Lewis & Thornhill, 2009). The interaction is usually dyadic, with clearly defined roles of interviewer vs interviewee or questioner vs. respondent.

Types of Interview

As a research method, there are a number of different types of interview, depending on how structured interview questions are, how many participants are involved at a time, how interviews are administered, and whether researchers' interest is in the content of answers or the way questions are answered. Each type is specifically suited to different research objectives.

Structured, Semi-Structured or Unstructured Interviews

Structured interviews are similar to written questionnaires (see Young, Chapter 11 of this volume), with set questions that do not vary from one interview to the next. In this type of interview, the interviewer reads the questions and records the answers, remaining neutral and avoiding any variation from one interview to the next. This type of interview tends to be used more for quantitative research, with larger samples, and is better suited to a deductive approach which aims to prove a hypothesis.

At the other extreme, an unstructured interview is well-suited for a qualitative, inductive approach which starts with data and allows patterns and tentative hypothesis to emerge from analysis. Another term for this type of interview is "in-depth interview," because it allows the researcher to explore a topic further, going deeper than it would be possible to do in a standardized format. For this reason, it is particularly useful for exploratory research. In an unstructured interview, the emphasis is not on questions developed in advance (although this should not be confused with a lack of preparation). Instead the focus is on the thoughts, perceptions, and experiences of the interviewee, and the interviewer may allow the interviewee to direct the conversation more, rather than just responding to questions. Charmaz (2006, p. 25) explains, "The interviewer is there to listen, to observe with sensitivity, and to encourage the person to respond. Hence, in this conversation, the participant does most of the talking."

A semi-structured interview may contain elements of both structured and unstructured types. It may include some standardized questions, but the order of the questions may vary; and the interviewer may explore some questions further, or omit others.

Group or Focus Interviews

In some cases, in particular when researchers are interested in gauging a variety of points of views or gathering opinions from a group quickly, it may be appropriate to interview more than one participant at a time. One type of group interview is the focus group interview, which is an organized discussion with a selected group of individuals to elicit their views on a topic. In this type of interview, interviewers, acting as facilitator or moderator of the discussion, encourage interviewees to discuss among themselves and to challenge each other's views. What is of interest for researchers in focus group interviews are diversity and consensus in points of views, interaction within the group, frequency and intensity of comments, and changes of opinions during the discussion. Focus interviews can be used at the preliminary or exploratory stages of a study to generate hypothesis and to prepare for a data collection instrument suitable for a larger sample. The main challenges for focus group interviews are the significantly increased demand on the interviewer to moderate and facilitate discussion and the logistic difficulty in conducting a group interview.

Technology-mediated Interviews

Interviews can be conducted face-to-face, or by telephone, video-conferencing, or other digital technology-mediated methods. The wide availability of video-conferencing now makes it technologically possible to conduct "virtual face-to-face" interviews. Consideration must be given to whether or not the virtual environment impacts openness, or hinders the interviewer's ability to pick up on nonverbal signals. The level of comfort with digital communication may vary based on factors such as age, education, and technological proficiency. So decisions on utilizing digital media for research interviewing must take these things into account. There may, however, be strong arguments in favor of utilizing these platforms, depending on your research aims and sample (i.e., a study examining online communication of university students in three countries).

Allett, Keightley, and Pickering (2011) developed a method they called "self-interviewing," which involves getting respondents to use an audio recorder to record themselves responding to a particular topic and to related media, objects, and/or spaces.

Eliciting Conversational Data through Interviews

Apart from finding out participants' opinions, interviews can be used to elicit conversational or narrative data. Interview is a long-standing means of data collection as part of sociolinguistic fieldwork (Hoffman, 2014) and is used in a relatively new method called narrative analysis (see De Fina, Chapter 22, this volume; Pavlenko, 2008). The conversational data collected through interview can be analyzed in terms of its interactional structural features (e.g. turn-taking, topic initiation and development, repair, etc.), linguistic features (e.g. variations and change in phonetic features, vocabulary, syntax, semantics, etc.), language use (e.g. politeness features, address terms, accommodation strategies, etc.), and narrative structures (e.g. opening, evaluation, details, etc.).

Why Use This Method?

There are a number of reasons to consider interviews as your data collection method, particularly if the nature of your research is *exploratory*, *explanatory*, or *emergent*.

Semi-structured and unstructured interviews are especially useful in exploring a general area in order to gain new insights and define further research questions (Saunders et al, 2009). For this reason, interviews may be useful in the early stages of your research, to inform the direction of the research and help to shape the research questions.

Interviews may provide insight when the research question is about "why." For example, studying "third culture individuals" (TCIs) to gain understanding of their perceptions of their own cultural identities, Moore and Barker (2012) used a method known as biographical phenomenology or life story interviewing. As shown in the following description, their semi-structured interviews utilized open-ended questions:

> The interviewees were first asked to give a chronological account of their intercultural experiences. Next, they were asked to describe how these experiences have influenced their sense of "who they are." In discussing their acculturation, identity formation, cultural identity as adults, and ongoing movement among different cultures, participants were allowed to choose the vocabulary that seemed most appropriate to them. The interviewer, herself a TCI, sought to be sensitive to the emotional issues involved and to prevent any personal biases or theoretical conceptualizations of the topic from influencing the interviews. The interviews proceeded with questions about how participants perceive themselves as able to function in different cultural contexts and concluded with a discussion on where interviewees see themselves as belonging. (Moore & Barker, 2012, p. 557)

In-depth interviews works well with emergent type of research approaches, e.g. grounded theory which was envisaged as a data-driven instead of theory-driven approach (Glaser & Strauss, 1967). In this type of research approach, theories are grounded in the data, and patterns and hypotheses emerge in the data rather than being determined prior to the start of the data collection.

The nature of the research subjects also drives the choice of method. For example, although one might argue that the structured questions in a survey-type interview could more easily be collected via a written or online survey, those methods might not be suitable for a sample with low literacy rates or limited internet access. Similarly, although written and online surveys are widely used in business research and may achieve a high response rate if the sample includes low- to mid-level employees, the response rate may drop significantly among senior executives, who are more likely to agree to be interviewed than to complete a questionnaire (Saunders et al., 2009).

How it Works with Other Methods

Interview is frequently used in combination with other methods.

For research with a grounded theory approach, Charmaz (2006) encourages using a mix of ethnographic and interviewing methods. "You may start observing to study a topic and as your analysis proceeds return to participants with more focused queries." (p. 28)

One example of this combination of observation and interviewing can be seen in Ducharme & Bernard (2001), a study exploring the issue of language use in native and non-native speakers of French. They utilized videotaped interactions followed by separate retrospective interviews with the student and the teacher. The videotaped interactions took the form of a conversation about the needs and expectations of the student, held on the second day of class. Later, retrospective interviews were conducted separately with each of the students and their teacher in which the videotaped exchanges were viewed with the researcher in order to discuss how the conversation unfolded and "what was going on" when communication breakdowns were apparent.

Challenges, Weaknesses, and Limitations

A researcher choosing interviews as a data collection method must be aware of and have plans to deal with a number of potential challenges.

Access

Depending on the nature of the research sample, recruiting interview participants may be very difficult. This is particularly true with so-called "elite" sample, as can be seen in the Case In Point which involved interviewing Chief Executive Officers of global companies. One group of researchers conducted an analysis of four studies in two countries involving interviews with 90 "corporate elites," and identified access as one of four common areas of challenge, along with power, openness, and feedback (Welch, Marschan-Piekkari, Penttinen, & Thavanainen, 2002). Even with non-elite samples, researchers may find it difficult or impossible to contact a potential participant directly, requiring that access be granted by a "gatekeeper." One example of this would be a project requiring access to employees within a large company. Without personal contacts on the inside, the researcher might be forced to request access from the company's human resources department, which might refuse access for any number of reasons.

Openness

Because of the face-to-face nature of interviews, a number of factors may impact the interviewee's willingness to talk openly and honestly. If the topic is a sensitive one, likely to cause embarrassment or emotional or psychological discomfort, it might be more effectively explored through an anonymous method.

Even with less sensitive topics, openness can be an issue. The interviewee may not trust the interviewer or the organization behind the research, or may be wary of the purpose of the research. For example, teachers being interviewed about their classroom practices might choose to downplay any problems for fear that it might reflect on their own performance or jeopardize their program's funding. Interviewees may also wish to present themselves in a favorable light (social desirability), or may provide answers they think the interviewer wants to hear. To overcome these challenges, the interviewer must be able to gain the trust of the interviewee. Assurances of anonymity, and discussions of how the data will be used may also help.

Language barriers

Intercultural Communication research often involves researching in another language. The key language issues that need to be considered are: which language to use, and how to avoid misunderstanding if operating in a second language or using interpreters while ensuring that interviewees are comfortable with language choice or the presence of interpreters. More language issues can be found in Holmes, Fay, Andrews, & Attia, Chapter 6 of this volume.

Geographic spread

Unless the study is limited to subjects based in a limited area, the travel costs and time required for a researcher to achieve the desired face-to-face interviews could be substantial.

Although telephone and video conferencing does make it technologically possible to conduct interviews long-distance, it is unlikely that a virtual interaction will be as effective as an in-person one for conducting in-depth interviews. Nonetheless, these options may work for structured or semi-structured interviews, or for briefer follow-up interviews.

Bias

Saunders et al. (2009) discuss a number of potential bias problems in relation to the use of semi-structured and in-depth interviews, which may affect reliability, validity and generalizability of research findings. There is a risk of the interviewer affecting the interviewee's responses. Phrasing of questions, tone, body language, and other responses could have an impact on the outcome. This could happen as a result of *interviewer bias*, or interviewer inexperience. Similarly, the openness issues discussed above are examples of *interviewee bias*. Bias may also be seen in the research sample, due to access, time and geography issues. Some scholars contend that *construct bias* and other forms of interviewer bias are more likely when the interviewer and interviewee are of different cultures and when the interview is conducted in a foreign language (Fink, Kölling, & Neyer, 2005). Others have found that gender dynamics may have an impact, particularly with sensitive topics (Charmaz, 2006).

Time limitations

In-depth interviews generally require a substantial time commitment from the interviewee, with interviews lasting 60 to 90 minutes or more. In today's busy world, that may have a major impact on potential participants' willingness to agree to an interview. Additionally, the researcher should take into account the overall length of time required for scheduling, travelling to, and conducting interviews.

Power differential

Due to the dynamic, two-way nature of an interview, differences in power and status between interviewee and interviewer may have an impact on the interview, affecting openness or potentially creating bias. The power differential could be in either direction:

> A successful working relationship with interviewees, on which qualitative research depends, can be difficult to develop if there is a power imbalance between the researcher and interview subject. However, it is usually assumed that in this relationship the researcher is the one with the higher status, whereas the informant is "one of society's

underdogs" or at the very least, a person who is unaccustomed to engaging in complex conceptual debates. By contrast, studies on elite interviewing are unanimous that the power balance is likely to favour the informant over the researcher. (Welch et al., 2002, p. 615)

Other differences between interviewer and interviewee (i.e., gender, race, culture, social class, age, and ideologies) may also affect the dynamics and the outcome of the interview (Charmaz, 2007). One example of this is a study reported by Welch et al. including 40 interviews conducted with male business managers in Latin countries, which found that the interviewees "would often respond to the 'flattery' of an attentive female audience."

Likewise, although some researchers believe that interviewees are more likely to be open when interviewed by someone from their own culture (Fink et al., 2005), others have found that subjects were "willing to comment more freely on issues to a foreigner rather than to someone with local contacts and allegiances" (Welch et al., 2002, p. 622).

Sample size

The question of sample size is not unique to interviewing, and as with other methods, there is no single answer. Baker & Edwards (2012), a review paper published by the National Centre for Research Methods titled "How many quantitative interviews is enough?", compiled the opinions of 14 qualitative methodologists and reached the conclusion, "it depends." Although even the experts could not provide a definitive answer, the article, available on the NCRM website, should shed enough light to give you confidence in answering the question for yourself.

Consistency

Related to sample size is the issue of consistency. Interviews are often conducted with a group of participants by one or several interviewers. Effort is required to ensure a high degree of consistency between each interview session (intra-interviewer consistency) and between each interviewer (inter-interviewer consistency).

Developing questions

For structured interviews, the exact wording of standardized questions must be developed in advance, much like a written questionnaire. Still, it will be helpful to ensure that the questions work well orally by reading them aloud to a test subject, perhaps a friend or colleague. Check for awkward phrasing and unclear vocabulary.

Even in an unstructured interview, where the interviewer is not reading from a list of questions, advance preparation is essential. Developing an interview guide will help you think through themes to be explored, open questions that may help to prompt rich discussions, and follow-up questions to probe further.

Charmaz (2006) provides an excellent list of sample questions and further prompts designed to elicit data-rich discussion. For example:

> "As you look back on _____, are there any other events that stand out in your mind? Could you describe [each one] it? How did this event affect what happened? How did you respond to _____ [the event]?" (p. 31)

Pay particular attention to questions you will use at the beginning and end of the interview. Many experienced interviewers recommend starting with an easy opening question designed to make the participant comfortable and talkative. Likewise, it can be useful to have a well-rehearsed wrap-up question or two to bring the interview to a natural conclusion and end on a positive note (see Case in Point for an example).

Prepare for every interview by reading through your interview guide again. While most experienced interviewers prefer not to read questions in an unstructured interview, in order to facilitate a conversational tone, it may be helpful to have a mind-map or bullet-point reminder list with you in the interview, in case your mind goes blank.

Recording the interview

In planning for interviews, you need to consider what method you will use to record the data, and possible implications of doing so. In a structured interview, it may be possible to simply write down the responses as questions are answered. But for most semi-structured or unstructured interviews, it will be necessary to audio- or video-record the interview. This requires gaining permission of the participant prior to recording, and making clear how the recording will be used. Even once permission is granted, the act of recording may have an impact on openness. If the interview topic is a sensitive one, participants may be inhibited by the "on the record" feel of a recording, or may not trust that their anonymity will be protected. It may be helpful to tell the participant that they may ask that the recording be paused or stopped at any point. Video-recording may make participants more self-conscious and stilted, and may increase the likelihood of social desirability bias. In some cases, researchers may determine that recording will prevent the gathering of rich data, and may choose to rely completely on note-taking.

If you do plan to record your interviews, consider what kind of equipment will be needed, and plan for a back-up in the event of technical problems. For example, one of the authors uses a hand-held digital audio recorder, but also has audio-recording software installed on her mobile phone, so that it can be deployed in the event of a problem. Test your equipment in advance, be sure you know how to work it properly, and carry spare batteries if needed. There is nothing worse than leaving an hour-long interview and realizing that something went wrong with the recording.

Interview location

For conducting in-depth interviews, ideally you want a private space that is free of distractions and background noises (which may affect your audio recording).

The setting may affect how comfortable the participant feels, and may impact openness.

Transcription

Transcribing interviews is no easy task. It is an "interpretative" (i.e. what is transcribed) and at the same time, a "representational" process (i.e. how it is transcribed) (Green, Franquiz, & Dixon, 1997). Things that need to be considered include:

- what to include and not to include,
- the transcriber's own methodological and analytical framework,
- audience,
- purpose of research,
- level of details (nonverbal cues, turn-taking, pauses, etc.),
- length of transcript,
- level of standardization,
- accessibility,
- standard orthography vs. phonetic transcription,
- translation,
- format,
- anonymity.

The amount of time transcription takes should not be underestimated. A single hour of audio recording can take anywhere from four hours (for an experienced transcriptionist) to ten hours (for a beginner) to transcribe. Even a handful of interviews can add up to weeks' worth of full-time transcribing. You'll need to consider whether you will do your own transcription or hire a professional transcriptionist and build in adequate time to your research schedule. If you do it yourself, transcription software can be helpful, allowing you to vary the playback speed (see a link for free software in the "Further Reading and Resources" list). Therefore, you need to determine what type of transcription is required in advance of beginning transcription.

After the interview

The use of field notes is a common practice in ethnographic research, and they can be invaluable for interviewing, as well. The field note can serve as a post mortem, recording details about the interview process, what went well and what didn't, which questions elicited rich responses and which fell flat. In this way, each interview can help inform the next, and help the interviewer improve techniques. In grounded theory and other emergent methodologies, the field note also becomes an important source of data (Dick, 2001).

Writing up a field note immediately after each interview, while the memories are still fresh, can help to capture the interviewer's impressions, themes or quotes that stood out. This becomes a valuable early step in the data analysis process. Figure 12.1 provides an example of a field note.

Interviewer:	▓▓▓▓▓▓▓▓
Date of interview:	17 Feb 2011
Time of interview start:	11:30 am
Interviewee's name/title/company:	▓▓▓▓▓▓▓▓
Location of interview:	Washington Mayfair Hotel, London (hotel bar/coffee shop)
Consent form signed:	Y
Permission to audi-record:	Y
Discussed options for anonymity:	Y or N __Option 1: Complete anonymity **X** Option 2: Identity included, direct attribution w/ review & permission

Themes that emerged, memorable quotes, anything that stood out:

Although he said he's never had any intercultural training or had any preparation for any of his overseas assignments, he displays a very high level of insight and self-awareness. He seems to be a "natural" intercultural communicator. Is that because of innate personality traits or is it due to his having lived and worked in many countries?

Used words like "humility," "empathy," "understanding," and "evolving" a great deal. His style, even with me, seemed to be one of reading people, and adjusting his own style to what he believes will work best. As he spoke, I found myself characterizing him as a "cultural chameleon" and he later used the word chameleon, so he may have an awareness of his own adaptation strategies. Are these natural traits to salesmen?

What worked:

- Overall, the mind-map worked, and interview lasted almost exactly the allotted 90 minutes.
- Getting him talking about specific incidents and examples
- Dealing with his personal experiences early (maybe consider starting there with all interviewees).

What didn't work:

- Didn't get a straight answer to success question, no matter how asked. Lots of hedging and circumlocution. Is it the question itself, or timing within the discussion? Will need to pay attention to this in future interviews.
- My use of the word "barrier"– he took it to mean "insurmountable," and couldn't think of any instances where he wasn't able to deal with a problem. Consider using other words to draw out smaller issues/obstacles.
- Location was a problem (it was selected by him, to fit between meetings while in Central London for the day). Way too much background noise (both people and loud coffee machine) for clear audio-recording – transcription may be a problem. Will insist on private locations for future interviews.

Areas for possible follow-up or further exploration:

- Perhaps speak later with his country managers to see if their perception of him matches his self-perception.

Figure 12.1 An example of a field note.

Ethical issues

Ethical issues to be considered may include protecting anonymity of the participants, and ensuring the security of the data, particularly recordings. If your research sample includes vulnerable participants (i.e., children, domestic abuse victims, HIV patients), there may be additional ethical issues to consider.

Analyzing Data from Interviews

Interview data are usually analyzed qualitatively. The most common method is thematic content analysis, whereby interview data are broken down into smaller units and coded according to themes or key words.

For those who adopt an emergent research approach, the process can be described as three concurrent flows of activity (Miles & Huberman, 1994): data reduction, data display, and conclusion drawing / verification. Data reduction refers to the process of selecting and simplifying the data, and it may include various kinds of coding and categorizing. A data display may include many types of matrices, graphs, charts, and networks, and again, according to Miles and Huberman, "the creation and use of displays is not separate from analysis, it is part of the analysis" (p. 10). The third stream, conclusion drawing and verification, is also interwoven throughout the process.

Seidel (1998) proposed a qualitative analysis model known as NCT, representing the three aspects of "Noticing things," "Collecting things," and "Thinking about things." Noticing refers to the process of finding interesting things when reading through transcripts, field notes, documents, and other data. As interesting things are noticed, they are given a label, or code. Collecting is the process of beginning to group together those interesting things, comparing and contrasting, renaming the codes, combining codes that are conceptually similar. The thinking part of the process takes place in both the noticing and collecting aspects, but also as a separate activity of analysis which looks for patterns and relations in the data.

Friese (2012) combines the NCT model with computer-aided qualitative data analysis software (CAQDAS) as a tool for supporting the process of qualitative data analysis. It should be noted that while the software provides a number of capabilities that enable all three steps in the model, as with all CAQDAS programs, it is the researcher not the software that performs the actual analysis.

Case In Point

Gibson, B. (2014). Intercultural competencies needed by global CEOs. Unpublished PhD thesis, Birkbeck, University of London. Available online at http://bbktheses.da.ulcc.ac.uk/64/.

A study conducted by first author of this chapter serves as a good case in point for the use of interviews. The research aimed to explore the intercultural challenges faced by Chief Executive Officers (CEOs) of companies doing business internationally and to identify the intercultural competencies needed by CEOs.

Getting access to participants

The research included in-depth interviews with 28 global CEOs. Gibson found that choosing to study CEOs presents a number of obstacles, perhaps the most challenging of which is gaining access to these busy executives. She found that in most organizations of any size, it may be impossible for an outsider to reach the CEO directly. Requests may be channeled through assistants or communication departments, who often choose to decline or ignore requests, or delegate them to other executives based on their judgment of the appropriateness of the topic. For example, a request to the CEO of a major supermarket chain was forwarded by his assistant to the company's director of communication because the topic dealt with communication. Gibson found that gatekeepers may play an important role even after participation has been agreed, because it is often necessary to work with them to schedule the meeting, and they may reschedule and even cancel meetings without regard for the researcher's needs.

Gibson's ability to gain access to the CEOs was helped by her previous experience in business, working at the senior level and serving as counsel to CEOs of a number of global companies. Her experience in the business world, her confidence as an interviewer, her age (which was close to the average age of her sample), and her vast professional network contributed to her ability to overcome many of the challenges.

Many of the participants were recruited through her professional contacts, personally introduced by someone with whom they had a relationship of trust, which helped to establish rapport and gain openness. Other CEOs were recruited through social media platform LinkedIn, which enabled potential participants to view not only the request but also Gibson's full professional profile before choosing to respond. So the profile, which reflects her long experience and spans both business and academic worlds, helped with gaining access and establishing credibility.

Verbal and written assurances of anonymity also supported openness. The decision to audio-record rather than use video was a deliberate one. Because of her background in corporate communication, Gibson was aware that most senior executives have been through media spokesperson training, and therefore the use of video might be more likely to turn the interview into a performance, resulting in crafted soundbites rather than authentic discussion.

In dealing with the time challenge, which was considerable in the pilot phase when the request was for 90 minutes, the meeting time requested was reduced to 60 minutes, with most of the interviews lasting about 50 minutes. All interviews were scheduled at the CEO's convenience, working around other meetings, and sometimes rescheduling at the last minute.

Carrying out the interviews

Before starting the interview, Gibson provided a brief overview of the research project, explained the objective and format of the interview, including confirming that the interview would conclude within the allotted 60 minutes. Participants were asked to sign a consent form, and permission was requested to audio-record the interview. It was reiterated that the recording would be used for transcription and analysis only, and that they could be assured of confidentiality and anonymity. The recording device was turned on and placed near the participant.

Although the overall format of the interviews was semi-structured, a short questionnaire was used to gather background information at the start of each interview, which would gather data for balancing the sample as well as providing a number of variables for possible analysis. These questions also served as a warm-up and provided a number of possible prompts for soliciting narratives. While asking the background questionnaire questions, Gibson read from and noted answers on paper. Upon completing that portion, the notes were set aside and the style of the discussion shifted to conversational.

Gibson explained that the format from that point forward would not be about asking and answering questions, but about the interviewee sharing stories from their own experiences of interacting, living, working, or managing cross-culturally, and that they could start wherever they chose. In some cases, that was all the prompting needed. In others, a prompt such as "it might help to start with the first time you found yourself outside your own culture" was usually enough to begin a narrative. Whenever another gap occurred, similar prompts were used to explore personal experiences, management experiences, and business challenges. If the participant spoke only in generalities, prompts included "can you remember a specific incident when you… ." If reference was made to having learned a lesson, prompts were used to explore how it was learned.

As the conversation began to wind down, or when the end of the hour approached, two concluding questions were asked which were designed to elicit the CEO's perspectives on which competencies are most important at their level (regardless of whether or not they believed they had them):

- "If you were hiring someone to replace yourself or for a similar role and you knew this person would need to be successful working across cultures, what traits or skills would you look for, or how would you know they have the competencies needed?"
- "What advice or tips would you give a CEO who is moving into a global position?"

Handling data

Although the data from the pilot study's four interviews could be analyzed manually with pen, paper, and basic word-processing software, Gibson knew that 28 interviews would require more. She utilized computer-aided qualitative data analysis software (CAQDAS) as a tool for supporting the process of qualitative data analysis. The software program selected was ATLAS.ti.

The 28 interviews generated approximately 24 total hours of digital audio recordings, which were transcribed verbatim, resulting in more than 250,000 words of textual data available for analysis. Both the digital recordings and the transcripts were imported into ATLAS.ti. This made it possible to synchronize recordings to transcripts, making it possible to review them together, and to go back and listen to particular passages at any time to clarify meaning or tone.

The process of coding was an interactive one, requiring many readings of the transcripts, viewing each one separately as well as comparing and contrasting it with the others, allowing patterns and themes to emerge. The data from the background questionnaires was also imported into ATLAS.ti and linked with the respective subjects to enable analysis by variables.

Conclusion

As this chapter has shown, interviews can be an effective method for data collection, but there are many factors to be considered in both the planning and implementation stages, including the researcher's own capabilities. For further practical advice about planning and carrying out interviews, see the "Further Reading and Resources" section.

Key Terms

Focus group interview A type of interview in which a selected group of individuals are invited to take part in an organized discussion on a topic.
Grounded theory A type of data-driven research approach pioneered by Glaser & Strauss (1967) in which the focus of the research is facilitating patterns and findings to emerge through the data.
Interview A data collection method in which the interviewer asks the interviewee questions to elicit the latter's views and opinions.
Semi-structured interview A type of interview in which the interviewer is allowed to adjust prepared questions or bring in new questions to give the interviewee opportunities to elaborate or to further probe a question.
Structured interview A type of interview in which interview questions are compiled prior to the interview. It is used when the researcher has a set of specific questions in mind.

References

Allett, N., Keightley, E., & Pickering, M. (2011). *Realities toolkit 16: Using self-interviews to research memory*. Retrieved June 16, 2015 from: http://www.socialsciences.manchester.ac.uk/morgancentre/realities/toolkits/self-interviews/.
Baker, S. E., & Edwards, R. (2012). *How many qualitative interviews is enough? Expert voices and early career reflections on sampling and cases in qualitative research*. Discussion paper, National Centre for Research Methods. Retrieved June 16, 2015 from: http://eprints.ncrm.ac.uk/2273/4/how_many_interviews.pdf.
Charmaz, K. (2006). *Constructing grounded theory: A practical guide through qualitative analysis*. Thousand Oaks, CA: Sage.

Dick, R. (2001) Making the most of emergent methodologies: A critical choice in qualitative research design. Paper prepared for the Association for Qualitative Research Conference, Melbourne 5–7 July. Retrieved June 16, 2015 from: http://www.aral.com.au/DLitt/DLitt_P48emerg.pdf .

Ducharme, D., & Bernard, R. (2001). Communication breakdowns: An exploration of contextualization in native and non-native speakers of French. *Journal of Pragmatics*, 33, 825–847.

Fink, G., Kölling, M., & Neyer, A. (2005). *The cultural standard method*. EI Working Papers / Europainstitut, 62. Europainstitut, WU Vienna University of Economics and Business, Vienna. Retrieved June 16, 2015 from: http://epub.wu.ac.at/450/.

Friese, S. (2012). *Qualitative data analysis with Atlast.ti*, Thousand Oaks, CA: Sage.

Gibson, B. (2014). Intercultural competencies needed by global CEOs. Unpublished PhD thesis, Birkbeck, University of London. Retrieved June 16, 2015 from: http://bbktheses.da.ulcc.ac.uk/64/.

Glaser, B., & Strauss, A. (1967) *The discovery of grounded theory*, Chicago: Aldine.

Green, J., Franquiz, M., & Dixon, C. (1997). The myth of the objective transcript: Transcribing as a situated act. *TESOL Quarterly*, 31(1), 172–176.

Hoffman, M. (2014). Sociolinguistic interviews. In J. Holmes & K. Hazen, (Eds.), (*Research methods in sociolinguistics: A practical guide* (pp. 25–41). Malden, MA: Wiley.

Miles, M.B., & Huberman, A.M. (1994). *Qualitative data analysis* (2nd ed.). Thousand Oaks, CA: Sage.

Moore, A.M., & Barker, G.G. (2012). Confused or multicultural: Third culture individuals' cultural identity. *International Journal of Intercultural Relations*, 36, 553–562.

Pavlenko, A. (2008). Narrative analysis. In Li Wei & M. Moyer (Eds.), *The Blackwell guide to research methods in bilingualism and multilingualism* (pp. 311–325). Oxford: Blackwell.

Saunders, M., Lewis, P., & Thornhill, A. (2009). *Research methods for business students* (5th ed.). Harlow: Prentice Hall.

Seidel, J. V. (1998). *Qualitative Data Analysis*. Retrieved June 16, 2015 from: http://www.qualisresearch.com/qda_paper.htm (originally published as Qualitative Data Analysis, in *The Ethnograph v5.0: A Users Guide, Appendix E*, 1998, Colorado Springs, CO: Qualis Research).

Welch, C., Marschan-Piekkari, R., Penttinen, H., & Thavanainen, M. (2002). Corporate elites as informants in qualitative international business research. *International Business Review*, 11(5), 611–628.

Further Reading and Resources

On overview of interviews:

Keats, D.M. (2000). *Interviewing: A practical guide for students and professionals*, Buckingham: Open University Press.

King, N., & Horrocks, C. (2010). *Interviews in qualitative research*. Thousand Oaks, CA: Sage.

On transcription:

Free transcription software, Express Scribe, is available for download at http://www.nch.com.au/scribe/ (Accessed June 16, 2015).

Bucholtz, M. (2000). The politics of transcription. *Journal of Pragmatics*, 32, 1439–1465.

Davidson, C. (2009). Transcription: Imperatives for qualitative research. *International Journal of Qualitative Methods*, 8(2), 36–52.

On analysis of interview data:

Silverman, D. (1993). *Interpreting qualitative data: Methods for analyzing talk, text and interaction*. Thousand Oaks, CA: Sage.

13 The Matched-Guise Technique

Ruth Kircher

> **Summary**
>
> The matched-guise technique is an indirect method of eliciting language attitudes that involves the experimental investigation of speech perception. The method is frequently used in both sociolinguistics and the social psychology of language. This chapter provides an overview of the key features of the matched-guise technique. Step by step, the chapter explains how to plan and conduct a matched-guise experiment by discussing the choice of an appropriate text, the recording of the experimental stimuli, the design of the evaluation booklet as well as the actual procedure to be followed for the experiment. Following this, the chapter explains how to analyze the findings of a matched-guise experiment. The chapter then discusses the limitations and the strengths of the technique, and it concludes by elaborating on the use of the technique in combination with other methods as well as more recent developments regarding indirect methods of attitude elicitation.

Language Attitudes Research in Sociolinguistics and the Social Psychology of Language

In general, *attitudes* are understood to consist of three separate components: a cognitive component, which concerns the beliefs held about the attitude object; an affective component, which consists of the feelings elicited by the attitude object; and a conative component, which comprises behavior directed at the attitude object (Bohner, 2001). It is generally agreed that individuals' attitudes towards their ingroups and any outgroups are at the core of intergroup cooperation and conflict because all intergroup relations are essentially characterized by stereotypes (i.e. beliefs), prejudices (i.e. affects), and discrimination (i.e. behaviors) – be they positive or negative (Bourhis & Maass, 2005).

Based on this understanding of attitudes in general, *language attitudes* are defined as any cognitive, affective or conative index of evaluative reactions towards different varieties and their speakers (Ryan, Giles, & Sebastian, 1982). The inclusion of the speakers of the varieties in this definition is due to the close connection between language and social identity, with the latter referring to "those aspects of an individual's self-image that derive from the social categories to which he [*sic*] perceives himself as belonging" (Tajfel & Turner, 1986, p. 16). Based on a large body of research evidence, it has long been acknowledged that language is an important symbol of social identity (e.g. Grosjean, 1982). In most modern research, attitudes towards particular varieties are therefore either taken to be direct reflections of the attitudes towards the speakers of those varieties (e.g. Garrett, Coupland, & Williams, 2003) or they are at least assumed to be very closely linked to them (e.g. Tabouret-Keller, 1997). Consequently, language attitudes cannot be said to indicate either linguistic or aesthetic quality *per se*. Instead, they should be considered as "expressions of social convention and preference which, in turn, reflect an awareness of the status and prestige accorded to the speakers of these varieties" (Edwards, 1982, p. 21).

There are three main types of methods that can be used to assess language attitudes: analysis of the societal treatment of language varieties, direct methods, and indirect methods of attitude elicitation (Ryan, Giles, & Hewstone, 1987). Analysis of the societal treatment of language varieties encompasses "[a]ll techniques which do not involve explicitly asking respondents for their views or reactions" (Ryan et al., 1987, p. 1068). This includes observational studies undertaken to investigate individuals' actual linguistic behavior – that is, the conative component of language attitudes. While such studies can provide rich information on the relative standing of different language varieties in particular societies, it has to be borne in mind that a person's linguistic behavior in a particular situation depends not only on their language attitudes but also on numerous other factors, including their addressee, the specific context, time and occasion, as well as the immediate consequences that their behavior can be expected to have (e.g. Gross, 1999). Hence, the fact that a person behaves in a particular way in one specific situation is by no means a guarantee that they will behave like that again – which makes single instances of linguistic behavior rather unreliable indicators of language attitudes in general (e.g. Gross, 1999).

Many researchers have therefore focused on the remaining components of language attitudes instead – that is, beliefs and feelings. However, investigating these is not easy either, because they have no overt substance and thus cannot be directly observed. This leads to methodological difficulties such as the determination of the right kind of data from which language attitudes can be inferred. As Romaine (1995, p. 288) notes, "[t]he translation of the notion 'attitude' from the subjective domain into something objectively measurable [...] is a common problem in any research that involves social categorization and judgements." Many researchers attempt to solve this problem by making use of direct methods of attitude elicitation, such as questionnaires and interviews (see Young, Chapter 11; Gibson & Zhu Hua, Chapter 12, this volume). Like the analysis of the societal treatment of varieties, these direct methods have been widely and profitably used to gather valuable information regarding language attitudes. However, their main drawback is that their purpose is usually recognizable – and as most individuals, consciously or unconsciously, put themselves in the best possible light when responding, the findings obtained by means of these methods tend to be influenced by social desirability biases (e.g. Garrett et al., 2003).

In order to obviate this problem, some researchers have devised indirect methods of attitude elicitation that involve speech perception experiments. The overall term used to describe such methods is the *speaker evaluation paradigm* (Ryan et al., 1982). The most well-known and sophisticated indirect, experimental method of attitude elicitation is the matched-guise technique, which was developed by Wallace Lambert and his associates (Lambert, Hodgson, Gardner, & Fillenbaum, 1960) in order to investigate attitudes towards English and French in Montreal, the urban center of the Canadian province of Quebec. The matched-guise technique is considered to form the foundation of the social psychological perspective on language attitudes (Ryan, Hewstone, & Giles, 1984). In fact, many of the roots of the entire discipline of the social psychology of language itself can be traced to Lambert et al.'s seminal investigation (Giles & Coupland, 1991).

In the basic set-up of a matched-guise experiment (Lambert et al., 1960), recordings are made of a number of perfectly bilingual or bidialectal speakers who deliver the same text twice, once in each of their varieties. (In more complex studies, the speakers may deliver the same text in even more varieties.) The participants whose language attitudes are being studied are not informed of the real research purpose. They listen to the recordings, unaware of the fact that they are hearing the same speakers more than once, in *matched guises*. (They are "matched" in the sense that the speaker and the semantic content of the text delivered by the speaker are the same each time – the only difference is the variety in which the speaker delivers that text.) Instead, the participants are under the impression that they are listening to a series of different speakers, some of whom use one variety, some another. They do know, however, that all speakers are delivering the same text. The effects of both the voices of the speakers and the text are thus minimized, and other potentially influential factors such as physical appearance are excluded. Based on voice cues only, the participants then have to rate the speakers in terms of personality characteristics – and any differences in reaction to the two recordings of the same speaker are presumed to be based on the participants' attitudes towards the varieties spoken, and thus also towards the social groups with which these varieties are associated (Lambert, 1967).

This chapter explains how to plan and conduct a matched-guise experiment by discussing the choice of an appropriate text, the recording of the experimental stimuli, the designing of the evaluation booklet as well as the actual procedure to be followed. The chapter then explains how to analyze the findings of a matched-guise experiment. Finally, the chapter discusses the limitations and the strengths of the technique, and it concludes by elaborating on the use of the technique in combination with other methods as well as more recent developments regarding indirect methods of attitude elicitation.

Planning a Matched-Guise Experiment

Choosing the Text

The first step of planning a matched-guise experiment involves choosing a suitable text. This does not need to be long – the length of the texts used in previous studies ranges between 30 seconds (e.g. Genesee & Holobow, 1989) and 150 seconds (e.g. Lambert, Anisfeld, & Yeni-Komshian, 1965). This is sufficient for participants to make systematic speaker evaluations. The use of a short text also has the advantage that more evaluations can be gathered from the participants in a relatively short period of time.

Evidently, neither texts nor the topics they deal with are ever entirely neutral – even if they have been composed by researchers explicitly in order to be uncontroversial or even trivial (Giles & Coupland, 1991). Nevertheless, there are some texts that are more appropriate than others for use in matched-guise experiments. Most importantly, the text should not deal with ideological or political issues. Moreover, it should be in no way language-related, and it should not contain any lexical items that identify it as originating from, or being more appropriate for, one of the varieties under investigation. A text that fulfils these criteria should have as little influence as possible upon the participants' evaluations of the speakers in their different guises. While some of the earlier studies used literary or philosophical texts (e.g. Lambert et al., 1960; Lambert et al., 1965), more recent studies have preferred "lighter" texts such as weather-related news items (e.g. Genesee & Holobow, 1989) and accounts of travels (e.g. Echeverria 2005).

Recording the Experimental Stimuli

The second step of planning a matched-guise experiment involves recording individuals who, when delivering the text, sound like native speakers of each of the varieties under investigation. In order to exclude the influence of any possible confounding variables, the speakers should be as similar to one another as possible in terms of their age, their socio-economic and ethnic backgrounds, as well as any other relevant characteristics. If speakers of different genders are used, equal numbers of women and men should be included because previous studies (e.g. Laur, 2008) have shown that there are systematic differences in the manner in which female and male speakers of the same variety are evaluated. Prosodic and paralinguistic features of the speakers' voices, such as their pitch and speech rate, should be kept constant as far as possible across their recordings (Giles & Coupland, 1991).

Once each speaker has been recorded delivering the same text twice (or more), once in each of their varieties, it is advisable to test the authenticity of the recordings. This should be done by playing them to test judges – that is, native speakers of the varieties under investigation who are asked what they think the native variety of each of the speakers is. In the actual matched-guise experiment, only the recordings of those speakers should be used whom the majority of test judges had found to speak each of their varieties natively (see e.g. Genesee & Holobow, 1989, who used 85% as a cut-off point). The recordings that are used in the actual experiment constitute the *experimental stimuli* – that is, they are the triggers for the participants' evaluative responses.

If more than one speaker is employed, the order of the experimental stimuli should be arranged so that no two recordings of the same speaker occur consecutively. If only one speaker is used, recordings of *filler voices* should be included (see e.g. Cargile, Giles, Ryan, & Bradac, 1994, p. 213). These are recordings of speakers who share the characteristics of the actual speaker and who also deliver the same text, but each of them in only one of the varieties under investigation, or even in another variety. These filler voices should be placed between the different recordings of the actual speaker so that these do not occur consecutively. This decreases the likelihood of the participants realizing that they are listening to the same speaker in matched guises. However, if possible, it is advisable to use more than one speaker to increase the reliability of the findings.

Regardless of how many speakers are included in the actual experiment, it is always advisable for the experimental stimuli to be preceded by *practice voices* (e.g. Lambert et al., 1965). Again, these are recordings of speakers who share the characteristics of the actual speakers and who also deliver the same text, but each of them only once. The aim of placing these practice voices before the recordings of the actual speaker(s) is to familiarize the participants with both the text and the experimental procedure. By the time the participants listen to the recordings of the actual speaker(s), they should thus no longer be paying much attention to the content of the text, or to the practicalities of the voice evaluation process. Instead, they should be able to focus solely on the experimental stimuli.

Designing the Evaluation Booklet

The third stage of planning a matched-guise experiment involves designing an evaluation booklet in which the participants can indicate their ratings of each of the experimental stimuli. On the front page, a brief explanation of the procedure as well as instructions should be provided (personal communication with Fred Genesee; see Figure 13.1). For instance, the participants should be informed that they will get to listen to brief audio-recordings of a number of different individuals, all of whom deliver the same text. The participants should be instructed to listen carefully to the different speakers' voices, and they should be asked to describe each speaker by rating them on the scales provided in the evaluation booklet. The participants should also be asked to respond as intuitively and as quickly as possible. Moreover, it is advisable to include a copy of the text on the front page of the evaluation booklet to aid the participants' familiarization with this. If different languages or dialects are under investigation, a copy of the text should be provided in each of them; if different accents are under investigation, one copy of the text is sufficient.

Each subsequent page of the evaluation booklet should contain the rating scales for one of the experimental stimuli. As the participants ought to remain unaware of the fact that they are listening to the same speakers more than once, in matched guises, each page should be labelled as containing the rating scales for a different speaker: speaker 1, speaker 2, speaker 3, etc. (see Figure 13.2). The rating scales in matched-guise experiments tend to be interval, Likert-like scales with opposite extremes of

> **Evaluation booklet**
>
> As part of this voice evaluation study, you will get to listen to brief audio-recordings of a number of different people who will all be delivering the same text. Please listen carefully to these recordings.
>
> After each recording, pleaserate the speaker on the semantic scales provided by circling the number which best corresponds to your impression of the speaker.
>
> Please try to respond as intuitively and as quickly as possible.
>
> This is the text that the speakers will deliver:
>
> [copy of the text]
>
> Please turn over for the rating scales for the different speakers.
>
> - front page -

Figure 13.1 Front page of an evaluation booklet.

certain traits at either end. Usually, half of these traits pertain to the status dimension and the other half of the traits pertain to the solidarity dimension. Empirical research from numerous parts of the world has revealed that status and solidarity are independent dimensions of language attitudes, and that it is indeed in terms of these two primary dimensions that the identities of speakers of different varieties tend to be evaluated (e.g. Ryan et al., 1984; Genesee & Holobow, 1989). A variety that is perceived to have much status is one that is associated with power, economic opportunity and upward social mobility – that is, a variety which carries much overt prestige in the society as a whole (e.g. Echeverria, 2005). A variety that is evaluated highly on the solidarity dimension, on the other hand, is one that elicits feelings of appreciation and belong – which is typically the case for the variety of one's family life and intimate friendships, as this "acquires vital social meaning and comes to represent the social group with which one identifies" (Ryan et al., 1982, p. 9). The dimensions of status and solidarity are considered to have "a universal importance" for the understanding of language attitudes (Ryan et al., 1987, p. 1073). Typical status-related traits used in matched-guise experiments include *intelligence*, *education*, *ambition*, *leadership* and *dependability*; typical solidarity-related traits include *kindness*, *warmth*, *likeability*, *sociability* and *humor* (e.g. Genesee & Holobow, 1989; Kircher, 2014; Lambert et al., 1960).

```
┌─────────────────────────────────────────────┐
│                  Speaker 1                  │
│ Please rate Speaker 1 in terms of the personality traits listed │
│ below. For each trait, circle the number which best │
│ corresponds to your impression of the speaker. │
│                                             │
│ a) [status trait 1]                         │
│       1    2    3    4    5    6    7      │
│    not at all ...                  very ... │
│                                             │
│ b) [solidarity trait 1]                     │
│       1    2    3    4    5    6    7      │
│    not at all ...                  very ... │
│                                             │
│ c) [status trait 2]                         │
│       1    2    3    4    5    6    7      │
│    not at all ...                  very ... │
│                                             │
│ d) [solidarity trait 2]                     │
│       1    2    3    4    5    6    7      │
│    not at all ...                  very ... │
│                                             │
│ e) [status trait 3]                         │
│       1    2    3    4    5    6    7      │
│    not at all ...                  very ... │
│                                             │
│ f) [solidarity trait 3]                     │
│       1    2    3    4    5    6    7      │
│    not at all ...                  very ... │
│                                             │
│                - sample page -              │
└─────────────────────────────────────────────┘
```

Figure 13.2 Sample page of an evaluation booklet.

In order to obtain some qualitative data to complement the quantitative data obtained by means of the rating scales, it is possible to include an open-ended question, asking the participants to provide their own description – or a list of the most pertinent additional perceived personality traits – for each of the experimental stimuli. Some researchers also ask the participants what they think each speaker's occupation is because this provides further information about their perceived status (e.g. Genesee & Holobow, 1989).

The penultimate page of the evaluation booklet should be used to ask the respondents for the necessary demographic data, such as their age, gender, native variety, and/or whatever other information is relevant in order to assess the effect of the social variable(s) under investigation as part of a particular research project.

On the final page of the evaluation booklet, it is customary to ask the participants what they believed the study was about, and whether they thought that there was anything unusual about any of the voices (e.g. Genesee & Holobow, 1989; see Figure 13.3). The purpose of these questions is to filter out those participants who guessed the real purpose of the experiment, and those who realized that they had heard the same speakers more than once. Since ignorance with regard to the methodology is a precondition to the elicitation of valid results, such participants should be removed from the subsequent analysis.

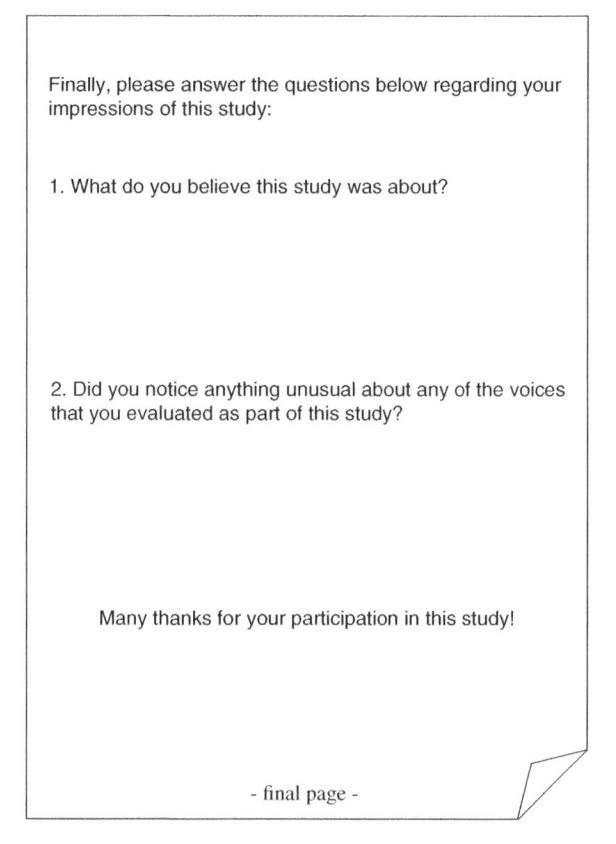

> Finally, please answer the questions below regarding your impressions of this study:
>
> 1. What do you believe this study was about?
>
> 2. Did you notice anything unusual about any of the voices that you evaluated as part of this study?
>
> Many thanks for your participation in this study!
>
> - final page -

Figure 13.3 Final page of an evaluation booklet.

Conducting a Matched-Guise Experiment

To avoid the problem of participants evaluating speakers in a socially desirable and therefore possibly dishonest manner, they are not told the real research purpose before the experiment. Instead, a matched-guise study is traditionally introduced as "an experimental investigation of the extent to which people's judgments about a speaker are determined by his [sic] voice," as is done when trying to estimate the personality of an unfamiliar speaker on the radio or at the other end of a telephone (Lambert et al., 1960, p. 44). Since Pear's (1931) classic study, in which he invited BBC audiences in the UK to provide personality profiles of voice recordings they heard on the radio, numerous further studies have been conducted to determine whether voice parameters really are an external mirror of someone's dispositional states. As Giles and Coupland (1991) point out, most researchers have concluded that there is only a very modest overlap between listeners' judgemnts and speakers' actual personalities. It can therefore be assumed that in matched-guise experiments, the speakers' actual personality characteristics are highly unlikely to be the cause of any of the evaluations.

When the evaluation booklets are distributed, the participants should be provided with the necessary instructions, and they should then be given time to familiarize themselves with the materials. They should also be offered an opportunity to ask questions, should any aspect of the experimental procedure be unclear to them.

The recordings should then be played to the participants, one after the other. As noted above, the underlying idea is that the matched-guise technique elicits language attitudes that are "less sensitive to reflection and social desirability biases" than those elicited by direct methods (Cargile et al., 1994, p. 213). Since the participants can begin rating each of the experimental stimuli while listening to it, they do not need to be given much time in between one stimulus and the next. Approximately thirty to fifty seconds should be sufficient. Once all experimental stimuli have been rated, the participants should be asked to complete the two final pages of the evaluation booklet.

After the completion of the experiment, the participants should be debriefed: they should be informed of the real purpose of the experiment, and of the fact that they heard the same speakers more than once. It should be explained to them why their naïvety was necessary for the successful completion of the experiment, and the researcher should apologize to any participants who might feel unhappy about this procedure. Once they have been debriefed, all participants should be offered the opportunity to withdraw their data from the research project if they wish to do so.

As with all other linguistic methods, it is advisable to conduct a pilot study, using a smaller participant sample that is as similar as possible to the actual sample with regard to the relevant social characteristics. The pilot should be used to test the instructions, the items in the evaluation booklet, and the experimental stimuli before using them in the actual experiment.

Analyzing the Findings of a Matched-Guise Experiment

Once the evaluation booklets have been collected from those participants who did not wish to withdraw their data, the data should be coded and entered into a statistical package such as SPSS. A simple way of analyzing the data is by means of repeated measures analyses of variance (ANOVAs). The between-subject variable(s) to be entered in SPSS depends on the independent variable(s) under investigation; the different varieties used by the same speaker function as the within-subject variable.

Initially, repeated measures ANOVAs should be run for each speaker separately to ascertain that there is no significant variation in the evaluation of the different speakers. Usually, the same evaluative pattern is found for all speakers. Should the speakers all be evaluated quite differently from each other, it is likely that there is a problem with the authenticity of the recordings. This should be tested. Should only one of the speakers be evaluated differently from the others, this is likely to be the result of an idiosyncratic speech style, and the evaluations made of this speaker should be excluded from the analysis.

Once the evaluative patterns for the different speakers have been ascertained, the ratings of those speakers that are consistently similar to each other should be combined, and new repeated measures ANOVAs should be performed on the recoded data.

Any systematic differences in reaction to the different varieties used can be presumed to be based on the participants' attitudes towards these different varieties, and therefore also towards the groups with which these varieties are associated (Lambert, 1967).

Limitations and Strengths of the Matched-Guise Technique

Limitations

Naturally, the matched-guise technique is not without faults. Agheyisi and Fishman (1970), for example, have pointed out the unsuitability of this method for attitude elicitation in diglossic settings. In such settings, language choices are highly dependent on factors such as domain, topic, location, role and interaction type. The fact that the text used is the same in each of the varieties thus poses a problem as there might be an incongruity between the variety in which the text is recorded and the domain to which it belongs. Participants might give low evaluations to speakers in one variety but not in the other, not because they have negative attitudes towards the variety itself but because they think that it is inappropriate for use in that particular domain.

Another aspect of the matched-guise technique that has been criticized is its alleged artificiality. While asking participants to evaluate speakers on the basis of nothing but their voices provides maximum control over other potentially influential variables, some researchers see this method as "a bit far removed from real-life contexts" (Fasold, 1984, p. 154) and consider matched-guise experiments to be "pencil and paper-studies" (Laur, 1994, p. 76).

Furthermore, there is a danger of participants being overly influenced by the fact that they are given rating scales and told to evaluate the speakers, as this might "set [them] up to make evaluative judgments in a way that doesn't happen in ordinary interactive settings" (Fasold, 1984, p. 155). The juxtaposition of two (or more) varieties could be what causes participants to feel "compelled to look for contrasts," and their evaluative reactions to each variety if it were encountered individually might be different to the evaluations obtained in a matched-guise study (Luhman, 1990, p. 340).

A final criticism that has been brought forward against the matched-guise technique is that language attitudes that are elicited from "interactively non-involved" participants are necessarily different from those of individuals actually participating in a particular speech exchange (Ryan et al., 1987, p. 1076).

Strengths

Admittedly, the suitability of the matched-guise technique as a means of attitude elicitation in diglossic settings is limited. However, in non-diglossic, stratified societies in which the status and power of different groups is associated with distinctive and stable speech style variation, many researchers consider the advantages of the technique to compensate for its drawbacks. Indeed, the method has become virtually standard in language attitudes research (Fasold, 1984). Since it was first used by Lambert and his associates in order to investigate language attitudes in the Canadian province of Quebec, the technique has been used there on numerous further occasions (e.g. Genesee & Holobow, 1989; Laur, 2008; Kircher, 2014) as well as being applied in a wide range of other settings – including Israel (Lambert et al.,1965), the UK (Sachdev, Elmufti, & Collins, 1998) and Spain (Echeverria, 2005), to name just a few.

The major strength of the technique lies in "the elicitation of spontaneous attitudes less sensitive to reflection and social desirability biases than are directly assessed attitudes" (Ryan et al., 1987, p. 1072). It is assumed that in studies of this kind, more private reactions are revealed than in direct attitude measures such as questionnaires or interviews because "respondents have the attitude object (a language, a variety, or even a feature of a variety) presented to them indirectly, triggering *subconscious* evaluation of the linguistic element (the attitude object) under the guise of being asked for an evaluation of the speaker, not his or her linguistic production" (Preston, 2009, p. 270, emphasis added).

As Lambert (1967, p. 94, emphasis added) himself states, "[t]he technique is particularly valuable as a measure of *group* biases in evaluative reactions [because] it has very good reliability in the sense that essentially the same profile of traits for a particular group appears when different samples of judges, drawn from a particular subpopulation, are used."

Consequently, many researchers consider the matched-guise technique to be "a rigorous and elegant design" for investigating people's language attitudes that has generated a considerable number of studies in various intergroup contexts with a very reasonable degree of comparability, thereby allowing for cumulative development of theory and laying "the foundations for cross-disciplinary work at the interface of the social psychology of language and sociolinguistics" (Garrett et al., 2003, p. 57).

The Matched-Guise Technique in Combination with Other Methods

While triangulation – that is, the use of more than one method to answer a particular research question – is advisable in the study of any aspect of language, it is particularly important in language attitudes research. Ryan et al. (1987), for example, strongly advocate the use of all three of the aforementioned types of methods, but at least direct and indirect ones, by explaining that if only one type of measurement is employed, it is impossible to make definitive statements about language attitudes. Furthermore, they note that it is quite possible, and even to be expected, that on many occasions, direct and indirect methods of attitude elicitation will yield contradictory results. This is by no means an issue of relative methodological merit but is due to the fact that direct and indirect methods of attitude elicitation simply produce results at different levels of analysis.

> This is so because of the often-forgotten fact that language attitudes are not like minerals there to be mined and unearthed, they are *social constructions* constantly changing to meet the demand of the situation in which they are *expressed* [...]. The direct and indirect methods lay claim to quite different layers of experience and as such manifest sometimes quite contradictory, yet highly rational, attitude constellations. (Ryan et al., 1987, p. 1076, emphasis in original)

Hence, Ryan et al. (1987, p. 1076) conclude that "[t]o use only one method, and particularly so in pursuit of socio-political ideals and/or policy implementation, is to be guilty of misunderstanding the nature of language attitudes."

Ideally, the participant sample involved in the direct and indirect methods should be the same. However, if this is not possible, the participant samples used for the different methods should be as similar as possible to each other with regard to their age, their gender, their social, ethnic and linguistic background, and any other social factors that are relevant to the study. This increases the degree of comparability.

Case in Point

Kircher, R. (2014). Thirty years after Bill 101: A contemporary perspective on attitudes towards English and French in Montreal. *Canadian Journal of Applied Linguistics, 17(1)*, 20–50.

Research question: What is the effect of mother tongue on the attitudes that adolescents in Quebec's urban center, Montreal, hold towards English compared to French?
Data collection methods: A questionnaire and a matched-guise experiment.
Participants: 147 college students from Montreal whose mother tongues were English, French and several immigrant languages.
Results: Regarding the status dimension, the results of both research methods indicate that the participants of all mother tongue groups have more positive attitudes towards English than towards French. This is interpreted as a consequence of the utilitarian value that English holds as the language of upward mobility in North America at large, as well as its role as the global lingua franca. These more positive attitudes towards English appear not only to be privately held, as evidenced by the matched-guise experiment, but also considered to be socially acceptable, as evidenced by the questionnaire.

Regarding the solidarity dimension, the outcome of the questionnaire indicates more positive attitudes towards English amongst the Anglophones, more positive attitudes towards French amongst the Francophones, and equally positive attitudes towards both languages amongst those participants who had a mother tongue other than English or French. The findings of the matched-guise experiment, on the other hand, show more positive attitudes towards English amongst all mother tongue groups. The outcome of the questionnaire is interpreted as revealing what the respondents consider to be socially acceptable and desirable – most likely as a consequence of previous language policy and planning measures implemented in Quebec. The findings of the matched-guise experiment, on the other hand, are seen to reveal more privately held attitudes – probably resulting from social identities that involve English as the ingroup language, including a Montreal-based identity and/or an international youth identity.

The comparison of the results from the questionnaire and the matched-guise experiment allows for a more nuanced comprehension of the language attitudes held by adolescent Montrealers than any one method could have provided on its own.

Variations and More Recent Trends in the Use of the Matched-Guise Technique

Some researchers have used variations of the matched-guise technique, such as the *verbal-guise technique*, which involves using a different speaker for each of the experimental stimuli. This procedure is usually employed out of necessity, when there is no possibility of locating speakers who can produce different guises with a comparable degree of fluency (e.g. Nesdale & Rooney, 1996). Other researchers have made use of the *segmented-dialogue technique*, a variation of the matched-guise technique which employs recordings of conversations and which can be used to assess attitudes towards linguistic behaviors such as code-switching (e.g. Genesee & Bourhis, 1982). A further variation of the matched-guise technique is the *theater-audience technique* in which theatergoers are asked over the speaker system, in different guises on different evenings, to complete a questionnaire related to the performance they attended. Their attitudes are measured by whether or not they complete the questionnaire during the interval of the performance, and by the variety in which they choose to complete it (e.g. Bourhis & Giles, 1976). Each of these variations of the matched-guise technique has its own set of advantages and drawbacks; however, a discussion of these goes beyond the scope of this chapter.

The majority of studies in the past has made use of the matched-guise technique in its pure form – and while the pioneering work of Wallace Lambert and his associates as well as many of the subsequent matched-guise experiments were conducted in person, the development of technology means that such studies can now easily be conducted online. This makes it much easier to reach larger numbers of participants, in more diverse locations, within a shorter period of time.

While the matched-guise technique was originally developed by Lambert et al. (1960) to investigate attitudes towards entire language varieties, the past decade has seen a rise in speaker evaluation studies that have also investigated attitudes towards specific linguistic features. Again, technology has played an important role in this development: computer software now allows researchers to modify recordings of speakers in a manner that results in almost identical experimental stimuli which differ only with regard to the specific linguistic variable(s) under investigation (e.g. Levon, 2007, who manipulated pitch range and sibilant duration to investigate the perceptual identification of gayness in male speech). The speaker evaluation paradigm thus now allows for the investigation of speech perception in a wide variety of contexts, both in person and electronically.

Key Terms

Evaluation booklet The booklet distributed to the participants in a matched-guise experiment that contains the instructions, a copy of the text, the rating scales for the experimental stimuli, as well as questions regarding the relevant social variables

Experimental stimuli In matched-guise experiments: the recordings of the bilingual/bidialectal speakers that are the triggers for the participants' evaluative responses

Language attitudes Any beliefs held about, feelings elicited by, or behaviors directed at different language varieties and their speakers

Speaker evaluation paradigm An umbrella term comprising indirect methods of attitude elicitation that involve speech perception experiments, such as matched-guise experiments

Triangulation The use of more than one method in order to answer a particular research question – for example, a matched-guise experiment in combination with a questionnaire

References

Agheyisi, R., & Fishman, J. A. (1970). Language attitude studies: A brief survey of methodological approaches. *Anthropological Linguistics*, 12(5), 137–157.

Bohner, G. (2001). Attitudes. In M. Hewstone, & W. Stroebe (Eds.), *Introduction to social psychology*, (3rd ed., pp. 239–282). Oxford: Blackwell.

Bourhis, R. Y., & Giles, H. (1976). The language of cooperation in Wales: A field study. *Language Sciences*, 42, 13–16.

Bourhis, R. Y., & Maass, A. (2005). Linguistic prejudice and stereotypes. In U. Ammon, N. Dittmar, K., Mattheier, J., & Trudgill, P. (Eds.), *Sociolinguistics: An international handbook of the science of language and society* (vol. 2, 2nd ed., pp. 1587–1601). Berlin: Walter de Gruyter.

Cargile, A.C., Giles, H., Ryan, E.B., & Bradac, J.J. (1994). Language attitudes as a social process: A conceptual model and new directions. *Language and Communication*, 14(3), 211–236.

Echeverria, B. (2005). Language attitudes in San Sebastian: The Basque vernacular as challenge to Spanish language hegemony. *Journal of Multilingual and Multicultural Development*, 26(3), 249–264.

Edwards, J.R. (1982). Language attitudes and their implications among English speakers. In E.B. Ryan, & H. Giles (Eds.), *Attitudes towards language variation: Social and applied contexts* (pp. 20–33). London: Edward Arnold.

Fasold, R. (1984). *The sociolinguistics of society*. Oxford: Blackwell.

Garrett, P., Coupland, N., & Williams, A. (2003). *Investigating language attitudes: Social meanings of dialect, ethnicity and performance*. Cardiff: University of Wales Press.

Genesee, F., & Bourhis, R.Y. (1982). The social psychological significance of code switching in cross-cultural communication. *Journal of Language and Social Psychology* 1(1), 1–27.

Genesee, F., & Holobow, N.E. (1989). Change and stability in intergroup perceptions. *Journal of Language and Social Psychology*, 8(1), 17–39.

Giles, H., & Coupland, N. (1991). *Language: Contexts and consequences.* Milton Keynes: Open University Press.

Grosjean, F. (1982). *Life with two languages: An introduction to bilingualism.* Cambridge, MA: Harvard University Press.

Gross, M. (1999). *Psychology: The science of mind and behaviour* (3rd ed.). Sevenoaks: Hodder and Stoughton.

Kircher, R. (2014). Thirty years after Bill 101: A contemporary perspective on attitudes towards English and French in Montreal. *Canadian Journal of Applied Linguistics*, 17(1), 20–50.

Lambert, W.E. (1967). A social psychology of bilingualism. *Journal of Social Issues*, 23(2), 91–109.

Lambert, W.E., Anisfeld, M., & Yeni-Komshian, G. (1965). Evaluational reactions of Jewish and Arab adolescents to dialect and language variations. *Journal of Personality and Social Psychology*, 2(1), 84–90.

Lambert, W.E., Hodgson, R.C., Gardner, R.C., & Fillenbaum, S. (1960). Evaluational reactions to spoken language. *Journal of Abnormal and Social Psychology*, 60(1), 44–51.

Laur, E. (1994). À la recherche d'une notion perdue: Les attitudes linguistiques à la Québécoise. *Culture*, 14(2), 73–84.

Laur, E. (2008). *Contribution aà l'étude des perceptions linguistiques: La méthodologie des faux-couples revisitée.* [Québec]: Office québécois de la langue francçaise.

Levon, E. (2007). Sexuality in context: Variation and the sociolinguistic perception of identity. *Language in Society*, 36, 533–554.

Luhman, R. (1990). Appalachian English stereotypes: Language attitudes in Kentucky. *Language in Society*, 19, 331–348.

Nesdale, D., & Rooney, R. (1996). Evaluations and stereotyping of accented speakers by preadolescent children. *Journal of Language and Social Psychology*, 15, 133–154.

Pear, T. H. (1931). *Voice and personality.* New York: Wiley.

Preston, D. (2009). Are you really smart (or stupid, or cute, or ugly, or cool)? Or do you just talk that way? In M. Maegaard, F. Gregerson, P. Quist, & J.N. Jørgensen (Eds.), *Language attitudes, standardization and language change – perspectives on themes raised by Tore Kristiansen on the occasion of his 60th Birthday* (pp. 105–129). Oslo: Novus Forlag.

Romaine, S. (1995). *Bilingualism* (2nd ed.). Oxford: Blackwell.

Ryan, E.B., Giles, H., & Hewstone, M. (1987). The measurement of language attitudes. In U. Ammon, N. Dittmar, & K.J. Mattheier (Eds.), *Sociolinguistics: An international handbook of language and society* (pp. 1068–1081). Berlin: Walter de Gruyter.

Ryan, E.B., Giles, H., & Sebastian, R.J. (1982). An integrative perspective for the study of attitudes towards language variation. In E.B. Ryan, & H. Giles (Eds.), *Attitudes towards language variation: Social and applied contexts* (pp. 1–19). London: Edward Arnold.

Ryan, E.B., Hewstone, M., & Giles, H. (1984). Language and intergroup attitudes. In J. Eiser (Ed.), *Attitudinal judgment* (pp. 135–160). New York: Springer.

Sachdev, I., Elmufti, N., & Collins, P. (1998). Oral assessment and accent evaluation: Some British data. In R.K. Agnihotri, A.L. Khanna, & I. Sachdev (Eds.), *Social psychological perspectives on second language learning* (pp. 187–203). New Delhi: Sage.

Tabouret-Keller, A. (1997). Language and identity. In F. Coulmas (Ed.), *The handbook of sociolinguistics* (pp. 315–326). Oxford: Blackwell.

Tajfel, H. & Turner, J. C. (1986). The social identity theory of intergroup behavior. In S. Wochel, & W. G. Austin (Eds.), *Psychology of intergroup relations* (pp. 7–24). Chicago: Nelson-Hall.

Further Reading and Resources

Abbul, R., Gass, S., & Mackey, A. (2013). Experimental research design. In R.J. Podesva, & D. Sharma (Eds.), *Research methods in linguistics* (pp. 116–134). Cambridge: Cambridge University Press.

Drager, K. (2013). Experimental methods in sociolinguistics. In J. Holmes, & K. Hazen (Eds.), *Research methods in sociolinguistics: A practical guide* (pp. 58–73). Oxford: Wiley Blackwell.

Garrett, P. (2010). *Attitudes to Language*. Cambridge: Cambridge University Press.

Myers, J., Well, A., & Lorch, R. (2010). *Research design and statistical analysis*. London: Routledge.

14 Discourse Completion Tasks

Emma Sweeney and Zhu Hua

> **Summary**
>
> This chapter explores the data collection method known as a discourse completion task, a production questionnaire in which the participant responds to a given prompt. Distinguishing features, strengths and limitations are analyzed, and practical advice is given on using this elicitation technique effectively. Several points are highlighted: DCTs are convenient to use and easy to control, but careful attention must be paid to the sensitivity of responses to the design of the instrument, and steps must be taken to provide additional validity to the data. Importantly, the data elicited from a DCT cannot be seen to replicate authentic, naturally occurring data, and as such it should be recognized that this instrument is best suited to answering research questions about attitudes to communication or pragmalinguistic knowledge of a certain language. Whilst allowing for these provisos, the chapter concludes that DCTs have potential in intercultural communication research if used to address realistic research questions

Discourse completion tasks (DCTs) are a type of production questionnaire in which speech acts are elicited in the written form by some kind of situational description (Billmyer & Varghese, 2000). They were first used for speech act data by Blum Kulka (1982), and then in the CCSARP (Cross-cultural Speech Act Realization Patterns) project, which sought to compare how two specific speech acts, requests and apologies, were realized across eight languages, according to different conditions of social distance, and, in addition, to compare realization by native speakers and non-native speakers of the languages in question (Blum Kulka & Olshtain, 1984). Since then, DCTs have been widely used as a data collection method for research in cross-cultural pragmatics. Some studies (e.g. Felix-Brasdefer, 2010) have used DCTs to investigate the cultural variation in the realization of speech acts in natural speech. However, it is now widely acknowledged that DCTs are much better suited to investigating respondents' knowledge of pragmalinguistic norms, or understanding of what is appropriate to say in certain situations (Golato, 2003; Hinkel, 1997; Sweeney & Zhu, 2010). Very little research to date has used DCTs in an investigation of what happens in intercultural communication, where people from from different cultures interact. One study by Sweeney and Zhu (2010), analyzed later on in this chapter, suggests that this instrument if applied to answer appropriate questions has great potential for intercultural communication research.

DCTs elicit response from some kind of situational prompt, but there are variations in the way the prompt is framed, the detail of the situation or context provided, and the response required. In the examples below, both A and C provide quite detailed context, albeit differently – C gives detailed information in order to establish social constraints, whilst A provides a rejoinder (or predetermined response to the strategy provided by the participant in the DCT) which clearly establishes a sense of the relationship between the participants. In contrast, Example B allows the writer more latitude to interpret the situation and balances that by offering the respondent the option of additional choices. All three elicit specific speech acts: Example A – request and apology, Example B – response to compliment, and Example C – request.

Example A

1 *At a students' apartment:*
   Larry, John's room-mate, had a party the night before and left the kitchen in a mess.

   John: Larry, Ellen and Tom are coming for dinner tonight and I'll have to start cooking soon; _____
   Larry: Ok, I'll have a go at it right away.

2 *At the professor's office*
   A student has borrowed a book from her teacher, which she promised to return today. When meeting her teacher, however, she realizes that she forgot to bring it along.

   Teacher: Miriam, I hope you brought the book I lent you.
   Miriam: _____
   Teacher: OK, but please remember it next week.

                          (Blum Kulka & Olshtain, 1984, p. 198)

> **Example B**
>
> *Directions:* Please react to the following situations. In some of the situations, you may find more than one response/reaction appropriate. In this case, please write down all the appropriate responses on the lines provided. Please do not discuss this questionnaire or your responses with others while you are filling it out.
>
> You have invited friends over for a casual dinner. At the end of the evening (when leaving your house) one of your friends says: "it was a nice evening!"
> You answer:
> a) _____ b) _____
> c) _____ d) _____
>
> (Golato, 2003, p. 115)

> **Example C**
>
> It is 10.30 p.m. on a Wednesday night and you have a paper due the next day. You are trying to finish the paper and you can't concentrate because you hear loud music coming from another student's room down the hall. You decide to ask her to turn the music down. The music has been on at this volume for half an hour. You have occasionally seen the student, Lucy Row, in the same dorm during the past six months. She is a student like you but you have never spoken to her. You have heard other people in the dorm complain about the volume of her music on several occasions, although you never have because you usually study in the library. However, today the library closed early. You are only halfway through and you know that the professor for this class is very strict and does not give extensions. What would you say?
>
> (Billmyer & Varghese, 2000, p. 548)

Another type of DCT which has developed in recent years is the oral DCT. It administers DCT through audio-recording and verbally. The situations from the written DCT are audio-recorded first and then played to participants who give an oral response. The oral responses are audio-recorded as they are elicited.

Despite being used widely in data gathering in the 1980s and 1990s, DCTs have also attracted their fair share of controversy and criticism. Their undoubted strengths lie for the most part in practical factors, whereas their weaknesses are largely based on their elicited rather than natural nature. Both will be discussed in the section below.

Evaluation of Discourse Completion Tasks

What DCTs measure

In the last couple of decades there have been a number of studies investigating the validity of DCT data in comparison to other elicited data and to naturally occurring talk (Economidou-Kogetsidis, 2013; Golato, 2003; Hinkel,1997; Yuan, 2001). The results of these studies, which are generally consistent, suggest that DCT data are not suited to answering questions about how language is realized naturally, but is much better suited to investigations into how much respondents know about what is appropriate to say in certain situations.

Differences between DCTS, other types of elicited data and natural speech are reported in the following areas:

- Although there are some similarities in the strategies used in both the DCT and the naturally occurring data, some strategies reported in the DCT do not occur in the recorded natural data and vice versa (Golato, 2003).
- Responses in DCTS are given to the prompts where they would be ignored in the natural data (Golato, 2003).
- Responses in the natural data develop over several turns, whereas in elicited data, responses are given over one turn (Golato, 2003; Yuan, 2001).
- Responses to DCTs are sensitive to questionnaire design which means responses may not be comparable (Billmyer & Varghese, 2000; Johnston, Kasper, & Ross, 1998).
- Compared with written DCTS, the response to oral DCTS is closer to the natural data (Yuan, 2001).

It is important to note that evidence around elaboration of DCT responses is rather inconsistent between speakers of different languages. As examples, Yuan (2001) investigated compliment responses in Chinese, comparing responses given to written DCTs, oral DCTs, open role plays, and naturally occurring speech, and found that written DCTs elicited the least elaboration. Whereas, Golato (2003) investigating the same speech act in German found that even though respondents may have struggled to know what to write initially, written DCT responses were longer than the naturally occurring responses in her study. She speculated that this may reflect the lack of physical interlocutor and thus nobody to intervene. Alternatively, respondents might have felt an obligation to respond to the DCT which they did not feel in the natural data, where some compliments were completely ignored. This cross-linguistic difference is significant for researchers working with different languages, as it raises the issue of comparability.

Strengths

The greatest strength of DCTs and, arguably, the reason for their widespread use, is the convenience they provide. Authentic, naturally occurring talk can be very hard to come by. This is frequently because of difficulties surrounding access. Even when access to data is possible, there remains a danger that the desired speech act or interaction will not occur. In contrast, DCTs are convenient and quick to use, do not require a lengthy or costly transcription, and responses can be easily and swiftly classified.

Another, equally important, strength of DCTs lies in the fact that they are carefully planned and designed to capture desired data and therefore variables such as relationship, power, status, gender, and age differentials can be controlled, converse to the situation with natural speech (Yuan, 2001). DCT data can be comparable, although this claim has to be tempered with recognition that DCT design can have a significant impact on participant responses, and that responses to different DCTs may not be comparable (Billmyer & Varghese, 2000; Johnston et al., 1998; Yuan, 2001). An additional benefit from planning is that it allows for participants to be fully informed of the goals and implications of the research, and to give their consent to their responses being used, making DCTs arguably more straightforward than naturally occurring talk or field notes from the perspective of fulfilling the ethical guidelines for data collection.

Limitations and Controversies

DCTs have been criticized for two main reasons. Firstly, the possibility of huge variation in style or design (evidenced by the examples above) raises some doubts over their comparability and efficacy (Billmyer & Varghese, 2000; Johnston et al., 1998). The second is authenticity and validity issue. As explained in the previous section, DCTs are suited to revealing participants' accumulated experience with language use, and not to be confused with natural data.

With regard to the design of DCTs, one of the issues under debate which potentially has implications on Intercultural Communication studies is the extent to which contextual information or prompts impact on participants' responses, or, to put it another way, "is the more contextual information, the better"? The short answer is "it depends," for two reasons. Firstly, available research suggests that the impact of contextual information on participants' responses varies between different speech acts. For example, Johnston et al. (1998) investigated the DCTs response to three different speech acts – requests, complaints, and apologies – and noted that the inclusion of a rejoinder (as seen in Example A above) had an impact on all three, but to varying degrees. Apologies were most affected by rejoinder, followed by request. Complaints were the least affected. The researchers argued that differences in the degree, direction, and certainty of face threat in different speech acts seem to have been a significant factor.

Secondly, some conflicting research evidence exists regarding whether additional contextual information help with non-native speakers or not. For example, Billmyer and Varghese (2000) examined the effect of providing greater depth of situational information and found that for both native speakers and non-native speakers, longer prompts elicited a greater number of moves. In contrast, however, Hinkel (1997) compared DCT and multiple-choice questionnaire data from Chinese speakers' responses in English to appropriateness of advice, and reported that the Chinese speakers in her study found it more difficult to complete the written DCT responses in English than to choose from responses on a multiple-choice questionnaire.

In sum, design clearly has an impact on the responses elicited and, hence, extra care should be taken in designing the questions and contextual information to maximize authenticity and validity. Cross-linguistic variations exist in elaboration of response and the usefulness of additional contextual information, and therefore, studies on speakers of different languages may not always be comparable. Great attention should be given to the claims that are made.

Case in Point

Sweeney, E., & Zhu, H. (2010). Accommodating towards your audience: Do native speakers of English know how to accommodate their communication strategies towards nonnative speakers of English? *Journal of Business Communication, 47(4),* 477–504.

Research question: This small-scale, exploratory study was inspired by the concept of "the native speaker problem" (Crystal, 2003; Graddol, 2006; Nickerson, 2005; Seidlhofer, 2000, 2001) which concerns the potentially problematic role of the native speaker in intercultural interactions in English. The objective of the research was to discover the differences in the use of communication strategies or pragmalinguistic norms between native speakers and non-native speakers in negotiation, and to assess the extent to which this sample of native speakers accommodated towards non-native speakers in intercultural interactions. Accomodation in this sense means the degree to which the native speakers adapted their communication in order to assist the effectiveness of the interaction, by either making their communication similar to (convergence) or different from (divergence) the communication of their interlocutor.

Research design: A DCT was chosen as the main data-gathering instrument for two principle reasons: firstly, it bypassed practical problems such as access to sufficient instances of the required speech acts and confidentiality issues connected with gathering data from authentic business interactions; secondly, it ensured complete comparability of the data and ease of analysis given a tight research schedule. In addition, it was recognized that although the DCT was unlikely to elicit natural speech paterns, it was likely to represent what the participants thought they should say. Therefore, it could arguably inform on the extent of native speakers' knowledge of intercultural communication difficulties and their ability to deal with them.

The DCT was carefully planned in order to maximize its validity in capturing the required data. Participants were informed that they were the retail buyer for an organization, were negotiating a new contract with an established supplier, and their interactant was new to the role. Although this supplier still maintained a leading position in the field, market conditions made it necessary to push for the best deal. It was hoped that the combination of established institutional relationship and new personal relationship would nullify any potential bias, and the balance of overall customer satisfaction and economic needs would moderate extremes of communication. This contextual section was followed by a series of prompts designed to represent a developing negotiation:

> **Sample of questions**
>
> Write down what you would say as an opening to the bargaining procedure.
> The seller offers a very small discount and strict payment terms. Write down what you would say to reject it.
> Make what you consider a reasonable concession from your opening position.
> The seller is taking too much time and doesn't seem to be willing to compromise. Write down what you would say to increase the pressure.
> The seller makes an offer you consider to be a step in the right direction. Write down what you would say to encourage further consessions.
>
> (Sweeney & Zhu, 2010, p. 502)

Following the prompts, participants were asked to answer four general questions about appropriate communication with non-native speakers of English, in order to understand the rationale behind their language choices.

> **General Questions**
>
> 1 When you are speaking to non-native speakers of English, what kind of language do you use? Give examples:
> 2 When speaking to non-native speakers of English, what kind of language do you avoid? Give examples:
> 3 What, if any, are the most significant potential problems of communication between native speakers of English and non-native speakers of English?
> 4 Rate the difficulty of this test. Why did you find it easy/difficult?
>
> Easy 0 1 2 3 4 5 6 7 Difficult

The planning stage was followed by pilot testing, completed by both native and non-native speakers who were not participants in the study itself. Once the pilot testing had accertained that the required data were elcited, participants were invited to complete the task. The native speaker participants were asked to complete the DCT twice, the first time with an unspecified interactant, and the second time imagining a non-native speaker interactant. The non-native speakers completed it only once and with an unspecified interactant

Fourteen native speakers and 13 non-native speakers took part in the DCT. The native speaker participants were drawn from the first researcher's personal and business contacts, came from a range of business backgrounds and were all between 30 and 60 years old. They had all attained a management level in their career and interacted with non-native speakers in a business capacity at least occasionally. The non-native participants were attending a full-time intensive course on Business English at the time of the research and using English for busines purposes in their everyday lives. Based on the Common European framework, all had an English level of at least

B2. Eleven of the non-native speakers were working at management level, and the other two were graduate trainees.

As an additional measure the responses were reviewed by three non-native speakers who had not participated in the DCT. It had been predicted that native speaker communication strategies that diverged from non-native speaker strategies, would be problematic for effective interpretability, and that the reviewers' comments would act as predictive validation. The reviewers were all proficient speakers of English using it frequently for business purposes.

Data analysis: The resultant data were subsequently analyzed both quantitatively and qualitatively. The former consisted of measuring the length of responses, average length of responses and standard deviation from the mean for each of the DCTs. The latter involved measuring how direct the responses were and identifying the type and amount of modification that was used to either soften or strengthen the force of the message.

Results: The results of the analysis indicated that the native speakers in this sample used far more nonconventionally indirect strategies or hints than the non-native speakers, although the most frequent strategy type for both groups was direct. In addition, the native speakers' turns were longer, their choice of strategies and vocabulary more varied, and the number and variety of supportive moves they used was greater. In terms of accommodation, the results suggested that to a certain degree the native speakers were adjusting their language towards that of the non-native speakers: the utterances for the DCT completed with the non-native speaker interlocutor were slightly shorter and contained fewer supportive moves, and there were more direct strategies and fewer indirect strategies. However, there was no reduction in internal modification, and the other changes were not consistently applied. Four of the non-native speakers did not modify their communication at all, whilst others overaccommodated.

The answers to the general questions at the end of the DCT suggested a general understanding of the communicative issues of intercultural communication, albeit an underestimation of the significance of the issues. Comments from the non-native speaker reviewers seemed to reinforce the results of the DCT: very indirect strategies embedded in long utterances were often misconstrued or missed entirely, while overly direct, unmitigated utterances were responded to negatively.

The authors concluded firstly, that the native speaker participants in this study had a greater linguistic repertoire at their fingertips which enabled them both to calibrate their strategies to convey a specific message, and to express their own personal variations of style. Secondly, that whilst these native speakers did understand in general the communication problems that can occur in intercultural interactions, they lacked an effective understanding of how to apply appropriate strategies.

Reflection on methodological issues: The DCT enabled the researchers to gather interesting and relevant data on what were believed to be appropriate communication strategies. Despite diverse responses in the native speakers' DCTs, there is sufficient similarity in the trend of the data from the DCT, the answers to the general questions and the comments from the review, to allow observations and generalization. However, if the aim was to discover the actual differences between native speaker and non-native speaker strategies and the actual ability of native speakers to accommodate their communication towards non-native speakers, then the data collection limits any claims that can be made.

Conclusion

Drawing on the discussion of the features of DCTs, their advantages and limitations, and the study reviewed above, there are three practical steps to be followed when using DCTs as a tool for data collection.

First and foremost, researchers should carefully consider the research questions they would like to answer. DCT data can only be confidently regarded as an approximation of realization of communication strategies, and the extent of claims that can be made should be limited accordingly.

Secondly, design is a key factor in increasing validity. The study reviewed above went some way to overcoming some shortcomings of DCTs such as an interaction over one turn, and tried to provide sufficient context to guide the participants and make the data comparable, without overly influencing participants' responses. However, these effort do not change the "off-line" (Golato, 2003) nature of DCTs, which permits excessive thought to go into the process of giving a response that would normally be automatic. An improvement that could have been made to the DCT in the study reviewed above might have been the oral DCT which brings the interaction a step closer to a real life situation. But, this is arguably more time-consuming and intrusive than a written DCT, and so may not be appropriate in all situations. Additionally, if language behavior is the target for the data collection, an oral DCT may still not provide suficiently useful data, and in this case an open role play may be preferable (Yuan, 2001).

Finally, measures should be in place to ensure the validity of the data captured. It is essential to carry out a pilot testing at the initial stage to ensure that the design does actually elicit the desired data. In the study reviewed here, a short retrospective questionnaire provided some useful additional explanation for the language choices made by the native speaker participants. The study also used a review of the data to test its predictive validity. In this case, the reviewers were interviewed and the researcher noted their comments. Alternatively, this kind of review could have been organized as a questionnaire with a five point lickert scale, which may have been more time efficient if a large number of responses were required.

DCTs will continue to be widely used in research which aims to understand speakers' language behavior, not only because of their convenience and ease of use, but also because they offer value in illuminating attitudes to communication and knowledge about appropriate communication. These attributes make them a valuable resource for researchers of intercultural communication, where the focus is on how people from different cultural backgrounds interact.

Key Terms

Discourse completion task A technique used in eliciting discourse data from participants by asking them to report either verbally or in writing what they would say in a given situation.

Elicited conversation Compared with naturally occurring speech, conversation can be elicited through a range of methods and techniques, such as discourse completion task, role play or interviews.

Oral DCT A type of discourse completion task in which participants are asked to listen to audio recordings of the situation first before giving their response verbally.

Role play A technique of collecting conversational data in which participants are asked to act out specified roles within a context.

Speech acts The performance of an act in speaking, such as requesting, greeting, apologizing, etc

References

Billmyer, K., & Varghese, M. (2000). Investigating instrument-based pragmatic variability: Effect of enhancing discourse completion tests. *Applied Linguistics*, 21(4), 517–552.

Blum Kulka, S. (1982). Learning to say what you mean in a second language: a study of the speech act performance of learners of Hebrew as a second language. *Applied Linguistics*, 3(1), 29–59.

Blum Kulka, S., & Olshtain, E. (1984). Requests and Apologies: Cross-cultural study of Speech Act realization patterns (CCSARP). *Applied Linguistics*, 5(3), 196–213.

Blum Kulka, S., House, J., & Kasper, G. (1989). *Cross cultural pragmatics: Requests and apologies*. Norwood, NJ: Ablex.

Crystal, D. (2003). *English as a global language*. Cambridge: Cambridge University Press.

Economidou-Kogetsidis, M. (2013). Strategies, modification and perspective in native speakers' requests: A comparison of WDCT and naturally occurring requests. *Journal of Pragmatics*, 53, 21–38.

Felix-Brasdefer, J. (2010). Intra-lingual pragmatic variation in Mexico City and San Jose, Costa Rica: A focus on regional differences in female requests. *Journal of Pragmatics*, 42, 2992–3011.

Golato, A. (2003). Studying compliment responses: A comparison of DCTs and recordings of naturally occurring talk. *Applied Linguistics*, 24(1), 90–121.

Graddol, D. (2006). *English next*. Retrieved June 16, 2015 from: http://englishagenda.britishcouncil.org/publications/english-next.

Hamid, A., & Amin, N. (2011). A cross-linguistic study of refusals: An analysis of pragmatic competence development in Iranian EFL learners. *Journal of Pragmatics*, 43, 385–486.

Hinkel, E. (1997). Appropriateness of advice: DCT and multiple choice data. *Applied Linguistics*, 18(1), 1–26.

Johnston, B., Kasper, G., & Ross, S. (1998). Effect of Rejoinders in production questionnaires. *Applied Linguistics*, 19(2), 157–182.

Kasper, G. (2004). Data Collection in Pragmatics Research. In H. Spencer-Oatey (Ed.), *Culturally speaking: Managing rapport through talk accross cultures* (pp. 316–341). London: Continuum.

McEwen, V., & Coupland, N. (2000). Accommodation theory: A conceptual resource for intercultural sociolinguistics. In H. Spencer-Oatey (Ed.), *Culturally speaking: Managing rapport through talk accross cultures* (pp. 191–214). London: Continuum.

Nickerson, C. (2005). English as a lingua franca in international business contexts. *English for Specific Purposes*, 24, 367–380.

Seidlhofer, B. (2001). Closing the conceptual gap: The case for description of English as a lingua franca. *International Journal of Applied Linguistics*, 11, 133–158.

Seidlhofer, B. (2000). Mind the gap: English as a mother tongue vs. English as a lingua franca. *Vienna English Working Papers*, 26, 51–69.

Sweeney, E., & Zhu, H. (2010). Accommodating toward your audience: Do native speakers of English know how to accommodate their communication strategies toward nonnative speakers of English? *Journal of Business Communication*, 47(4), 477–504.

Yuan, Y. (2001). An inquiry into empirical pragmatics data-gathering methods: Written DCTs, oral DCTs, field notes, and natural conversations. *Journal of Pragmatics*, 33, 271–292.

Further Reading and Resources

Blum Kulka, S., & Olshtain, E. (1984). Requests and apologies: Cross-cultural study of speech act realization patterns (CCSARP). *Applied Linguistics*, 5(3), 196–213.

Golato, A. (2003). Studying compliment responses: A comparison of DCTs and recordings of naturally occurring talk. *Applied Linguistics*, 24(1), 90–121.

Yuan, Y. (2001). An inquiry into empirical pragmatics data-gathering methods: Written DCTs, oral DCTs, field notes, and natural conversations. *Journal of Pragmatics*, 33, 271–292.

Kasper, G., & Rose, K. R. (2002). *Pragmatic development in a second language*. Oxford: Blackwell. Chapter 3 contains an introduction to a number of methods used in developmental pragmatics research including DCT, authentic discourse, elicited conversation, role play, and others.

15 The Critical Incident Technique

Helen Spencer-Oatey and Claudia Harsch

> **Summary**
>
> The Critical Incident Technique is particularly useful when researchers are interested in understanding the details of interactional events. For intercultural researchers the technique can help throw light onto issues such as the impact of different intercultural events, the range and effectiveness of the strategies used for handling them, and the cultural values or principles that may underlie them. Data can be collected using a range of research methods which need to be adjusted according to the specific research focus. The accounts can then not only be analyzed for research purposes, but also developed into training resources. The method is used by researchers holding different paradigmatic positions.

What is the Critical Incident Technique (CIT)?

The Critical Incident Technique (CIT) was first developed in the 1950s by the psychologist John Flanagan, in order to help identify behavior in the workplace that made a crucial difference between effective and ineffective performance on a particular task. Flanagan described the procedure as follows:

> Essentially, the procedure was to obtain first-hand reports, or reports from objective records, of satisfactory and unsatisfactory execution of the task assigned. The cooperating individual described a situation in which success or failure was determined by specific reported causes. (Flanagan, 1954, p. 329)

In the 60 or more years since Flanagan's classic paper, the CIT has been used extensively across a very wide range of fields, including medicine, counselling, international management, organizational behavior, and education. In the intercultural field, it has also been very widely used, not only for research but especially as a source of data for intercultural training.

As Chell (1998) points out, Flanagan developed the CIT at a time when the positivist approach (for more on positivist approach, see Zhu Hua, Chapter 1, this volume) to scientific investigation was dominant, and this entailed an assumption that there was an objective reality or truth that could be identified. Since that time, different paradigms have emerged and this has led to a more variable interpretation of the CIT (Butterfield, Borgen, Amundson, & Malio, 2005).

Two fundamental questions are: what is meant by "critical" and what is meant by an "incident". In terms of the former, Flanagan (1954, p. 338) defined it in terms of "extreme behavior, either outstandingly effective or ineffective with respect to attaining the general aims of the activity." Along similar lines, Edvardsson (1992, p. 17) regards it as something that "deviates significantly, either positively or negatively, from what is normal or expected," and Cope and Watts (2000) have associated it with high emotional content. However, Keatinge (2002) suggests that the term "critical" might be replaced with "significant" or "revelatory." This fits more comfortably with a constructionist paradigm and allows for the interpretive role of the participant to be incorporated. This is captured very well in the following interpretations:

> The "critical incident" is a complex phenomenon that does not occur independently of the entrepreneur but in many cases is a change in perception and awareness that stimulates the entrepreneur into action. (Cope & Watts, 2000, p. 113)
>
> Critical incidents are not "things" which exist independently of an observer and are awaiting discovery like gold nuggets or desert islands, but like all data, critical incidents are created. Incidents happen, but critical incidents are produced by the way we look at a situation: a critical incident is an interpretation of the significance of an event. To take something as a critical incident is a value judgement we make, and the basis of that judgement is the significance we attach to the meaning of the incident. (Tripp, 1993, p. 8)

Similar variability applies to the term "incident." Flanagan (1954, p. 327) defined an incident as "any observable human activity that is sufficiently complete in itself to permit inferences and predictions to be made about the person performing the act." Cope and Watts (2000), on the other hand, refer to critical "periods" or "episodes" because it is often difficult to determine the boundaries of some experiences, and insisting on doing so could trivialize the diversity and complexity of the experiences that people go through.

Chell (1998) therefore argues that researchers need to think through how the CIT may be interpreted and applied most appropriately for their own particular research focus. This is as true for the intercultural field as for any other.

Intercultural Research Themes and Use of the CIT

Up to now, research into intercultural communication using the CIT has mainly focused on four main areas: the identification of cultural values/standards, insights into cross-cultural transitions/adaptation, insights into intercultural interaction, and the development and evaluation of training resources.

Cultural Values/Standards

The CIT has been employed in research to identify culture-specific values and cultural standards, for example by Thomas and colleagues (e.g. 1996, 2000, 2010). Thomas (2010, p. 21) understands culture as "a national and linguistic entity, which provides its members with a sense-giving orientation" [cf. Holliday, Chapter 2, this volume]. He assumes culture-specific standards underlie and influence people's behavior, judgments and expectations. He argues that participants perceive behavior as unexpected if it is not in line with their underlying culture standards. Hence, interactions which do not evolve as anticipated and expected may cause criticality. Consequently, Thomas in his 1996 study focused on members of two (national) cultures, in this case China and Germany. He interviewed sojourners as well as members of the two cultures in question.

The focus was on frequently occurring difficulties in work-related tasks, where interactions did not take place as anticipated or entailed unexpected behavior; he also collected narrations of interactions which worked surprisingly well. Along with the critical interaction narratives, Thomas elicited explanations of the interactions and behaviors. The narratives and explanations were translated into both languages and the quality of the explanations was evaluated by experts from both cultures. This approach allowed Thomas to identify cultural standards which were at work during the narrated interactions and caused criticality. Using expert analysis across a range of situations also allowed generalizing these standards beyond the collected situations to the wider work domain for the two cultures in question. If these work-related cultural standards are validated by other domains, for example by literature, sociology, or philosophy, one can identify core cultural standards which provide a basic guide to understanding; they are, however, not intended to explain the complexity of human behavior (Thomas, 2010). Thomas and colleagues used this approach in further studies to analyze cultural standards for other cultures (e.g. France, England, Spain, the Czech Republic, the US, Japan, Korea, and Indonesia, Thomas, 2000). They applied their findings to develop culture-specific training materials for work sojourners, amongst other materials (e.g. Thomas & Schenk, 2001).

Cross-cultural Transitions/Adaptation

Another important research topic in the intercultural field is intercultural adaptation. The CIT is particularly valuable for researching this topic when the aim is to gain insights into the specific, concrete experiences that people go through, as well their reactions to them. It can yield insights into many of the components of this topic, including the types of challenges that people may experience, the impact those challenges may have on the individuals, the strategies they may use for dealing with the challenges, and any perspective change/personal growth that may occur. Arthur explains the strengths of the CIT for this topic area as follows:

> a critical incident methodology provides a "running experiential commentary" of meaningful events and reactions to those events (Brookfield, 1995). It permits tracking of experiences at various times rather than a single "snap shot" of cross-cultural transition. (Arthur, 2001, p. 44)

The CIT thus allows a focus on what is significant and meaningful to the participants, putting their perspectives at the heart of the study. Examples of studies that have used the CIT for researching this topic include Arthur (2001) and Chang (2009).

Intercultural Interaction

Intercultural interaction is a very broad topic area that is studied by researchers in several disciplines, including applied linguistics, communication studies, organizational behavior, and international management. It can cover topics such as intercultural teamwork, workplace relations, politeness/rapport, and discrimination. The aims of the studies can be various, including the identification of interactional problems, challenges, successes and achievements that people experience in intercultural interaction; the behavior/strategies that people use in different intercultural interaction contexts for achieving certain goals; and the behaviors that are more or less effective and/or are more or less acceptable to members of different multicultural groups or organizations. Often such foci have the higher-level aim of yielding an enhanced theoretical understanding of the issue at stake and/or of intercultural competence. Some illustrative studies are touched on below.

Chen, Tjosvold, and Su (2005) used the CIT to explore the conditions under which foreign managers and local employees are able to find productive ways of working together. Similarly, Dekker, Rutte, and Van den Berg (2008) collected incidents of interactional behavior among members of virtual, global teams which they believed were particularly critical for effective team functioning. The researchers then compared whether Dutch, Belgian, American and Indian participants held the same perceptions of what counted as critical behavior for effective teamwork.

In applied linguistic intercultural research that has used the CIT, the main focus has been on politeness/rapport. For example, Spencer-Oatey (2002) used the CIT to explore the motivational concerns underlying the management of intercultural relations. She elicited incidents that the participants found to be particularly noticeable in some way, in terms of their relationship with the other person(s). She referred to them as "rapport sensitive" incidents rather than "critical" incidents, but this was simply because of the content focus. A very similar approach was used in Culpeper,

Marti, Mei, Nevala, & Schauer (2010), although they concentrated only on incidents that had a particularly negative effect on interpersonal relations. They collected data in a number of different countries, and then made some cross-cultural comparisons. In both of these studies, the aim was to gain insights into ways of conceptualizing (im)politeness and rapport across cultures.

Another aspect of intercultural relations, perceived discrimination, has also been studied through the CIT. Orbe and Camara (2010), for example, collected 957 accounts of incidences of perceived discrimination. They analyzed these incidents in order to explore two research questions: What are the core elements of perceived discrimination experiences? Additionally, what similarities and differences in perceived discrimination exist across different cultural groups?

In all these cases, the CIT enabled the researchers to gain insights into participants' perceptions of, and reactions to, different aspects of intercultural interaction in different contexts.

Training Resources

Probably the most widespread use of critical incidents in the intercultural field is for training purposes (e.g. Brislin, 1986; Fowler & Blohm, 2004; Wight, 1995). The CIT is frequently used for underpinning research by serving to elicit examples of intercultural interactions that could potentially be used as training resources (e.g. Thomas & Schenk, 2001, see above). The research aims not only at eliciting a set of critical incidents, but also at evaluating the suitability of these incidents for inclusion in a training program.

Dela Cruz, Salzman, Brislin, and Losch (2006), for instance, wanted to develop a Hawaiian Intercultural Sensitizer (ICS) for training purposes. They explain the ICS as follows:

> One of the highly successful tools used in cross-cultural training is the "Intercultural Sensitizer" (ICS), also known as the "Cultural Assimilator" [...]. The ICS is a cross-cultural training method that utilizes the critical incident approach (Flanagan, 1954) to portray culture conflicts between individuals from different cultural backgrounds. Critical incidents are short case studies or vignettes depicting a cross-cultural interaction and potential misunderstandings between culturally different individuals. (Dela Cruz et al., 2006, p. 120)

To develop such an instrument, they first needed to gather a large sample of critical incidents that reflected common situations of misunderstanding, uncertainty, confusion or discord between people from different cultures, and they used the CIT to gather such incidents.

Needless to say, these four broad theme areas are illustrative rather than exhaustive. The CIT can be used to investigate any aspect of intercultural communication when there is a desire to examine specific encounters that are particularly meaningful in some way for the participants. Walker and Truly (1992) argue that it is "a particularly useful method when studying complex interpersonal phenomena" and intercultural interaction can certainly be regarded as that.

Collecting Critical Incident Data

Having considered an illustrative range of research themes that can usefully be explored through using critical incident data, the next question is how exactly such data can be elicited. In fact, there is a range of possibilities. According to Flanagan (1954, p. 335), the CIT should be regarded as a "flexible set of principles which must be modified and adapted to meet the specific situation at hand." He identified four data-collection possibilities: interviews, questionnaires, record sheets, and observations. All of these have been used in the intercultural field. CIs can be collected at one point in time or in a longitudinal approach, again depending on the research aims and the kinds of incidents or occurrences one tries to elicit and research.

Interviews

One of the methods used most frequently to collect CI data is the interview [see also Gibson & Zhu Hua, Chapter 12, this volume]. Interview techniques employed in the CIT range from open to highly structured approaches to suit a variety of research aims and foci.

Chell (2004) describes the "critical interview technique" as a means to elicit a narration of significant occurrences as perceived by the interviewee, encompassing affective, behavioral and cognitive aspects of events, strategies and outcomes. She offers a list of "wh-probes" for the critical interview approach to help participants focus on what happened, how it was managed and what the outcomes were:

> *What* happened next?
> *Why* did it happen?
> *How* did it happen?
> *With whom* did it happen?
> *What* did the parties concerned feel?
> *What* were the consequences – immediately and longer term?
> *How* did the respondent cope?
> *What* tactics were used?
>
> (Chell, 2004, p. 49)

Chen et al. (2005, see above) employed a similar approach, asking participants to describe concrete situations in which they had worked (un-)successfully with their boss, detailing on the setting, what happened and any consequences.

An interesting approach was employed by Dekker, Rutte, and Van den Berg (2008), who sent out detailed and specific questions to participants a week before the interviews to facilitate recollection and elicit specific interaction events. They used, among others, the following questions:

> Now I want you to think back to specific incidents that you have seen occur in the last year. Can you think of an incident in which your virtual team members showed a critical interaction behavior? Would you describe for each example: (1) what were

the circumstances surrounding this incident, (2) what exactly did the team member(s) do that was critical, and (3) how did the behavior (positively or negatively) affect the satisfaction of the team members and/or the performance of the team? (Dekker et al., 2008, p. 446)

Thomas and colleagues (see above) had a different aim: They tried to identify cultural standards which underlie encounters between members of two cultural groups. Hence, they interviewed a large sample of participants with experience in the respective cultures, with a view to eliciting recurrent inexplicable behavior in these encounters which they could analyze as prototypical behavior. Thomas (2010) describes the elicitation process as follows:

> For instance, German managers in France were asked to describe encounters with their French partners, in which they frequently experienced unexpected behavior. (…) The situational context, the Germans' own goals and expectations, as well as their observations, considerations, intentions and actions were noted. The French reaction to unexpected behavior on the part of the Germans and the Germans' assumptions about the underlying causes for the reactions were also documented. (Thomas, 2010, pp. 25–26)

(Focus) group interviews (see Gibson & Zhu Hua, Chapter 12, this volume) are another option if the researcher is interested in the co-construction of interpretations and explanations of events. If it is possible to interview participants involved in the same incident, this dyadic approach (Gremler, 2004) can bring together the different perspectives relevant for interpreting a specific incident.

Regardless of the interview approach chosen, the interviewer has to maintain control over the focus, which is more challenging in narrative and open interviews. The aim is to strike a balance between openness to allow the interviewee to remember and narrate events on the one hand, and on the other hand enough focus and guidance to elicit the kind of events and explanations one is searching for.

Questionnaires

Another frequently used method for collecting CI data is the questionnaire (see also Young, Chapter 11, this volume). Such a questionnaire usually includes a demographic section followed by a section to elicit a CI. How much structure or prompting is included in the CI section varies across studies, and this is a key issue for the researcher to consider. For example, Orbe and Camara (2010, p. 286) simply asked each participant to provide "a short story about an incident, representing one of the listed forms of discrimination (e.g. based on race, sex, sexual orientation, disability, and age), that impacted them the most." They received stories that ranged in length from 1–2 sentences to 1–2 pages.

This variability can sometimes be a problem, especially when the researcher wants to know certain key features like the setting, whether other people were involved, how different participants reacted, or wants to elicit certain types of CIs, and so some researchers state their expectations explicitly. For example, Dela Cruz et al. (2006) asked participants to write about two situations. They explain this as follows:

> The first was a situation when they interacted with a professor or other university personnel and felt culturally and/or personally respected, understood or encouraged. The second was a situation when they interacted with a professor or other university personnel and felt culturally and/or personally disrespected, misunderstood or confused. Respondents documented what happened, their reactions, feelings, and thoughts, the ethnicity of the faculty member, why they thought the incident occurred and how the incident could happen again or be prevented. (Dela Cruz et al., 2006, p. 126)

The researchers do not provide a copy of the questionnaire or any more details about the questionnaire design than reported above, but judging from the description, they provided respondents with a fair amount of guidance not only as to what types of CIs they were seeking to collect but also the types of detail they would like included.

Record Sheets

A third method for collecting CI data is to use record sheets, and for the sheet to be completed not simply on a one-off basis (although this is possible), but potentially on an ongoing basis. Once again the amount and type of structuring provided in the sheet can be variable. The Council of Europe (2009) and Spencer-Oatey and Davidson (2014) both provide templates for recording a portfolio of encounters, providing prompts as to the information that is useful to note down. The latter suggest the "3R" acronym to try and aid memory, and provide further prompts within each of the steps: *Report* the facts of what happened; *Reflect* on why it happened; *Re-evaluate* after discussing with others. These kinds of templates are particularly valuable when researching the challenges that people face when adjusting to a different cultural environment, the insights and personal growth that they can experience through reflecting on their encounters, and the steps that they can take to enhance their intercultural competence.

Another approach, especially when researching the experiences of a cohort of people over a fixed period of time, is to send them regular prompts, usually with the focus of the prompt differing from week to week. This is the approach that Arthur (2001) took. She explains it as follows:

> The prompts for the critical incidents were posed in the form of open-ended questions as follows:
>
> 1 What experience this week did you find to be stressful?
> 2 How did you deal with the situation that you found to be stressful this week?
> 3 What action did anyone take this week that you found to be affirming or helpful?
> 4 How do you view yourself this week in relation to international development issues?
> 5 What are the most important insights that you realized about yourself this week?
>
> The first prompt queried an outstanding stressful event in the experience of participants, and the second prompt was focused on coping efforts used to manage the stressors

related to the event. Rather than attempting to account for all stressors in the experience of students, an attempt was made to understand in greater depth one meaningful event per week and students' related coping efforts. The third prompt was designed to uncover perceptions about meaningful social support in a cross-cultural context. Therefore, students generated both the events and the coping strategies that were meaningful for them. The last two prompts were more general in nature, in an effort to track the process in which students' potentially altered their worldview regarding self and their understanding of international development. (Arthur, 2001, pp. 44–45)

Arthur goes on to explain that each of the prompts was sent out in successive weeks, so that the participants could focus on reporting the unfolding demands of their experiences at the beginning of their sojourn, then clarify in their minds the coping strategies that they were using and helpful strategies used by others. Towards the end of their sojourn, the prompts turned their attention to reflecting on the development of their self-awareness and their growth in intercultural competence.

Observations

Flanagan (1954, p. 338), in his original specification of the CIT, argued that "direct observations are to be preferred" and identified the following elements that need to be planned for this:

Specifications regarding observations

(a) Persons to make the observations.
  - Knowledge concerning the activity.
  - Relation to the observed.
  - Training requirements.
(b) Groups to be observed.
  - General description.
  - Location.
  - Persons.
  - Times.
  - Conditions.
(c) Behaviors to be observed.
  - General type of activity.
  - Specific behaviors.
  - Criteria of relevance to general aim.
  - Criteria of importance to general aim (critical points).
      (Flanagan, 1954, Figure 2, p. 339)

Observation is rarely used nowadays on its own as a CIT data collection method in the intercultural field. However, it is sometimes used in combination with other methods [cf. Jackson, Chapter 16 this volume on ethnography]. Chang (2009), for example, who researched the adjustment experiences of international aid workers, combined interviews with field observation. She reports that the field observation was particularly helpful in providing the researcher with a good contextual understanding of the situations that the aid workers were experiencing, including daily life challenges.

Observation can thus provide very useful background contextual information which can enhance the researcher's understanding and interpretation of CIs obtained through other methods. It may also suggest questions that could be used in interviews. We take up this combination of methods in greater detail in the next section.

CIT and Multiple Methods

As has been mentioned in passing in some of the sections above, the CIT is often used in conjunction with other methods. This can occur in two ways. One is for the additional method to provide useful supplementary evidence about the critical incidents. For example, Chen *et al.* (2005) were interested in the relations between foreign managers and local employees in companies in Shanghai and they wanted to test a model which linked cooperative and competitive goals with constructive controversy, innovation and job commitment. They collected the CIs through interviews, but in order to be able to test their model, they supplemented this with questionnaire data that probed specific information about the CIs. In other words, they combined interview and questionnaire methods to collect more comprehensive CI information. Another example is Chang's (2009) study mentioned above. Chang's field observations complemented her interviews, enabling her to interpret the CIs with greater contextual understanding.

Another way in which multiple methods can be used with the CIT is when the CI data forms part of a broader study. For example, Spencer-Oatey and Xing (2008) were interested in Sino-British business relations and they decided to explore this through a case study approach, researching a Chinese delegation visit to a company in the UK. They collected various types of data: they video-recorded the formal meetings, they played back the recordings to the participants to get their post-event comments, they interviewed all the participants, and Xing accompanied the delegation on all their trips, dinners and so on. During the course of the visit a number of critical incidents occurred, and the researchers were able to build a more comprehensive picture of the issues through combining the various sources of data. In other words, the researchers did not deliberately try to elicit CIs; rather, the CIs emerged "in real time" during the visit, while the researchers were collecting a variety of data for a broader purpose. A similar situation is the case with Wang and Spencer-Oatey (in preparation) who studied a Chinese ministerial visit to the United States. Once again, a variety of data were collected, but rather unusually, the Chinese delegation leader called a meeting every evening to discuss how their day of meetings with their American hosts had gone. The delegation members spontaneously focused on discussing incidents that had been particularly face-enhancing or face-threatening to their delegation, and the researchers were able to gain further insights into these CIs by looking at the video-recordings of the sessions they referred to.

Analyzing Critical Incident Data

The ways in which CI data are analyzed is dependent, of course, on the researcher's purpose. One of the most common approaches is to conduct a thematic analysis; this is illustrated in both Arthur's (2001) and Dela Cruz et al.'s (2006) studies. Arthur (2001) wanted to use critical incident data to investigate cross-cultural transitions, so she used three trained raters to carry out a thematic content analysis of the CIs, which resulted in a classification taxonomy. She was then able to work out the number (and proportion) of responses coded for each theme, as well as to examine whether there was any change over time in the frequency of codings for each theme. Based on this, she could identify *(inter alia)* some commonly occurring stressors for this cohort of participants and any variation that occurred over time.

Dela Cruz *et al.* (2006) also used thematic analysis with the critical incidents that they collected, but for a different purpose than Arthur. As explained above, she and her colleagues wanted to develop an intercultural sensitizer training resource, and the first step needed in that process was to categorize CIs into different themes. However, this was merely to help them select a set of incidents that were as comprehensive as possible and had a minimum amount of redundancy. The next analytic step was to invite a panel of respected bicultural community leaders to examine the set of selected CIs and to provide interpretations of the incidents. This input was then used to develop the intercultural sensitizer. In the final step of the study, the draft intercultural sensitizer was piloted with 285 students at Hawaiian educational institutions to test its validity.

Another analytic possibility is to examine the CIs for behavioral items, an approach taken by Dekker et al. (2008). As explained above, Dekker and her colleagues wanted to identify critical behavior for effective virtual teamwork and to explore whether there were any cultural differences in people's perceptions of what counted as critical virtual teamwork behavior. In an earlier study they had already established a set of behavioral categories, and two raters then independently distributed the behavioral items in the critical incidents across this pre-established set of behavioral categories. If any did not fit, they added a new category. Since the CIs had been collected from interviewees of different nationalities, the mapping of CI behaviors to the behavioral categories could be done by nationality. This enabled the researchers to investigate whether national culture affected people's perceptions of what counted as critical behavior for effective virtual teamwork.

Yet another approach was taken by Thomas and colleagues (e.g. 1996, 2000, 2010, discussed in an earlier section of this chapter – "Intercultural Research Themes and Use of the CIT/Cultural Values/Standards"), who employed cross-cultural comparisons and expert analysis of causes and effects in recurrently reported critical interactions. Based on the interviews, "a single sentence that contributes to the critical interaction" was identified (Thomas, 2010, p. 26), which was then analyzed by experts "in order to filter out the cultural standards that come into play during the interaction." The results were compared to earlier findings, allowing the researchers to identify a set of cultural standards which can provide helpful points of orientation and reflection (2010, p. 26).

If the researchers give very specific instructions as to the types of CIs they wish to be told about, it may be possible to ask respondents a set of follow-up questions which can then be analyzed statistically. For example, as explained previously, Chen et al. (2005) used the CIT to explore the conditions under which foreign managers and local employees are able to find productive ways of working together. The respondents were asked to describe a specific instance in which they had worked closely with their boss on a specific issue, either successfully or unsuccessfully. They were then asked to rate a number of specific questions on 5-point scales in order to provide further background information on the incident. This data allowed the researchers to test the four specific hypotheses that they had identified in advance of the study.

Reflections on the CIT

Strengths

The CIT allows the collection of reports and recollections on observed interactions and behavior for contexts where direct observation may not be feasible. It facilitates access to participants' perceptions and interpretations of events, enabling the researcher to identify the importance of events from the participant's viewpoint. The CIT permits the collection and interpretation of context-rich data, linking context, events and outcomes (Chell, 1998).

Another strength of the CIT is that it can facilitate reflection and personal growth for the participants, which is particularly true when record sheets or autobiographic tools are employed.

Challenges

Despite the strengths of the CIT, implementing it is not without its challenges. A fundamental issue is deciding how to define a CI in any given study. As discussed above, there is considerable variation over the ways in which both "critical" and "incident" can be interpreted, and each researcher needs to decide what his or her own position on this is. For example, Dekker et al. (2008, p. 446) interpret "critical" in a very similar way to Flanagan (1954) and report that they ensured the interviewer collected only incidents that met the following criteria:

1. Actual behavior was reported;
2. The actual behavior had been observed by the interviewee;
3. The interviewee was able to provide relevant factors of the situation;
4. The interviewee was able to judge the criticalness of the behavior (contributed to a positive or negative outcome); and
5. The interviewee was able to make clear why he or she believed the behavior had been critical.

(Dekker et al., 2008, p. 446)

In contrast, Arthur (2001), as mentioned above, seems to have been much less specific as to how the critical incident should be reported, merely sending a prompt such as "What experience this week did you find to be stressful?" Here "critical" is equated with "stressful" and the participants seem to have been given little guidance as to how much detail to report. Other prompts, such as "How do you view yourself this week in relation to international development issues?" do not relate to an "incident" at all but rather aim to promote reflection on unique experiences. Thus, like Tripp (1993), Arthur treats criticality more as something that emerges through reflection than something that is objectively present.

In terms of the concept of "incident," some researchers (e.g. Dekker et al., 2008; Orbe & Camara, 2010) treat it as a single, one-off event while others (e.g. Chen et al., 2005) focus more on an issue and the events that occur around it which might unfold over a short period of time. So another key set of questions for the researcher to think through are as follows: What is the most suitable timeframe to use? Is it best to collect one-off encounters, or a series of encounters relating to a particular issue, or a period of time during a longer stretch during which some kind of major development or personal growth occurred?

Another challenge is to be found in eliciting the CIs. Recollecting CIs is retrospective in nature and participants may find it difficult to access memories, particularly if these are emotionally loaded (Cope & Watts, 2000). In order to facilitate remembering CIs, interview questions can be sent in advance, as done by Dekker et al. (2008). Another helpful means is to accompany the instructions used in participant records or questionnaires with an example of the kind of CIs one is seeking to elicit.

Limitations

One limitation of the CIT is related to the accuracy of recollections, which could impede reliability and validity of the findings. Self-reports are based on subjective memories, which are in themselves interpretations of an event experienced by the participant. When recollecting and re-telling the past events, participants may re-interpret the story, which in addition may be altered by memory effects or by emotions attached to the event (e.g. Cope & Watts, 2000). These limitations may in part be addressed by guiding participants to the perspective of other people involved in the incident, by collecting complementary data, e.g. from other interactants' perspectives, or by using group interviews which allow co-construction and negotiation of interpretations.

Another limitation is found in the nature of interviews as self-reports, which often present a one-sided perspective, and may lack reliability and validity. This can be mitigated for example by collecting data on the perspective of other people involved in the interaction (e.g. dyadic studies as suggested by Gremler, 2004), or by taking into consideration relevant other data sources (e.g. Chell, 2004; see the section above).

Studies using the CIT in the intercultural field tend to have a limited sample size, which could influence the generalizability of the findings. Nevertheless, the data elicited by CIT allow deep insights and have "greater explanatory power" (Chell, 2004, p. 57).

New Directions

A potential extension of the CIT can be found in researching the use of CIs for training or assessment purposes. CIs for such pedagogical purposes can be constructed from the narrations collected by the CIT. When CIs are used in training or in assessment, think-aloud techniques can be employed to examine the cognitive processes and competencies needed to interpret CIs. This research can feed into validating the construct of CI-based training and assessment.

Key Terms

Critical incident A critical incident is an event or episode that is significant in some way, such as in its impact on people's emotional reactions or on the subsequent unfolding of events. It can also refer to an event that is perceived as puzzling or surprising by a participant.

Critical incident technique The critical incident technique encompasses a range of data collection procedures (i.e. it is not a single, specific procedure) that enable the researcher to gain insights into the "critical" events or episodes that s/he is interested in.

Criticality In relation to critical incidents, different researchers interpret criticality in different ways, but most regard it as something perceived or constructed as "critical" by one or more of the participants of the event.

Incident With regard to the critical incident technique, an incident is usually an event that is relatively complete in itself. However, for some researchers it can be a period or an episode with less clear-cut boundaries.

References

Arthur, N. (2001). Using critical incidents to investigate cross-cultural transitions. *International Journal of Intercultural Relations*, 25, 41–53.

Brislin, R. (1986). A culture general assimilator: Preparation for various types of sojourn. *International Journal of Intercultural Relations*, 10, 215–234.

Butterfield, L. D., Borgen, W. A., Amundson, N. E., & Malio, A.-S. T. (2005). Fifty years of the critical incident technique: 1954–2004 and beyond. *Qualitative Research*, 5(4), 475–497.

Chang, W-W. (2009). Schema adjustment in cross-cultural encounters: a study of expatriate international aid service workers. *International Journal of Intercultural Relations*, 33, 57–68.

Chell, E. (1998). Critical incident technique. In G. Symon & C. Cassell (Eds.), *Qualitative methods and analysis in organizational research: A practical guide* (pp. 51–72). Thousand Oaks, CA: Sage.

Chell, E. (2004). Critical incident technique. In C. Cassell & G. Symon (Eds.), *Essential guide to qualitative methods in organizational research* (pp. 45–60). Thousand Oaks, CA: Sage.

Chen, Y-f., Tjosvold, D., & Su, S.F. (2005). Goal interdependence for working across cultural boundaries: Chinese employees with foreign managers. *International Journal of Intercultural Relations*, 29, 429–447.

Cope, J. & Watts, G. (2000). Learning by doing. An exploration of experience, critical incidents and reflection in entrepreneurial learning. *International Journal of Entrepreneurial Behavior and Research*, 6(3), 104–124.

Council of Europe, Language Policy Division (2009). *Autobiography of Intercultural Encounters*. Retrieved June 23, 2015 from: http://www.coe.int/t/dg4/autobiography/default_EN.asp?%20%20and%20http://www.coe.int/t/dg4/linguistic/autobiogrweb_EN.asp.

Culpeper, J., Marti, L., Mei, M., Nevala, M. & Schauer, G. (2010). Cross-cultural variation in the perception of impoliteness: a study of impoliteness events reported by students in England, China, Finland, Germany and Turkey. *Intercultural Pragmatics*. 7(4), 597–624.

Dekker, D.M., Rutte, C.G., & Van den Berg, P.T. (2008). Cultural differences in the perception of critical interaction behaviors in global virtual teams. *International Journal of Intercultural Relations*, 32, 441–452.

Dela Cruz, K.C.K., Salzman, M.B., Brislin, R., & Losch, N. (2006). Hawaiian attributional perspectives on intercultural interactions in higher education: Development of an intercultural sensitizer. *International Journal of Intercultural Relations*, 30, 119–140.

Edvardsson, B. (1992). Service breakdowns: A study of critical incidents in an airline. *International Journal of Service Industry Management*, 3(4), 17–29.

Flanagan, J.C. (1954). The critical incident technique. *Psychological Bulletin*, 51(4), 327–358.

Fowler, S. M. and Blohm, J. M. (2004). An analysis of methods for intercultural training. In D. Landis, J.M. Bennett, & M.J. Bennett (Eds.) *Handbook of Intercultural Training*. (3rd ed., pp. 37–84). Thousand Oaks, CA: Sage.

Gremler, D. D. (2004). The critical incident technique in service research. *Journal of Service Research*, 7(1), 65–89.

Keatinge, D. (2002). Versatility and flexibility: Attributes of the Critical Incident Technique in nursing research. *Nursing and Health Sciences*, 4, 33–39.

Orbe, M.P., & Camara, S.K. (2010). Defining discrimination across cultural groups: Exploring the [un-]coordinated management of meaning. *International Journal of Intercultural Relations*, 34, 283–293.

Spencer-Oatey, H. (2002). Managing rapport in talk: using rapport sensitive incidents to explore the motivational concerns underlying politeness. *Journal of Pragmatics*, 34, 529–545.

Spencer-Oatey, H., & Davidson, A. (2014). *The 3R Tool. Developing evaluation sensitivity in intercultural encounters*. Retrieved July 30, 2015 from: http://www.warwick.ac.uk/globalpadintercultural/globalpad_3r_v2.pdf

Spencer-Oatey, H., & Xing, J. (2008). A problematic Chinese business visit to Britain: issues of face. In H. Spencer-Oatey (Ed.), *Culturally speaking: Culture, communication and politeness theory* (pp. 272–288). London: Continuum.

Thomas, A. (1996). Analyse der Handlungswirksamkeit von Kulturstandards. In A. Thomas (Ed.), *Psychologie interkulturellen Handelns* (pp. 107–135). Göttingen: Hogrefe.

Thomas, A. (2000). Globalisierung und interkulturelle Managementkompetenz. In B. Fahrenhorst, and S.A. Musto (Eds.) *Grenzenlos. Kommunikation, Kooperation, Entwicklung* (pp. 162–174). Berlin: Gesellschaft für internationale Entwicklung.

Thomas, A. (2010). Culture and cultural standards. In A. Thomas, E.-U. Kinast & S. Schroll-Machl (Eds.), *Handbook of Intercultural Communication and cooperation. Basics and areas of application* (pp. 17–27). Göttingen: Vandenhoeck & Ruprecht.

Thomas, A., & Schenk, E. (2001). *Beruflich in China. Trainingsprogramm für manager, fach- und führungskräfte*. Göttingen: Vandenhoeck & Ruprecht.

Tripp, D. (1993). *Critical incidents in teaching. Developing professional judgement*. London: Routledge.

Walker, W., & Truly, E. (1992). The critical incidents technique: Philosophical foundations and methodological implications. *American Marketing Association Winter Educators' Conference Proceedings* (pp. 270–275).

Wang, J., & Spencer-Oatey, H. (in preparation). The ups and downs of face in ongoing intercultural interaction: A case study of participant perspectives.

Wight, A. R. (1995). The critical incident as a training tool. In S.M. Fowler (Ed.): *Intercultural sourcebook: Cross-cultural training methods. Vol.1* (pp. 127–140). Yarmouth, ME: Intercultural Press.

Further Reading and Resources

Butterfield, L. D., Borgen, W.A., Amundson, N.E., & Malio, A.-S.T. (2005). Fifty years of the critical incident technique: 1954–2004 and beyond. *Qualitative Research*, 5(4), 475–497.
Chell, E. (2004). Critical incident technique. In C. Cassell & G. Symon (Eds.), *Essential guide to qualitative methods in organizational research* (pp. 45–60). Thousand Oaks, CA: Sage.
Flanagan, J.C. (1954). The critical incident technique. *Psychological Bulletin*, 51(4), 327–358.
Spencer-Oatey, H. (2013). Critical incidents. A compilation of quotations for the intercultural field. *GlobalPAD Core Concepts*. Available at GlobalPAD Open House. Retrieved June 23, 2015 from: http://go.warwick.ac.uk/globalpadintercultural.
Tripp, D. (1993). *Critical Incidents in teaching. Developing professional judgement.* London: Routledge.

16 Ethnography

Jane Jackson

> **Summary**
>
> This chapter explains what is meant by ethnography, delving into its historical roots, purpose, and characteristics. Various types of ethnographic research are described and suggestions are offered for ethnographic investigations and applications in the field of language and intercultural communication. The ethnographic research process is outlined, with attention paid to ethnographic forms of data collection and analysis, including the use of specialized software. As well as underscoring the merits of this mode of research, this chapter draws attention to limitations and constructive ways to enhance the quality of ethnographic work.

Introduction

Ethnographic research or ethnography (from the Greek *ethnos* = nation and *graphein* = writing) is increasingly used today within the field of language and intercultural communication. While perhaps one of the most challenging of all forms of research, it has numerous strengths and advantages; quality ethnographies have the potential to significantly enrich our understanding of linguistic and cultural practices. In this chapter, we briefly explore the historical development of this mode of research, review the core characteristics and elements of ethnographic studies, and discuss the benefits, limitations, and challenges that ethnography can pose for both novice and experienced language and Intercultural Communication researchers, as well as scholars in other disciplines.

What is Ethnographic Research?

A definition of ethnography is not easy to pin down, and some features are contested. As noted by O'Reilly (2005, p. 1), "ethnography is difficult to define because it is used in different ways in different disciplines with different traditions." To complicate matters, the term "ethnography" may refer to ethnographic research (e.g. ethnography as an activity), or the product of the research (e.g. the narrative or report that presents the findings of an ethnographic study) (Davies, 2008; Pole & Morrison, 2003; Watson-Gegeo, 1988).

In the past few decades, many definitions of ethnography have emerged. One of the most widely quoted is a succinct description offered by Brewer (2000, p. 10):

> Ethnography is the study of people in naturally occurring settings or "fields" by means of methods which capture their social meanings and ordinary activities, involving the researcher participating directly in the setting, if not also the activities, in order to collect data in a systematic manner but without meaning being imposed on them externally.

For Wacquant (2003, p. 5), ethnography is depicted as "social research based on the close-up, on-the-ground observation of people and institutions in real time and space, in which the investigator embeds herself near (or within) the phenomenon so as to detect how and why agents on the scene act, think and feel the way they do."

As indicated in these definitions, the primary goal of ethnography is to develop a deeper understanding of the meanings that cultural or behavioral practices and beliefs hold for a particular group of people in a specific time and context.

> The underlying purpose of ethnographic research… is to describe what the people in some particular place or status ordinarily do, and the *meanings* they ascribe to the doing, under ordinary or particular circumstances, presenting that description in a manner that draws attention to regularities that implicate cultural process (Wolcott 2008, pp. 72–73). (italics in original)

Hence, culture is a core element in ethnographic studies, which is not the case in all forms of qualitative research. For a study to be ethnographic, it "must provide the kind of account of human social activity out of which cultural patterning can be discerned" (Wolcott, 2008, p. 72).

While some ethnographers examine social units that may be as broad as an entire cultural group (e.g. Spencer's (2011) study of American expatriates in Costa Rica), others may limit their study to a single social unit or cultural setting (e.g. Markose, Symes, & Hellstén (2011), an investigation of two immigrant families in Australia). Whatever the scope of the research, the defining characteristic of ethnography is attention to the description and interpretation of cultural behaviors.

Ethnographic Traditions

Before taking a closer look at the methodologies associated with ethnography, it is helpful to have some knowledge of its historical development, which is deeply rooted in cultural anthropology and sociology (Agar, 1996; Atkinson, 1994; Geertz, 1973; Hammersley & Atkinson, 2007; Heath & Street, 2008; Hymes, 1974, 1996; Kottak, 2012; Spradley, 1979; Watson-Gegeo, 1988). Closely linked to this mode of research is ethnology, the branch of anthropology that compares and analyzes the characteristics of different peoples and the relationship between them (Hammersley & Atkinson, 2007).

In the first part of the twentieth century, cultural anthropologists primarily explored "exotic" non-Euro-American cultures and spent several years or more living in the field, learning the local language and dialect, while observing and participating in the group's activities. During the First World War, for example, anthropologist Bronislaw Malinowski lived with residents in the Trobriand Islands, where he immersed himself in the local language and cultural practices. On his return to the UK, he published several ethnographies about the beliefs and customs he had observed (e.g. Malinowski, 1922). His work inspired both novice and experienced anthropologists to carry out ethnographic fieldwork in other faraway lands. As noted by Roberts, Byram, Barro,, Jordan, & Street (2001, p. 89), during this time period, "living with the 'natives' became a necessary rite of passage for entering the discipline of anthropology, and the core texts of the discipline became those ethnographies written by fieldworkers."

While this tradition has continued, there have also been many changes in ethnographic research since Malinowski's early studies. Interest in "ordinary" cultural practices and social life has become much more prevalent. Accordingly, "urban ethnography" is now popular (Deegan, 2001; Duneier, Kasinitz, & Murphy, 2014; McCurdy, Spradley, & Shandy, 2005; Roberts et al., 2001), with more research focusing on cultures or subcultures within one's own neighborhood (e.g. language centers, bilingual or multilingual classrooms, prisons, multicultural community associations, immigrant groups, charity shops). Damen (1987, p. 57) explains:

> In the past, the terms ethnology and ethnography have been applied respectively to the study and description of the so called "primitive societies." Indeed, dictionary definitions still reflect early ethnocentric biases... Today ethnology and ethnographies (written descriptions) are no longer concerned exclusively with the far-away and exotic but also examine the near, the more familiar and the modern.

Traditional ethnographic research and contemporary urban ethnographies both have a role to play in better understanding cultural elements. As noted by Jordan and Roberts (2000, p. 1), "both traditional anthropology which involved making the strange familiar, and modern urban ethnography which involves making the familiar strange are the two perspectives that allow us to gain a better understanding of the nature of cultural patterns and practices."

Another key development relates to a shift in "ownership" of ethnographic research. Ethnography is no longer predominantly the work of anthropologists and sociologists. Nowadays, more and more students and researchers from other disciplines (e.g. applied linguistics, education, intercultural communication, law, geography, health, management, business, psychology, ethnic and gender studies) are engaging in some form of ethnographic research. In sociolinguistics, for example, Dell Hymes and John Gumperz developed the "Ethnography of Communication" (also known as the "Ethnography of Speaking") to better understand the language–culture connection in context (Gumperz & Hymes, 1964, 1972). Building on their work, sociolinguists in many parts of the world are now conducting ethnographic investigations of the communication patterns of speech communities, that is, groups of peoples who share "rules for the conduct and interpretation of speech, and rules for the interpretation of at least one linguistic variety" (Hymes, 1986, p. 54).

In a related development, an ethnographic approach is also now being used in educational settings to nurture students' language and cultural awareness (of both self and Other). In the last few decades, a growing number of applied linguists and interculturalists have designed programs to help second-language students acquire an understanding of ethnographic concepts and methods, with the expectation that they will be more actively engaged in the host culture and develop a higher level of sociopragmatic awareness and intercultural competence (e.g. Byram & Feng, 2005; Jackson, 2006, 2008; Roberts et al., 2001).

Finally, while early ethnographers typically spent many months or even years in the field, it has become more common for researchers to do focused studies that involve only a few months or even weeks of contact with the group under study. The implications of this development are discussed further near the end of the chapter, when we examine the limitations and controversies associated with ethnographic research.

Genres of Ethnography

Today, there are many types or genres of ethnographic research. Some of the most common ones that can be found in the literature on language and Intercultural Communication are: critical ethnography, feminist ethnography, visual ethnography/hyper ethnography, virtual/online ethnography/, and autoethnography. Let's take a brief look at each.

Critical Ethnography

Drawing on cultural studies, feminist and neo-Marxist theories, and research on critical pedagogy, critical ethnography has grown in popularity in recent decades (Gordon, Holland, & Lahelma, 2001; Madison, 2012). Overtly political and critical, this approach is designed to draw attention to inequalities in social structures and institutions in order to effect change. As O'Reilly (2009, p. 51) explains, the primary aim of this type of ethnography is "to expose hidden agendas, challenge oppressive assumptions, describe power relations, and critique the taken-for-granted." In the field of language and intercultural communication, critical ethnographers expose inequalities in intercultural interactions and diverse cultural settings, including institutions and organizations (e.g. discriminatory practices in the education of second-language speakers, the treatment of refugees or migrant workers).

For more insight into critical ethnography, you may consult Carspecken (1996), Madison (2012), and Thomas (1993). Examples of book-length critical ethnographies include Heller (2011), Herrera & Torres (2006), and Ibrahim (2014).

Feminist Ethnography

Feminist ethnography is concerned with the study of females and the cultural practices that females engage in in particular contexts and situations. Work of this nature may involve comparisons of how gender operates within different ethnic groups or societies (e.g. roles of women in the workforce in various cultural settings). Gordon et al. (2001, p. 194) explains that feminist ethnographers strive to "observe processes in the construction of gender hierarchy and gendered power relations at the level of the micro politics of the educational institution... ." For more on feminist ethnography see Buch & Staller (2014), and Craven & Davis (2013).

Visual Ethnography/Hyperethnography

Nowadays, ethnographers may amass and analyze a large amount of visual data (e.g. digital images) during the course of their research. As noted by Pink (2007, p. 1):

> Photography, video and hypermedia are becoming increasingly incorporated into the work of ethnographers – as cultural texts, as representations of ethnographic knowledge and as sites of cultural production, social interaction and individual experience that themselves constitute ethnographic fieldwork locales.

Advances in specialized computer software now enable researchers to make use of hypermedia, that is, they may create links between text elements and/or multimedia objects such as motion video, graphics, sound, and virtual reality (Dicks, Mason, Coffey, & Atkinson, 2005). Hypermedia enables the researcher to "create complex linkages within datasets, and across datasets. It allows one to link analytic commentaries, methodological reflections and theoretical speculations with data" (Dicks et al., 2005, p. 4).

For a more thorough discussion of visual ethnography and hypermedia see Coover (2004), Dicks et al., (2005), and Pink (2007).

Virtual/Online Ethnography/Netnography

With an increase in the use of the Internet, more ethnographers are investigating online communities, including (inter)cultural interactions in cyberspace (e.g. chatrooms, discussion forums, blogging, microblogging, videocasting, podcasting, social networking sites, virtual worlds, etc.). Netnography, also known as virtual/online ethnography, refers to "a form of ethnographic research adapted to include the Internet's influence on contemporary social worlds" (Kozinets, 2010, p. 1). Conducted over the Internet, this approach is specifically designed to study cultures and communities online. For more on netnography, see Boellstorff, Nardi, Pearce, & Taylor (2012), Kozinets (2010) and Lenihan & Kelly-Holmes, Chapter 17, this volume.

Autoethnography

Rooted in autobiography and ethnography, autoethnography entails reflective self-examination by the researcher (Ellis, 2004; Jones, Adams, & Ellis, 2013). In this approach, the ethnographer attempts to document, describe, and analyze his or her own personal experiences within a particular cultural context. This form of ethnography "challenges canonical ways of doing research and representing others," and positions research as "a political, socially-just and socially-conscious act..." (Ellis, Adams, & Bochner, 2011, p. 1). In this genre, the ethnographer is "simultaneously the subject and the object of observation" (Hammersley & Atkinson, 2007, p. 204). Further, as a method, autoethnography is deemed both process and product.

Autoethnography is not without critics. "While reflexivity implies the unavoidable implication of the observer in what she or he observes," Hammersley & Atkinson (2007, p. 205) argue that there is "little justification for substituting self-absorption for a thoroughgoing sociological or anthropological imagination." In their view, "personal reflection should always be a part of theoretical and methodological development, and not the opportunity to put the ethnographer's self ahead of the 'others' about whom she or he writes" (p. 205).

For more on critical and interpretive autoethnography see Boylorn, Orbe, Ellis, & Bochner (2014), Denzin (2014), Ellis (2009) and Jones, Adams, & Ellis (2013). For examples of autoethnographic work see Ellis (2004, 2009) and Wyatt & Adams (2014).

Characteristics of Ethnographic Research

While ethnographies can take many shapes and forms, they generally share the following common characteristics:

- A focus on a specific group, event(s), or cultural scene in a natural setting rather than a laboratory.
- Involves negotiation and rapport-building with gatekeepers and informants (e.g. permission to enter the cultural scene and gather data, the cultivation of respect and trust so that participants feel assured that their views and actions will be fairly and accurately represented).
- The "holistic" nature of a particular sociocultural phenomenon or event is investigated, often getting under way with a general problem or focus instead of specific research questions or hypotheses to test.
- Research questions tend to develop as new understandings emerge through fieldwork (e.g. the process of participant observation and ethnographic conversations or interviewing), along with hypotheses about their answers.
- Interest in sociocultural behavior within the setting or event under study, including language use.
- Sustained personal contact with participants (e.g. face-to-face, online).
- Multiple methods of data collection (e.g. ethnographic conversations, interviewing, focus groups, participant observation, videotaping, surveys, the collection

and analysis of documents/diaries/journals, visual materials, and artifacts), with the aim of better understanding the behavior (e.g. linguistic, sociocultural) from inside the event or setting.
- Aims to present an accurate portrayal of participants' perspectives and actions (the "emic" or insider perspective).
- Ongoing, continual data collection within the setting or group that is being investigated.
- A gradual shift from detailed, rich descriptions of the participants and cultural scene to the identification of concepts and local cultural theories, which are grounded in the data collected (grounded theory).
- A concern for rigor with an emphasis on thick, rich descriptions of particular scenes, events, or behavior rather than generalizations that extend beyond the scene under study.
- As well as the emic or insider voice, the researcher's (or outsider's) analysis or perspective is present in the analysis of data and subsequent report.
- Evidence of reflexivity, that is, "the process of reflecting critically on the self as researcher, the 'human as instrument'" (Lincoln & Guba, 2000, p. 183) or "turning back on oneself" (Davies, 2008, p. 4). Ethnographers acknowledge and explain their biases, relevant background/life experiences, worldview, and assumptions that may impact their research.

(Adapted from Brewer, 2000; Crang & Cook, 2007; Davies, 2008; Gobo, 2008; Hammersley & Atkinson, 2007; O'Reilly, 2005, 2009; Pole & Morrison, 2003).

Data Collection in Ethnographic Research

In the course of their work, ethnographers may draw on the full range of qualitative data-collection methods, including participant observation, informal or formal interviewing, focus group discussions, ethnographic conversations, and document analysis (e.g. diaries, journals, policy statements). Throughout any study, detailed field notes are a core element.

Participant observation is essential for effective fieldwork and lies at the heart of ethnography (Spradley, 1980). Wolcott (2008) has identified three different roles that ethnographers may play: active participant, privileged observer, and limited observer. An active participant takes on the role of participant and fully engages in activities, whereas the privileged observer has access to the cultural scene and events under study but does not act as a participant. The limited observer role is less frequent in true ethnographic research. In this category, it is not possible to gain full access to the cultural scene or participate in activities, and there is more reliance on other forms of data collection, such as interviews.

Besides participant observation, ethnographers may gather oral data from participants through formal interviewing, ethnographic conversations, or focus groups (Gobo, 2008; O'Reilly, 2005, 2009; Spradley, 1979). Focus groups may be employed early in a study to gain more insight into key issues that are prevalent in the cultural scene that will be the focus of a study. A focus group typically involves four to twelve people associated with the cultural scene who have some things in common as well as several key differences (O'Reilly, 2005). Through discussion facilitated by the researcher, the participants are encouraged to offer their views about such aspects as group beliefs and practices.

While some interviews may be formal with a set list of questions, an ethnographic interview or "unstructured interview" tends to be very relaxed and informal, so that informants may feel more willing to divulge their thoughts and feelings (Spradley, 1979). In this type of interview, an interview protocol is not prepared in advance, although the ethnographer usually has some questions or probes in mind.

Some ethnographic studies involve the collection and analysis of documents (e.g. diaries narratives, responses to email prompts, policy statements) or the use of such techniques as mapping (e.g. illustrations or drawings of the cultural scene). Photography and videography (e.g. digital images or videotapes) may also be employed to gather additional information about the area under investigation (Pink, 2007; Dicks *et al.*, 2005). (See Lyons, Chapter 18, this volume, for a more in-depth discussion of visual data).

Throughout an ethnographic study, the researcher maintains detailed field notes, that is, a written record of observations and fragments of remembered conversations with informants as well as other speech. Although researchers may use recordings (e.g. video- or audiotapes of interviews), field notes are one of the most important elements in ethnographic research as they provide an account of what the researcher observes, thinks, and feels while collecting and later reflecting on the data. For more on writing field notes see Emerson (2011), Van Maaen (2011), and Wang (2012). Pole & Morrision (2003) provide examples of field notes.

Data Analysis in Ethnography

As data are being collected, the ethnographic researcher triangulates data types and sources in a process that is ongoing throughout the study. Triangulation refers to "the use of multiple methods, data collection strategies, and data sources to get a more complete picture of the topic under study and to cross-check information" (Gay, Mills, & Airasian, 2009, p. 416).

Through naturalistic, systematic observation and interaction with informants, ethnographers aim to develop a "thick, rich description" of cultures or aspects of a culture from an emic, or insider's, perspective (Atkinson, 1994; Watson-Gegeo, 1988). Throughout this reiterative process, the ethnographer strives to refrain from jumping to subjective conclusions about observations.

Ethnography "generates or builds theories of cultures – or explanations of how people think, believe, and behave – that are situated in local time and space" (LeCompte & Schensul, 1999). To accomplish this, the ethnographer identifies recurrent themes and issues, integrates them into existing categories, and adds new categories or subcategories as new understandings or topics emerge. The success of the study depends, in part, on the researcher's ability to analyze and synthesize a large amount of qualitative data into coherent, detailed descriptions of the cultural scene. To represent the emic perspective as truthfully as possible, the ethnographer employs member checks, that is, the field participants review transcripts or statements in the researcher's report to check for accuracy and completeness (Gay et al., 2009). The researcher's voice ("etic perspective") should also be present in the analysis and subsequent report, to make connections with existing literature and help readers make sense of the cultural elements that have been observed and recorded.

Computer-aided Data Analysis

Ethnographers are increasingly making use of computers to organize and analyze texts (e.g. field notes, interview transcripts), and hypermedia data (e.g. graphics, audio files, video clips). The term "CAQDAS" refers to computer-assisted qualitative data analysis software. Some of the most popular software used in ethnographic research are NUDIST, NVivo, Atlas-T1, and Ethnograph. Some packages allow for the incorporation of quantitative (numeric) data and/or include tools that enable quantitative approaches to qualitative data.

For more information about CAQDAS consult the website sponsored by the CAQDAS Networking project at the University of Surrey (CAQDAS, n.d.). See also Silver & Lewins (2014) for a comparison of various software packages for qualitative data analysis. This publication can also help you to decide if software is necessary or helpful for your project.

Ethnographic Report

The product of the research is the development of a narrative or report that describes the study and the key findings. "The research report includes a holistic description of the culture, the common understandings and beliefs shared by participants, a discussion of how these beliefs relate to life in the culture, and discussion of how the findings compare to literature already published about similar groups" (Gay et al., 2009, pp. 13–14). Thus, the report should be richly detailed and include both emic and etic perspectives, with evidence of reflexivity.

Strengths and Limitations of Ethnography

Strengths

Ethnographic research has a number of strengths, which make it appealing to language and Intercultural Communication specialists, as well as scholars in many other disciplines. The guiding questions can be revised and refined as the ethnographer becomes more familiar with the cultural group and new understandings emerge. Sustained contact with the group under study can also lead to a much deeper understanding of cultural elements than is possible in many other modes of research.

> Ethnographic approaches are particularly valuable when not enough is known about the context or situation to establish narrowly defined questions or develop formal hypotheses… Because ethnographies typically employ multiple methods for gathering data, such as participant observations and open-ended interviews as well as written products, ethnographic research may be able to provide an holistic, culturally grounded, and emic perspective of the phenomenon under investigation (Mackey & Gass, 2005, p. 170).

In particular, ethnography can bring to light nuances and subtleties that other methodologies overlook, as noted by Frankel, Wallen, & Hyun (2012, p. 509):

> What people think and say happens (or is likely to happen) often is not really the case. By going out into the world and observing things as they occur, we are (usually) better able to obtain a more accurate picture. This is what ethnographers try to do – study people in their natural habitat in order to "see" things that otherwise might not even be anticipated. This is a major advantage of the ethnographic approach.

Systematic, first-hand observation can be a significant strength of ethnography. By paying close attention to the actual behavior (e.g. language use, actions) of people in their natural environment, ethnographers can gain a deeper understanding of their actions. Through ethnographic interviews and conversations and the analysis of written documents (e.g. diaries, field notes), the thoughts, ideas, and emotions of the participants can also become more evident. This process can generate theories of cultures.

> The strength of ethnography as we see it is in the capacity to offer conceptual and theoretical accounts of discrete social action… ethnography is capable of engaging with issues which go beyond the particular and the discrete, not to general or macro-theoretical explanations but in such a way that there is connection and resonance with wider social behavior, social processes and broader structural issues (Pole & Morrison, 2003, p. 160).

Ethnographic investigations are also well suited to longitudinal studies, as they can capture and track behaviors and attitude changes over time and space, e.g. for many months or years. For example, an ethnographer may document the linguistic and intercultural learning of a particular immigrant family from their arrival in the new land until several years later. Instead of capturing the thoughts and feelings of the participants at one single moment in time (e.g. through the administration of a quantitative survey), the ethnographer can systematically observe and record their struggles and triumphs over several years to better understand the process of acculturation.

Limitations and Challenges

Every approach to research has shortcomings and critics, and ethnography is no exception. In fact, Hammersley (1992) devoted an entire volume to this, with the aim of enhancing the quality and rigor of studies of this nature. Most criticisms center on the lack of specific hypotheses to direct the study, the duration and quality of fieldwork, lack of generalizability and limited potential for replicability, researcher bias, and lack of validity.

The dynamic, flexible nature of ethnography can have both advantages and disadvantages. While it can be liberating for a researcher to develop hypotheses as his or her understanding of a context grows, it can also mean that a study can lack focus and direction, and this can be very confusing for novice researchers. "Because the researcher usually begins his or her observations without a specific hypothesis to confirm or deny, terms may not be defined, and hence the specific variables or relationships being investigated (if any) may remain unclear" (Frankel et al. 2012, p. 520).

Ethnographies generally require extensive and intensive data collection over a lengthy period, which necessitates a major investment in time and resources:

> ethnographies involve intense research over an extended period of time. They require a commitment to long-term data collection, detailed and continuous record keeping, and repeated and careful analysis of data obtained from multiple sources... If the researcher participates in an event he or she is observing, this may leave little time for the carefully detailed field notes that ethnographies may require (Mackey & Gass, 2005, p. 170).

While early ethnographers typically spent many months or years in the field, it has become more common for studies to be conducted in much less time. Consequently, many questions are being raised about the quality of ethnographies that result from much shorter periods of observation. Richards (2003, p. 16), for example, rails against inadequate fieldwork:

> It is methodologically unacceptable to settle for quick forays into the field in order to scoop up data and retreat (an approach known by the pejorative term "blitzkrieg ethnography"), so while it may be legitimate to use methods characteristic of ethnography, these do not in themselves mean that you are working within this tradition... the term "ethnographic" is much abused, being invoked for any work that might be described as broadly "ethnographic." In ethnography there is no substitute for extended immersion in the field, and where this is not possible researchers should consider traditions where participant observation is not essential, the two most obvious being grounded theory and the case study.

Since most ethnographic studies involve a small number of participants and cultural scenes, generalizability, that is, the application of research findings to settings and contexts different from the one in which they were attained, is problematic. Replicability (the process of repeating a study with different participants under similar situations) is nearly impossible to achieve. As noted by Heath & Street (2008, p. 45),

> all ethnographic research is inherently interpretive, subjective, and partial... comparison between one study and another can only be based on descriptions of who, what, where, when, and how. Time moves on, people change, and circumstances differ, yet ethnographers have an obligation to make clear their *decision rules* as though they could imagine that someone else might step back into the same location or group.

It is incumbent on the ethnographer to provide a rich, detailed picture of the cultural scene under study so that readers of the ethnographic report can draw their own conclusions about the relevance of the study and findings for their own context and situation.

Another concern about ethnography relates to researcher bias and validity, that is, the extent to which a conclusion or concept is well-founded and representative of the real world (Gay et al., 2009). Frankel et al. (2012, pp. 520–521) point out that ethnography is "highly dependent on the particular researcher's observations and interpretations, and since numerical data are rarely provided, there is usually no way to check the validity of the researcher's conclusions. As a result, observer bias is almost impossible to eliminate." While some scholars lament the lack of objectivity in studies of this nature, others stress the vital role that reflexivity plays in ethnographic work. Hymes (1996, p. 13), for example, calls on researchers to declare their biases and any personal characteristics that may impact their observations and interpretation of the data: "Since partiality cannot be avoided, the only solution is to face up to it, to compensate for it as much as possible, to allow for it in interpretation." While reliance on the researcher's interpretations makes it challenging to ascertain the validity of an ethnography, using member checks, presenting sufficient qualitative data (e.g. original quotes from interview transcripts/diary entries), and fully declaring one's biases can enhance confidence in the findings.

Project Ideas and Resources

An ethnographic approach can be used to investigate a seemingly endless range of issues in language and intercultural communication, such as: identity formation and change, language and intercultural development through study and residence abroad, acculturation in a new land, etc. Using an ethnographic approach, Donelan (2010) investigated an Intercultural Performance Project in a secondary school, Spencer (2011) explored the cultural and linguistic integration of American expatriates in Costa Rica, and Broughton (2011) studied a transnational Internet-based community of fans of Spaghetti Westerns.

> ### Case in Point
>
> Jackson, J. (2008). *Intercultural journeys; From study to residence abroad.* Basingstoke: Palgrave Macmillan.
> Ethnographers may choose to analyze a person, cultural event, activity, or process that occurs within a particular cultural setting. An example of an ethnographic study of a group's behavior over time was conducted by Jackson (2008).

This study examined the experiences of 14 Chinese university students (English majors) from Hong Kong who took part in a short-term study abroad program in England. Using the tools of ethnographic research (e.g. fieldwork at home and abroad, including participant observations, informal conversations, interviews, sojourner diaries, field notes), the students' language use and intercultural developmental trajectories were tracked from their home environment to England, throughout their five-week stay abroad, and for one semester after their return to Hong Kong. The developmental trajectories of four of the participants were then selected for closer scrutiny. By closely observing and interacting with them for more than a year, it was possible to identify a range of internal and external factors that impacted their second language and (inter)cultural learning, as well as their evolving self-identities. The findings challenged the proposed linkage between second language proficiency and intercultural competence, and raised awareness of specific program features and individual attributes and behaviors that can lead to differing outcomes. These new understandings led to adjustments in all phases of the study abroad program: pre-sojourn preparation, sojourn support, and re-entry debriefings. Hence, ethnographic studies of this nature can lead to both theoretical and practical advances.

Conclusion

While ethnography is arguably one of the most challenging approaches to research, it can also be highly rewarding. When done well, it can lead to deeper understandings of issues in language and intercultural communication, bring about the emergence of new theories, and provide direction for innovative practice.

Key Terms

Anthropology The study of humankind, past and present, that draws and builds upon knowledge from the social and biological sciences, as well as the humanities and natural sciences.
Ethnography of communication (Ethnography of speaking) An approach to the study of discourse which focuses on a group's ways of seeing and experiencing the world and how these worldviews are expressed through particular ways of speaking
Field notes Detailed written accounts of the ethnographer's observations, reflections, and analytical thought
Fieldwork The portion of research that is conducted in the location of the group or individuals under study
Participant observation The researcher actively engages in events in the setting under study

References

Agar, M. (1996). *The professional stranger* (2nd ed.). San Diego, CA: Academic Press.
Atkinson, P. (1994). *The ethnographic imagination: Textual constructions of reality*. London: Routledge.

Boellstorff, N., Nardi, B., Pearce, C., & Taylor, T. L. (2012). *Ethnography and virtual worlds: A handbook of method*. Princeton, NJ: Princeton University Press.

Boylorn, R. M., Orbe, M. P., Ellis, C., & Bochner, A. P. (2014). *Critical autoethnography: Intersecting cultural identities in everyday life*. Walnut Creek, CA: Left Coast Press.

Brewer, J. (2000). *Ethnography*. Buckingham: Open University Press.

Broughton, L. (2011). Crossing borders virtual and real: a transnational Internet-based community of Spaghetti Western fans finally meet each other face to face on the wild plains of Almeria, Spain. *Language and Intercultural Communication*, 11(4), 304–318.

Buch, E. D., & Staller, K. M. (2014). What is feminist ethnography? In S.N. Hesse-Biber (Ed.), *Feminist research practice: A primer* (pp. 107–143). Thousand Oaks, CA: Sage.

Byram, M., & Feng, A. (2005). Teaching and researching intercultural competence. In E. Hinkel (Ed.), *Handbook of research in second language teaching and learning* (pp. 911–930). Mahwah, NJ: Lawrence Erlbaum.

CAQDAS (n.d.). CAQDAS Networking project at the University of Surrey. Retrieved June 22, 2015 from: http://www.surrey.ac.uk/sociology/research/researchcentres/caqdas/support/choosing/caqdas_definition.htm.

Carspecken, P. F. (1996). *Critical ethnography in educational research: A theoretical and practical guide*. New York: Routledge.

Coover, R. (2004). Using digital media tools in cross-cultural research, analysis, and representation. *Visual Studies*, 19(1), 6–25.

Crang, M., & Cook, I. (2007). *Doing ethnographies*. London: Sage.

Craven, C, & Davis, D-A. (Eds). (2013). *Feminist activist ethnography: Counterpoints to neoliberalism in North America*. Lanham, MD: Lexington Books.

Damen, L. (1987). *Culture learning: The fifth dimension on the language classroom*. Reading, MA: Addison-Wesley.

Davies, C. A. (2008). *Reflexive ethnography: A guide to researching selves and others* (2nd ed.). London: Routledge.

Deegan, M. J. (2001). The Chicago School. In P.A. Atkinson, A. Coffey, S. Delamont, J. Lofland & L. Lofland (Eds.), *The handbook of ethnography* (pp. 11–25). Thousand Oaks, CA: Sage.

Denzin, N. (2014). *Interpretive autoethnography* (2nd ed.). Thousand Oaks, CA: Sage.

Dicks, B., Mason, B., Coffey, A., & Atkinson, P. (2005). *Qualitative research and hypermedia: ethnography for the digital age*. Thousand Oaks, CA: Sage.

Donelan, K. (2010). Drama as intercultural education: An ethnographic study of an intercultural performance project in a secondary school. *Youth Theatre Journal*, 24, 19–33.

Duneier, M., Kasinitz, P., & Murphy, A. (2014). An invitation to urban ethnography. In M. Duneier, P. Kasinitz & A. Murphy (Eds.), *The Urban Ethnography Reader* (pp. 1–8). Oxford: Oxford University Press.

Ellis, C. (2004). *The ethnographic I: A methodological novel about autoethnography*. Walnut Creek, CA: AltaMira Press.

Ellis, C. (2009). *Revision: Autoethnographic reflections on life and work*. Walnut Creek, CA: Left Coast Press.

Ellis, C., Adams, T. E., & Bochner, A. P. (2010). Autoethnography: An Overview. *Forum Qualitative Sozialforschung/ Forum: Qualitative Social Research*, 12(1), Art. 10. Retrieved June 23, 2015 from: http://www.qualitative-research.net/index.php/fqs/article/view/1589.

Emerson, R. M. (2011). *Writing ethnographic fieldnotes* (2nd ed.). Chicago: Chicago University Press.

Frankel, J.R., Wallen, N. E., & Hyun, H. H. (2012). *How to design and evaluate research in education*. New York: McGraw-Hill.

Gay, L. R., Mills, G. E., & Airasian, P. (2009). *Educational research: Competencies for analysis and applications*. Upper Saddle River, NJ: Pearson Education.

Geertz, C. (1973). Thick description: Toward an interpretive theory of culture. In C. Geertz, *Interpretation of cultures* (pp. 4–30). New York: Basic Books.

Gobo, G. (2008). *Doing ethnography*. Thousand Oaks, CA: Sage.

Gordon, T., Holland, J., & Lahelma, E. (2001). Ethnographic research in educational settings. In P. Atkinson, A. Coffey, S. Delamont, J. Lofland & L. Lofland (Eds.), *Handbook of ethnography* (pp. 188–203). Thousand Oaks, CA: Sage.

Gumperz, J.J., & Hymes, D. (Eds.) (1964). *The ethnography of communication. Special issue of American Anthropologist*, 66 (6).

Gumperz, J.J., & Hymes, D.H. (Eds) (1972). *Directions in sociolinguistics*. New York: Holt, Rinehart, & Winston.

Hammersley, M. (1992). *What's wrong with ethnography? Methodological explorations*. London: Routledge.

Hammersley, M., & Atkinson, P. (2007). *Ethnography: principles in practice* (3rd ed.). London: Routledge.

Heath, S. B., Street, B. with Mills, M. (2008). *On ethnography: Approaches to language and literacy research*. New York: Teachers College Press.

Heller, M. (2011). *Paths to post-nationalism: a critical ethnography of language and identity*. Oxford: Oxford University Press.

Herrera, L., & Torres, C. A. (2006). *Cultures of Arab schooling: critical ethnographies from Egypt*. Albany: State University of New York Press.

Hymes, D. (1974). *Foundations in sociolinguistics: An ethnographic approach*. London: Tavistock Publications Ltd.

Hymes, D. (1986). Discourse: scope without depth. *International Journal of the Sociology of Language*, 57, 49–89.

Hymes, H. (1996). *Ethnography, linguistics, narrative inequality: Toward an understanding of voice*. London: Taylor and Francis.

Ibrahim, A. (2014). *The rhizome of Blackness: A critical ethnography of hip-hop culture, language, identity, and the politics of becoming*. New York: Peter Lang.

Jackson, J. (2006). Ethnographic preparation for short-term study and residence in the target culture. *The International Journal of Intercultural Relations*, 30(1), 77–98.

Jackson, J. (2008). *Intercultural journeys: From study to residence abroad*. Basingstoke: Palgrave Macmillan.

Jones, S. H., Adams, T.E., & Ellis, C. (2013). *Handbook of autoethnography*. Walnut Creek, CA: Left Coast Press.

Jordan, S., & Roberts, C. (2000). *Introduction to ethnography*. (Learning and Residence Abroad (LARA) Project). Oxford: Oxford Brookes University.

Kottak, C. (2012). *Cultural anthropology: Appreciating cultural diversity*. New York: McGraw-Hill.

Kozinets, R. V. (2010). *Netnography: Doing ethnographic research online*. Thousand Oaks, CA: Sage.

LeCompte, M., & Schensul, J. (1999). *Designing and conducting ethnographic research*. Lanham, MD: AltaMira Press.

Lincoln, Y. S., & Guba, E. G. (2000). Paradigmatic controversies, contradictions, and emerging confluences. In N. K. Denzin & Y. S. Lincoln (Eds.). *Handbook of qualitative research* (2nd ed., pp. 163–188). Thousand Oaks, CA: Sage.

McCurdy, D. W., Spradley, J. P., & Shandy, D. J. (2005). *The cultural experience: ethnography in complex society*. Long Grove, IL: Waveland Press.

Mackey, A., & Gass, S. M. (2005). *Second language research: Methodology and design*. Mahwah, NJ: Lawrence Erlbaum.

Markose, S., Symes, C., & Hellstén, M. (2011). "In this country education happen at the home": Two families in search of the instruments of appropriation for school success. *Language and Intercultural Communication*, 11(3), 248–269.

Madison, D. S. (2012). *Critical ethnography: Method, ethics, and performance.* Thousand Oaks, CA: Sage.
Malinowski, B. (1922). *Argonauts of the Western Pacific.* New York: Dutton.
O'Reilly, K. (2005). *Ethnographic methods.* London: Routledge.
O'Reilly, K. (2009). *Key concepts in ethnography.* Thousand Oaks, CA: Sage.
Pink, S. (2007). *Doing visual ethnography* (2nd ed.). Thousand Oaks, CA: Sage.
Pole, C., & Morrison, M. (2003). *Ethnography for education.* Maidenhead: Open University Press.
Richards, K. (2003). *Qualitative inquiry in TESOL.* Basingstoke: Palgrave Macmillan.
Roberts, C., Byram, M., Barro, A., Jordan, S., & Street, B. (2001). *Language learners as ethnographers.* Clevedon: Multilingual Matters.
Silver, C., & Lewins, A. (2014). (2nd ed.). *Using software in qualitative research: A step-by-step guide.* Thousand Oaks, CA: Sage.
Spencer, A. (2011). Americans create hybrid spaces in Costa Rica: a framework for exploring cultural and linguistic integration. *Language and Intercultural Communication,* 11(1), 59–74.
Spradley, J. (1979). *The ethnographic interview.* New York: Holt, Rinehart and Winston.
Spradley, J. (1980). *Participant observation.* New York: Holt, Rinehart and Winston.
Thomas, J. (1993). *Doing critical ethnography.* Thousand Oaks, CA: Sage.
Van Maaen, J. (2011). *Tales of the field: On writing ethnography* (2nd ed.). Chicago: University of Chicago Press.
Wacquant, L. (2003). Ethnografeast: A progress report on the practice and promise of ethnography. *Ethnography,* 4(1), 5–14.
Wang, T. (2012). Writing live fieldnotes: Towards a more open ethnography. Retrieved 23 June 2015 from: http://ethnographymatters.net/blog/2012/08/02/writing-live-fieldnotes-towards-a-more-open-ethnography/.
Watson-Gegeo, K. (1988). Ethnography in ESL: Defining the essentials. *TESOL Quarterly,* 22(4), 575–592.
Wolcott, H. (2008). *Ethnography: A way of seeing.* Lanham, MD: Altamira Press.
Wyatt, J., & Adams, T. E. (2014). *On (writing) families: Autoethnographies of presence and absence, love and loss.* Rotterdam: Sense Publishers.

Further Reading and Resources

Crang, M., & Cook, I. (2007). *Doing ethnographies.* Thousand Oaks, CA: Sage.
Fetterman, D. M. (2009). *Ethnography: Step-by-step* (3rd ed.). Thousand Oaks, CA: Sage.
Hammersley, M. (2007). *Ethnography: Principles in practice,* London: Routledge.
Murchison, J. (2010). *Ethnography essentials: Designing, conducting, and presenting your research,* San Francisco: Jossey-Bass.
Watson-Gegeo, K. A. (1988). Ethnography in ESL: Defining the essentials. *TESOL Quarterly,* 22(4), 575–592.

17 Virtual Ethnography

Aoife Lenihan and Helen Kelly-Holmes

Summary

As the border between online and offline culture and communication becomes increasingly blurred, there is a need to develop and expand methods of systematically investigating online spaces as both dynamic cultures and cultural artefacts (Hine, 2000). Virtual ethnography transfers the principles of ethnography as a way of describing and observing cultures to online communicative contexts. It is a mixed-methods approach underpinned by an ethnographic sensitivity and a grounded, data- and context-driven approach to understanding culture. When ethnography goes virtual its remit remains the same, what has changed with technological development is how cultural stories are told.

With the normalization of the Web and its integration into and omnipresence in everyday life, there is a recognition among researchers that virtual spaces are no longer an extraordinary or separate domain but spaces in which culture can and should be examined. With this assumption in mind, the current chapter explores virtual ethnography as a research method for intercultural communication. First of all the origins and conceptual basis of virtual ethnography are examined before going on to describe the method and various approaches to it. Following this, the strengths and limitations of the method are considered as well as the challenges faced by researchers using this method. Next, the actual process of virtual ethnography/doing ethnography virtually is outlined and current studies and themes are explored. Finally, mixed and combined approaches as well as future methodological trends are outlined.

Virtual Ethnography: Origins and Conceptual Basis

Ethnography is all about describing and analyzing culture, and virtual ethnography takes the same principles and applies them to online cultures (cf. Jackson, Chapter 16, this volume). An early definition by Cavanagh (1999) outlines virtual ethnography as a variation of more traditional ethnomethodological methods which uses a range of observational and other qualitative methods such as observation, questionnaires, interviews, conversation analysis, the researchers' field notes etc., to study how meaning is constructed in online spaces. It uses ethnography (see Jackson, Chapter 16, this volume) to consider the culture of a group from their perspective. At its simplest, ethnographic research online involves the researcher learning how to live there and how to account for what goes on in this space (Carter, 2005). Virtual ethnography as a distinct research approach was primarily developed by Christine Hine (2000) and is used across disciplines including anthropology, sociology, economics, psychology and intercultural communication.

The key idea of virtual ethnography is the same as that of ethnography, namely the immersion of the researcher in the social or cultural situation, attempting to learn how life is lived there as opposed to the researcher approaching it with a particular preemptive research question(s) or assumption(s). It is a method grounded in the field or site of research; it is driven by the context and data; and it informs rather than is informed by theory or an approach. Virtual ethnography extends the ethnographic field and observation from the examination of co-present and face-to-face interactions, to mediated and distributed online ones (Wouters, 2005) in the social spaces of the Internet (Hine, 2008).

It is important to distinguish virtual ethnography from other qualitative methods, such as interview studies, case studies, grounded theory, narrative analysis, etc. (Markham, 2008). Virtual ethnography shares commonalities with other research methods such as website content analysis, (for example, both use qualitative and quantitative methods to investigate websites, discourse online, etc. (Wouters, 2005)) the distinguishing feature of virtual ethnography is the goal of "thick description" (Geertz, 1983) from the participants' perspective. Thick description is the ability to discuss or describe the experience of, in the case of virtual ethnography an Internet user, while retaining a critical outlook on this experience as the virtual ethnographer.

Virtual ethnography has become acknowledged in academia as an appropriate method to investigate how users make sense of the Internet and its possibilities (Hine, 2008). Ethnography as an approach has moved on from its earlier field sites which were distant and bounded cultures and is now concerned with ethnography "at home" or in multiple locations (O'Reilly, 2009). The potential for virtual ethnography is strengthened by the development of multi-sited ethnography, the ethnography of organizations (businesses, hospitals, etc.), the use of discourse analysis (see Monaghan, Chapter 4, this volume) and the overall broadening of ethnography as a method for investigating culture. Virtual ethnography emphasizes the sociocultural dimensions of the Internet rendering it a space of dynamic cultures, practices and customs (Hjorth, 2011).

Hine (1994) argues for the development of virtual ethnography not to replace old methods but to focus on the assumptions underlying ethnography and also on the features of new technologies that are perceived as different or "special." There are two main perspectives on virtual ethnography in the literature: the view of those who consider virtual ethnography a distinct methodological approach, and the view of those who do not. Hine (2005) acknowledges that her virtual ethnographic approach polarizes opinions: it is considered by some as the same as ethnography in face-to-face contexts, while others believe it to be so different it is not ethnography at all. Hine (2008) views virtual ethnography as developing in dialogue with the principles of ethnography in other domains. Park (2004) concurs, believing that virtual ethnography fits well within the wider field of ethnography in its current self-reflexive phase (see Jackson, Chapter 16, this volume). For us, when ethnography goes virtual its remit remains the same, it is about telling cultural stories, what has changed with technological development is how these are told (Murthy, 2008).

Strengths and Limitations of this Method

Virtual ethnography can be employed to ascertain a grounded sense of the meanings of both the technology and the cultures which facilitate it and are facilitated by it. In other words, virtual ethnography allows the researcher to understand the Internet as both *culture* and *cultural artefact* (Hine, 2000). Firstly, the Internet is a culture, a place where culture is created and recreated. Indeed, as Hine (2000) notes, the ethnographic research of online spaces has contributed to the establishment of the perception of the Internet as a culture and the idea that the uses people make of this technology could and should be studied, which will be discussed further below. Secondly, the Internet can be viewed as a cultural artefact. It is a product of culture: a technology created and developed by particular people with their own goals and priorities specific to their context. It is a technology shaped by how it is marketed, taught, used, etc. What the Internet is and what it does is the result of understandings which are culturally produced and can vary (Hine, 2000). This approach allows ethnographers to investigate local or specific cultural contexts of interpretation and use.

Considering the Internet as a cultural artefact questions the viewpoint of the Internet as simply a site for the consequences of culture. Rather, it highlights the status of the Internet as a cultural realization founded on contextually situated understandings of the technology. Studies of computer mediated communication (CMC) have moved on from viewing the Internet as a poor medium of communication to now seeing it as a rich communication medium, which aids the development of cultures (Hine, 2000). Hine (2005) suggests that a methodological shift in the field of Internet research, namely the demarcation of the worldwide web as an ethnographic field site was vital to the development of the status of Internet communication as culture. Virtual ethnographic methods allow researchers to demonstrate the cultural richness of the Internet domain. Hine (2005) continues to argue that, given our understanding of the Internet as a cultural context is intertwined with the application of ethnography to this domain, the method and the phenomenon are in a mutually dependent relationship, and define each other through this connection. Since, as highlighted above, ethnography is a method for investigating culture, and by demonstrating that ethnography can be applied to the online context, the Internet is then delineated as a cultural – and intercultural – context.

Some researchers are not satisfied with Hine's (2000) or others' approaches to virtual ethnography as a means for investigating culture, and consider it as having a number of limitations. Catterall and Maclaran (2001, p. 234) wonder what an ethnography of a virtual community can actually represent: membership can be transient, the identities of participants unknown/unverifiable, interactions online have a private/public nature, and research online is opportunistic in nature. In other words, given how fluid, dynamic, and varied the online context is, they question how the ethnographer can give an account of living and making meaning here. Also, a similar concern is raised about the ease of the Internet as a field and site of research: as it is "all there," i.e. nothing is missed due to archives, etc., and the text is already there, not mediated by transcription, what does the ethnographer offer to the study (Beaulieu, 2004)? In other words, when meaning-making leaves a textual, audio, visual, etc., trace, can these not just be studied, described and analyzed themselves?

Some researchers identify a limitation in virtual ethnographic studies where the field of research is the online context only (Teli, Pisanu, & Hakken, 2007). Ethnography, and thus virtual ethnography, is a holistic approach and should not focus only on online practice(s) in their view; rather it should overlap with the offline context and offline practices. Teli et al. (2007) argue for the ethnography of online groups to include online and related offline contexts, human and nonhuman actors in both of these, a more hybrid, or to use their term cyborg, a "cyberethnography." One of the core objectives of ethnography as a way of investigating cultures is to reveal complexity; hence, both traditional and virtual forms of ethnography must integrate the relevant context. In particular, in virtual ethnographic studies, Wittel (2000) warns how the connections between online and offline spaces can be underestimated; he believes the lack of consideration or inclusion of the offline environment reduces the complexity of such studies.

Doing Virtual Ethnography/Ethnography Virtually

Virtual ethnography is a mixed-methods approach and can involve a number of methodologies. In short, this means that every virtual ethnographic study and methodological approach is different in context, methods employed, analysis, and outcomes. It is therefore difficult to give an overall account of how to do virtual ethnography. Hine (2000) views the lack of frameworks for doing virtual ethnography as a strength of the approach. She outlines ten principles of her practice of "virtual ethnography" but notes that these should not been seen as rules, since ethnography primarily involves adaptation and divergence from prior assumptions. Furthermore, she believes that as a method, it is a "lived craft" as opposed to a distinct approach or framework devoid of a particular ethnographic study and ethnographer.

In line with Gajjala (2006), we consider virtual ethnography as a method that "unfolds" as the researcher progresses in their study and continues to do so as the research advances. Although there are more prescriptive methods for doing virtual ethnography (e.g. Abdelnour Nocera, 2002; Mann, 2006) we see three guiding aspects as essential to a virtual ethnographic approach, namely the *field*, *field notes* and the *ethnographer*. One point to bear in mind is that virtual ethnography is labor-intensive, it "requires inductive, interactive, and recursive data collection and analysis" (Greenhow, 2011 p. 78). In other words, it involves initial or introductory work, interaction by the researcher on some level, and data collection/analysis shaped by the ever-changing research site and by the developing knowledge and insights of the researcher.

We will now look at the three essential ingredients for investigating Intercultural Communication using virtual ethnography.

Field

Virtual ethnography shifts the focus from place to interaction, in other words, the communities and cultures being investigated are not bounded entities before the ethnographer enters the field, as in traditional ethnography, but are created as part of the virtual ethnographic process (Markham, 2008). In terms of the research field, the virtual ethnographer must be mindful that finding the research field and defining sensible boundaries around it is part of the research project and one of the primary concerns in undertaking this method of research (cf. Hine, 1994, Markham, 2008). Virtual ethnographers have their own version of an arrival story, discussing how they negotiated access, observed online interactions, communicated with Internet users, etc. (Hine, 2000). The arrival story of Lenihan's (2013, 2014) virtual ethnography is twofold, the first part being how the researcher came across the Facebook Translations application in her personal life and then selected this as the ethnographic field for her study, and, secondly, when the researcher actually began the virtual ethnography, i.e. began collecting data and engaging with the domain ethnographically. Attention must be paid and acknowledgement given to the impact of mundane research decisions and choices, such as how data sites are found, what search engine is used, etc., as these are the criteria used to create boundaries around the field. These choices and practices delineate and affect the research field for the virtual ethnographer and form their arrival story to the ethnographic field.

Field notes/diary

There is no consensus on what field notes are meant to describe; broadly, these notes are the record and verification of events during the period of the virtual ethnography. They should record all details of the ethnography, from notes on data collected to reflections on research decisions made, and should be kept in chronological order. Adhering to this ensures that the record will reflect the dynamic changes in both the context and participants' individual and group lives, as well as the researchers' decision making (Lindlof & Taylor, 2002).

The first stage in the virtual ethnography and therefore the fieldwork diary is to get a working idea on the main aspects of the research field, who is involved, how it is structured and facilitated, etc. Lenihan's (2014) early field notes outlined the various aspects of the Facebook Translations application itself and how it worked, and asked further questions as they arose for follow up. As Utz (2010, p. 97) notes, "observation begins from the moment the researcher enters the online group" or cultural field. It is usually unfocused at the beginning and the primary goal is simply to get familiar with the online setting. Next, the researcher will turn to more specific topics or areas of interest. At the beginning, large amounts of data will be gathered, anything that the ethnographer considers as being of relevance will be collected, as in the early stages, "nothing is too trivial or too obvious to be noticed and documented" (Lindlof & Taylor, 2002, p. 162). The fieldwork diary can also be supplemented in virtual ethnography with other methods of capturing the field such as screen-capture recordings, screenshots and/or downloading of material.

Ethnographer

Prior knowledge of the field can vary amongst virtual ethnographers and can shape their entry into the field. Some researchers may do research on an online community of which they are a member, while others may be completely unfamiliar with the context. Fay (2007) describes her research on an academic group of which she was a member as requiring a "repositioning" of herself towards the academic project, the participants and her research aims. From this the researcher has personal experiences to reflect critically on as a resource. If already familiar with the research field, the virtual ethnographer should reflect on their prior familiarity, knowledge and viewpoints before re-entering the field. Furthermore, if doing research on an online community of which the researcher is part, they may need to announce their new role to the community (Baym, 2000) and consider the impact of the research on their connections/relationships within that context.

There is a spectrum of participation which ethnographers grapple with in their fieldwork; however, most virtual ethnographers advocate the inclusion of some participation in the research field to "experience embedded cultural understanding" (Kozinets, 2010, p. 75). For Lenihan (2014) it was only after six months of observation, data collection, and recording of field notes that she decided some level of participation was needed to gain an insight into the culture of the particular Facebook community at the level or perspective of the users. In this case the researcher participated only on a handful of occasions and this was sufficient to gain new insights and experiences in the ethnographic field. When participating in the ethnographic field the virtual ethnographer must then acknowledge that it is not a 100 % naturalistic ethnography, however; as discussed above, the impact of the virtual ethnographer on the ethnography is felt in every aspect of the study given the online context.

Research Themes and Current Studies

One of the earliest studies which used ethnographic methods online is Markham (1998). In this study she considers cyberspace, as she terms it, as an "evolving cultural form" in which users create social networks, groups, and communities through electronic messages. She is interested in the consequences of these social contexts, and investigates what cyberspace means to Internet users, how it affects or changes their lives. In particular, she is interested in how users make sense of their online experiences: do they shift between the offline physical world and the online context where they can re-create their bodies or leave them behind? Markham chose a number of contexts for her observations. Firstly, she considered the common metaphors used to refer to online interaction(s) in online conversations, in magazines, on television and in books. Secondly, she assumed the role of a "lurker" in an online community and analyzed an eight-month conversation from this context. Also, she considered how members of the community organize its boundaries and norms though conversation. Finally, she interviewed a hacker to discuss how they made sense of identity online.

Identity is a common theme of virtual ethnographic research, and this is illustrated in recent research on social media/Social Network Sites (SNS) (e.g. boyd & Ellison, 2008). Rybas and Gajjala (2007) investigated the construction of racial identity on SNSs, or social network systems as they term them, using virtual ethnographic research methods grounded in epistemologies of doing. In another study, boyd and Heer (2006) used virtual ethnography in conjunction with visualization to study profiles and social identity on the then SNS Friendster (it is now marketed as a social gaming site). They gathered data via participant observation over a nine month period in 2003, including interviews, qualitative surveys, and focus groups. 1.5 million user profiles were collected from three source profiles. Informed by this ethnographic data, they developed an "egocentric interactive visualization" to explore and analyze the collected profiles (boyd & Heer, 2006, p. 3).

Virtual ethnography was also used to examine user interaction(s) for a variety of concerns and from a broad range of approaches. Fernàndez and Gil-Rodríquez (2011) were concerned with Facebook as a collaborative platform in higher education and used virtual ethnography to investigate the interaction(s) on forums. Brink-Danan (2010) investigated a Ladino email list, Ladinokomunita, looking at the relationship between vernacularity and postvernacularity and how community boundaries were established and maintained.

Case in Point

Lenihan, A. (2014) Investigating language policy in social media: Translation practices on Facebook. In P. Seargeant & C. Tagg (Eds.), *The language of social media: Community and identity on the internet* (pp. 208–227). Basingstoke: Palgrave Macmillan.

Research question: To investigate the online culture and communication of the Facebook Irish language translations application (app) community as a means of understanding how language policy works in this online setting.
Research design: Observation with a small level of ethnographer participation. Data collection was via fieldwork diary, screenshots and downloading of material.
Participants: Facebook, the Irish Translations app community, and the ethnographer.
Data: Documentation of observations of Facebook activities and developments over a three year period in this online culture, Facebook publications in written and video format and related data sources outside of the Facebook website. Documentation of

observations of the online communication among the members of the Irish Translations app community over a three year period and some participation in the Facebook app as a "translator" from this community.
Results: In terms of language policy theory, this research demonstrates that the assumed dichotomy of "bottom-up" forces as opposed to "top-down" forces is not always in evidence. Rather, language policy is now realized as not just unidirectional, but can be found in "multiple discursive relations" (Androutsopoulos, 2009) and cannot be separated from the shared norms and normative discourses of language communities (Leppänen & Piirainen-Marsh, 2009). An expanded view of language policy is necessary, one that challenges the accepted dichotomies, since the object of its study, the social media context, is ever changing, fluid and dynamic.

Another theme virtual ethnographic research has addressed is the development of multilingualism and the experience of minority language communities and speakers online.

Case in Point

Doutsou, I. (2013) Ethnicity mediated: Identity practices of Greek diaspora on a social network site. PhD Thesis, Kings College, London. Available from: https://kclpure.kcl.ac.uk/portal/en/theses/ethnicity-mediated-identity-practices-of-greek-diaspora-on-a-social-network-site(dbf56ca5-2043-4fe3-8b8d-ae80f54471f3).html

Research question: To investigate "the processes by which new media practices may result in redefining ethnic belonging for diasporic populations," by "describing how a set of participants – Greeks in London – practice their ethnicity and move between online and offline sites, countries, cultures and languages" (Doutsou, 2013).
Research design: Discourse-centered online ethnography (DCOE) (see below) of Facebook sites used by London-based members of the Greek diaspora; online and offline; interviews, questionnaires, screen observation and fieldwork.
Participants: The ethnographer, London-based members of the Greek diaspora, Facebook.
Data: multimodal data (visual, textual); content shared on profile, status updates, wall posts, and group pages on Facebook; interview data.
Results: "The study points to a range of creative and innovative online practices of hybridization which contest stereotypical notions of Greek ethnicity, create a new identity for "place" and "home" and expand the resources from which ethnic identity can be imagined. ... The analysis reveals the existence of an online space which facilitates transnational identities and challenges discourses of ethnicity and diaspora" (Doutsou, 2013).

Kelly-Holmes, (2006a, b) also used a similar approach in her study of commercial language practices on the Web to consider how they engage with a multilingual user base and audience. These studies examined static websites and pages. In the first study, the Irish language version of the Google search engine was the starting point for examining the feasibility and range of resources of online communication in Irish (Kelly-Holmes, 2006b). In the second, (Kelly-Holmes, 2006b), she observed the languages used on the global homepages of a number of commercial brands and also on their county/region and language-specific websites, a total of 548 websites. Based on these results she also distributed a questionnaire about language issues and multilingualism to the brand managers of the organizations studied. None of these were completed, with some companies citing confidentiality reasons and the majority simply not responding. Kelly-Holmes (2006b) considered her approach a combination of virtual ethnography with linguistic landscape analysis. This mixed approach, along with Discourse Centered Online Ethnography (DCOE), which combines ethnographic observation with analysis of discourse (cf. Doutsou, 2013), will be discussed next.

Mixed and Emerging Approaches

Virtual ethnography can be used in conjunction with a linguistic landscape analysis. Linguistic landscape (Landry & Bourhis, 1997) is a methodology used to investigate multilingualism in the public space (e.g. Shohamy & Gorter, 2009). It presents an account of the visual presence of particular language(s) in a particular domain and the technique involves recording visual multilingualism (and also monolingualism) by systematically counting the presence and frequency of languages on public signs, both signs which are and are not subject to language policy and planning directives. The linguistic landscape approach asserts that the visibility of particular languages could reflect their relative position in the sociolinguistic hierarchy of that context, and that a greater visibility of one particular language could imply that this was the dominant language. Therefore, the visibility and visual positioning of particular languages could be used as a way to reveal common-sense ideologies about language(s) that are established in a particular society.

Recently, focus in linguistic landscape studies has moved from the landscape of cities and public spaces to the Web (e.g. Ivkovic & Lotherington, 2009; Kelly-Holmes 2006a, b). Kelly-Holmes (2006b, 2013) combined aspects of virtual ethnography and linguistic landscape analysis to investigate corporate multilingualism online by examining corporate websites. She observed, recorded and counted the available different language versions of corporate websites in conjunction with accessing these localized versions and contrasting the experience of using these versions to the English or another language iteration of the site. This approach, like linguistic landscape analysis, takes the view that the availability and extent of content in languages other than English on corporate websites indicates their position in the sociolinguistic reality of the corporate Web.

Androutsopoulos (2008) proposed DCOE as a method of investigating people's motivations for the use of particular linguistic resources online and the meanings they attach to those resources. DCOE (see the example of Doutsou, 2013 above) is a combination of methods which involves the systematic observation of particular sites of online discourse in conjunction with direct contact with the social actors of these. It uses insights gathered ethnographically to influence the selection, analysis and interpretation of log data to investigate the relationship between digital texts and their production/reception practices. Androutsopoulos outlined twelve practice-derived guidelines for DCOE, based on the two pillars of this approach: systematic observation and contact with Internet users. Systematic observation assumes that insights into discourse practices and patterns of language use are gained from ongoing observation of online sites of discourse, both in terms of their relationships within a particular site and also across a series of sites of discourse. The six guidelines for the first pillar advise the researcher to: "examine relationships and processes rather than isolated artefacts, move from core to periphery of a field, repeat observation, maintain openness, use all available technology and use observation insights as guidance for further sampling" (Androutsopoulos, 2008, p. 5). The second pillar draws on and uses insights from the observation and log-based analysis of Computer Mediated Discourse (CMD) of the first pillar. Guidelines 7 to 12 advise the following: "contacts should be limited, non-random, and include various participation formats, pay attention to the initial contact, formulate and customize interview guidelines, confront participants with (their own) material, seek repeated and prolonged contacts and make use of alternative techniques wherever possible" (Androutsopoulos, 2008, p. 5).

Key Terms

Computer-mediated communication Communication that occurs via computers, this term acknowledges the potential influence and effect of the technology on the communication. It can include text, visual and oral communication, which can occur synchronously and/or asynchronously, across a variety of online domains and contexts, such as text-based chat rooms, email, video conferencing, etc., and there may be a number of participants, from two people to larger groups.

Online culture Culture is the summation of the norms, customs, beliefs, values, etc., of a particular community or society. Online culture emphasizes that online contexts are places where culture is created and recreated (Hine, 2000) and also that there may be a distinct online culture, with its own norms, values, etc., different to other communities or contexts.

Social network sites Following boyd and Ellison (2008) we use the term "social network sites," as opposed to the popular anecdotal term of "social networking sites," to emphasize how connections on these sites, such as Facebook, are typically between those who already know each other and that the novelty of these sites lies in the articulation and presentation of one's existing social network.

Virtual ethnography The ethnographic approach to data collection and analysis in an online context. It involves the researcher assuming the role of ethnographer and experiencing the online context and interactions at the level of the Internet user. It furthermore, includes the use of a range of ethnographic methods, such as observation, interviews, participation, etc. to gather data and the inclusion of the reflections of the virtual ethnographer in the analysis of this online context.

Virtual field Ethnography is grounded in a physical bounded field or site of research. The virtual field can also be grounded in a particular bounded website or application but in this context the ethnographer must often set and delineate the boundaries of their virtual field as part of their research process. The boundaries can be delineated by time-period, area(s) of interest, availability of/access to material, aim/focus of the study or as mentioned above, by existing website or application limits.

References

Abdelnour Nocera, J.L. (2002). Ethnography and hermeneutics in cybercultural research accessing IRC virtual communities. *Journal of Computer Mediated Communication*, 7(2). doi: 10.1111/j.1083-6101.2002.tb00146.x

Androutsopoulos, J. (2008). Potentials and limitations of discourse-centred online ethnography. *Language@Internet*, 5(9). Retrieved June 24, 2015 from: http://www.languageatinternet.org/articles/2008/1610

Androutsopoulos, J. (2009). Policing practices in heteroglossic mediascapes: A commentary on interfaces. *Language Policy*, 8, 285–290. doi: 10.1007/s10993-009-9142-y

Baym, N. K. (2000). *Tune in, log on: Soaps, fandom and online community*. Thousand Oaks, CA: Sage.

Beaulieu, A. (2004). Mediating ethnography: Objectivity and the making of ethnographies of the internet. *Social Epistemology*, 18(2–3), 139–163. doi: 10.1080/0269172042000249264

boyd, D. M., & Ellison, N. B. (2008). Social network sites: Definition, history, and scholarship. *Journal of Computer Mediated Communication*, 13(1), 210–230. doi:10.1111/j.1083-6101.2007.00393.x

boyd, D., & Heer, J. (2006). Proceedings of the Hawai'i International Conference on System Sciences (HICSS-39): Profiles as Conversation: Networked Identity Performance on Friendster. Kauai, HI: IEEE Computer Society.

Brink-Danan, M. (2010). The meaning of Ladino: The semiotics of an online speech community. *Language and Communication*, 31, 107–118. doi:10.1016/j.langcom.2010.08.003

Carter, D. (2005). Living in virtual communities: An ethnography of human relationships in cyberspace. *Information, Communication and Society*, 8(2), 148–167. doi: 10.1080/13691180500146235

Cavanagh, A. (1999). Behaviour in public? Ethics in online ethnography. *Cybersociology*, 6. Retrieved June 24, 2015 from: http://www.cybersociology.com/files/6_2_ethicsinonlineethnog.html

Catterall, M., & Maclaran, P. (2001). Researching consumers in virtual worlds: A cyberspace odyssey. *Journal of Consumer Behaviour*, 1(3), 228–237. doi: 10.1002/cb.68

Doutsou, I. (2013). Ethnicity Mediated: Identity Practices of Greek Diaspora on a Social Network Site. PhD Thesis, Kings College, London. Retrieved June 24, 2015 from: https://kclpure.kcl.ac.uk/portal/en/theses/ethnicity-mediated-identity-practices-of-greek-diaspora-on-a-social-network-site(dbf56ca5-2043-4fe3-8b8d-ae80f54471f3).html.

Fay, M. (2007). Mobile subjects, mobile methods: Doing virtual ethnography in a feminist online network. *Forum: Qualitative Social Research*, 8(3). Retrieved June 24, 2015 from: http://www.qualitative-research.net/index.php/fqs/article/view/278/611

Fernàndez, C., & Gil-Rodríguez, E. (2011). Facebook as a collaborative platform in higher education: The case study of the universitat oberta de Catalunya. In T. Daradoumis, S. Caballé, A.A. Juan, & F. Xhafa, (Eds.), (*Technology-enhanced systems and tools for collaborative learning scaffolding* (pp. 27–46). Berlin: Springer-Verlag.

Gajjala, R. (2006). Cyberethnography: Reading South Asian digital diasporas. In K. Landzelius (Ed.), *Native on the net: Indigenous and diasporic peoples in the virtual age* (pp. 272–291). London: Routledge.

Geertz, C. (1983). *Local knowledge: Further essays in interpretive anthropology*. New York: Basic Books.
Greenhow, C.M. (2011). Research methods unique to digital contexts: An introduction to virtual ethnography. In N.K. Duke, & M.H. Mallette (Eds.), *Literacy Research Methodologies* (2nd ed., pp. 70–86). New York: Guilford Press.
Hine, C. (1994). Virtual ethnography. Pater presented at When Science Becomes Culture. International Symposium. Montreal, 10–13 April.
Hine, C. (2000). *Virtual ethnography*. Thousand Oaks, CA: Sage.
Hine, C. (2005). Virtual methods and the sociology of cyber-social-scientific-knowledge. In C. Hine (Ed.), *Virtual methods: Issues in social research on the internet* (pp. 1–13). Oxford: Berg.
Hine, C. (2008). Virtual ethnography: Modes, varieties, affordances. In N.G. Fielding, R.M. Lee, & G. Blank (Eds.), *The Sage handbook of online research methods* (pp. 257–270). Thopusand Oaks, CA: Sage.
Hjorth, L. (2011). *Games and gaming: An introduction to new media*. Oxford: Berg.
Ivkovic, D., & Lotherington, H. (2009). Multilingualism in cyberspace: Conceptualising the virtual linguistic landscape. *International Journal of Multilingualism*, 6(1), 17–36. doi: 10.1080/14790710802582436
Kelly-Holmes, H. (2006a). Irish on the World Wide Web: Searches and sites. *Journal of Language and Politics*, 5(1), 217–238. doi: 10.1075/jlp.5.2.05kel
Kelly-Holmes, H. (2006b). Multilingualism and commercial language practices on the Internet. *Journal of Sociolinguistics*, 10(5), 507–519. doi: 10.1111/j.1467-9841.2006.00290.x
Kelly-Holmes, H. (2013). "Choose your language!" Categorisation and control in cyberspace. *Sociolinguistica*, 27, 132–145. doi: 10.1515/soci.2013.27.1.132
Kozinets, R. V. (2010). *Netnography: Doing ethnographic research online*. London: Sage.
Landry, R., & Bourhis, R. (1997). Linguistic landscape and ethnolinguistic vitality. *Journal of Language and Social Psychology*, 16(1), 23–49. doi: 10.1177/0261927x970161002
Lenihan, A. (2013) The interaction of language policy, minority languages and new media: A study of the Facebook translations application. Unpublished PhD dissertation, University of Limerick.
Lenihan, A. (2014). Investigating language policy in social media: Translation practices on Facebook. In P. Seargeant & C. Tagg (Eds.), *The language of social media: Community and identity on the internet* (pp. 208–227), London: Palgrave Macmillan.
Leppänen, S. & Piirainen-Marsh, A. (2009). Language policy in the making: An analysis of bilingual gaming activities. *Language Policy*, 8(3), 261–284. doi: 10.1007/s10993-009-9130-2
Lindlof, T.R., & Taylor, B.C. (2002). *Qualitative communication research methods*. Thousand Oaks, CA: Sage.
Mann, B.L. (2006). Virtual ethnography and discourse analysis. In B. L. Mann (Ed.), *Selected styles in web-based educational research* (pp. 439–456). Hershey, PA: Information Science Publishing.
Markham, A.N. (1998). *Life online: Researching real experience in virtual space*. Walnut Creek, CA: AltaMira Press.
Markham, A. N. (2008). The methods, politics, and ethics of representation in online ethnography. In Y. S. Lincoln & N. K. Denzin (Eds.), *Collecting and interpreting qualitative materials* (3rd ed., pp. 247–284). Thousand Oaks, CA: Sage.
Murthy, D. (2008). Digital ethnography: An examination of the use of new technologies for social research. *Sociology*, 42(5), 837–855. doi: 10.1177/0038038508094565
O'Reilly, K. (2009). *Key concepts in ethnography*. Thousand Oaks, CA: Sage .
Park, J. K. (2004). Virtual ethnography or ethnography of virtuality? Methodological analysis of ethnographic research of the Internet. Paper presented at the Annual Meeting of the International Communication Association. New Orleans, 27–31 May.

Rybas, N., & Gajjala, R. (2007). Developing cyberethnographic research methods for understanding digitally mediated identities. *Forum: Qualitative Social Research*, 8(3). Retrieved June 24, 2015 from: http://www.qualitative-research.net/index.php/fqs/article/view/282

Shohamy, E., & Gorter, D. (Eds.) (2009). *Linguistic landscape: Expanding the scenery*. New York: Routledge.

Teli, M., Pisanu, F., & Hakken, D. (2007). The internet as a library-of-people: For a cyberethnography of online groups. *Forum: Qualitative Social Research*, 8(3). Retrieved June 24, 2015 from: http://www.qualitative-research.net/index.php/fqs/article/view/283

Utz, S. (2010). Using automated "field notes" to observe the behavior of online subjects. In S. D. Gosling, & J. A. Johnson (Eds.), *Advanced methods for conducting online behavioral research* (pp. 91–108). Washington, DC: American Psychological Association.

Wittel, A. (2000). Ethnography on the move: From field to net to internet. *Forum: Qualitative Social Research*, 1(1). Retrieved June 24, 2015 from: http://www.qualitative-research.net/index.php/fqs/article/view/1131/2517

Wouters, P. (2005). The virtual knowledge studio for the humanities and social Sciences. Paper presented at the First International Conference on e-Social Science. Manchester, 22–24 June.

Further Reading and Resources

Androutsopoulos, J. (2014) Computer-mediated communication and linguistic landscapes. In J. Holmes, & K. Hazen (Eds.), *Research methods in sociolinguistics: A practical guide* (pp. 74–90). Oxford: Wiley-Blackwell.

Androutsopoulos, J. (2008). Potentials and limitations of discourse-centred online ethnography. *Language@Internet*, 5(9). Retrieved June 24, 2015 from: http://www.languageatinternet.org/articles/2008/1610

Carter, D. (2005). Living in virtual communities: An ethnography of human relationships in cyberspace. *Information, Communication and Society*, 8(2), 148–167. doi: 10.1080/13691180500146235

Hine, C. (Ed.) (2005). *Virtual methods: Issues in social research on the internet*. Oxford: Berg.

Hine, C. (2008). Virtual ethnography: Modes, varieties, affordances. In N.G. Fielding, R.M. Lee, & G. Blank (Eds.), *The Sage handbook of online research methods* (pp. 257–270). London: Sage.

18 Multimodality

Agnieszka Lyons

> **Summary**
>
> This chapter is devoted to the notion of multimodality and multimodal analysis as a theoretical and methodological approach. Following a discussion of the conceptual basis of multimodality and its applicability to the study of intercultural communication, I turn to the practical aspects of conducting multimodal research, as well as strengths and limitations of this approach. In the last section, I present the current themes addressed in multimodal studies and consider the potential of mixed-method approaches including multimodal analysis.

Multimodality: Origins and Conceptual Basis

The rise in the use of digital photography and video-recordings in the analysis of human communication has led to a growing interest in modes of communication other than speech and writing. The visual, along with the verbal, is now widely recognized as bearing meaning-making potential and worthy of close analysis across a variety of contexts. While the popularization of technology and new media may have foregrounded the multimodal character of communication, meaning has always been constructed multimodally through the use of semiotic resources (language, or code) and sensory resources, such as smell or taste. These resources are often referred to as *modes* and the theoretical approach concerned with their use in communication is known as *multimodal analysis*.

Attempts to define the notions of *mode* and *modality*, fundamental to the field of multimodal analysis, were rarely undertaken in the early literature. Two common assumptions may have contributed to this: the ostensibly self-evident and unproblematic nature of the modalities under investigation and the fact that semiotic modalities naturally align with sensory modalities (Bateman, 2011). Those who have worked on defining the notion of mode come from a variety of backgrounds and have therefore focused on a range of features and classification criteria. Whereas some researchers (e.g. Kress, 2009; Van Leeuwen, 2004) proposed sets of criteria for classifying particular resources as modes, others (e.g. Bateman, 2011) moved beyond descriptions in order to theorize the notion of mode itself.

Multimodal studies are based on three main assumptions: Firstly, it is assumed that communication always involves the use of multiple modes (speech, writing, gestures, images, and others), and their intermodal relationships contribute to meaning-making. Secondly, meaning is constructed through selection and configuration of different modes in interactions. Finally, resources used by interactants are socially shaped over time to create a shared cultural sense of the way in which they can convey meaning. Multimodal expression, thus, is highly context-dependent, with multimodal meanings constructed within specific social and cultural contexts, based on the communicative needs of different communities or cultures. As a result, multimodal research can benefit immensely from the insights of Intercultural Communication studies. At the same time, when researching Intercultural Communication, multimodal approaches bring to light aspects of great significance to communicating interculturally. It is, indeed, not only verbal or textual expression that conveys meaning in particular cultures, but a whole array of other culturally contextualized semiotic means.

Based on the assumption that expressive resources of a culture are not limited to those of speech and writing, mode is understood as socially established in conjunction with the affordances and constraints of the material substrate of a resource and its specific semiotic uses within a community. Taking a cue from social semiotic theory – which investigates human communication (visual, verbal, or oral) in specific social and cultural contexts and understands meaning-making as a social practice – Kress (2009) defines mode as "a socially shaped and culturally given resource for making meaning" and problematizes this notion from the perspective of qualifying criteria as well as features and descriptive planes which help differentiate between individual modes. He says that resources have to fulfil three criteria in order to be recognized as modes. They need to be able to represent 1) states, actions, or events (ideational function); 2) social relations of participants in a given communicative act (interpersonal function); and 3) both of the above need to be represented as coherent (both internally and within their environments) texts (textual function). According to Bateman (2011), on the other hand, the minimal requirement for a semiotic resource to be recognized as mode is that a particular material substrate is sufficiently controllable as to be used purposefully in the meaning-making process. It is important to acknowledge a different understanding of mode and modality, which was proposed by Van Leeuwen (2004). He defines modality as deriving from the concept of modality in grammar (cf. modal verbs) and extends this notion to mean a stance that may be taken by communicators. As is evident even from this brief outline, the term "modality" is polysemous in that it can refer to the presence or employment of modes of communication or the grammatical system of stances.

Irrespective of the exact definition and criteria of classifying resources as modes, scholars who adopt multimodal approaches to discourse recognize that all communication is constructed across a number of planes (e.g. verbal, nonverbal, and visual), and realized through semiotic resources (language being only one of them) drawn upon to create meaning (Jewitt, 2009). Communication within various modalities is achieved through hybrid communicative acts which, Van Leeuwen (2004, p. 8) states, constitute "multimodal microevents in which all the signs present combine to determine their communicative intent," a view that ties in with the second of the three assumptions that form the basis of multimodal studies. Scholars working on multimodal communication focus on interactions between different communicative modes and challenge the oft-repeated view that language (spoken or written) is the most important meaning-making tool. They recognize meaning as constructed based on the meaning potential of material artefacts, of the social and cultural contexts in which communication occurs, as well as the intentions and prior experiences of those who communicate (Price & Jewitt, 2013).

In line with the third of the earlier cited assumptions, the social and cultural aspects of multimodal meaning-making bring to the fore the fact that a message expressed in a certain mode may have a different meaning in the cultural setting in which it was produced and in other cultures or societies. Following from this, a mode is what a community takes to be a mode, based on its representational needs and practices (Kress, 2009, pp. 58–59), and a resource can only be recognized as a mode for a particular group of users if it is used by this group regularly, consistently, and with shared assumptions about its meaning potential (cf. the notion of communicative competence proposed by Dell Hymes, 1974). What is clear is that individual semiotic modes, rather than pre-established, are developed by groups of users. Such development results from exploring affordances of modes which are deemed useful for meaning-making within a particular physical, social, or cultural context (Bateman, 2011). Lack of certain expressive possibilities in a language, mode, or community may, and does, lead to the development of alternative ways of expressing the same concepts or meanings, either in the same or other modes (for example, the elaborate linguistic system of gestures that constitutes sign language compared to a narrow scope of gestures accompanying other modes of communication; and the use of punctuation, originally intended as the representation of intonation in writing). There is no equivalence between modes and the meanings they can express in different cultures. What in one culture is best expressed in writing, in another may be best expressed through gestures, images, or objects. The same can be said about other types of groups and functions of code use.

Despite the differences in their potential for communication between instances of a particular mode as used in different cultures, there are also some commonalities. For example, sequence in time is fundamental to making meaning in speech, as sounds are produced in sequence and their order determines the meaning of an utterance. In comparison, in images all elements are displayed simultaneously and it is their arrangement in space that constitutes a major means for making meaning (Kress, 2009), and picture frames mark image boundaries and separate them from the surrounding environment. The choice of a form of expression depends on a number of factors and both the construction and – importantly – the interpretation of a multimodal text are socially and culturally grounded.

Scholars have discussed the question of the epistemological status of claims made within multimodal studies (cf. Kress & Van Leeuwen, 1998), i.e., the basis on which we build our interpretations of semiotic codes and values we attribute to them. Some of the suggestions include interpreting spatial orientation based on our prior visual literacy (e.g. Dyer, 1989), familiarity with semiotic registers (emergent due to the changing contexts in which they are produced), with their sets of linguistic or nonlinguistic signs (Agha, 2007), or on the cognitive theory of metaphor proposed in Lakoff & Johnson (1980), according to which most abstract concepts are interpretable with reference to other concrete metaphors.

With growing interest and prominence of multimodal approaches to the analysis of communication, scholars have attempted to separate contributing modes for the purpose of analysis, which has proven difficult due to their parallel and co-dependent development. This has resulted in modes now being seen as functioning as multimodal ensembles rather than as groups of modes co-existing independently. Another difficulty that scholars working with multimodal discourse face is their diverse character and, consequently, the lack of uniform approach to the analysis of all types of multimodal texts.

Doing Multimodal Research

Since multimodal approaches can be applied to a wide range of different types of data, the ways in which a researcher deals with the data collection and data analysis stages can differ significantly. Multimodal analysis can be applied to print materials (e.g. press advertisements, comic books, children's books, or text books (Baldry & Thibault, 2006)), face-to-face interactions (Norris, 2004), or film/video (e.g. Kress & Van Leeuwen, 1996). Each of these types of data requires a different method of collection, handling, and analysis, and an altered ethical approach.

Collecting and analyzing multimodal data in face-to-face interactions involves conducting observations and writing field notes as well as collecting texts that may have been part of the interactions. For example, in the case of classroom interaction, handouts could be collected for analysis, as the students' and teachers' interactions with them can be seen as bearing meaning-making potential, while in the case of operating theaters, the collection of forms and reports can inform the analysis of situated action, as in the study in the Case in Point presented below.

The use of video recordings is very common due to the specific characteristics of this type of data. Video preserves the temporality and sequentiality of interactions, enabling researchers to replay (including replaying in slow- or fast-motion) or fast forward recorded material, which in turn provides a different view of observed events. Also, since video is able to record events as they happen, capturing all the aspects of interactions, it gives researchers access to a large amount of fine-grained detail which can be analyzed, e.g. facial expressions, gestures, or gaze. In addition, the material collected is easy to disseminate. Video recording provides a durable account of what took place, which can be viewed repeatedly to extract meaningful patterns and enable detailed microanalysis of interactions. Researchers at MODE (http://mode.ioe.ac.uk/) argue for repeatedly viewing videos and engaging with the data in a range of different configurations and with a number of different people to get as wide a perspective as possible. Viewing a video extract with and without sound, listening to the sound only, watching in fast-forward and slow mode – all allow for different perspectives and the potential of noticing a range of different patterns.

> **Case in Point**
>
> Bezemer, J., Cope, A., Kress, G., & Kneebone, R. (2011). "Do you have another Johan?" Negotiating meaning in the operating theatre. *Applied Linguistics Review*, 2, 313–334.

Research questions: How do surgeons formulate requests for instruments in the operating theater and how nurses and surgical trainees disambiguate these requests on the basis of their prior experience with surgical instruments and equipment, the surgical procedure, and the surgeon's idiolect?

How does multimodal communication unfold in situated encounters?

What strategies do nurses and surgeons deploy to deal with instability and diversity in professional communication?

Research design and data collection method: The study adopts a linguistic-ethnographic approach, bringing together close analysis of multimodal communication and ethnographic analysis of the context. Descriptive and analytic procedures from applied linguistics, social semiotics and ethnography are used.

The study is based on fieldwork conducted at a teaching hospital in London between June 2009 and July 2010. The researchers observed 40 operations, lasting between 45 minutes and 6 hours (approximately 70 hours in total) and observed medical staff and students during preparation and cleaning up in the operating theatre and its adjacent rooms. Between cases, the researchers spoke to staff and students and observed them elsewhere in the hospital. The data collected was discussed in data sessions in a multidisciplinary research team.

Participants: Medical staff performing operations at a teaching hospital in London, including five consultant-surgeons, five surgical registrars, five (senior) house officers, ten medical students, 25 nurses and operation department practitioners and five anesthetists.

Data: audio and video recordings of ten operations, collected using a wireless microphone worn by one of the surgeons, inbuilt video cameras in the handle of the operating lamp and the laparoscope (a camera that is inserted into body cavities), field notes of all operations observed, photographs of the interactions around the operating table, documents circulating in the operating theater (e.g. forms and reports), and interviews with the nurses and the consultant.

Results and issues for consideration: The analysis shows how changes affecting the communicational landscape of the society, such as growing instability and diversity, play out in the moment-by-moment use of language at the operating table and how they are dealt with by team members who have different professional backgrounds and who draw on different, social, cultural, and linguistic resources.

The same approach of examining data in a range of different configurations can be applied to static multimodal texts, for instance, print advertisements and promotional materials, as in the case study referred to below. Viewing them in a range of different ways, removing certain modes or changing the layout can point to meanings being achieved by the existing multimodal ensemble.

Case in Point

Aiello, G., & Thurlow, C. (2006). Symbolic capitals: Visual discourse and intercultural exchange in the European Capital of Culture scheme. *Language and Intercultural Communication*, 6(2), 148–162.

Research questions: What are the dominant visual resources used in the branding of European Capital of Culture cities?
What ideologies of Europeanness are communicated by these resources?
What opportunity does each visual resource offer for intercultural exchange?
Research design and data collection method: The research adopts a social semiotic approach to a range of visual texts. The authors view visual discourse as the deployment of *resources* (rather than codes) for social action, and whose meaning *potentials* (rather than meanings) may be exploited for political, economic, and ideological ends.

The data-collection process involved identifying the cities currently holding, and in the process of competing for, the European Capital of Culture title between 2005 and 2011 and writing to each of these cities to ask for copies of any promotional materials related to their bid. The research team also accessed an archived collection of all available official websites of the cities. In their analysis, they chose to focus only on visual images and designs, recognizing, however, that meaning is always situated and contextualized.
Participants: 30 of the 43 cities either nominated or competing for the title of European Capital of Culture between 2005 and 2011.
Data: The official promotional texts of 30 of the 43 cities either nominated or competing for the title of European Capital of Culture between 2005 and 2011, including print publicity materials and archived collection of all available official websites of the cities.
Results and issues for consideration: The study found that although there are no centralized rules about promotional materials or specific requirements concerning images or design, the visual discourse of the European Capital of Culture scheme is generally uniform, irrespective of any claims to diversity. Texts in these promotional materials were found to be constituted through the selection of basic visual content and figurative images with iconic meaning potential (e.g. cityscapes, fireworks, children, maps, "high culture"), with additional meaning realized through the particular way images were presented.

The examination of the semiotic resources employed by different European Capital of Culture cities in their efforts to express the "European dimension" of their candidacy shows how certain discursive themes are privileged in the re-presentation of this cross-cultural narrative about Europe. For a cross-cultural audience, Europeanness is presented through the repetition of generic cultural details or identity markers.

Having completed their observation and recording, researchers prepare an account of what happened during their observation and illustrate it with relevant images (e.g. sketches of events, stills from a video, room layout and record of movement). Sampling is a key issue: taking into account the (usually) copious amount of collected data, it is necessary to select representative clips to process. A set of video data can also be coded in a number of ways. It is at this stage of initial processing that researchers may start noticing recurring themes in the data, noting down any analytical thoughts they may have. It is important, however, to keep them separate from the data to avoid the situation where researchers' questions form part of the dataset.

The initial stage of collecting other types of data which lend themselves to multimodal analysis, such as printed pages from a book, web pages, or promotional materials, while not involving observation and field notes, follows a similar process of initial "logging." Baldry and Thibault (2006) propose conducting cluster analysis of the data and constructing tables with relevant information, such as that about movement, space, proximity, frames, and actions, possibly accompanied by stills or crops of relevant parts of a printed text or a website.

Since all modes are taken into account, multimodal analysis and transcription are very time-consuming and labor-intensive. Even a short clip from a video recording or a single web page can take hours to transcribe. Therefore, it is not usually feasible to provide transcription of a long stretch of a video recording or more than a few pages of static multimodal texts. Bearing specific research questions in mind, a researcher needs to select a sample of a multimodal text to transcribe and analyze in detail. Whatever the selection, however, it needs to be compared with the whole corpus rather than analyzed as an isolated instance.

Multimodal Transcription

As a crucial stage of research, transcription is no longer considered a "straightforward" turning of speech into writing. Instead, the process conveys the researcher's interpretative, theoretical, or analytical point of view, especially in the way in which transcripts inevitably foreground certain features and omit others (Cowan, 2014). By the time of transcription, a researcher would have already made decisions which bear consequences for the analysis: only a certain part of the whole context has been recorded, which means that no other elements will be possible to transcribe. This shows the importance of a clear idea about what our research questions are and what aspects of multimodal interactions should be analyzed in order to answer the questions set.

Selective as it is, video data contains a breadth of details which can be transcribed and analyzed. Since it is neither possible nor practical to transcribe every single aspect of a multimodal interaction, transcribers are always faced with a choice of what to transcribe and what to leave out, which modes to attend to and what level of details to include. There are different ways of making multimodal transcripts (see, e.g. Baldry & Thibault, 2006; Norris, 2004) and a range of software that supports multimodal transcription. For example, ELAN is a professional tool for adding complex annotations to audio and video streams, which runs on Windows, Mac OS X, and Linux. Annotations can take a variety of forms, such as sentences, glosses, translations, or descriptions, and are created on separate "tiers." An added benefit is the fact that a wide variety of audio and video formats (including Windows Media Player, QuickTime or Java Media Framework) is supported.

In her article on multimodal transcription, Cowan (2014) compares three types of transcription – orthographic transcription, conversation analysis transcription, and multimodal transcription using a tabular and timeline layouts – and discusses their advantages and shortcomings. The tabular transcript separates particular modes (e.g. gaze, vocalization, interaction with artefacts and objects) into columns, while maintaining information about how they work together. This approach allows for a number of different readings: across a row to analyze the co-occurrence of modes at a point in time, or one mode through time, for example. Reading and interpreting tabular representations takes time, but it allows us to notice patterns in the use of different modes and their interrelations. On the other hand, the timeline layout uses a more visual form of representation. Time is represented as a horizontal line with different aspects of interaction represented underneath and accompanied by stills from the video. Here again, it is possible to analyze modes occurring simultaneously as well as the use of a single mode over time. This type, Cowan (2014) argues, allows for a better representation and identification of patterns in the data.

Some more examples and materials pertaining to multimodal transcriptions and examples of their use can be found on the MODE website; particularly useful for the choice of the appropriate method may be the multimodal transcription bank (http://mode.ioe.ac.uk/category/transcription-bank). Importantly, the choice will always depend on the particular research and research questions, and not all forms will be equally suitable for a given research project.

Ethics in Multimodal Research

Doing any kind of research requires taking into account the question of ethics, i.e., deciding what is right and what is wrong in a given research context. The choices that need to be made are influenced by a number of factors: one's individual moral framework stemming from one's cultural background, legal and ethical regulations within a particular discipline, and a number of ethical frameworks (for example, the principle of confidentiality or voluntariness of taking part in research). Data has to go through the usual anonymization process, however. Although in some types of research it is enough to change participants' names and other identifying details to ensure reasonable levels of anonymity, in multimodal research there is the added need to consider ways of anonymizing participants' faces and voices in video clips, a much less straightforward process. Questions arise also with regard to other aspects of a participant's physical self that may need to be anonymized and the extent to which it is possible to ensure anonymity in the case of multimodal data at all. Additionally, the type of data collected has implications on how research is disseminated and findings shared; for example, it may be possible to embed a whole video clip in an academic article online, making it easily searchable by the general public.

Strengths and Limitations of this Method

Adopting a multimodal approach to data analysis has clear benefits: Multimodal communication is central to human interactions, and multimodal analysis enables a more systematic insight into how multiple modes are employed in multimodal ensembles to convey complex meanings. Also, social and cultural meanings are often conveyed in modes other than speech and writing. Video data provides a wealth of details for analysis in a durable and sharable form and provides scope for microanalysis of fine-grained detail.

Like any analysis of representation and communication, multimodal research has clear benefits for the study of intercultural communication, but it is also characterized by significant limitations. Firstly, there is the question of how many modes to include in analysis and how much attention to pay to a single mode. There is a danger of devoting too much attention to individual modes, which may result in too much importance being given to only one of the ways in which people make meaning. At the same time, interest in multiple modes may mean that researchers do not devote enough attention to individual modes and the way they work within a certain multimodal ensemble. It is this interplay between modes within an ensemble, rather than a set of individual modes, that needs to be analyzed as bearing meaning-making potential.

The fact that multimodal analysis focuses on microinteractions (examination of short stretches of video recordings or individual printed pages) leads to questions about its applicability to answering more general questions about culture and society. It is, therefore, vital that multimodal analysis is linked to social theory, and that texts are analyzed within particular socio-historical contexts.

From a practical and technological point of view, the collection of video data requires familiarity with recording equipment and decision-making about the camera positioning and the focus of the recording. Video itself is selective in that it is the researchers' decision what to include in the recording and what to exclude from it. Finally, multimodal analysis and transcription require a lot of processing time. Time consuming and labor-intensive, the process forces a researcher to be selective in how much and what part of collected data to transcribe, which means that any further analysis is influenced by the researcher's initial selection.

Research Themes and Current Studies

Multimodal analysis is capable of providing in-depth insights into communication in a variety of expressive modalities. As pointed out by Jewitt (2013), multimodal research undertaken to date can be classified as having four major foci:

1. The systematic description of modes and their semiotic resources;
2. Multimodal investigation of interpretation and interaction with specific digital environments;

3   Identification and development of new digital semiotic resources and new uses of existing resources in digital environments;
4   Contribution to research methods for the collection and analysis of digital data and environments within social research.

Some of the fields in which the importance of multimodal expression has been recognized include advertising, personal publishing in the form of social networking sites and poetry albums, decoration, children's books, comic books, print multimodal narratives, and visual design in general (Kress & Van Leeuwen, 1996). Research covered areas such as opera, music, and tangible interfaces. Enregistering identity and expressing intertextual meanings in TV series have also been analyzed. Numerous examples of studies representing these and other interests can be found in recent volumes edited by Page (2010) and O'Halloran and Smith (2011).

In the field of film editing, Burn and Parker (2001) proposed the notion of *kineikonic mode* to denote the moving image as a multimodal form in cinema and film, orchestrated in the process of filming and editing. Multimodal approaches have been frequently applied to researching communication and learning with digital technologies and exploring concepts around embodiment in the context of emergent digital technologies from the point of view of analyzing body position, posture, gesture, gaze, and talk as well as the idea of multimodal flow of interaction (e.g. Price & Jewitt, 2013).

In electronically mediated interactions, research has focused on representation of the self and performing identity on online platforms, multimodal aspects of participatory web (Androutsopoulos, 2010) as well as the use of avatars and the importance of their nonverbal behavior in online environments. Multimodal literacy in the context of electronic multimodal narratives has also been considered.

The list of disciplines provided above is not exhaustive. Its aim is to draw attention to the range of forms and breadth of research in which multimodal expression has been recognized.

Mixed-method Approach with Multimodality

Multimodal analysis is not usually seen as a research method *per se* but as a perspective or theoretical approach which is combined with other approaches, such as ethnography or literacy studies. Studies that adopt multimodal approaches are diverse (see "Research Themes and Current Studies" above). The diversity inherent in multimodal studies seems to be related to the wide range of communicative resources available to humans and the diverse social contexts in which multimodal communication occurs. For example, the analysis of the same person's output on different online platforms (e.g. Twitter, Facebook, and blog) can demonstrate what meaning-making potential each resource carries on each of these platforms. Looking further at principles of organization in these different texts and taking into account the modal affordances of each medium as well as the wider social and cultural contexts in which these texts were produced, one can draw conclusions about the meaning-making potential of each of these instances of multimodal communication.

One of the major contributors to contemporary developments in multimodal studies has been social semiotic theory. Multimodal approaches, concerned with the socially and culturally situated construction of meaning, can be applied to investigate power and ideology in human interactions. Applying sociological and anthropological lens allows us to examine how communities use multimodal conventions to establish and maintain identities and human perception of modes and their impact on communication can be analyzed applying psychological theories.

Conclusions

Multimodal analysis offers a wealth of possibilities for the study of intercultural communication. Meanings expressed in different modes are characteristic of communities and cultures that produce them, and it is within these social and cultural contexts that multimodal meanings can be analyzed. Communities shape the way in which modes are commonly understood and what tools are considered to be modes.

Appropriate selection of multimodal data, data collection process and analysis provide ample opportunity for scholars working in the field of intercultural communication and can shed light on this important, yet still under-researched aspect of communication.

Key Terms

Mode A set of socially and culturally shaped resources for making meaning. Modes, rather than fixed, are created through social processes, and thus fluid and context-dependent. In order for a particular resource to be a mode, the community in which it is used needs to recognize it as a mode and share a cultural sense of how this resource can be organized to construct and convey meaning. The choice of mode is a central aspect of interaction and meaning-making. Mode is often contrasted with medium, i.e., the substance through which texts are disseminated, e.g. a printed book or an audio file.

Modal affordance The term *affordance* originated in Gibson's (1977) work on cognitive perception. Kress (1993) uses it to refer to the material and the cultural aspects of modes, i.e., what can be expressed and represented easily with a particular mode. From this perspective, *affordance* refers to the materially, culturally, socially and historically developed ways in which meaning is made with particular semiotic resources. The affordance of a mode is shaped by its materiality, by what it has been repeatedly used to mean and do, and by the social norms and conventions that inform its use in context.

Semiotic resource The actions, materials and artefacts we use for communicative purposes – these can be physiological (e.g. our use of muscles to make facial expressions) or technological (as in the use of a pen and paper to produce written texts) – and the ways in which these resources can be organized.

Multimodal ensemble Interrelationships between co-present modes. As the resources of different modes are combined, meanings are corresponding, complementary, and dissonant in an integrated whole. Scholars talk about intersemiotic (semantic) relationships between the different semiotic systems within a multimodal text.

Semiotic landscape The way semiotic resources are used in a specific historical and social-cultural setting. It includes the kinds of resources used, the degree to which they are used, the purposes for which they are used, and the ways in which they are combined into multimodal texts or used separately. Semiotic landscape also includes people's attitudes towards specific semiotic resources, and the way in which their use is learned and regulated.

References

Agha, A. (2007). *Language and social relations.* Cambridge: Cambridge University Press.

Aiello, G., & Thurlow, C. (2006). Symbolic capitals: Visual discourse and intercultural exchange in the European Capital of Culture scheme. *Language and Intercultural Communication*, 6(2), 148–162.

Androutsopoulos, J. (2010). Localizing the global on the participatory web. In N. Coupland (Ed.), *The handbook of language and globalization* (pp. 203–231). Oxford: Wiley-Blackwell.

Baldry, A., & Thibault, P.J. (2006). *Multimodal transcription and text analysis: A multimedia toolkit and coursebook with associated on-line course.* Sheffield: Equinox.

Bateman, J. A. (2011). The decomposability of semiotic modes. In K.L. O'Halloran & B.A. Smith (Eds.), *Multimodal studies: Exploring issues and domains* (pp. 17–38). London: Routledge.

Bezemer, J., Cope, A., Kress, G., & Kneebone, R. (2011). "Do you have another Johan?" Negotiating meaning in the operating theatre. *Applied Linguistics Review*, 2, 313–334.

Burn, A., & Parker, D. (2001). Making your mark: Digital inscription, animation, and a new visual semiotic. *Education, Communication & Information*, 1(2), 155–179.

Cowan, K. (2014). Multimodal transcription of video: Examining interaction in Early Years classrooms. *Classroom Discourse*, 5(1), 6–21.

Dyer, G. (1989). *Advertising as communication.* London: Routledge.

Gibson, J. J. (1977). The theory of affordances. In R. Shaw, & J. Bransford (Eds.), *Perceiving, acting and knowing* (pp. 67–82). New York: Wiley.

Hymes, D. (1974). Ways of speaking. In R. Bauman & J. Sherzer (Eds.), *Explorations in the ethnography of speaking* (pp. 433–452). London: Cambridge University Press.

Jewitt, C. (2009). Introduction: Handbook rationale, scope and structure. In C. Jewitt (Ed.), *Handbook of multimodal analysis* (pp. 1–7). London: Routledge.

Jewitt, C. (2013). Multimodal methods for researching digital technologies. In S. Price, C. Jewitt, & B. Brown (Eds.), *The Sage handbook of digital technology research* (pp. 250–265). Thousand Oaks, CA: Sage.

Kress, G. (1993). Against arbitrariness: The social production of the sign as a foundational issue in critical discourse analysis, *Discourse and Society*, 4(2), 169–191.

Kress, G. (2009). What is mode? In C. Jewitt (Ed.), *Handbook of multimodal analysis* (pp. 54–66). London: Routledge.

Kress, G., & Van Leeuwen, T. (1998). Front pages: (the critical) analysis of newspaper layout. In A. Bell & P. Garret (Eds.), *Approaches to media discourse* (pp. 186–219). Oxford: Blackwell.

Kress, G., & Van Leeuwen, T. (1996). *Reading images: The grammar of visual design*. London: Routledge.
Lakoff, G., & Johnson, M. (1980). *Metaphors we live by*. Chicago: University of Chicago Press.
Norris, S. (2004). *Analyzing multimodal interaction: A methodological framework*. London: Routledge.
O'Halloran, K.L., & Smith, B.A. (Eds.). (2011). *Multimodal studies: Exploring issues and domains*. London: Routledge.
Page, R. (Ed.). (2010). *New perspectives on narrative and multimodality*. London: Routledge.
Price, S., & Jewitt, C. (2013). *A multimodal approach to examining "embodiment" in tangible learning environments*. Paper presented at Seventh International Conference on Tangible, Embedded and Embodied Interaction. 10–13 February, 2013, Barcelona, Spain.
Van Leeuwen, T. (2004). Ten reasons why linguists should pay attention to visual communication. In P. Levine & R. Scollon (Eds.), *Discourse & technology: Multimodal discourse analysis* (pp. 7–19), Washington, DC: Georgetown University Press.

Further Reading and Resources

Baldry, A., & Thibault, P.J. (2006). *Multimodal transcription and text analysis: A multimedia toolkit and coursebook with associated on-line course*. Sheffield: Equinox.
Jewitt, C. (Ed.). (2014). *Handbook of multimodal analysis* (2nd ed.). London: Routledge.
Kress, G., & Van Leeuwen, T. (2001). *Multimodal discourse: The modes and media of contemporary communication*. London: Arnold.
Norris, S. (2004). *Analyzing multimodal interaction*. London: Routledge.
O'Halloran, K.L., & Smith, B.A. (Eds). (2011). *Multimodal studies: Exploring issues and domains*. London: Routledge.

19 Critical Discourse Analysis: A Sample Study of Extremism

John P. O'Regan and Anne Betzel

> **Summary**
>
> Critical discourse analysis (CDA), or the critical analysis of discourse, refers to a collection of sociotheoretical perspectives on discourse in society, encompassing a range of applications and approaches in discourse analysis. This chapter takes a broad view of CDA which highlights how there are different avenues into the critical analysis of discourse, and not always with the same understandings or objectives. With this purpose, this chapter begins by giving an overview of the theoretical rationale and dispositions which have often informed a critical approach to discourse and summarizes the principal issues at stake. Having outlined the main parameters of interest and debate, we select a particular model of CDA – the dialectical–relational approach – and using an adapted version of this methodology apply it to a selection of discourse data derived from the (inter)cultural contexts of islamism, white supremacism, and multiculturalism.

Introduction

Critical discourse analysis (CDA) refers to a diverse collection of sociotheoretical perspectives on discourse in society, encompassing a wide range of applications and approaches in discourse analysis (Blommaert, 2005, 2010; Chilton, 2004; Fairclough, 1992, 2003, 2010a; Graham & Luke, 2013; Lazar, 2008; Pennycook, 1994, 2001,

2007; Slembrouck, 2001; van Dijk, 1998, 2011; Wodak & Chilton, 2005; Wodak & Meyer, 2009) and drawing upon an equally broad range of perspectives in critical social theory, including for example Althusser (1971), Foucault (1972, 1980), Gramsci (1971), Habermas (1984), Marx & Engels (1998/1845), Pêcheux (1982), and more recently Bhaskar (1986, 1998, 2008). It is the link to social theory and the critique of social formations which provides the impetus and rationale for describing this approach to discourse analysis as critical. For the purposes of this overview we are including as part of this group a number of researchers working critically in discourse analysis who due to the poststructuralist orientations of their work, might not, or would not, describe themselves as practitioners of CDA, but whom we nevertheless consider to be critical analysts of discourse (see Block, 2007; Blommaert, 2005, 2009, 2010; Blommaert & Omoniyi, 2010; Luke, 2005; Pennycook, 1994, 2001, 2007; Rajagopalan, 2004, 2012). We have done this in order to highlight how there are different avenues into the critical analysis of discourse and not always with the same understandings or objectives. With this purpose, this chapter begins by giving an overview of the theoretical rationale and dispositions which often inform a critical approach to discourse and summarizes the principal issues at stake. Having outlined the main parameters of interest and debate, we select a particular model of CDA, which we have adapted for our purpose, and offer an illustrative sample of analysis following this methodology.

Critical discourse analysis (CDA) has attracted considerable attention over several years, usually as an approach to language which is concerned with the critique of relations of power and ideology in society at large. The objects which CDA has used for this critique have in the main consisted of texts, either spoken or written, where asymmetrical power relations are often in play, e.g. police interviews, courtroom exchanges, political speeches, policy documents, and asylum interrogations and applications (cf. Blommaert, 2009; Ehrlich, 2001; Fairclough, 2001; Phipps, 2013). CDA, as it has been commonly understood, is thus concerned with the production, circulation, and interpretation of texts in which relations of domination and control may be said to be at stake (Fairclough 2001, 2010a; Fairclough & Wodak, 1997; van Dijk, 1993, 2011).

Crucial to the critique which CDA presents is the perception that it is ideology in concert with power which provide the legitimation for relations of inequality and domination. Ideology can be described as referencing explicit and even vocal opinions which may then be aligned with an implicit, presupposed and often naturalized "worldview," or overarching perspective on the reality in which we are participating. In the words of Fairclough (2010b), "Ideologies are seen as one modality of power, a modality which constitutes and sustains relations of power through producing consent or at least acquiescence, power through hegemony, rather than power through violence or force" (p. 73). It is a critical concept of ideology, which owes its articulation to the Marxist philosophical thinking of Gramsci (1971) and Althusser (1971), in addition to Marx himself (Marx & Engels, 1998/1845) (see also, Blommaert, 2005; Bourdieu, 1984, 1991; Eagleton, 1991; Hall, Lumley, & McLennan, 1978; Holborow, 2012; Larrain, 1979; McLennan, Molina, & Peters, 1978; Thompson, 1984; van Dijk, 1998; Williams, 1977). There are, however, a number of reservations about this concept of ideology, and critical analysts of discourse who take a more poststructuralist stance will often prefer to use the term discourse (as a count and noncount noun) in its place (see for example, Block, 2007; Blommaert, 2005;

Pennycook, 2001; Weedon, 1997). This is because of the implication, following Foucault (1980), that when the term ideology is used, it often, "stands in virtual opposition to something else that is supposed to count as truth" (p. 118). In poststructuralism, veridical truth is denied. The result is that in CDA both terms are used, often interchangeably.

The Dialectical–Relational Approach

As noted, there are a variety of approaches to critical discourse analysis. These include sociocognitive (Chilton, 2005; van Dijk, 2008), discourse-historical (Reisigl & Wodak, 2009), and multimodal perspectives (Kress, 2010; Kress & van Leeuwen, 2000). While there are overlaps between them, there is also a good deal of diversity and dispersion in the way in which they go about (critical) discourse analysis, as well as in the ways in which they define constructs such as ideology, power, discourse, and the term critical itself. As Wodak & Meyer (2009) note, "CDA has never been and has never attempted to be or to provide one single or specific theory" (p. 8). For reasons of space we are not able to give an account of these individual perspectives and so we direct the reader to the literature to learn more about them (see, Blommaert & Bulcaen, 2000; Fairclough & Wodak, 1997; Fairclough, Mulderrig, & Wodak, 2011; Pennycook, 2001, Wodak & Chilton, 2005; Wodak & Meyer 2009). Instead, we will focus upon a particular model in the light of the foregoing discussion. This is the dialectical–relational approach, and is to be found in the recent work of Norman Fairclough (see, Chouliaraki & Fairclough, 1999; Fairclough, 2001, 2003; 2006; 2010a; 2012). We have chosen this approach in order (1) to highlight the dialectical–relational approach as a significant model of CDA; (2) to show how this approach may be adapted depending upon the epistemological position from which you as a researcher are working; and (3) to illustrate how the dialectical–relational approach can be applied to a sample body of discourse data.

The dialectical–relational approach is greatly influenced by the philosophy of critical realism (Bhaskar, 1986, 1998, 2008), and works according to a (critical) realist ontology in which it is argued that reality is distinct from our knowledge of it, and that our knowledge does not exhaust that reality (Collier, 1994; Sayer, 2000). In a critical realist ontology, and thus also in the dialectical–relational approach, discourse *construes* reality, in the sense that reality must be conceptually mediated if we are to have any knowledge of it. It is discourse or *semiosis* which is the mediating mechanism for our knowledge of reality. Discourse (as a noncount noun) and semiosis are synonymous terms, and in the dialectical–relational approach it is often the latter term which is preferred because of the confusion which can arise with discourse as a count noun for referring to a perspectival way of seeing and knowing. The fact that discourse construes reality, and that there is no possibility of meaning creation in the absence of it, entails that discourse itself is a powerful facet of social life, and in the dialectical–relational approach, and in other iterations of CDA (in addition to poststructuralist ones), discourse (or semiosis) as well as the discourses which are part of it are viewed as having distinctive – albeit contingent upon other social elements – causal powers and "liabilities" (i.e. effects) of their own

(Fairclough, Jessop, & Sayer, 2010). Reality in this sense is made up of discursive and nondiscursive dimensions of which discourse is one *moment* in a dialectical relationship with other moments of the social process (Best & Kellner, 1991; Fairclough et al., 2010; Harvey, 1996). These other "moments" may be economic, political, environmental, legal, educational, religious, dispositional, concrete, and so on. Moments are constituted within *fields* (Bourdieu & Wacquant, 1992) – such as politics, education, and the legal system – and are bound up with power, itself another moment within the social relations of fields. In Fairclough's words, "power is partly discourse, and discourse is partly power – they are different but not discrete, they 'flow into' each other" (2010d, p. 4). If power and discourse – and therefore knowledge too – are intertwined, then it follows from a dialectical–relational perspective that, "economic forces and socio-political institutions are in part semiotic, and [so] analysis has to be in part semiotic analysis" (Fairclough, 2010c, p. 252).

The discourse-theoretical complex which the dialectical–relational approach presents is augmented by a structural conception of the social process as consisting in, "an interplay between three levels of social reality: *social structures*, *practices* and *events*" (Fairclough, 2010c, p. 232) to which correspond three dimensions of semiosis: *semiotic systems* (language and other semiotic codes), *orders of discourse* (a specific configuration of discourses, genres, and styles), and *texts* (written, spoken, and other semiotic modalities). If social structures conform with social reality in the broadest sense, then semiotic systems (of which one code is language) are the means by which social reality is mediated and comprehended. Social reality – and the social structures of which it is comprised – are in turn made up of a range of social practices, i.e. people *doing things* within diverse social spaces by acting conventionally (genres), articulating beliefs (discourses), adopting identities (styles), and generally performing their mode of being, or *habitus* (Bourdieu, 1984, 1991). These spaces are not randomly made but can and do coalesce into discursive regularities, for example, as social institutions (political systems, legal systems, faith systems, security systems etc.), as workplaces (parliaments, universities, hospitals, banks, legal practices, police stations, registration centers, etc.), and as ideologies (perspectival discourses and habitus). Fairclough (1992) has taken from Foucault (1972, 1981) the term *order of discourse* to describe these discursive regularities. Orders of discourse are the semiotic dimension of social practices and represent different configurations of discourses, genres, and styles. These are each ways of acting and interacting semiotically. Discourses are ways of representing (and therefore also ways of *believing*); genres are ways of acting conventionally (e.g. in writing, and in spoken and nonverbal communication): "they are ways of regulating (inter)action" (Fairclough et al., 2010, p. 213); and styles are ways of taking up identities in their semiotic aspect – i.e. of enacting one's being as part of a subject position or "role" (e.g. father, mother, policeman, asylum seeker, receptionist, CEO). As a result of changes in the economic, social and political fields, new discourses (i.e. ideological ways of seeing and knowing) can be *enacted*, which lead to the *inculcation* of new ways of (inter)acting, which in turn produce new ways of being (identities). Since 9/11 for example, the discourses around counterterrorism globally have led, amongst other things, to radical changes in airport security procedures, leading to changed ways of acting and interacting (new genres and styles) on the part of passengers and airport staff in airports in response to the perceived threat. Such social events always have a semiotic dimension. These are texts (in the broadest sense) in multiple semiotic modalities, of which language

Social processes	Semiotic fields	Semiotic codes
Social structures ↑	Semiotic systems ↑	Language, image, sound, space, gaze, shape etc.
Social practices │	Orders of discourse │	Discourses, genres, styles
Social events ▼	Texts ▼	Writing, talk, and other semiotic modes

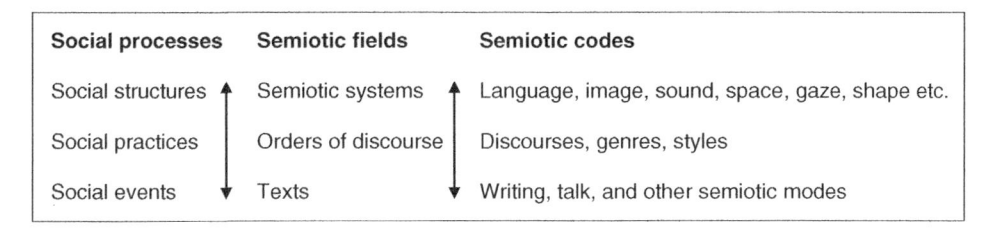

Figure 19.1 Levels of structures, practices, and events, and their respective fields and codes.

as either writing or talk is one. Figure 19.1 illustrates these different levels and their relations.

As is usual in this model, between the levels of structures, practices, and events, and their respective fields and codes, a dialectic is in play so that no level is discrete, but is in a constant process of flowing into and between the other elements in each of the levels. Fairclough (2010c) refers to the dialectical relation of discourses, genres, and styles as one of *interdiscursivity* and as a component in the analysis of texts: "textual analysis includes both linguistic analysis (and if relevant, analysis of other semiotic forms, such as visual images) and interdiscursive analysis (analysis of which genres, discourses and styles are drawn upon, and how they are articulated together)" (p. 238). An important issue here is that Fairclough sees interdiscursivity as a mediating "interlevel" between the micro-level linguistic analysis of the text (in conjunction with relevant social analysis) and the analysis of social structures. In other words, relations of interdiscursivity via orders of discourse are what connect the analysis of the text with an analysis of social structures.

Methodology

The dialectical–relational approach is a methodology and not just a method. Methodology is understood as theory in combination with method in the construction and analysis of an object of research (Bourdieu & Wacquant, 1992; Fairclough, 2010c). In this sense it is not simply a matter of taking a method and applying it to an object of research. The object first has to be theorized itself drawing upon relevant social theories in a "transdisciplinary way," "either in research teams which bring together specialists in relevant disciplines, or by engaging with literature in such disciplines" (Fairclough, 2010c, p. 236). In this process the object of research is constructed. Having done this, the task is to seek a semiotic point of entry into it (Fairclough, 2010c). The point of entry in most iterations of CDA is usually written or spoken texts which circulate as social practices within the order of discourse that corresponds to them, and which act as interdiscursive *cues*. As far as texts based on language are concerned, in this approach, a principal purpose is to identify and discuss the linguistic features of texts which appear to act as cues to interdiscursive relations.

The methodology of the dialectical–relational approach is derived from Bhaskar's explanatory critique (Bhaskar, 1986; Chouliariaki & Fairclough, 1999) and consists of four stages. The dialectical–relational approach as formulated by Fairclough (2010c) is consistent with critical realism in having a normative (i.e. emancipatory) agenda. This leads to the stages to be followed being articulated so that a principal concern is the righting of social "wrongs":

1 Focus upon a social wrong, in its semiotic aspect.
2 Identify obstacles to addressing the social wrong.
3 Consider whether the social order "needs" the social wrong.
4 Identify possible ways past the obstacles.

This kind of normative focus can have the effect of circumscribing to some extent the kind of critical discourse analysis that it is possible to do, because by taking such a defined epistemological stance, the prospective CDA researcher within this frame is obliged to commit to a form of analysis whose objective is the creation of a better world. Such a transformational agenda, while no bad thing in itself, is in conflict with epistemological positions, such as poststructuralism, which do not accept such grand narrative approaches to reality and social life, and where the concept of truth itself is problematic and provisional. Despite this difference, we agree with Fairclough that the research of topics which have significant implications for human wellbeing, such as immigration, terrorism, globalization, and security, are necessary activities in any critical analysis of discourse (Fairclough, 2010c). To accommodate these concerns and interests, we have adapted the four stages of the dialectical–relational approach in the following way:

1 Focus upon a social phenomenon in its semiotic aspect (Draw upon relevant theories about the phenomenon and look for a semiotic point of entry.)
    (a) Step 1 Identify the phenomenon you want to research.
    (b) Step 2 Theorize the phenomenon in a transdisciplinary way (Use relevant theory). Once you have the theory, you can then look for a semiotic point of entry.
2 Identify the causes of the phenomenon and (if relevant) the obstacles to changing it (Why is the phenomenon like this?)
    (a) Step 1 Select texts in the light of the object of research and adopt an analytical framework for categorizing and interpreting their features.
    (b) Step 2 Analyze texts by linking linguistic analysis to interdiscursive and social analysis.
3 Does the social order require the phenomenon to be the way that it is? Who benefits most from the phenomenon remaining unchanged?
4 Identify ways past the obstacles. Can the dominant discourse be contested?

Case Study: Discourses of extremism and multiculturalism

1. Focus upon a Social Phenomenon in Its Semiotic Aspect

The social phenomenon we focus upon is the discursive construction of identities in discourses of extremism and multiculturalism, on the part of islamists and white supremacists on the one hand and UK politicians on the other, and the way in which cultural essentialism and outsiderness may be seen to dominate the lenses of both discourses. We have selected these examples because of their relevance to key issues in Intercultural Communication, and because CDA often concerns itself with the analysis of discourses and texts of social import and consequence. In addition, we have selected them because we see similarities between the ways in which these discourses are articulated by their distinctive protagonists. More precisely, we wish to show how in discourses of extremism and multiculturalism a distinct division between Us and Them serves as an organizing principle which isolates certain cultural elements and identity markers within an essentialist view that reduces and "others" the Other, and which closes off – intentionally in the case of islamists and white supremacists, and at least consequentially in the case of politicians – any possibility of a dialogic understanding of culture and intercultural relations which might alter the (inter)cultural status quo. In this manner, "the dominant group justifies its power with stories – stock explanations – that construct reality in ways to maintain their privilege" (Ladson-Billings & Tate, 1995, p. 58).

We locate the discussion of discourses of extremism and multiculturalism within an "interdiscourse approach" to Intercultural Communication which, "set(s) aside any a priori notions of group membership and identity and ... ask(s) instead how and under what circumstances concepts such as culture are produced by participants as relevant categories for interpersonal ideological negotiation" (Scollon & Scollon, 2000, p. 544). Whereas a good deal of Intercultural Communication studies have adhered, often implicitly, to a predominant essentialism and have been inclined to take membership categorization as a given, interdiscourse approaches emphasize the social and linguistic practices which bring identity and culture into being (Blommaert, 2005; Holliday, 1999; Piller, 2007), and so complement interdiscursivity in the dialectical–relational approach. In addition, we also draw upon critical race theory (Cole, 2009; Delgado, 2001; Ladson-Billings & Tate, 1995) as a wider theoretical frame. Critical race theory operates from the perspective that racism is deeply ingrained in social life both institutionally and structurally (Delgado, 2001) and that in discussions of race, "social reality is constructed by the formulation and the exchange of stories about individual situations. These stories serve as interpretive structures by which we impose order on experience and it on us" (Ladson-Billings & Tate, 1995, p. 57).

Within these theoretical frames, and in keeping with the dialectical–relational approach, we seek a semiotic point of entry into extremism and multiculturalism as social phenomena through discursively mapping how references to polarized collective identities in the discourse of islamists, white supremacists and political leaders lead to the discursive construction and maintenance of an essentialized difference. To this end, and for the purposes of this illustration, we have chosen to analyze discourses of extremism and multiculturalism as they are constructed in statements made by the following individuals:

1. Mohammad Siddique Khan, a suicide bomber believed to be the leader responsible for the London "7/7" bombings of 7 July 2005. Khan recorded a suicide video message before his murder of six civilians on the Circle underground line, Edgware Road.
2. Michael Adebolajo, one of two islamist converts who attacked and killed soldier Lee Rigby on the afternoon of 22 May 2013 near the Royal Artillery Barracks

in Woolwich, London. Adebolajo was recorded on the phone of an eyewitness making a statement justifying the killing.
3 Anders Behring Breivik, a white supremacist responsible for the bombing of government buildings in Oslo and a mass shooting at a Workers' Youth League (AUF) camp on the island of Utøya on 22 July 2011 which left a total of 85 people dead. Breivik gave notice of his right-wing militant leanings in an online compendium entitled "2083: A European Declaration of Independence" (Breivik, 2011).
4 British prime minister David Cameron's speech at the Munich Security Conference in February 2011 in which he sets out his view on radicalization and Islamic extremism (sic) (Cameron, 2011).

The selected text excerpts are indicative of contemporary discourses of extremism and multiculturalism on the part of islamists, white supremacists, and conservative British politicians. Both discourses are contained within a wide range of texts, including speeches, interviews, press releases, radio and television addresses, and policy documents. Furthermore, discourses of extremism and multiculturalism are constructed in other semiotic modes in the form of symbolic and emblematic representations such as flags, insignia, iconic images, or memorials. These texts are interdiscursively related as they are constituted by a combination of elements in orders of discourse, on the one hand configuring extremism and on the other configuring conceptions of multiculturalism, and set out relevant parameters and categories which consequently influence social practices and structures. For example, discourses about multiculturalism in a speech by David Cameron may find their way into policy initiatives, which through implementation and inculcation are reproduced and amplified as generally accepted genres and styles in response to the perceived terrorist threat.

In our analysis we primarily focus upon the process of Othering, i.e. "the process whereby the 'foreign' is reduced to a simplistic, easily digestible, exotic or degrading stereotype" (Holliday, 1999, p. 245). The analytical categories are identity and the discursive construal of identities which we understand to be dialectically related to social practices and structures. We consider the process of Othering and the categorization of collective identities as both deliberate and deriving from "common sense," i.e. they originate from our ideological conceptualizations of reality and social groups, and a shared set of beliefs in relation to them.

2. Identify the Causes of the Phenomenon and the Obstacles to Changing It

The discourses of Khan, Adebolajo, Breivik, and Cameron display shared features which consist of (1) an appeal to a legitimating authority, (2) reference to unifying ideological constructs which are either religious, political, or philosophical, or a combination of these, and (3) pervasive Self/Other dichotomies. They can be described as generic as they are based upon, "a common structure of functional units (obligatory and optional) that is repeated again and again from text to text" (Lemke, 1998, pp. 1182–1183).

Appeals to a legitimating authority in islamist discourse include religious references, for example, to "the one true God, Allah," to "the final messenger and prophet

Muhammad" (Khan, 2005), and to religious verses: "we are forced by the Quran in Sura at-Tawba, through many, many ayah throughout the Quran that we must fight them as they fight us" (Adebolajo, 2013). The white supremacist Breivik, for his part, makes references to supposed resistance organizations such as the "Western European Resistance" and "the Knights Templar" (Breivik, 2011). Cameron's references to a legitimating authority include "my country, the United Kingdom," "Western values" and most frequently the inclusive pronoun "we" to refer to the British nation (Cameron, 2011). Khan and Adebolajo mention Islam as the unifying construct legitimizing their actions, whereas Breivik (2011) construes these forces in a negative way, by reference to, "the name of the devil: cultural Marxism, multiculturalism, globalism, feminism, emotionalism, suicidal humanism, egalitarianism – a recipe for disaster." Cameron (2011) in his speech appeals to a conception of the UK as a liberal country which believes in certain essential British values, such as, "freedom of speech, freedom of worship, democracy, the rule of law, equal right regardless of race, sex or sexuality." These values are identity markers essential for Cameron's ideological rendering of the British nation and his construction of an idealized sense of British community and identity. They represent an unequivocal appeal to reassert "British" values in the face of radicalization and extremism. They furthermore constitute a key element in a politico-national discourse according to which Britain is a good society because of the values it holds. The statements about values can be understood as a product or artefact of ideology, rather than a direct description of *actual* British values.

The most ubiquitous features of the discourses of extremism and multiculturalism are the appeal to identity and pervasive Self/Other dichotomies. Breivik (2011) emphasizes "our moral inheritance" and "our Judeo-Christian values," which necessarily entails, like Cameron's speech, an act of differentiation and exclusion. He explains, "It is not only our right but also our duty to contribute to preserve our identity, our culture and our national sovereignty by preventing the ongoing Islamisation." Self/Other dichotomies also appear in Khan's suicide video statement (2005), although they are appropriated according to his political and historical positioning, i.e. he reclaims himself as a victim: "And our words have no impact upon you, therefore I'm going to talk to you in a language that you understand. Our words are dead until we give them life with our blood." Self/Other dichotomies lock social groups into a particular form of identity and effectively immobilize the relationship between them. In order to establish where the moral responsibility and blame for his actions lie, he engages in a concerted effort to present the identities of "my Muslim brothers and sisters" as victims and to emphasize the responsibility of "your democratically elected governments":

> And your support of them makes you directly responsible, just as I am directly responsible for protecting and avenging my Muslim brothers and sisters. Until we feel security, you will be our targets. And until you stop the bombing, gassing, imprisonment and torture of my people we will not stop this fight. We are at war and I am a soldier. Now you too will taste the reality of this situation. (Khan, 2005)

A similar justification is provided by Michael Adebolajo. After the killing of Lee Rigby, Adebolajo makes a statement, recorded on a witness's phone, in which he justifies violence as a reaction to the violence of others: "The only reason we have killed this man today is because Muslims are dying daily by British soldiers. And this British soldier is one. It is an eye for an eye and a tooth for a tooth" (Adebolajo, 2013).

In Cameron's speech (2011), the construction of polarized identities, or Othering, is evident in the emphasis on Britishness and a call for unity constructed around a choice of being either with "Us" or with the "Other": "At stake are not just lives, it is our way of life. That is why this is a challenge we cannot avoid; it is one we must rise to and overcome." The emphasis on "our way of life" reduces diversity to a binary logic which simplifies intercultural relations according to an idealized conception of Britishness while also dismissing alternative viewpoints. Cameron considers Britishness to be endangered due to "a weakening of our collective identity":

> Under the doctrine of state multiculturalism, we have encouraged different cultures to live separate lives, apart from each other and apart from the mainstream. We've failed to provide a vision of society to which they feel they want to belong. We've even tolerated these segregated communities behaving in ways that run completely counter to our values. (Cameron, 2011)

Cameron's discourse is defensive as it intends to counteract forces from "without" through presenting "Britishness" as an uncontested, given category; and it is antagonistic as it seeks to (re)structure membership and "Britishness" via the common endeavor of providing "a vision of society" and overcoming "a challenge we cannot avoid." The discourse, furthermore, functions to discipline domestic society by marginalizing dissent or protest, and enforces national unity by reifying a particular conception of community. Accordingly, Cameron emphasizes the need for others to integrate with an essentialized and idealized "British" Self, and a culture which is conceived and constructed as a static and homogenous entity (Faulks, 2006).

3. Does the Social Order Require the Phenomenon to be the Way That It Is?

The Other cast as alien is not only a feature of islamist and white supremacist discourse, but, as we have seen, is also a feature of political discourse, such as that of Cameron, and others on the European right (Fekete, 2012). All the protagonists in this analysis employ concepts of culture and belonging in fundamentalist and absolutist ways which entail a perception of the Other as a separate and completely *other* counterpart to an essentialized pure Self. The unity of the Self and the unity of the Other are simplistic categorizations which allow the different protagonists to overcome any cognitive dissonance concerning their actions and to construct Self-affirming ways of thinking about difference, while also reinforcing a preconceived (inter)cultural status quo. The focus on difference in discourses of multiculturalism allows for the implementation of a political and (inter)cultural agenda which is centered upon a principally "White" nation, as well as the inculcation of new ways of acting (genres) and new ways of being (styles) in response to a particular construal of the terrorist threat (e.g. via security protocols, border restrictions, and surveillance practices). The political implications of the discourse of multiculturalism show how new genres and styles have become ideologically accepted across societal structures as networks of social practices within orders of discourse. However, through employing pervasive Self/Other dichotomies, the alienation and continued ostracism of the Other is perpetually renewed. In the case of extremists such as Khan, Adebolajo, and Breivik, the Self/Other dichotomy legitimizes their indifference to the suffering of the Other. In the case of Cameron it works in tragic mimicry of those he wishes to condemn. By adopting the same cultural binaries which are to be found in the discourse of extremists, Cameron excludes from "Britishness" everyone who does not share the values of his "British" Self. Attention is thus focused onto perceptions of cultural difference in such a way which relegates members of ethnic minority communities, many of whom are British citizens and consider themselves British, to a secondary relationship with an idealized ethnocultural British Self. In the absence of an intercultural consciousness which acknowledges the presence of the Other in the Self, the prospect of a dialogue which might facilitate structural and institutional change is thereby rendered intentionally remote (Jackson, 2005; Phipps, 2014; Shaw, 2012).

4. Identify ways past the obstacles

When identifying ways past the obstacles, your route will depend upon your epistemological and/or political stance. For example, through taking a more emancipatory or critical realist stance you may engage in a normative project and a discussion of how societal "wrongs" might be "righted." For this purpose, you might refer to models of intercultural dialogue which focus on openness, difference-creation, difference management, and difference training as solutions to the practice of Othering (Lederach, 2003). Alternatively, you might understand such a transformative agenda as problematic due to the claims it makes regarding truth and knowledge (Kramsch, 2009; MacDonald & O'Regan, 2012; Nair-Venugopal, 2012). This may lead you to adopt a more poststructuralist or problematizing stance, which means understanding the act of analysis and the destabilization of rigid dominant interpretations as a form of contestation. Your objective may then be to engage in a discourse politics through mapping discourses and problematizing givens which present themselves as truths. In either approach, it is extremely doubtful that critique of itself can overcome or destabilize the dominant discourse, but by subjecting the dominant discourse to criticism, critical approaches to discourse analysis may be said to "underlabour" (Bhaskar, 1998, p. 179) for activities whose interests lie in that direction.

Concluding Remarks on CDA

For researchers new to CDA, there are a number of pointers to bear in mind. First, there is the issue of having some familiarity with social theory, particularly with concepts such as discourse, ideology, and power, and a considered view on what these mean. Second, is the need to have some understanding of language in order to be able to analyze texts – CDA is not just commentary. Third, it is important to provide a reasoned account of the interpretation which is placed upon the discourse that is analyzed, which is to say that the analysis should seek to be faithful to the internal workings of the text rather than, for example, simply in disagreement with it. Finally, and closely related to the previous point, is that simply applying the linguistic analytical categories of CDA to a text is insufficient. Not all features of a text are going to be discoursally significant, so identifying which are and which are not requires careful judgment and argument as well as reference to wider theoretical and empirical frames within which the analysis should be located.

Key Terms

Critical An attitude or stance which questions given assumptions or propositions. The term is also used to refer to research approaches which have been informed by social theory, particularly from the perspectives of Marxism, critical realism, or poststructuralism.

Dialectic/Dialectical A relationship between two or more elements which is not simply one way, but is multiple and dynamic. In a CDA perspective, the relation between discourse and the social context for discourse is dialectical in that discourse and context are both mutually constituted as well as mutually conditioned.

Discourse(s) The noncount noun "discourse" refers to language on its own, and to *semiosis*, i.e. all forms of meaning construction in their social context, and of which language is one instance. Discourse as a count noun refers to perspectival ways of seeing and knowing as they are constituted through semiosis. Discourses and ideologies can in this respect be viewed as synonymous, although ideology is often dispreferred in favor of discourse in poststructuralist perspectives. In CDA both terms are used, often interchangeably.

Order of discourse Orders of discourse are the semiotic dimension of social practices and represent different configurations of discourses, genres, and styles. Discourses are ways of representing (and therefore also ways of *believing*); genres are ways of acting conventionally (e.g. in writing, and in spoken and nonverbal communication); and styles are ways of taking up identities in their semiotic aspect – i.e. of enacting one's being as part of a subject position or "role" (e.g. father, mother, policeman, asylum seeker, receptionist, CEO). The relationship between these three dimensions is known as *interdiscursivity*.

Poststructuralism An epistemological perspective which questions the grounds for knowledge and veridical truth. Poststructuralism is the subset of postmodernism which is devoted to the study of discourse, and is closely associated with continental, particularly French, philosophy. Poststructuralists tend to prioritize discourse over other material factors such as the economy in explaining social reality and change.

References

Adebolajo, M. (2013). Woolwich attack: Terrorist proclaimed "an eye for an eye" after attack. [Online]. Retrieved June 26, 2015 from: http://www.telegraph.co.uk/news/uknews/terrorism-in-the-uk/10073910/Woolwich-attack-terrorist-proclaimed-an-eye-for-an-eye-after-attack.html.
Althusser, L. (1971). *Lenin and philosophy*. New York: Monthly Review Press.
Best, S., & Kellner, D. (1991). *Postmodern theory: Critical interrogations*. London: Macmillan.
Bhaskar, R. (1986). *Scientific realism and human emancipation*. London: Verso.
Bhaskar, R. (1998). *The possibility of naturalism: A philosophical critique of the contemporary human sciences* (3rd ed.). London: Routledge.
Bhaskar, R. (2008). *A realist theory of science*. London: Verso.
Block, D. (2007). *Second language identities*. London: Continuum.
Blommaert, J. (2005). *Discourse*. Cambridge: Cambridge University Press.
Blommaert, J. (2009). Language, asylum and the national order. *Current Anthropology*, 50(4), 415–441.
Blommaert, J. (2010). *The sociolinguistics of globalization*. Cambridge: Cambridge University Press.
Blommaert, J., & Bulcaen, C. (2000). Critical discourse analysis. *Annual Review of Anthropology*, 29, 447–466.
Blommaert, J., & Omoniyi, T. (2010). Email fraud: Language, technology, and the indexicals of globalisation. *Social Semiotics*, 16(4), 573–605.
Bourdieu, P. (1984). *Distinction*. London: Routledge.
Bourdieu, P. (1991). *Language and symbolic power*. Oxford: Polity.
Bourdieu, P., & Wacquant, L. (1992). *An invitation to reflexive sociology*. Cambridge: Polity Press.
Breivik, A.B. (2011). *2083 – A European Declaration of Independence*. Retrieved June 25, 2015 from: http://www.deism.com/images/breivik-manifesto-2011.pdf.
Cameron, D. (2011). *PM's speech at Munich Security Conference*. Retrieved June 25, 2015 from: https://www.gov.uk/government/speeches/pms-speech-at-munich-security-conference.
Chilton, P. (2004). *Analysing political discourse*. London: Routledge.
Chilton, P. (2005). Missing links in mainstream CDA: modules, blends and the critical instinct. In R. Wodak, & P. Chilton (Eds.), *A new agenda in (Critical) Discourse Analysis* (pp. 18–51). Amsterdam: John Benjamins.
Chouliaraki, L., & Fairclough, N. (1999). *Discourse in late modernity: Rethinking Critical Discourse Analysis*. Edinburgh: Edinburgh University Press.
Collier, A. (1994). *An Introduction to Roy Bhaskar's philosophy*. London: Verso.
Cole, M. (2009). *Critical race theory and education: A Marxist perspective*. Basingstoke: Palgrave Macmillan.
Delgado, R. (2001). Two ways to think about race: Reflections on the id, the ego, and other reformist theories of equal protection. *Georgetown Law Journal*, 89, 2279–2296.
Eagleton, T. (1991). *Ideology: An introduction*. London: Verso.
Ehrlich, S. (2001). *Representing rape: Language and sexual consent*. London: Routledge.
Fairclough, N. (1992). *Discourse and social change*. Cambridge: Polity.
Fairclough, N. (2001). *Language and power*. Harlow: Longman.
Fairclough, N. (2003). *Analysing discourse: Textual analysis for social research*. London: Routledge.
Fairclough, N. (2006). *Language and globalization*. London: Routledge.
Fairclough, N. (2010a). *Critical discourse analysis: The critical study of language* (2nd ed.). London: Longman.

Fairclough, N. (2010b). Language and ideology. In N. Fairclough (Ed.), *Critical discourse analysis: The critical study of language* (pp. 56–83). London: Longman.

Fairclough, N. (2010c). A dialectical–relational approach to critical discourse analysis in social research. In N. Fairclough (Ed.), *Critical discourse analysis: The critical study of language* (pp. 230–254). London: Longman.

Fairclough, N. (2010d). General introduction. In N. Fairclough (Ed.), *Critical discourse analysis: The critical study of language* (pp. 1–21). London: Longman.

Fairclough, N. (2012). Critical discourse analysis. In J. P. Gee & M. Handford (Eds.), *The Routledge handbook of discourse analysis* (pp. 9–20). London: Routledge.

Fairclough, N., Jessop, B., & Sayer, A. (2010). Critical realism and semiosis. In N. Fairclough (Ed.), *Critical discourse analysis: The critical study of language* (pp. 202–222). London: Longman.

Fairclough, N., Mulderrig, J., & Wodak, R. (2011). Critical discourse analysis. In T. A. van Dijk (Ed.), *Discourse studies: A multidisciplinary introduction* (pp. 357–378). Thousand Oaks, CA: Sage.

Fairclough, N., & Wodak, R. (1997). Critical discourse analysis. In T. van Dijk (Ed.), *Discourse as social interaction* (pp. 258–284). Thousand Oaks, CA: Sage.

Faulks, K. (2006). Education for citizenship in England's secondary schools: A critique of current principle and practice. *Journal of Education Policy*, 21 (1), 59–74.

Fekete, L. (2012). The Muslim conspiracy theory and the Oslo massacre. *Race & Class*, 53(3), 30–47.

Foucault, M. (1972). *The archaeology of knowledge*. London: Tavistock Publications.

Foucault, M. (1980). *Power/knowledge: Selected interviews and other writings*. Brighton: Harvester.

Foucault, M. (1981). The order of discourse. In R. Young (Ed.), *Untying the text* (pp. 48–78). London: Routledge.

Graham, P. W., & Luke, A. (2013). Critical discourse analysis and political economy of communication: Understanding the new corporate order. In R. Wodak (Ed.), *Critical discourse analysis: Concepts, history, theory (Vol. 1)*. Thousand Oaks, CA: Sage.

Gramsci, A. (1971). *Selections from prison notebooks*. London: Lawrence and Wishart.

Habermas, J. (1984). *The theory of communicative action: Reason and the rationalisation of society (Vol.) 1*. London Heinemann.

Hall, S., Lumley, B., & McLennan, G. (1978). Politics and ideology: Gramsci. In B. Schwarz (Ed.), *On ideology* (pp. 45–76). London: Hutchinson.

Harvey, D. (1996). *Justice, nature and the geography of difference*. Oxford: Blackwell.

Holborow, M. (2012). What is neoliberalism? Discourse, ideology and the real world. In D. Block, J. Gray, & M. Holborow (Eds.), *Neoliberalism and applied linguistics* (pp. 33–55). London: Routledge.

Holliday, A. (1999). Small cultures. *Applied Linguistics*, 20(2), 237–264.

Jackson, R. (2005). *Writing the war on terrorism: Language, politics and counter-terrorism*. Manchester: Manchester University Press.

Khan, M. S. (2005). *London bomber: Text in full*. Retrieved June 25, 2015 from: http://news.bbc.co.uk/1/hi/uk/4206800.stm.

Kramsch, C. (2009). *The Multilingual Subject*. Oxford: Oxford University Press.

Kress, G. (2010). *Multimodality: A social semiotic approach to contemporary communication*. London: Routledge.

Kress, G., & van Leeuwen, T. (2000). *Multimodal discourse*. London: Arnold.

Ladson-Billings, G., & Tate, W.F. (1995). Toward a critical race theory of education. *Teacher's College Record*, 97(1), 47–68.

Larrain, J. (1979). *The concept of ideology*. London: Hutchinson Education.

Lazar, M. M. (2008). *Feminist critical discourse analysis: Studies in gender, power and ideology*. London: Palgrave MacMillan.

Lederach, J.P. (2003). *Little Book of Conflict Transformation: Clear Articulation Of The Guiding Principles By A Pioneer In The Field*. Intercourse, PA: Good Books.
Lemke, J. L. (1998). Analysing Verbal Data: Principles, Methods and Problems. In K. Tobin and B. Fraser (Eds), *International handbook of science education* (pp. 1175–1189). New York: Kluwer.
Luke, A. (2005). Normativity and the material effects of discourse. *Critical Discourse Studies*, 2(2), 198–202.
MacDonald, M.N., & O'Regan, J.P. (2012). The ethics of Intercultural Communication. *Educational Philosophy and Theory*, 45(10), 1005–1017.
Marx, K., & Engels, F. (1998/1845). *The German ideology*. New York: Prometheus Books.
McLennan, G., Molina, V., & Peters, R. (1978). Althusser's Theory of Ideology. In B. Schwarz (Ed.), *On ideology* (pp. 77–105). London: Hutchison.
Nair-Venugopal, S. (2012). *The gaze of the West and framings of the East*. Basingstoke: Palgrave Macmillan.
Pêcheux, M. . (1982). *Language, semantics and ideology: Stating the obvious*. London: Macmillan.
Pennycook, A. (1994). Incommensurable discourses? *Applied Linguistics*, 15(2), 115–138.
Pennycook, A. (2001). *Critical applied linguistics: A critical introduction*. Mahwah, NJ: Lawrence Erlbaum.
Pennycook, A. (2007). *Global Englishes and transcultural flows*. London: Routledge.
Phipps, A. (2013). Unmoored: language pain, porosity, and poisonwood. *Critical Multilingualism*, 1(2), 96–118.
Phipps, A. (2014). "They are bombing now": "Intercultural Dialogue" in times of conflict. *Language and Intercultural Communication*, 14(1), 108–124.
Piller, I. (2007). Linguistics and Intercultural Communication. *Language and Linguistics Compass*, 1(3), 208–226.
Rajagoplan, K. (2004). On being critical. *Critical Discourse Studies*, 1(2), 261–263.
Rajagoplan, K. (2012). "World English" or "World Englishes"? Does it make any difference? *International Journal of Applied Linguistics*, 22(3), 374–391.
Reisigl, M., & Wodak, R. (2009). The discourse–historical approach (DHA). In R. Wodak & M. Meyer (Eds.), *Methods of critical discourse analysis* (pp. 87–121). Thousand Oaks, CA: Sage.
Sayer, A. (2000). *Realism and Social Science*. Thousand Oaks, CA: Sage.
Scollon, R., & Scollon, S.W. (2000). *Intercultural Communication: A discourse approach*. Oxford: Blackwell.
Shaw, I.S. (2012). Stereotypical representations of Muslims and Islam following the 7/7 London terror attacks: Implications for Intercultural Communication and terrorism prevention. *The International Communication Gazette*, 74(6), 509–524.
Slembrouck, S. (2001). Explanation, interpretation and critique in the analysis of discourse. *Critique of Anthropology*, 2(1), 33–57.
Thompson, J. (1984). *Studies in the theory of ideology*. Cambridge: Polity.
van Dijk, T.A. (1993). Principles of critical discourse analysis. *Discourse and Society*, 4(2), 249–283.
van Dijk, T.A. (1998). *Ideology: An interdisciplinary approach*. Thousand Oaks, CA: Sage.
van Dijk, T.A. (2008). *Discourse and context: A sociocognitive approach*. Cambridge: Cambridge University Press.
van Dijk, T.A. (Ed.). (2011). *Discourse studies: A multidisciplinary approach*. Thousand Oaks, CA: Sage.
Weedon, C. (1997). *Feminist practice and poststructuralist theory*. Chichester: Wiley.
Williams, R. (1977). *Marxism and literature*. Oxford: Oxford Univerity Press.
Wodak, R., & Chilton, P. (Eds.). (2005). *A new agenda in (critical) discourse analysis*. Amsterdam: John Benjamins.

Wodak, R., & Meyer, M. (Eds.). (2009). *Methods of critical discourse analysis* (2nd ed.). Thousand Oaks, CA: Sage.

Further Reading and Resources

Blommaert, J. (2005). *Discourse*. Cambridge: Cambridge University Press.
Fairclough, N. (2001). *Language and power*. Harlow: Longman.
Fairclough, N. (2010). *Critical discourse analysis: The critical study of language* (2nd ed.). London: Longman.
Pennycook, A. (2001). *Critical applied linguistics: A critical introduction*. Mahwah, NJ: Lawrence Erlbaum.
Wodak, R., & Meyer, M. (Eds.). (2009). *Methods of critical discourse analysis* (2nd ed.). Thousand Oaks, CA: Sage.

20 Conversation Analysis

Adam Brandt and Kristian Mortensen

> **Summary**
>
> Conversation analysis (CA) is the study of the organization of social interaction. Through the fine-grained microanalysis of naturally occurring social interaction, CA aims to uncover the ways in which participants employ verbal, vocal and bodily conduct in order to make sense in and of the unfolding interaction. In this chapter, we (1) introduce conversation analysis and the ethnomethodological theory which underpins it, (2) outline how this approach has been applied to the study of, and contributed to our understanding of, Intercultural Communication to date, and (3) propose ways in which this line of research might move forward.

Introduction

This chapter provides an overview of conversation analysis (CA) by describing its epistemological background and methodological practices. This will then pave the way for an overview of how CA researchers have approached the study of Intercultural Communication (IC), and some proposals for future directions CA-for-IC research might take.

Conversation analysis can be described as both a research field and as a research methodology, and it is primarily in the latter that issues of "interculturality" (cf. interculturality as a general term for intercultural studies) have been examined. That is, the methodology of CA can be, and has been, used (1) to investigate interactions that are describable as "intercultural" from a macro-perspective, and (2) to unpack how issues of interculturality emerge as relevant in and through the interactional work of participants. These means of applying CA to the study of IC will be discussed in more detail later.

Conversation analysis is an inductive research field that studies the organization of social interaction as it naturally occurs in moments of everyday life. "Inductive" here refers to the general methodological principle of avoiding any theorizing that does not originate from empirical analysis of the data at hand. The aim is to reveal the methods through which participants occasion sense-making practices for social action. That is, the verbal, vocal and bodily conduct through which participants display their *in situ* understanding of the sequential unfolding of the interaction. Since the 1960s, CA has been primarily known for the description of how verbal and vocal resources are systematically used to produce locally ordered turns-at-talk. This is not to say, however, that conversation analysts are interested in language *per se*; rather, the interest lies in the *social actions* that participants perform through various resources, among them verbal and vocal conduct. Additionally, social actions as performed through bodily conduct have also been studied from early on in CA's lifecourse (Goodwin, 1981; Heath, 1986) and are increasingly accepted as essential aspects of CA's field of inquiry (e.g. Rasmussen, Mortensen, & Hazel, 2014; Streeck, Goodwin, & LeBaron, 2011). It is in this emphasis on action over language that CA differs from other forms of discourse analysis.

From a CA perspective, the social conduct of participants in interaction is a public display of how they understand one another, and jointly create and sustain intersubjectivity, as they go about their social business. "Understanding" and "misunderstanding" has long been a central concern for many social science researchers, and not least those interested in IC. However, CA's position here is somewhat unique, in that understanding is treated as a praxeological matter, that is, as something participants display in and through their social actions (see e.g. Mondada, 2011). Understanding is negotiated on a moment-by-moment basis, where each action is seen and understood in relation to the prior action (referred to as indexicality) and, at the same time, opens up for a new understanding of it (referred to as reflexivity).

Through this kind of analytic mindset, we can begin to get an insight into how understanding and knowledge can be claimed, displayed, and expected (or otherwise) by participants, through their social conduct in interaction. This microanalytic approach to the study of human action, and approach to cognition as socially situated in central to CA research on IC, and CA research in general.

In the following two sections, we consider in more detail the epistemological position of CA, and then the procedures for doing conversation analytic research, before returning to the application of CA to IC research.

Sociological Background

Conversation analysis emerged out of ethnomethodology (EM), a sociological approach to the commonsense knowledge of everyday life as a basis for human action (hence "ethnomethods," or "people's methods"), and, for most of its practitioners, still resides firmly in sociology. However, CA has influenced a range of other disciplines such as linguistics and applied linguistics, education, anthropology, and social psychology. As a research methodology, CA is frequently used in these fields, often as a critical voice against more interpretive approaches and methodologies that tend to invoke external concepts such as gender, power or culture as explanations for human behavior. The reluctance of CA research to allow *a priori* categories, such as gender or "culture," to inform analysis follows from Harold Garfinkel's work in the 1950s and 1960s (e.g. 1956), in which he challenged a range of scientific assumptions and working methods which prevailed across the social sciences. Most predominantly, he criticized the functionalist/structuralist approach of, in particular, Talcott Parsons (1951) and the fundamental sociological claim that individuals are subject to externally given (social and linguistic) structures that define – or even determine – human behavior. Instead, Garfinkel argued, researchers should investigate the methods that participants *themselves* make use of in creating their social world. In this sense, EM and its related methodological approaches are the most radically emic of all social scientific methods.

Conversation analysis originated in the work of Harvey Sacks, who was a student of Garfinkel, and heavily influenced by his work. In particular, Sacks was trying to solve one of EM's methodological problems, namely, how to get access to the commonsense knowledge that "members" share and make use of in the practical reasoning of their everyday life (Garfinkel, 1967). Commonsense knowledge is such an integral part of our social lives – or, as Garfinkel put it, is "seen but unnoticed" – that it is hard to study. Applying the technology available at that time, Sacks turned towards audio recordings of real-life spoken interaction in order to achieve this, and began to investigate commonsense knowledge as it became visible through the systematic organization of talk. Hence, the birth of CA, and its emphasis on the verbal and vocal conduct of participants in interaction, was not due to any particular interest in language, but simply because language-in-use was the most convenient source of data through which to gain insight into people's methods for making sense of their social world. Or, as Sacks says "because I could get my hands on it, and I could study it again and again" (Sacks, 1992, vol. 1, p. 622). Recently, as mentioned in the opening section, new technological advances (i.e. the availability and easy use of video recording equipment) have led to increased consideration of other aspects of social interaction, including bodily conduct and the use of material artefacts, in CA studies.

Early CA studies examined telephone calls and other sites of everyday conversations, the fine-grained systematic analysis of which led Sacks and his colleagues – Emmanuel Schegloff and Gail Jefferson – to uncover some foundational principles of how spoken interaction is organized. The findings were published in two seminal papers. In the first, the authors described how turn-taking is normatively organized (Sacks, Schegloff, & Jefferson, 1974). In the second paper, they described how participants deal with situations in which "intersubjectivity" is under threat, i.e. how participants identify and deal with problems of speaking, hearing, or understanding (Schegloff, Jefferson, & Sacks, 1977) (note that "problem" here does not relate to an external "truth," but to what members orient to as problematic). Subsequent CA research has built and expanded upon the key observations first laid down by this work in the 1970s, and examined a huge range of interactional media and contexts beyond the telephone.

CA sees activities and identities as constructed by participants in and through social interaction. This opposes the view of individuals as merely "cultural dopes" (Garfinkel, 1967) who blindly follow given social structures. For example, Garfinkel (1967) argues that the ways in which participants in the jury room can be categorized is numerous (e.g. man, husband, tennis player, democrat and so on) and that a reference to their for-the-purpose-position (i.e. "jury member") is just one such category. As such, Garfinkel asks, on what grounds can *this* category be used to describe their actual social behavior? Jury members are recognized *as* jury members in and through their publicly available practices. That is, their ways of working, the practical reasoning on which their work is done, defines them *as* jury members rather than as, say, husbands. Similarly, the authors of this chapter can be relevantly described in terms of their nationality ("British," "Danish"), gender ("male"), family affiliation ("father," "son," "brother"), profession ("academic") or personal hobbies. And yet, there are times when some identities (e.g. "man," "Dane," "buddy," "Dad," etc.) are not relevant to the activity in which one finds oneself (such as writing a book chapter on CA, for which the identity of "academic" may be relevant). We will return to the distinction between correctness and relevance of identity categories when considering CA approaches to IC.

An area of CA which is of particular relevance to the study of IC is membership categorization analysis (MCA). Membership categorization analysis reveals how categories and category-bound activities are used in interaction to serve local social and interactional purposes. That is, MCA focuses on how participants orient to one another as certain *types* of people that belong to certain social categories. As noted above, the ways in which we can refer to other people are numerous so what does one achieve by employing one category rather than another? For example, what are the interactional consequences in orienting to someone's identity as, say, a professor, instead of other (also true) categories such as male, husband, father, Dane, football fan, etc.? MCA aims to make sense of how systematic use of categories is employed in social interaction (Stokoe, 2012; Angouri, Chapter 3, this volume).

This can be extended not only to the ways that social categories are employed in interaction, but also (for example) how one category can make another category relevant. In his classic example "The baby cried, the mommy picked it up" (Sacks, 1992, vol. 2, pp. 236–242) Sacks argues that we hear "the mommy" as "the mother of this particular baby" as they belong to the same category (i.e., family members). In addition, picking up babies is the sort of things that mothers do; it is a category-bound activity. Sacks's point is then that *if* we can understand "baby" and "mommy" as belonging to the same social category (family) then that's how we hear them. The extension from family members to cultural (and other social) categories may or may not seem far, but the ways in which participants categorize themselves and each other during courses of interaction have been central in CA approaches to IC. We will return to this later.

Data and Method

CA works with audio- and/or video recordings of naturally occurring interaction, i.e. interactions that would have taken place regardless of the presence of the researcher. With participants' consent, video cameras and audio recorders are used to capture interactions in whatever setting is of interest to the researcher. Everyday mundane conversation is taken to be the most basic site of society (see e.g. Schegloff, 2006) and many of the early descriptions of the methods participants use in their sense-making practices are based on empirical analyses of everyday conversation. But CA researchers have also looked at institutional interaction such as classrooms, police interrogations, and medical interaction (for an overview, see Mortensen & Wagner, 2012), and have shown how interaction in such settings is organized differently from everyday conversation (see e.g. Arminen, 2005; Drew & Heritage, 1992). This has paved the way for so-called "applied CA," which not only describes interaction in institutional settings, but also aims at providing practical implications on the basis of empirical analysis to the practitioners in questions (Antaki, 2011).

In order to outline members' practices for the accomplishment of intersubjectivity as it surfaces in social interaction, CA works with meticulous transcriptions of the data (i.e. the video/audio recordings). Here CA differs from other approaches to the study of human interaction (e.g. most discourse analytic approaches) in that not only *what* is being said, but also *how* it is being said is annotated in the transcriptions. This includes fine details such as the precise timing of periods without talk (down to tenths of a second), change in pitch and intonation, changes in volume, sound stretches, shifting of body positions, shifting of eye gaze, and many other aspects of verbal and nonverbal conduct. Even the exact details of laughter, such as number of beats, have been found to be socially organized and performing a wide range of social actions (e.g. Jefferson, 1984; Jefferson, 1985; Jefferson, Sacks, & Schegloff, 1987). As Schegloff notes:

> the elements of conduct taken up in (CA analyses) are not "details".... . They are just the sorts of building blocks out of which talk-in-interaction is fashioned by the parties to it; they are the ordinary size (Schegloff, 1988: 100)

It is, however, important to note that the transcript does not substitute for the recordings nor does it count as "the data." A transcript is, regardless of the level of detail, "'theory laden' renderings of certain aspects of what the tape has presented of the original interaction" (ten Have, 1999, p. 77) and should never be studied in isolation from the recording on which it was based.

The recording and transcription are then subject to detailed analysis. During this process, each turn at talk is examined carefully with the following questions in mind:

- Why does this happen, in the way that it does, at this precise moment? (Summarized by CA researchers as "why that, in that way, now?")
- What does that display about the participant's understanding of the situation and, in particular, the prior turn?
- What are the consequences for this in the next turn?

While many studies employing CA methods – including the majority of those which have examined IC to date – are based on a "single case analysis" (analyzing one particular sequence), others aim to identify a particular interactional phenomenon and find multiple cases of it. Building a "collection" in this way helps to see systematicities of interaction and participants' orientations towards the action(s) as a social practice.

A CA Approach to Intercultural Communication

The small body of research employing a CA approach to the study of IC emerged, in the mid-1990s, in much the same way as EM/CA itself emerged – in response, and as an alternative, to the top-down, structuralist approaches which were seen to dominate the research landscape. In such approaches to IC research, national cultural memberships are typically treated, implicitly or explicitly, as prediscursive, pretheoretical, given categories, which directly affect the behavior of the participants. These cultural categories and cultural differences (or "dimensions of culture," cf. Hofstede, 2001) are treated as describable and measurable, and typically used in questionnaire-based studies as independent variables against which other, dependent, variables, such as communicative abilities or values, can be measured (cf. the work of Geert Hofstede (2001) and Trompenaars & Hampden-Turner (1997), as exemplars of this approach; also see Holliday, Chapter 2, this volume). As such, from this approach, so-called "misunderstandings" are frequently described as emerging from the cultural or linguistic difference of the participants.

Of course, this treatment of nationality, ethnicity and/or "culture" as influencing or prescribing communicative behaviors is not limited to researchers operating within a structuralist paradigm; discourse analysts too have long adopted similar approaches, albeit through very different means of analyses. One of the earliest, most influential discourse analysts and IC researchers, John Gumperz (e.g. 1978) also made similar claims regarding the impact of "culture" on behavior (or more specifically, in Gumperz's case, communication).

Alternatively, some discourse-analytic approaches (including, as can be seen from the below quotation, that of "interactional sociolinguistics," of which Gumperz is said to be the founding father) seem to suggest that, not only is this way of conceptualizing the relationship between culture and communication theoretically and empirically problematic, but that researching IC may not be even possible, since IC does not exist on a micro-level:

> From an interactional sociolinguistic perspective, discourse is communication between or among individuals. Cultures, however, are large, superordinate categories; they are not individuals. Cultures are a different level of logical analysis from the individual members of cultures. Cultures do not talk to each other; individuals do. In that sense, all communication is interpersonal communication and can never be intercultural communication. (Scollon & Scollon, 2001, p. 138)

A long-lasting tension for researchers, then, is to consider how to analyze IC and interculturality (1) without using "culture" as an analytic construct in the study of (mis)communication, and (2) without indulging in "analytic stereotyping" by characterizing the object of analysis (only) by the cultural differences which are ostensibly present (Sarangi, 1994). A CA approach offers one solution to this conundrum by moving the burden of determining if (and how) "culture" is relevant in any given interaction from the analyst to the participants themselves.

A CA position aims for analytical "neutrality," in that it is not the researcher's position to provide (nor deny) any kind of *a priori* description of an interaction. Rather, it is for the participants to demonstrate – through their interactional practices – if, and how, categories are relevant to them as they go about their social business. This is no less true for the interculturality of an interaction – researchers ought not to deem if an interaction is or is not intercultural, the goal of CA for IC research is to unpack if, and how, an interactional event is *treated as* intercultural by those involved. That is, the goal is to see how interculturality is *achieved by,* rather than *impacts on,* interactional conduct.

From a CA perspective, then, the relevance of participants' national (or any other) cultural membership is determined only by what those participants do and say with one another as they conduct their social business, rather than according to researchers' hypotheses, research questions, theoretical assumptions, or personal beliefs. These displays can manifest, as was touched upon in earlier sections, through participants' orientations to relevant identity categories and/or claims, category-bound activities or displays and expectations of knowledge and understanding.

Nishizaka (1995, 1999) was the first to employ a CA approach to the study of IC, and in so doing "treat this [interculturality] as a phenomenon to be investigated, instead of using interculturality – the fact that the participants come from different cultures – as a given fact from which the argument should start" (Nishizaka, 1995, p. 302).

Through his microanalysis of a Japanese radio program interview between the Japanese host and an international student in Japan, Nishizaka showed how the "cultural differences" (1995, p. 303) of the participants are *made relevant through their interactional conduct*. These cultural differences, Nishizaka noted, were mostly manifest through (1) displays of expectations of, and rights to, knowledge of cultural artefacts (such as Japanese food), and (2) notions of "ownership" of language.

This latter observation, on the ways in which different "language expertise" (or at least expectations thereof) emerges through interaction, has been subsequently explored in some detail by CA researchers. "Second language (L2) interaction" has developed into a substantial subfield of CA research, arguably spurred on by Firth and Wagner's (1997) hugely influential work on using CA for research into second language acquisition. Many other studies since have examined the ways in which L2 interactions are organized and do or do not differ from L1 interaction, both in institutional settings and in ordinary conversations (e.g. Gardner & Wagner, 2004).

However, while CA studies looking at different linguistic knowledge has flourished, those looking at cultural knowledge have not. While there are some valuable contributions to the field of IC, they remain small in numbers. Nishizaka's seminal work had two interrelated themes which have regularly reemerged in CA for IC research: (1) making national/cultural/ethnic identities relevant, and (2) expectations of cultural knowledge. In considering the first of these, it is worth providing a Case in Point.

> **Case in Point**
>
> Fukuda, C, (2006). Resistance against being formulated as a cultural other: The case of a Chinese student in Japan. *Pragmatics, 16(4),* 429–456.
>
> **Research question:** How do interculturality, and Edward Said's (1978) notion of "exoticization" (the process of establishing a superiority over a cultural "other"), emerge through talk-in-interaction?
> **Research design and data-collection method:** The data analyzed was the audio-recordings of naturally occurring mealtime talk.
> **Participants:** A Japanese couple, in their 60s and 70s, who are hosting a Japanese-speaking graduate student from China. The researcher was also present at the mealtime gathering.
> **Data:** Following data collection and transcription, the researcher identified sequences of talk in which the participants oriented to their different linguistic and/or cultural backgrounds, and when "categorizations and identities are constructed, assigned, or asserted" (Fukuda, 2006, p. 433).
> **Analytic observations:** Through analysis of those sequences, Fukuda noted how, through reference to paired categories (such as "developing nation"/"developed nation," "native speaker"/"non-native speaker," and "Japanese cultural novice"/"Japanese cultural expert"), the Japanese hosts were seen to make interculturality relevant, and to engage in a process of "exoticizing" the "cultural other." However, Fukuda also noted that the participant being "constructed as a cultural other" resisted these practices through her responses.

Similar findings have been noted by other researchers employing CA and MCA to the study of identities, such as ethnicity. For example, Day (1994, 1998) showed how staff in an international workplace treated their colleague's Chinese ethnicity as relevant to the organization of a party, while the Chinese staff member contested this. From a CA perspective, then, the study of identity is key ground for examining interculturality, since:

> membership of a category is ascribed (and rejected), avowed (and disavowed), displayed (and ignored), in local places and at certain times, and it does these things as part of the interactional work that constitutes people's lives. (Antaki & Widdicombe, 1998, p. 2)

In other words, in examining categorizations and orientations to identities through this analytic lens, researchers can shed light on how, when and why identities are made relevant, and used to achieve various social goals, in intercultural interaction.

The second main theme of CA for IC research to date – expectations regarding knowledge (or non-knowledge) of cultural practices and artefacts – has tended to place greater emphasis on CA's traditional primary focus – the organizational structure of interaction – and considered how this might differ (at times) when interculturality becomes relevant. For example, Mori (2003) examined interaction between Japanese and American students and showed how, as they got acquainted, the students organized their talk, and participation therein, according to expectations about cultural knowledge (e.g. "What Japanese food do you like?"). Mori argued that the cultural differences of the participants is used as a "resource for organizing their participation and, at the same time, recreates the salience of the interculturality of the interaction" (Mori, 2003, p. 144).

Zimmerman (2007) has taken this further, reiterating the point that interculturality is not omnirelevant, but also observing, importantly, that claims to cultural knowledge and expertise can be at times expected but not forthcoming, and also do not always come from a participant who holds a passport to that country.

More recently, Bolden (2014) has also built on the work of Mori, but rather than a single case analysis of interaction between unacquainted parties, or friends (as in Zimmerman, 2007), her analysis is based on a *collection* of orientations to cultural expertise within one transnational family.

Case in Point

Bolden, G.B., (2014). Negotiating understanding in "intercultural moments" in immigrant family interactions. *Communication Monographs, 81(2)*, 208–238.

Research questions: How do participants' divergent linguistic and/or cultural expertise become "live and relevant" (Moerman, 1988: 70) in family conversation, and how are these "intercultural moments" interactionally organized?
Research design and data-collection method: The sequences of interaction analyzed for this study are taken from a corpus of approximately 40 hours of video-recorded, naturally occurring, face-to-face conversation between family members.
Participants: A three-generation Russian-American family, all of whom are living in the USA following long-term immigration from the former Soviet Union.
Data: Bolden separates the sequences she analyzes into types, in all of which the ongoing conversation is put on hold in order to deal with potential or actual issues of non-understanding. The three sequence types are: (1) when one participant checks another's knowledge of a word or concept; (2) when one participant displays an assumption that another does not know a particular word or concept; and (3) when a participant initially displays an assumption of understanding, but then has to revise their assumption following a repair initiation from the addressee.
Analytic observations: The analysis of the above sequences of interaction, in which participants deal with possible issues of understanding, showed that expectations of cultural and linguistic knowledge are not uniform or stable, and can be shaped by the local sequential context and/or the social activity at hand. Again, it shows that interculturality is not omnirelevant, and is made relevant through participants' visible social conduct. It also shows that, how, and to what purposes, in these "intercultural moments," shared competences and knowledge are no longer the default.

It is generally agreed then, from a CA perspective that interculturality is not always relevant to participants in interaction, regardless of their cultural backgrounds, but is something which emerges from their conduct, as they go about certain social activities, such as getting acquainted. With these empirically grounded observations now made, though, what lies ahead for research applying this approach? What else can CA and MCA offer the field of IC? Despite the impact and value of the above-mentioned studies, they are admittedly thin on the ground, and it is not clear in what direction future research will go. In the next section, we propose some possible avenues that IC research with a CA approach might follow.

Possible Future Directions of CA for IC

As is apparent from the previous section, analysis of displays and expectations of knowledge have been key in research employing CA for IC. And in keeping with developing trends in CA broadly (Heritage, 2012; Stivers, Mondada, & Steensig, 2011), we expect that future research explore this in more detail. Future research in this area would do well to build on the findings of Mori (2003) and Bolden (2014) by uncovering, across a broader range of datasets, how and when "intercultural moments" occur, and to what end. For example, how is cultural knowledge (and all that entails) employed in the performance of other social actions? One preliminary example of this, by Brandt and Jenks (2011), has shown how unacquainted parties can use cultural stereotypes (presented as knowledge) as a means to tease and make fun of one another as they get acquainted.

The same study showed how "third cultures" (i.e. practices and/or artefacts from a cultural group not represented by parties in the interaction) can be employed in the pursuit of social goals (in this case, refuting stereotypes); further research may also consider how knowledge of "third cultures" can be used as interactional resources.

Displays and expectations of knowledge are also likely to be investigated in institutional settings, such as workplaces, service encounters and educational environments. Few studies to date have examined interculturality from a CA perspective in institutional settings, although one exception examined orders in a Japanese sushi restaurant in California, and unpacked how "trust and acceptance of the customer's cultural knowhow" (p. 862) can impact upon the ordering process (Kuroshima, 2010). Further research of this kind would be welcome, and instrumental in furthering understanding of how interculturality impacts upon professional encounters of varying sorts.

An alternative CA approach to the examination of intercultural interactions, including in workplaces, is to investigate settings in which where participants come together *because* of their national or ethnic identities. Studies of this kind are also in limited supply, although exceptions include investigations into internship interviews with immigrants in Denmark (Tranekjær, 2015) and encounters between international students and university staff at a student helpdesk (e.g. Hazel, 2013; Hazel & Haberland, 2013). In such research, even if interculturality does not become demonstrably relevant to the participants, analytic observations can be discussed – subsequent to completed analysis – in terms of theories of IC. Outside of IC, this approach has been employed to inform research fields (e.g. second language acquisition; cf. Kasper, 2006) and ideological agendas (e.g. feminism; cf. Kitzinger, 2010) with great success.

Whatever it is which lies ahead for CA for IC, it seems that analysis of systematicities across large collections of interactional phenomena will be preferable to further single case analyses; while the single case studies mentioned in the preceding section have made invaluable contributions to a CA interpretation of interculturality, perhaps now is the time for researchers to build on these. For example, research into the systematic uses of categories and identities in various forms of interactional settings is essential. In her "call to arms" for the future direction of MCA, Stokoe (2012) argued that large-scale analyses of when participants in interaction "go categorial" (2012, p. 295) is essential for "interrogating culture, reality and society, without recourse to its reputed "wild and promiscuous" analytic approach" (p. 277).

Despite the first CA investigations of "interculturality in action" emerging almost two decades ago, this subfield of IC research remains in its infancy. This means, however, there are an enormous range of possibilities which lie ahead for this approach, which will contribute hugely not only the field of IC itself, but also to our understanding of social interaction in general.

Key Terms

Conversation Analysis Conversation analysis (CA) can be said to be both a theory of the systematics of social action, and a methodology for its analysis. Drawing upon its ethnomethodological foundations (see further on), researchers employing CA engage in the finely detailed microanalysis of recordings of naturally occurring interactions, in order to unpack the systematic ways in which they are organized.

Ethnomethodology A sociological approach for understanding the methods which members of society use in order to jointly create meaning of their social world and day-to-day experiences. It was developed by Harold Garfinkel and has led to the emergence of CA and MCA as established approaches to sociological study.

Interculturality The nature of an encounter, or interaction, as taking place between participants of different cultural backgrounds. The term tends to be used in post-structural or ethnomethodological approaches to intercultural communication, and emphasizes that an encounter can only be described as intercultural if it is demonstrably being treated as such by those involved. As such, interactions ought not to be externally labelled as intercultural, but may have "intercultural moments," or may be treated as intercultural for particular social or rhetorical purposes.

Membership Categorization Analysis The methodological sibling of CA, which also adopts an ethnomethodological approach, but differs in that the focus is not on the sequential organization of social (inter)action, but on how participants in interaction jointly and systematically employ and/or negotiate their presumed commonsense knowledge of social structures – including (but not limited to) categories group of relevance to IC, such as gender, nationality, ethnicity and profession, and the category-bound activities that go with them – in and through their various everyday activities.

References

Antaki, C. (Ed.). (2011). *Applied conversation analysis*. Basingstoke: Palgrave Macmillan.
Antaki, C., & Widdicombe, S. (Eds.). (1998). *Identities in talk*. Thousand Oaks, CA: Sage.
Arminen, I. (2005). *Institutional interaction. Studies of talk at work*. Aldershot: Ashgate.
Bolden, G. B. (2014). Negotiating understanding in "intercultural moments" in immigrant family interactions. *Communication Monographs*, 81(2), 208–238.
Brandt, A., & Jenks, C. J. (2011). "It is okay to eat a dog in Korea… like China?" Assumptions of national food-eating practices in intercultural interaction. *Language and Intercultural Communication*, 11(1), 41–58.
Day, D. (1994). Tang's dilemma and other problems: Ethnification processes at some multicultural workplaces. *Pragmatics*, 4(3), 315–336.
Day, D. (1998). Being ascribed, and resisting, membership of an ethnic group. In C. Antaki & S. Widdicombe (Eds.), *Identities in talk* (pp. 151–170). Thousand Oaks, CA: Sage.
Drew, P., & Heritage, J. (Eds.). (1992). *Talk at work: Interaction in institutional settings*. Cambridge: Cambridge University Press.
Firth, A., & Wagner, J. (1997). On Discourse, communication and (some) fundamental concepts in SLA research. *The Modern Language Journal*, 81(3), 285–300.
Fukuda, C. (2006). Resistance against being formulated as cultural other: The case of a Chinese student in Japan. *Pragmatics*, 16(4), 429–456.
Gardner, R., & Wagner, J. (Eds.). (2004). *Second language conversations*. London: Continuum.
Garfinkel, H. (1956). Some sociological concepts and methods for psychiatrists. *Psychiatric Research Reports*, 6, 181–195.
Garfinkel, H. (1967). *Studies in ethnomethodology*. Englewood Cliffs, NJ: Prentice-Hall.
Goodwin, C. (1981). *Conversational organization: Interaction between speakers and hearers*. New York: Academic Press.
Gumperz, J. (1978). The conversational analysis of interethnic communication. In: E. Lamar Ross (Ed.), *Interethnic Communication* (pp. 13–31). Athens, GA: University of Georgia Press.
Hazel, S. (2013). Interactional competence in the institutional setting of the international university: Talk and embodied action as multimodal aggregates in institutional interaction. Unpublished PhD thesis, Roskilde University, Roskilde.
Hazel, S., & Haberland, H. (2013). Negotiated exclusion: On the constitution of "Otherness" in a multilingual workplace setting. Working paper for the Workshop on Diversity and Difference in the Contemporary Workplace, Copenhagen Business School, January 31–February 1, 2013. Retrieved June 27, 2015 from: http://lingcorp.ruc.dk/lingcorp/Working_Papers_files/Hazel%20%26%20Haberland%20Working%20Paper%20CBS%202013%5B1%5D.pdf.
Heath, C. (1986). *Body movement and speech in medical interaction*. Cambridge: Cambridge University Press.
Heritage, J. (2012). Epistemics in action: Action formation and territories of knowledge. *Research on Language and Social Interaction*, 45(1), 1–29.
Hofstede, G. (2001). *Culture's consequences: Comparing values, institutions and organizations across nations*. Thousand Oaks, CA: Sage.
Jefferson, G. (1984). On the organization of laughter in talk about troubles. In J. M. Atkinson, & J. Heritage (Eds.), *Structures of social action: Studies in conversation analysis* (pp. 79–96). Cambridge: Cambridge University Press.
Jefferson, G. (1985). An Exercise in the Transcription and Analysis of Laughter. In T.A. v. Dijk (Ed.), *Handbook of discourse analysis* (pp. 25–34). New York: Academic Press.

Jefferson, G., Sacks, H., & Schegloff, E. A. (1987). Notes on laughter in the pursuit of intimacy. In G. Button & J. R. E. Lee (Eds.), *Talk and social organization* (pp. 152–205). Clevedon: Multilingual Matters.

Kasper, G. (2006). Beyond repair: Conversation analysis as an approach to SLA. *AILA Review*, 19, 83–99.

Kitzinger, C. (2010). Doing feminist conversation analysis. *Feminism & Psychology*, 10(2), 163–193.

Kuroshima, S. (2010). Another look at the service encounter: Progressivity, intersubjectivity, and trust in a Japanese sushi restaurant. *Journal of Pragmatics*, 42, 856–869.

Moerman, M. (1988). *Talking culture: Ethnography and conversation analysis*. Philadelphia: University of Pennsylvania Press.

Mondada, L. (2011). Understanding as an embodied, situated and sequential achievement in interaction. *Journal of Pragmatics*, 43, 542–552.

Mori, J. (2003). The construction of interculturality: A study of initial encounters between Japanese and American students. *Research on Language and Social Interaction*, 36(2), 143–184.

Mortensen, K., & Wagner, J. (2012). Conversation Analysis and applied linguistics. In C. A. Chapelle (Ed.), *The Encyclopedia of Applied Linguistics* (pp. 944–1127). Oxford: Wiley-Blackwell.

Nishizaka, A. (1995). The interactive constitution of interculturality: How to be a Japanese with words. *Human Studies*, 18, 301–326.

Nishizaka, A. (1999). Doing interpreting within interaction: The interactive accomplishment of a "henna gaijin" or "strange foreigner." *Human Studies*, 22, 235–251.

Parsons, T. (1951). *The social system*. New York: Free Press.

Rasmussen, G., Mortensen, K., & Hazel, S. (Eds.) (2014). *A body of resources – CA studies of social conduct*. Special issue of *Journal of Pragmatics*, 65, 1–156.

Sacks, H., Schegloff, E. A., & Jefferson, G. (1974). A simplest systematics for the organization of turn-taking for conversation. *Language*, 50(4), 696–735.

Sacks, H. (1992). *Lectures on conversation* (edited by Gail Jefferson). Oxford: Blackwell.

Said, E. (1978). *Orientalism*. London: Vintage.

Sarangi, S. (1994). Intercultural or not? Beyond celebration of cultural differences in miscommunication analysis. *Pragmatics*, 4(3), 409–427.

Schegloff, E. A. (1988). Goffman and the Analysis of conversation. In P. Drew & A. Wootton (Eds.), *Erving Goffman: Exploring the interaction order* (pp. 89–135). Cambridge: Polity Press.

Schegloff, E. A. (2006). Interaction: The Infrastructure for social institutions, the natural ecological niche for language, and the arena in which culture is enacted. In N.J. Enfield & S.C. Levinson (Eds.), *Roots of human sociality: Culture, cognition and interaction* (pp. 70–96). Oxford: Berg.

Schegloff, E. A., Jefferson, G., & Sacks, H. (1977). The Preference for self-correction in the organization of repair in conversation. *Language*, 53, 361–382.

Scollon, R., & Scollon, S. W. (2001). *Intercultural communication: A discourse approach*. Oxford: Blackwell.

Stivers, T., Mondada, L., & Steensig, J. (Eds.). (2011). *The morality of knowledge in conversation*. Cambridge: Cambridge University Press.

Stokoe, E. (2012). Moving forward with membership categorization analysis: Methods for systematic analysis. *Discourse Studies*, 14(3), 277–303.

Streeck, J., Goodwin, C., & LeBaron, C. (Eds.). (2011). *Embodied interaction: Language and body in the material world*. Cambridge: Cambridge University Press.

ten Have, P. (1999). *Doing conversation analysis: A practical guide*. Thousand Oaks, CA: Sage.

Tranekjær, L. (2015). *Interactional categorization and gatekeeping: Institutional encounters with otherness*. United Kingdom: Multilingual Matters.

Trompenaars, F., & Hampden-Turner, C. (1997). *Riding the waves of culture: Understanding cultural diversity in business*. New York: McGraw-Hill.

Zimmerman, E. (2007). Constructing Korean and Japanese interculturality in talk: Ethnic membership categorization among users of Japanese. *Pragmatics*, 17(1), 71–94.

21 Corpus Analysis

Michael Handford

> **Summary**
>
> Unlike other discourse-based approaches, corpus methods have not been widely employed in the analysis of intercultural interactions. This chapter outlines what tools are used in corpus linguistics and how they can be applied, then discusses the benefits of employing corpus linguistics methods in the analysis of intercultural encounters. It is argued that intercultural studies can benefit from the application of corpus methods in terms of improving rigor and reducing perceived arbitrariness, specifically through the creation and analysis of smaller specialized corpora. The chapter also discusses the compatibility of corpus methods with other methods, and examines the issue of empiricism in relation to corpus linguistics.

What is the Method About?

What is a corpus, and what is corpus linguistics? A corpus is a principled collection of real-life spoken, written or multimodal texts, stored on or accessible through a computer, which can be qualitatively and quantitatively analyzed (Biber, Conrad, & Reppen, 1998; Flowerdew, 2012; O'Keeffe, Carter, & McCarthy, 2007; Sinclair, 1991). Corpus linguistics (hereafter CL) is the empirical analysis of the language and signs within such texts, using computer software and combining quantitative and qualitative approaches. Corpora can be approached either bottom-up or top-down, that is from the lexical, grammatical and textual level, or from a more social contextual level. CL is positioned here as a methodology which fits under the umbrella of discourse analysis (Bhatia, Flowerdew, & Jones, 2008; Gee & Handford, 2012; McCarthy, 1998; for discussion of the ontological status of CL, see McEnery & Hardie, 2012). This chapter explores how this methodology relates to Collier and Thomas's (1988) call for the development and application of approaches for the discourse-based analysis of intercultural interactions, while acknowledging that outside of translation studies (e.g. Baker, 1995), there have been few intercultural communication studies (hereafter IC) which utilize a corpus methodology (Handford, 2014; Spinzi, 2011).

The above definition of a corpus states that it is a "principled" collection of texts, meaning that it should be suitably compiled to address a particular purpose. This purpose will dictate the size and content of the corpus, as corpora should be representative of the language used by the discourse community in question so that the specific research question can be answered. Many corpus linguists agree that the bigger the corpus the better (Biber et al., 1998; Sinclair, 1991; Stubbs, 1996,) although Flowerdew (2004) draws the important distinction between mega-corpora and specialized corpora. The former are made up of hundreds and millions of words or even billions of words (for example The British National Corpus, or the Cambridge International Corpus), and can be used to answer questions about "general" language, such as what the most frequent words are in English compared to French.

Specialized corpora, in contrast, will be much smaller in size, and are created with a specific question in mind, such as what are the key language items and discursive practices in written academic genres (e.g. Hyland, 2009), or what are the typical discursive patterns in a story by Samuel Beckett (Scott & Tribble, 2006, p. 179), or what cultural identities are indexed by the pronoun "we" in professional meetings (Handford, 2014). While large corpora are often decontextualized, specialized corpora can be ethnographically informed (Flowerdew, 2004), and hence of more relevance to IC. In terms of its applicability, CL can be employed to support either constructivist or more essentialist perspectives of culture (see Holliday, Chapter 2, this volume), can analyze small or large cultures, can shed light on identity (see Angouri, Chapter 3), and is a discourse approach (Monaghan, Chapter 4).

Why This Method and Why Not?

While the impact of corpus linguistics in applied linguistics over the past three decades has been considerable, its value not universally accepted (see Baker, 2006; Flowerdew, 2012). Many of the concerns within applied linguistics are concerned with the following three areas:

- Corpora contain decontextualized data (Widdowson, 1998)
- Corpora necessitate a bottom-up approach (Swales, 2002)
- Corpora are quantitative, number-crunching tools (see Baker, 2006, p. 8)

These points are certainly applicable to some studies, although more so with studies of mega-corpora (if you are analyzing billions of words, you cannot say much about context). For studies of specialized corpora, contextual information is essential, and as stated above, it is such corpora that tend to be more appropriate for IC.

The increasing influence of CL in discourse and other communication-related fields is a consequence of the methodology providing an attractive degree of replicability, rigor and relative objectivity (Mautner, 2009), producing "results and language patterns that have been discovered in a relatively neutral manner" (Baker, 2006, p. 18). Moreover these patterns may not be obvious prior to analysis. One of the delights of doing CL is the unearthing of the unexpected. Therefore, CL can benefit IC, provided the corpus research is combined with other tools that can allow for contextually relevant interpretations. This area will be discussed further below.

CL has been effectively employed in "cross-cultural" comparisons, for example, a comparison of US and UK language usage (Biber et al., 1998), a study of Spanish and US pharmaceutical labels (Connor, Ruiz-Garrido, Rozycki, Goering, Kinney, & Koehler, 2008), a study of apologies in Chilean and Irish soap operas (Fahey, 2005), and a comparison of response tokens (e.g. "really") in spoken British and Irish English (O'Keeffe & Adolphs, 2008). An earlier study by Stubbs (1996) explored a large corpus of British English to reveal the way certain "cultural keywords" (that is words that are deemed to be salient within a particular culture, such as "democracy") are used across various contexts.

While such studies are of clear value, they are all predicated on a "received culture" perspective that sees culture as a given, rather than something that is constructed and which emerges through the discourse (see Holliday, Chapter 2, this volume). And while the considerable majority of corpus-based IC have approached culture as a given, often conflating culture with nationality, there is nothing inherent in a corpus methodology that necessitates such an approach. Indeed, if we accept the compatibility between CL and discourse analysis, corpora lend themselves to studies of the dialogic emergence of culture across synchronically or diachronically recurrent contexts. The section on what are the relevant themes below describes an example of a study that explores the discursive construction of emergent cultural identities.

How is CL Conducted?

Planning and Design

In theory, we can either decide the research question or problem first, and then collect appropriate corpus data, or collect data first and then to decide the research question. Unless you are considering building a mega-corpus of a language (such as the BNC), which would require very considerable resources, the former approach is more appropriate. It will ensure your corpus has a higher chance of being *representative* of the community or genre or register in question. However, there are an ever-increasing number of freely available corpora on the web (see "Further reading and resources" below), which may be very suitable for your particular research question. While many of the first corpora were in English, recently more corpora are being compiled in a variety of languages.

If you cannot find a suitable corpus and decide to build your own, issues to consider include:

1. Is your corpus of spoken language, written language, or both?
2. Is it a multimodal corpus, comprising a range of semiotic modes?
3. How can you obtain permission to collect the data (certain types of data, such as workplace communication, can be difficult to obtain)?
4. How big should my corpus be?
5. What type of background information do I need to collect?

Obviously, all these questions should be considered in terms of your research question, and therefore specific answers cannot be given here. However, when considering the size and content of your corpus, there are two key issues: representativeness, and practicality in terms of time and financial constraints. Specialized corpora tend to be between several thousand to one million words, depending on how specialized the variety of language or genre is, and the practical time and cost constraints. Spoken data, for instance is much more expensive to convert into machine-readable form. To transcribe one hour of speech often takes between ten and twenty hours. For written texts, especially those collectable in electronic format, the job of converting them into machine-readable format is more straightforward. This largely explains the tendency for corpora to be written rather than spoken, and for mega-corpora to be comprised of mainly written language. For IC of interactions, spoken and electronic corpora may be of more relevance than written. For IC, the issue of background information is particularly important, as plausible interpretation may only be achieved through triangulation of data sources. Useful discussions of the practicalities of building a corpus can be found in Baker (2006, Chapter 6), and Reppen (2010).

Analysis: software and analytical tools

There are three necessary components in CL: a researcher, the corpus data stored in electronic form on a computer, and corpus software. The software allows the researcher to conduct searches with large datasets virtually instantaneously. For instance, corpus software has allowed lexicographers to calculate the frequency of individual words in a language, across and within different genres and discourse communities, and to use such information in the compilation of learner and bilingual dictionaries. Corpora have revolutionized lexicography (Hunston, 2002).

While lexicogrammatically focused analyses in CL may seem to have less direct relevant to IC, it should be emphasized that the initial quantitative analysis conducted with corpus software is a stepping-stone to qualitative analyses. Furthermore, while many corpus studies employ a bottom-up, text-first approach, more critical and contextual analyzes that approach the data from sociolinguistic, situational, top-down perspectives are also compatible with CL (Hyland, 2009, p. 20).

Software

Different software packages, such as the freely available AntConc Tools (see "Further reading and resources" below) allow the researcher to conduct searches, calculate word frequency, pinpoint which linguistic items occur with statistical significance in comparison to a reference corpus, pinpoint a word's typical collocations, or calculate the most frequent multiword units (or clusters). From a more top-down, social perspective, software such as CQP-Web can pinpoint which group of speakers use one language form more than another. There is also groundbreaking research into which gestures are used with particular linguistic items and functions by particular speakers (Handford & Matous, 2011; Knight, 2011; Tsuchiya, 2013), and into preferred turn length and function according to inter- and intragroup relationships (Tsuchiya & Handford, 2014) using a variety of software. For a review of different types of software, see McEnery and Hardie (2012).

Analytical tools: Concordance, Collocation and Discourse Prosody

Concordance lines are generated by searching for a word or phrase in the corpus, and are often the second step in a corpus analysis (the first being choosing the linguistic item, usually because it is statistically or culturally interesting in some way; see Tognini-Bonelli (2001) on corpus driven versus corpus-based approaches). Collocation occurs "when a word appears near another word, and the relationship is statistically significant in some way" (Baker, 2006, p. 96). A common collocation in English is "blond hair," which is a stronger collocation than "brown hair". This is because "brown" may co-occur with many words, whereas "blond" is much more likely to be found with "hair" than other words. Software enables us to see which words are the most typical collocates of the item in question. According to Hoey (2005, p. 8), collocation is the mechanism through which language items become mentally "loaded with the contexts and co-texts in which they occur" through repeated usage, a process termed "lexical priming."

Collocation is also important because, according to Stubbs (1996, p. 172) it can clarify collocations' implicit associations and connotations, and "therefore the assumptions which they embody," as in his study of cultural keywords. This reference to the connotations and underlying assumptions of particular language-in-use is termed "semantic prosody" or "discourse prosody" (see McEnery & Hardie, 2012; Stubbs, 1996); one of the greatest benefits of CL is that it enables the inference of the discourse prosody of particular language items. Discourse prosody concerns whether, for instance, a word or cluster has an underlying meaning or usage that is positive or negative, which we can infer by analyzing the item across several concordance lines, and such an insight is often not accessible through intuition alone. As Sinclair (1991, p. 100) famously states "the language looks rather different when you look at a lot of it at once." Furthermore, discourse prosody can be indicative of a particular discourse (Baker, 2006, p. 87) – that is, a way of viewing and acting in the world (Gee, 2005). In critical discourse analysis, it has been a powerful tool to show the underlying or implicit discriminatory practices in, for instance, the media portrayal of various marginalized groups (see Baker, 2006).

Below are all the concordance lines for the words "thick skin" from the *TIME Magazine Corpus* of 100 million words (see Davies, 2008). I have chosen this phrase because I hypothesize that it is usually used in English in its metaphorical sense, to mean something that is useful in unpleasant situations, and that it collocates with "have." In terms of its discourse prosody, we could argue such a meaning would be positive, in that it is something desirable. This usage would contrast with the metaphorical use of "thick (face) skin" (面の皮が厚い) in Japanese, for instance, meaning to be insensitive (hence negatively nuanced), and might thus be a cause of intercultural miscommunication.

Concordances: thick skin (*TIME*)

1 (1929) O'Neill bits below the **thick skin** of New England farmer loneliness. Infidelity
2 (1929) This bristling hair, together with **thick skin,** is one of the mongoose's protections against
3 (1952) that he seemed to have a **thick skin**. As the baby grew, his skin darkened and
4 (1954) "Just pray for a **thick skin** and a tender heart. You need it when people just stare coldly and
5 (1966) Foss's good advice to Davis: "Wear a **thick skin** and a soft smile, and carry a sense of humor.
6 (1972) about the war, Humphrey?" But Humphrey has a **thick skin**. Always the tireless campaigner
7 (1983) doer" with the proper credentials: "A great big foot, a **thick skin** and a great big mouth."
8 (1984) constant glare of public scrutiny. If they do not have a **thick skin,** they get a thick entourage."
9 (1989) Then he shrugs. "You have to develop a **thick skin**. You can't bleed to death every time
10 (1992) few arabesques on its **thick skin** with the carving knife, but the sheer dumbness of the art
11 (1994) It takes **thick skin** to be a Jewish settler in Hebron. This is the only place in
12 (2000) politics has always required an unusual combination of warm heart and **thick skin**
13 (2001) The 56-year-old prosecutor is going to need his **thick skin**. Last week, when George W.
14 (2003) beware of the media. I know you think you have a thick skin, but take my word for it

There are 14 instances of "thick skin" in the whole corpus, and eleven of them are clearly metaphorical. In terms of collocations of the metaphorical instances, three of the preceding verbs are forms of the lemma "have." Along with several other verbs (require, need, have to develop) which co-occur, the discourse prosody does indeed seem to be that having a thick skin is desirable or positive, in negative situations that occur in public office or the public eye.

It has also been argued (Handford, 2010; Stubbs, 2007; Tognini-Bonelli, 2001) that vertically viewed concordance lines can show the repetitions which comprise a social practice within a particular discourse community. Stubbs (2007, p. 154) states, "Frequency of occurrence in the corpus is evidence of a social norm," because that groups of people usually communicate in the way they have been socialized, or constrained, to communicate. By examining concordance lines of frequent, statistically or culturally significant items, we can make inferences about the social practices of the community or communities in question.

Frequency lists and keywords

One of the most basic searches in CL is a frequency list, showing which words occur more frequently in our corpus. Corpora have shown "the" to be the most frequently used word in written and spoken English, and that the most frequent 2000 words account for around 83% of all words used in L1 English (see O'Keeffe et al., 2007, pp. 32–36). Frequency lists can also be produced for clusters, and one of the key insights of CL is that L1 and, to varying degrees, L2 English is far more phraseological (i.e. made up of collocations, fixed phrases and idioms) than traditional "slot and filler" theories can account for (see O'Keeffe et al., 2007, chapter 3). Such insights raise questions for language learning, translation and successful intercultural encounters in English as a Lingua Franca (ELF) contexts.

Another type of corpus search is termed a "keyword search," which involves comparing the language in your target corpus with a larger reference corpus to see what language is statistically more (or less) typical in your target corpus. Like frequency lists, keyword lists can be created in a matter of seconds. In my study of business meeting discourse (Handford, 2010), I made keyword lists to see which words are more typically used in meetings than in everyday situations. While I had expected the list of keywords to be full of business-related nouns, like "profit," in fact many of the keywords were interpersonal. The top keyword was the pronoun "we," which will be discussed further below. Statistically significant keywords can be a powerful tool in IC, because they bring to light important words, which can then be interpreted with reference to the context in question (Stubbs, 1996; Spinzi, 2011).

Discourse patterns

An alternative, more top-down, approach to the analysis of your corpus is through first categorizing the stages of the texts in terms of their communicative function (or "moves"), and then analyzing the constitutive lexicogrammar. Such an approach was combined with bottom-up approaches in Connor et al.'s (2008) interdisciplinary study of patient-directed medicine labeling in the US and Spain. They created two comparable corpora and analyzed what the differences were in terms of moves and lexicogrammar (through concordances and frequency and keyword lists). They found greater use of technical terms in the Spanish data (lexical difference), and higher repetition of possible side effects (move difference) in the American data. The move difference was explained in terms of the relatively litigious nature of US society. The study was deemed helpful for intercultural health education teachers and consultants because it allows for concrete points of comparison. It also highlights the potential value of comparative corpora for IC and intercultural pedagogy.

Discourse community patterns

Another top-down approach involves finding which groups of speakers use particular forms more or less frequently. For instance, in business meetings German speakers were found to use the modal verb "must" six times more frequently than other groups (e.g. British and Japanese), who tend to use the less face-threatening "need to" (Handford, 2010, p. 175). Such findings can be useful for shedding light on learners' preconceptions of "the other": in class this information can be presented, and then learners are encouraged to speculate why. This often unearths stereotypes concerning "direct" or "rude" Germans. The class can then be told that the German verb *mussen* is etymologically linked but pragmatically less forceful than the English "must"; that is, the issue is one of pragmalinguistic transfer (Thomas, 1983) rather than assumed national character.

What are relevant research themes?

Below is a list of some of the main research areas where CL has been applied (see Flowerdew, 2012; Hunston 2002; Hyland, Chau & Handford, 2012; O'Keeffe & McCarthy, 2010).

- Language teaching
  - Learner corpora
  - Second-language acquisition
  - Materials design
  - Classroom corpora (data-driven learning)
  - Language testing
- Translation studies
  - Parallel corpora
  - Comparable corpora
- Production of dictionaries and grammars for language learners and translators
- Critical linguistics, pinpointing ideologically important items
- Literary studies and stylistics
- Forensic linguistics
- Electronic communication
  - Websites
  - Social media
  - Emailing
- Multimodal corpora
  - Photographs
  - Gestures
  - Images
- Professional communication
- Academic discourse
- Gender studies
- Media studies
- English as a lingua franca
- Health care

While certain areas are not typically explored in IC (such as forensic linguistics), others have clear overlap with IC research themes, for instance translation studies and ELF.

The potential overlap between IC, CL and ELF is discussed by Seidlhofer, (2012, p. 146), whose team created the publically accessible VOICE corpus of spoken ELF interactions (see below). She states:

> If we want to understand how intercultural communication works in a globalized world and how it may be improved we need to revisit and revise established ideas about what constitutes a language or a community and how people actually draw on linguistic resources to communicate with each other in the real world. We need, in other words, to understand how ELF is used.

She goes on to argue it is a prerequisite for understanding real-world contexts such as peacekeeping, translation and interpretation, conflict resolution, and asylum seeker interrogations, where often ELF is the only means of communicating.

In terms of more general research themes, cultural approaches to discourse and pragmatics are compatible with a corpus methodology. A strong research theme in CL is concerned with cognitive and psycholinguistic approaches (see McEnery & Hardie, 2012), and thus overlaps with the IC research theme of language culture and thought. Two IC themes that have received less attention are the issue of cultural identities, and how we might conceptualize cultural difference as it emerges through spoken discourse. My 2014 study of cultural identities in professional meetings aims to explore this gap, and to show how CL might contribute to IC. This study will be described now in some depth, to demonstrate these aims.

> **Case Study**
>
> Handford, M. (2014). Cultural identities in international, interorganisational meetings: a corpus-informed discourse analysis of indexical "we." *Language and Intercultural Communication, 14(1)*, 41–58.

This study featured two research questions:

1 What cultural identities are explicitly indexed in business meetings through *we*?
2 What can corpus linguistics contribute to IC studies?

The data were drawn from two corpora of professional spoken interactions I have built, CANBEC[1] and an in-progress corpus of construction industry communication.[2] During the compilation of both corpora a considerable amount of background information has been collected, meaning qualitative interpretations were possible.

For this study, three meetings were chosen. The meetings involved people from (ten) different nationalities, organizations (both public and private sector), and professions (including finance, IT, civil engineering, logistics management, environmental consultancy, and design); in other words, each meeting was international, interorganizational, and interprofessional. Furthermore, the three meetings were from different industries (manufacturing, pharmaceuticals, and engineering). These meetings were chosen because they were the most varied in terms of the potential range of differing

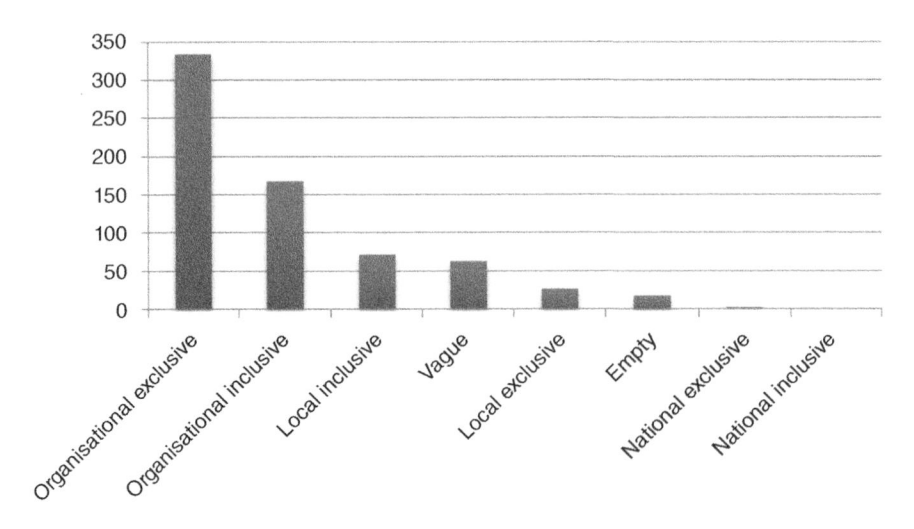

Figure 21.1 "We" identities. Combined total of "we"s from 30,000 words of meeting data from three meetings, classified by cultural identity.

large and small (Holliday, 1999) cultures; allowing the potential signaling of professional, organizational, local as well as national identities.

The paper builds on the finding that "we" is the top statistically significant keyword in business meetings (Handford, 2010), and then explores which cultural identities are indexed (Bucholtz & Hall, 2005) by "we" at different moments in the unfolding discourse. For instance, in the following concordance lines from the meeting between two pharmaceutical companies, the first "we" indexes both companies (i.e. inclusive organizational "we"), the second indexes the speaker's company only (exclusive organizational "we"), and the third indexes all people present at the meeting (inclusive personal "we").

1 Sounds good. So we've got a way ahead (1 sec.) on that.
2 So should we put we put them all through to Hezer?
3 So I g = I guess for me if we look at the logistics action we took cos I

The paper moves from the quantitative keyword findings, to a qualitative interpretation of the concordance lines, to a quantitative categorization of each instance of "we" in the meetings, to a qualitative analysis of the pronoun in longer extracts. Figure 21.1 shows the combined results from the three meetings, showing the number of "we"s from 30,000 words of meeting data according to different cultural identities.

Interview and other background data were referred to during analysis. In other words, a plausible interpretation of the identities was achieved through a mixed-methods approach, drawing on CL and discourse analysis, professional communication, organizational studies, IC and identity studies (Alvesson, 2002; Benwell & Stokoe, 2006; Gee, 2005; Handford, 2010; McCarthy 1998). Rather than imposing an etic categorization of the varying identities, for instance by focusing on nationality and then explaining behavior from that perspective, each instance of "we" in the transcripts was interpreted with relation to the interviews and observation notes to unearth the various identities the interlocutors signaled at different moments.

In terms of the first research question, there was a clear pattern across all three meetings: organizational identity was by far the most frequent, whereas the indexing of nationality through "we" was extremely rare (as it was by other more explicit nationality indexicals). This arguably problematizes the widespread essentialist Hofstedian (1991) prioritization of nationality above other cultural identities in business interactions. Within organizational references, exclusive "we" was far more common, and such "we"s are often evidence of the ascription and avowal of differing cultural identities. The paper also shows the extent to which individuals may index different identities – for instance in one typical 30-second extract the speaker indexes three differing identities.

The dearth of research to date which combines CL with a discursive approach to IC provided the rationale for the second research question. It was concluded that the approach allows the intercultural to be analyzed in discourse, thus providing a method to answer Collier and Thomas's (1988) call of more discourse-based approaches. However, there were limitations with the study in terms of the small number of qualitatively analyzed meetings, and the specific focus on one, admittedly important, item.

How Does it Work With Other Methods?

Corpus methods can be effectively combined with purely qualitative methods in the analysis of discourse and culture, including observations, case studies, and discourse analysis to enhance the analysis (Connor, 2013, p. 9). For instance, in a recent book-length study, Tsuchiya (2013) combines CL with conversation analysis to develop a "time-aligned corpus" to compare the turn-taking behaviors of people from different national cultures from quantitative and then qualitative perspectives. Using the same tool, Tsuchiya and Handford (2014) analyze an international, interorganizational, interprofessional meeting combining CL, conversation analysis, discourse analysis, and ethnographically informed field notes and interviews. Differences in length and functions of speaker turns were observed, depending on whether the speakers were communicating intergroup or intragroup. The findings also shed light on the culture-specific nature of face in professional contexts, and what is deemed conflictual communication.

CL is also useful in pinpointing the absence of something, which can then be discussed with the analyzed discourse community. In a corpus study of on-site international communication, on a construction site, Handford and Matous (2011) interviewed the Hong Kongese and Japanese engineers after we noticed the lack of relational communication in the recorded interactions. These interviews unearthed highly ethnocentric views of "the other," and concerns about relationship-building across cultures.

As we can see, with triangulated studies involving CL, the corpus analysis provided the first step into the data by bringing to light something interesting, which is then followed up with qualitative methods. Some qualitative approaches have instead used a corpus as a repository or source of examples, with which to check their assumptions, for example CDA (see McEnery & Hardie, 2012, pp. 16–18).

According to Hunston, CDA, which has traditionally been one of the most top-down and qualitative approaches in applied linguistics, has benefited from a mixed-method approach. It is argued here that many of the benefits of CL to CDA also apply to IC. Hunston (2002, p. 123) proposes that CDA arguments:

> depend on assumptions about the influence upon people and on society of repetitions of ways of saying things, and about the power of language whose meaning is covert. It seems apparent, then, that corpora are a very useful tool for the critical linguist, because they identify repetitions, and can be used to identify implicit meaning.

Such an argument is also relevant to IC, given the importance of understanding implicit meanings in real encounters between interlocutors with differing avowed and ascribed sociocultural identities (Collier & Thomas, 1988) in context, and CL augments analysis through exploring repeated usage across a relevant range of texts and contexts.

When considering the complementarity of corpus methods with other methods, the empirical, but not positivistic, nature of mainstream CL research is apposite, as there is often confusion that CL is informed by a positivistic ontology and is therefore incompatible with qualitative, interpretative approaches and methods. Given the importance of interpretation in IC, this issue deserves some consideration.

There is agreement among corpus linguists that it is an empirical approach (Biber, 1988; Hunston, 2002; McCarthy, 1998; McEnery & Hardie, 2012; O'Keeffe et al., 2007; Sinclair, 1991; Stubbs, 1996, 2007). As such, there are two key methodological principles on which corpus linguistics is based (Stubbs, 2007, p. 131). The first concerns data collection and the researcher: "the observer must not influence what is observed. Data and analysis must be independent… corpus data are part of natural language use and not produced for purposes of linguistic analysis." Therefore, corpora comprise texts that are not created for the purpose of the corpus – they are recordings or copies of "real life" discourse. A collection of interviews conducted by the researcher for the purpose of making a corpus thus would not be regarded as a corpus, no matter how interesting the results. Furthermore, while accepting the impossibility of pure objectivity, many corpus linguists would take issue with Blommaert and Verschueren's (1998) assertion that "In the field of intercultural communication, there is no real theoretical difference between talking with the other and talking about the other," as in CL there is a categorical theoretical difference.

The second methodological principle relates to what is seen as important: "repeated events are significant… The frequent occurrence of lexical or grammatical patterns in a large text collection is good evidence of what is typical and routine in language use." In other words, CL is centrally concerned with what is usual in certain contexts, which would occur independent of the researcher. And while the main focus is on typical usage, such a focus also allows for a clearer understanding of the unique and the unusual.

Although CL is an empirical approach, Stubbs (2007, p. 131) stresses the difference between our understanding of what the language *is* (the ontology) and how we think we can *discover* the underlying meaning of the language in question (the epistemology, see Zhu Hua, Chapter 1, this volume). While CL assumes an empirical epistemology and thus methodology (asserting that data must be observable), it rejects a materialist ontology. In other words, the texts in a corpus are not seen as the essence of the language, or by extension that the only reality is what can be observed – the texts are merely the traces (the products) of the communicative events (the processes) that took place. Therefore, CL requires considerable interpretation of the data to discover patterns and infer their meaning, which would not be evident through introspection or manual analysis alone. At the risk of stating the obvious, but to the chagrin of many novice analysts, in CL the computer cannot interpret patterns in language – this is the role of the researcher. What technology and corpus methods can do is make such patterns visible, and "demonstrate order where only randomness or idiosyncrasy were visible" (Stubbs, 2007, p. 131), for instance collocation, discourse prosody, and evidence of social practices.

Such an empirical epistemology places a corpus approach to IC in contrast with much of the work in the field that relies *solely* on questionnaires, surveys and interviews as the source of data, and is more in line with Collier and Thomas's (1988) and Dervin's (2012) calls for discourse-based approaches to IC. Although there has been considerable debate within the field of discourse analysis over the value or appropriateness of a corpus approach to the analysis of discourse, from both theoretical and methodological perspectives (see Baker, 2006; Hunston, 2002, for discussion of these issues). Mona Baker, the pioneer of CL in cross-cultural translation studies, argues that we should not reject empirical research through falsely confusing it with positivistic objectivity, while acknowledging the impossibility of achieving a truly objective account. She states (2001, p. 13):

> Researchers today have to accept that total objectivity is an illusion if they are to be at all realistic, and that focusing on discourses rather than structures strengthens this element of subjectivity even more. At the same time, they have to devise some criteria for assessing what counts as serious research and what might be regarded as "questionable," "anecdotal" or "unreliable" within a given scholarly community.

CL can thus improve methodological rigor by addressing concerns of arbitrariness and circularity of analysis, while not entailing a positivistic stance.

This chapter has outlined how corpus methods can be used in IC, and has addressed some of the concerns that IC researchers may have about the practicality and appropriateness of combining CL and IC. In conclusion, for researchers interested in the language, functions, social practices and various semiotic means employed in spoken, written, virtual, and visual interactions and the social or cultural identities invoked through such communication in particular discourse communities, the constantly developing field of CL may offer new methods and insights.

Key Terms

Corpora Plural of corpus.
Corpus A principled collection of real life spoken, written or multimodal texts, stored on or accessible through a computer, which can be qualitatively and quantitatively analyzed.

Corpus Linguistics The empirical analysis of the language and signs within such texts, using computer software and combining quantitative and qualitative approaches.
Keywords Words and phrases that have statistical significance, or cultural salience.

Notes

1. The Cambridge and Nottingham Business English Corpus, copyright Cambridge University Press. Project directors Profs Ronald Carter and Michael McCarthy.
2. Funded by a grant from the JSPS, project number 00466781. Project Director Michael Handford.

References

Alvesson, M. (2002). *Understanding organizational culture*. Newbury Park, CA: Sage.
Baker, M. (1995). Corpora in translation studies: An overview and some suggestions for future research. *Target*, 7(2), 223–243.
Baker, M. (2001). The pragmatics of cross-cultural contact and some false dichotomies in translation studies. In M. Olohan (Ed.), *CTIS Occasional Papers*, 1, 7–20. Manchester: UMIST Centre for Translation & Intercultural Studies, 2001.
Baker, P. (2006). *Using corpora in discourse analysis*. London: Continuum.
Benwell, B., & Stokoe, E. (2006). *Discourse and identity*. Edinburgh: Edinburgh University Press.
Bhatia, V. Flowerdew, J., & Jones, R. (Eds.). (2008). *Advances in discourse studies*. London: Routledge.
Biber, D. (1988). *Variation across speech and writing*. Cambridge: Cambridge University Press.
Biber, D., Conrad, S., & Reppen, R. (1998). *Corpus linguistics: Investigating language structure and use*. Cambridge: Cambridge University Press.
Blommaert, J., & Verschueren, J. (1998). *Debating diversity: Analysing the discourse of tolerance*. London: Routledge.
Bucholtz, M., & Hall, K. (2005). Identity and interaction: A sociocultural linguistic approach. *Discourse Studies*, 7(4–5), 585–614.
Collier, M.J., & Thomas, M. (1988). Cultural Identity: An Interpretive Perspective. In Y.Y. Kim, & W.B. Gudykunst (Eds.), *Theories in Intercultural Communication* (pp. 99–120). Newbury Park, CA: Sage.
Connor, U. (2013). Corpus linguistics in intercultural rhetoric. In D. Belcher, & G. Nelson (Eds.), *Critical and corpus-based approaches to intercultural rhetoric*, (pp.8–21). Ann Arbor: University of Michigan Press.
Connor, U., Ruiz-Garrido, M., Rozycki, W., Goering, E., Kinney, E., & Koehler, J. (2008). Patient-directed medicine labeling: Text differences between the United States and Spain. *Communication & Medicine*, 5(2), 117–132.
Davies, M, (2008). *TIME Magazine Corpus: 100 million words, 1923–2006*. Available online at http://corpus.byu.edu/time/.
Dervin, F. (2012). Cultural identity, representation and Othering. In J. Jackson (Ed), *Routledge handbook of Intercultural Communication* (pp. 181–194). London: Routledge.
Fahey, M. (2005). Speech acts as intercultural danger zones: a cross-cultural comparison of the speech act of apologizing in Irish and Chilean soap operas. *Journal of Intercultural Communication*, 8, 1404–1634.

Flowerdew, L. (2004). The argument for using English Specialized corpora to understand academic and professional settings, In U. Connor, & T. Upton (Eds.), *Discourse in the professions: perspectives from corpus linguistics* (pp. 11–36). Amsterdam: John Benjamins.
Flowerdew, L. (2012). *Corpora and language education*. Basingstoke: Palgrave Macmillan.
Gee, J.P. (2005). *An introduction to discourse analysis*. London: Routledge.
Gee, J.P., & Handford, M. (Eds.). (2012). *The Routledge handbook of discourse analysis*. London: Routledge.
Handford, M. (2010). *The language of business meetings*. Cambridge: Cambridge University Press.
Handford, M. (2014). Cultural identities in international, interorganisational meetings: a corpus–informed discourse analysis of indexical "we," *Language and Intercultural Communication*, 14(1), 41–58.
Handford, M., & Matous, P. (2011). Lexicogrammar in the international construction industry: A corpus–based case study of Japanese–Hong-Kongese on-site interactions in English. *English for Specific Purposes*, 30(2), 87–100.
Hoey, M. (2005). *Lexical priming*. Abingdon: Routledge.
Hofstede, G. (1991). *Culture and organizations*. New York: McGraw-Hill.
Holliday, A. (1999). Small cultures. *Applied Linguistics*, 20(2), 237–264.
Hunston, S. (2002). *Corpora in applied linguistics*. Cambridge: Cambridge University Press.
Hyland, K. (2009). *Academic discourse*. London: Continuum
Hyland, K., Chau, M. H., & Handford, M. (Eds.) (2012). *Corpus applications in applied linguistics*. London: Continuum.
Knight, S. (2011). *Multimodality and active listenership*. London: Continuum
Mautner, G. (2009). Checks and balances: How corpus linguistics can contribute to CDA. In R. Wodak & M. Meyer (Eds.), *Methods of critical discourse analysis* (pp. 122–143). Thousand Oaks, CA: Sage.
McCarthy, M. (1998). *Spoken language and applied linguistics*. Cambridge: Cambridge University Press.
McEnery, T., & Hardie, A. (2012). *Corpus linguistics*. Cambridge: Cambridge University Press.
O'Keeffe, A., & Adolphs, S. (2008). Using a corpus to look at variational pragmatics: Response tokens in British and Irish discourse. In K.P. Schneider, & A. Barron (Eds.), *Variational pragmatics* (pp. 69–98). Amsterdam: John Benjamins.
O'Keeffe, A., & McCarthy, M. (Eds.). (2010). *The Routledge handbook of corpus linguistics*. London: Routledge
O'Keeffe, A., Carter, R., & McCarthy, M. (2007). *From corpus to classroom*. Cambridge: Cambridge University Press.
Reppen, R. (2010). Building a corpus: what are the key considerations? In A. O'Keeffe & M. McCarthy (Eds.), *The Routledge handbook of corpus linguistics* (pp. 31–37). Abingdon: Routledge.
Scott, M., & Tribble C. (2006). *Textual patterns*. Amsterdam: John Benjamins.
Seidlhofer, B. (2012). Corpora and English as a Lingua Franca, In K. Hyland, M.H. Chau, & M. Handford (Eds.) *Corpus applications in applied linguistics* (pp. 135–149). London Continuum.
Sinclair, J. (1991). *Corpus, concordance, collocation*. Oxford: Oxford University Press.
Spinzi, C. (2011). Corpus linguistics and intercultural communicative approach: A synergy, *Cultus*, 4, 9–20.
Stubbs, M. (1996). *Text and corpus analysis*. Oxford: Blackwell.
Stubbs, M. (2007). On texts, corpora and models of language. In M. Hoey, M. Mahlberg, M. Stubbs, & W. Teubert (Eds.), *Text, discourse and corpora* (pp. 163–190). London: Continuum.
Swales, J. (2002). Integrated and fragmented worlds: EAP materials & corpus linguistics. In J. Flowerdew (Ed.), *Academic discourse* (pp. 150–164). Harlow: Longman.

Thomas, J. (1983). Cross cultural pragmatic failure. *Applied Linguistics*, 4, 91–112.
Tognini Bonelli, E. (2001) *Corpus linguistics at work*. Amsterdam: John Benjamins.
Tsuchiya, K. (2013). *Listener behaviours in intercultural encounters*. Amsterdam: John Benjamins.
Tsuchiya, K., & Handford, M. (2014). A corpus-driven analysis of repair in a professional ELF meeting: not "letting it pass." *Journal of Pragmatics*, 64, 117–131.
Widdowson, H. (1998). Context, community & authentic language. *TESOL Quarterly*, 32(4), 705–716.

Corpus Resources

Antconc Tools: www.antlab.sci.waseda.ac.jp/software.html
Corpus resources at the University of Washington (a useful link to many sites): http://courses.washington.edu/englhtml/engl560/corplingresources.htm
Mark Davies free corpora: www.corpus.byu.edu
The Sketch Engine: www.sketchengine.co.uk
VOICE corpus www.univie.ac.at/voice/

22 Narrative Analysis

Anna De Fina

> **Summary**
>
> In this chapter I review some of the main current trends in narrative analysis and discuss its applications to the study of Intercultural Communication. First I propose some broad theoretical–methodological distinctions among narrative approaches and then I focus on two main areas: research on narratives as ways of telling, and research on narratives as reflecting and shaping identities and experiences. Within the latter area I specifically discuss interactionally oriented studies, showing how they have evolved through time from focusing on groupings broadly defined in terms of ethnicity, race, or national origin, towards close studies of smaller communities and their practices. I close the chapter with the discussion of a case study.

Background

The field of narrative studies constitutes today a wide interdisciplinary area in which research from a variety of social science fields converge. The beginnings of a movement towards the use of narrative for the study of social phenomena can be traced back to the late 1980s and early 1990s. Indeed, with the exception of Labov and Waletzky's 1967 groundbreaking article on the structure of narratives of personal experience, the foundational work in narrative analysis was produced in those years by scholars who came from many different fields such as social psychology (Bruner, 1986), anthropology (Hymes, 1981; Rosaldo, 1993), history (White, 1987), sociology (Riessman, 1991), and sociolinguistics (Schiffrin, 1996), just to name a few, and gave birth to the so called "narrative turn." The thrust behind this turn was a growing dissatisfaction with experimental methods and positivist views of research in the social sciences, a stress on the significance of individual experience as a basis for social behavior and representations, a re-evaluation of subjectivity and interpretive complexity in the research process, and a concern with including social agents' own views and experiences. Although thriving, this wide field of studies is far from being unified in terms of methodologies and approaches, and so one of the objectives of this chapter will be to distinguish some of the main threads within the dizzying variety of methodologies of narrative analysis, to discuss their application to the study of Intercultural Communication and to provide examples of how different types of narrative analysis can enhance understanding of cultural issues.

Before discussing the questions that narrative analysts ask and how they may be pertinent to research in intercultural issues, I will try to describe broad methodological differences between approaches in the field. A first division concerns study foci: while some studies concentrate on the structure of stories, others focus on topics and topic presentation within stories, still others focus on aspects of storytelling as an event: for example the participation structure (that is, the roles of narrators and listeners) and storytelling strategies. Thus, there is a general divide in narrative approaches between a focus on stories as structured texts, a focus on stories as vehicles for the communication of content, and a focus on stories as communicative events (see De Fina & Georgakopoulou, 2012, pp. 23–25). Approaches to stories as texts and approaches to stories as vehicles for content generally pay less attention to the context in which narratives are produced, while approaches that regard storytelling as an event are very interested in the process through which stories emerge.

Another broad division concerns the types of data taken as the basis for analysis: while a great many studies work with research-generated data, for example stories elicited or spontaneously produced in interviews and other research contexts, in other approaches the focus is on naturally occurring data, for example on stories that arise in informal contexts such as conversations, or in formal contexts such as classrooms and other kinds of institutional environments. Finally, while most research in the field is qualitative and makes use of ethnography, there are also studies based on experimental designs. These methodological choices reflect differences in objectives and research questions, but also profound divergences in the way narratives themselves are defined and conceived. Describing these differences in detail is beyond the scope of this chapter, so I will just sketch the main point of disagreement between trends of narrative analysis. While approaches that focus on stories as texts usually take the view that stories can be defined in canonical terms according to well established characteristics, such as being recounts of past events, being chronologically organized, and containing climatic events and denouements, approaches that focus on storytelling events and practices do not work with presupposed assumptions about story structure but try to understand what counts as a story for participants.

Narrative Analysis and Intercultural Communication

A great deal of research in narrative analysis that uses the different approaches described above poses and tries to answer questions that are all relevant to Intercultural Communication studies. Indeed, narrative analysts try to establish how storytelling or stories shape and are shaped by practices and beliefs that are characteristic of communities sharing the same culture. Among the issues that have been investigated are the following:

- what specific forms stories take in particular communities and how storytelling events are structured
- how story topics and story content are related to ideologies and cultural practices associated with a particular community
- how identities are constructed and conveyed through stories by particular groups
- how stories construct and reflect intergroup relations.

All of these questions are pertinent to the study of Intercultural Communication in that the latter basically concerns the investigation of the characteristics, practices, and ideologies of different cultural groups (see Gudykunst, 2003 and Zhu Hua, Chapter 1, this volume for a discussion).

A further attempt to group different kinds of studies focused on or based on narrative analysis leads us to recognize two big categories: on the one hand there are researchers who focus on storytelling styles and ways of telling as cultural constructs, i.e. that describe the characteristics of stories or the way they are told and managed in particular cultural groupings. On the other hand, there are studies that use stories and storytelling as a methodological tool to investigate individual and group experiences and identities. Although there is a great deal of overlap between the two categories, I will treat them separately in order to facilitate a discussion of the theoretical methodological issues involved.

Stories as Ways of Telling

The study of storytelling ways and styles has as its main aim the discovery and analysis of cultural specificity. Research that belongs in this category is interested in describing and understanding such specificity and in drawing possible comparisons between story structures and aspects of the storytelling event across communities. The methods used to carry out this kind of research have been mostly ethnographic (although, as we will see, there are some exceptions) and analyses of the narratives have been based on the linguistic study of patterns at different levels. I will start with ethnographically inspired research carried out by anthropologists on non-Western communities. These are studies of particular groups in which researchers used ethnographic, participant observation of storytelling events as they were carried out in the community as a basis for their analyses, but also grounded their interpretations on knowledge that they gathered about such communities' culture more generally in order to connect storytelling practices with other salient cultural aspects. In these investigations, narrative is seen as a form of performance, and attention is paid to the mechanisms that make narratives pleasurable to an audience. Much of this research was carried out in the late 1980s and 1990s. Examples of these types of investigations are provided by the work of anthropologists Hymes and Scollon & Scollon. Hymes (1981) developed his ethnopoetic method, which is a close description of formal (phonological and syntactic) patterns of organization of narratives in the tellings of members of Native American tribes. He showed that such narratives indeed presented very distinctive patterning of sounds and meanings which reflected more general cultural models in the community, but also that forms of knowledge that were typical of that group were found in the content of stories told. Similarly, Scollon & Scollon (1981) described Atabaskan people's narratives also using a kind of ethnopoetic analysis – that is, dividing the stories into lines, stanzas, and episodes, and showed how both the forms of the narratives and their content responded to Atabaskan conceptions about the role of stories as main sources of transmission of knowledge and also specific views about agency.

Ethnographic based studies of storytelling by different groups have also been conducted by scholars interested in investigating the role of storytelling in education and socialization. For example Michaels (1981) and Gee (1986), who were interested in unequal school performance by minority children, studied narratives told at school by African American children in classroom. In particular, they investigated the way topics were presented in narratives in response to teachers' elicitations during telling time in school. They found that, as opposed to Caucasian children, African American children preferred a style in which connections between different episodes in a narrative were created based on free associations rather than on logical and temporal links. Gee (1989) attributed topic-associating style in narrative to a preference for oral styles of discourse in African American communities. Similar arguments were made by Brice Heath (1983) who analyzed storytelling within a wider study of literacy practices among American communities. She compared families living in two cities in the Piedmont region of North Carolina which were also different ethnically, since one was predominantly white and one predominantly African American. She found that storytelling practices reflected different views about socializing children. While in the African American community children were encouraged to experiment with storytelling and to be creative, in the white community the stress was on telling stories that were both factual and well formed.

Much research within socialization studies also contributed to this line of inquiry, openly focusing on cross-cultural comparison of storytelling styles. For example, Blum Kulka (1997) observed and compared how Jewish American and Israeli families managed storytelling during dinner-time. Instead of investigating solely story structure or topic, she also analyzed the structure of participation: that is who was allowed to tell stories, how children and adults were expected to take part in storytelling and what kinds of interactions developed around narratives. Among other things, Blum Kulka found that Israeli families preferred a much more involved style and that they gave children greater participatory rights as opposed to Jewish American families who favored more monological performances. Similar studies focused on individual national groups or subgroups (see for example Georgakopoulou, 1997 for Greeks, Johnstone, 1990 for Midwesterners) or on comparisons of different groups (see Miller, Wiley, Fung, & Liang, 1997).

Some research on cross-cultural differences in storytelling has been conducted also through experimental methodologies, in particular when inspired by interest in cognitive issues. Among the most significant examples of this trend was the "Pear Stories" study conducted by Chafe and associates in 1980. Chafe elicited retellings of a silent movie by members of a variety of national groups. Among his objectives was the investigation of ways in which culture may influence people's understanding and representations of reality. Chafe showed that there were differences among national groups, for example in the amount and manner of evaluation of the events and of protagonists in the silent movie and in the strategies chosen to refer to characters. Some more recent studies have compared the way stories are told to children by mothers belonging to different national groups through semi-experimental designs involving for example the use of the same story book to elicit narratives by mothers in the two groups (see Harkins & Ray, 2004).

To summarize: studies of storytelling styles have focused either on individual cultures or on open cross-cultural comparisons. While the former have offered descriptions of narrative practices and performances relying mainly on ethnographic observation, the latter have used a greater variety of methods, including experimental designs. What these studies have in common is that they show that different cultural groups exhibit systematic differences in the way in which they structure stories, the preferred topics, and telling and participation rights and patterns, and that these divergences reflect wider differences in ideologies and the organization of social life. Studies that directly address cultural differences also highlight some of the difficulties of intercultural and cross-cultural inquiry in general, in particular the difficulty of defining culturally homogeneous communities and the risks of falling into stereotyped conceptions deriving from descriptions that are not based on participant-generated categories (see De Fina & Georgakopoulou, 2012, and Koven, 2015, on this point). Indeed, recent reflections on cultural and intercultural phenomena point to the fact that groupings in terms of national or ethnic identity are too sweeping and that there may be a great deal of internal variability even within communities that are supposed to be homogeneous (see Scollon, Scollon, & Jones, 2012). As a consequence, more recent research on storytelling has turned away from direct cross-cultural comparison and from descriptions of individual cultural practices based on national or ethnic groupings focusing instead on smaller groupings and communities of practices and concentrating on emic (that is participant-based) definitions of categories and practices.

Storytelling, Experience and Identity

A great deal of research in narrative, particularly in the last two decades, uses storytelling as a window into the way experiences and identities are communicated and constructed in particular groups. The latter are not necessarily defined in terms of a homogeneous culture, but more in terms of common ground that may be constituted by a more varied set of elements such as shared practices, experiences and characteristics (both more stable like gender or ethnicity and temporal like being an immigrant), etc. Thus, studies of narrative have targeted a great variety of communities: such as immigrants (De Fina, 2003; De Fina & King, 2011; Koven, 2013; Pavlenko, 2001; Relaño Pastor, 2014), asylum seekers (Maryns, 2005), women (Coates, 2002; Georgakopulou, 2007; Holmes, 2006; Shiffrin, 1996), men (Kiesling, 2006), members of the LGBQ community (Gray, 2009) marginal group members such as homeless (Boydell, Goering, & Morrell-Bellai, 2000), or travelers (Piazza, 2014), divorcees (Riessman, 1990), professionals (Linde, 1993) just to mention a few. As we will discuss, narrative has also been used as a tool to elicit the affirmation of new identities and the construction of new apprehensions of experience.

As mentioned at the beginning of this chapter, the popularity of the use of stories in the study of experiences and identities derives from the imperative of striving to incorporate participant's own voices in the study of social phenomena and from the stress on qualitative methods that characterized the narrative turn in the social sciences. Indeed, narrative turn proponents saw narrative not only as tool of research, but also as a fundamental mode of apprehension of experience in all cultures and among all human groupings. Bruner (1986) famously opposed the narrative to the logico-scientific "mode of thought," legitimating the former as an authentic and widespread form of knowledge capable of representing humans' search for catharsis and aesthetic pleasure. As we will discuss, this fundamental evaluation of storytelling as an authentic and unmediated representation of experience is present in a great deal of research based on autobiographical narrative.

As it was the case with research on culture and narrative, investigators who study relationships between narrative, identities and the representation of experience use different paradigms and methods, however most of the work in the area is qualitative and often ethnographic in nature and only rarely resorts to quantitative and experimental design.

The big questions that research on narrative identities and experiences asks are:

- How are particular experiences recounted by members of communities whose life is in many ways marked by those experiences?
- How do members of communities define in-group and out-group membership in and through stories?

Common ways of describing experiences and of creating memberships boundaries can be seen as defining elements of particular cultures; therefore, work on narratives and identities is very relevant to intercultural studies.

Studies within this camp vary along a series of parameters:

1 what kinds of stories they use as tools of research: for example autobiographies or life stories versus other narrative types, elicited versus nonelicited narratives, oral versus written narratives
2 whether they use case studies or more extended corpora
3 what kind of research environment they choose: for example interviews vs research-independent settings, mixed settings, etc.
4 which element/aspect of storytelling they focus upon: whether on content, for example story topic, or aspects of the storytelling interaction, for example strategies or participation frameworks
5 whether they include a longitudinal component or not

6   whether they use stories as tools to elicit identity displays or they target storytelling as a discourse activity that reveals ways of doing identity.

These parameters are not necessarily exclusive of each other, as researchers mix methods and compound objectives, but they are useful both to evaluate research and to design projects. They also reflect different conceptions of the relations between narrative and identities even though they also share much common ground. Indeed, most researchers in the field nowadays subscribe, at least in theory, to a social constructionist and postmodern view of identity as process, not as product (see De Fina, Schiffrin, & Bamberg, 2006; Angouri, Chapter 3, this volume). The latter implies that there is a stress on the performative aspects that characterize identity displays and constructions as forms of "doing" rather than as forms of "being." Most also accept the idea that identities are plural, polyphonic and at times conflicting, and that people may claim membership into a variety of groups and communities. They also tend to agree that identities are evolving and emergent so that they cannot be conceived of as fixed tags that people use to describe self and others. However, differences still exist in the emphasis given to coherence and unity in narrated selves, in the attention paid to the local context in which stories are produced, including the presence and activity of interlocutors and their participation in the creation of identities, and conversely in the stress given to the linking of local contexts with wider sociohistorical contexts. These differences are at the basis of divergent choices in methodological terms. A broad division can be traced between studies that target or use autobiographical narrative and studies that target other kinds of narratives such as narratives of personal experience, anecdotes, small stories, etc.

Research on autobiographical narrative tends to use elicited narratives or existing written biographies and focuses on the texts produced, for example studying the themes dealt by narrators and their hierarchical organization, the metaphors and rhetorical figures employed to convey those themes, the ways linguistic choices relate to agency and the narrators' roles in the story world and in the world more generally. These choices are then examined in the light of more general cultural constructs such as ideologies and shared representations. In life story research there is a tendency to see the project of storying the self as always involving the creation of coherent identities (McAdams, 1993). An example of this type of study is Linde's (1993) examination of narratives told by professionals, in which she interviewed subjects and asked them to tell their life story. Stories were collected over the course of several interviews and their content was then analyzed in terms of overarching themes used by narrators to give coherence to experience. Such "coherence principles" reflect cultural systems and commonsense understandings of reality that can be seen as shared by members of a culture. For instance, the interviewees resorted to psychoanalysis or astrology as systems that provided coherence to their life choices.

Life and biographical narratives are also often used to investigate language experiences. In her study of "cross cultural" autobiographical narratives Pavlenko (2001) used a corpus of published and written autobiographies and autobiographical essays to investigate issues of identity related to language learning. She collected a total of 28 autobiographical texts and analyzed explicit references by the authors to issues of language and identity, explicit statements related to "repositioning," that is, changes in identity and implicit alignments with characters in the story or "members of the audience" (p. 323). Pavlenko then related these identity negotiations to the need to fight monolingual ideologies and to create new identities and also to the internalization of certain mainstream ideas about language, ethnicity, race, and so forth.

Applications of narrative methods to the field of language teaching and learning have expanded exponentially in the last decade thanks to the "sociolinguistic turn" (Dornyei & Usioda, 2011) in applied linguistics and second language acquisition, the stress on the subjectivity and complexity of learning experiences (Miller et al., 1997), and the importance placed on investment by language learners (Norton, 2000). Thus, scholars in second language learning and acquisition have used autobiographical narratives about language learning to investigate how individuals evaluate and live the experience of learning a language and the types of agency that they convey in the language-learning stories (see Miller, 2014; Barkhuizen, 2015).

Autobiographical narratives such as journals and diaries have become popular in research about language learning and teaching not simply as research instruments, but also as tools for bringing about changes in attitudes and to develop learners' or teachers' awareness and sense of self. Learners' diary studies, which have been used since the 1970s (see Bailey, 1983; Schumann & Schumann, 1977) and continue to be used (see Casanave, 2012), consist of entries about the process of learning a language written in chronological order for a period of time and then collected and thematically analyzed to produce a report. Thematic analyses look not only at the topics and foci of concern that come up in the writing, but also at their progression and transformation over time (see Kohronen, 2014). Studies based on diaries and journals have also been done with teachers. The objective is to both better understand one's teaching practices and to raise awareness about them. For example Canagarajah (2012) used a type of autobiographical narrative to discuss the situation of peripheric teachers in the TESOL community and to raise awareness about their possibility of inhabiting new identities.

To sum up, life story and biographical analyses present a series of advantages for studying groups and communities: through thematic analyses they highlight topics and perspectives that are unique to such communities and provide a deeper understanding of how members deal with particular experiences. As noted by Barkhuizen (2015), diary studies for example, "are useful for researchers who aim to explore and understand affective factors, learning strategies, and the learners' own perceptions of their language learning through information that is recorded while learners are actually engaged in the process of learning. They make accessible data unobservable by other methods (Faerch & Kasper, 1987) providing a rich, detailed picture of learning, particularly the social and cognitive dimensions of learners from their particular point of view." (p. 101). Studies based on autobiographical writing also have a significant action component in that they help members of communities (both research and professional ones) to make sense of their experiences, to build new identities and to cast a critical look on presuppositions and conventional ideas about their activities and profession.

There are, however, some limitations to both life-story research and research based on autobiographical writing. The main limitation has been until recently the heavy reliance on thematic analysis with a lack of attention to context, and therefore the tendency to equate autobiographical writing with an "authentic" expression of the self. In addition, life story research, in contrast to autobiography-based studies, also tends to put too much stress on continuity and coherence in identity constructions as opposed to fragmentation and chaos.

The most recent research in narrative analysis has followed the general shift in sociolinguistics towards a much more grounded view of identity and a much more practice-based conception of semiotic activity. This is already visible in the field of research on narratives of language learning that we just reviewed above, where new approaches have started to focus more on the process itself of constructing a narrative as a meaning-making activity (see for example the concept of "narrative knowledging" as proposed by Barkhuizen, 2011). These changes reflect the fact that narrative-based research, like identity research, has shifted its attention towards nuanced and close analyses of narratives in interactional contexts and to a consideration of how narrative practices are embedded within other practices (see De Fina & Georgakopoulou, 2008). Researchers do not relate identities and cultures directly through categories of national, ethnic or racial belonging since it is now much clearer that such wide grouping may share a great deal in terms of ideologies and practices, but that they also harbor as many divisions and conflicts within themselves. Thus, studies focused on identity target smaller communities and often rely on the construct of "communities of practice" (henceforth CoP) as proposed by Lave and Wenger (1991). The CoP framework regards identity as a form of doing that happens and develops through time within common enterprises and shared activities. As a consequence, rather than studying wide groupings and wide identities, researchers focus on particular groups in specific contexts. To take a narrative example, this approach has been applied by Holmes (2006) to the analysis of the role that narratives, in particular anecdotes, play in the construction and negotiation of gendered professional identities within specific work organizations in New Zealand. This type of study exemplifies many of the characteristics of more recent approaches to identities in narratives:

- it focuses on narratives embedded in interactions;
- it targets a specific group within a particular context;
- it looks at identity as a type performance;
- it takes relationality and dialogism as central to the display and interpretation of identities.

Similarly, studies that apply narrative analysis to the investigation of identities in the last decade have moved away from exclusive reliance on thematic analysis and have started to take the context of interaction and the embedding of different contexts in the production and interpretation of narratives much more seriously. As a result, narrative analysis has focused more and more on the processes of negotiation of identities, on the strategies used by narrators to engage and influence their audiences, on audience and participants' co-construction of narrative identities, and on how different types of stories besides the life story or the extended canonical narrative can also have different functions and roles in the construction of identities.

This new focus has produced important changes in both studies based on research-elicited narratives and studies based on naturally occurring narratives. It is noticeable, for example, how narrative analysts have recently revisited the traditional division between interview narratives and conversational ones, underscoring the importance of treating all narratives as contextually embedded. De Fina and Perrino (2011) make the point that opposing interview data to "natural" data creates a false dilemma, since interview narratives are as subject to the constraints imposed by the local context as any other interactional event. They argue that ignoring those constraints, not including the interviewer's voice and presence in the analysis, trying to erase any trace of the research context, is what has led to a widespread rejection of interview narratives by interactionally oriented researchers. Thus, analyses of interview narratives today tend to incorporate those aspects much more readily.

As mentioned, another significant consequence of the "interactionist shift" in narrative studies, that is the view of narrative as always embedded in concrete interactional contexts rather than as free-standing text, has been the growing interest in how different kinds of stories can be used as research tools and objects. Besides the canonical story described by Labov (1972) as consisting of an abstract, orientation, complicating action, evaluation, and coda, other kinds of stories have been used as a focus and tool of research. We already saw that Holmes described anecdotes. Georgakopoulou (2007) has proposed the use of "small stories," that is, brief narratives often related to recent and not very momentous events, sometimes embedded in social media or topically related to social media, as a source of data and of interpretation on identities. In her study of adolescent girls in a London school, she found that small stories were used by these adolescents not only to comment and bond around romantic interests, but also as terrains to construct and present different kinds of positions vis-à-vis gender discourses and ideologies.

Interactionist analyses of narrative regard as important the interplay of two worlds in stories: the storytelling world, that is the interactional context of the telling, and the story world, that is the world of the story with its protagonists and actions. They look for connections between those two worlds and how they in turn reflect and shape identities and representations. One way of accounting for this interplay is through the construct of positioning as proposed by Bamberg (1997). The author argues that positioning by narrators can be examined at three levels:

1   positioning vis-à-vis story characters;
2   positioning vis-à-vis other participants in the interaction;
3   positioning vis-à-vis more general categories of being such as those proposed in dominant discourses.

Positioning analysis has been widely applied to the study of identity display in narratives in different environments: from conversational stories to interview based narratives (for a discussion see Depperman, 2013).

Case in Point

De Fina, A. (2003). *Identity in narrative. A study of immigrant discourse.* Amsterdam: John Benjamins.

In order to illustrate some of the methods and issues related to interactionist approaches in narrative analysis, I will use my own study on the construction and negotiation of identities among Mexican economic immigrants to the United States. Below I summarize the research questions, design of the study, analytic instruments and findings.

Research questions: The general research question was: How do Mexican immigrants construct and negotiate identities in and through narratives?

Subjects and methods: The study subjects were 14 immigrants (nine men and five women), 12 of whom came from the same village in Mexico. Since it was difficult to approach immigrants directly, as being mostly undocumented they were afraid of being interviewed, I used a snowball sampling technique in order to find people to interview. Before starting the interviews, I had made contact, through a common friend, with a young Mexican man, called Ismael, who was himself an immigrant and who had become very interested in the topic of this research, and had offered to introduce me to people from his village, all of whom lived in Maryland. Thus, I had the opportunity to visit the interviewees' homes several times in some cases, to observe and discuss their lifestyle, and the conditions in which they lived and worked. I was introduced to them as a friend and was treated as a friend. I planned and carried out interviews based on a loose set of questions about migration motives and experiences, but also followed the conversation as it developed. To elicit narratives of personal experience I always asked the question: "Is there an experience that you had here in the United States that has particularly struck you?" That question elicited narratives in many cases, but not always. I discussed all the interviews with Ismael who helped me contextualize the talk and information.

Analysis: From the corpus of interviews, I selected narratives of personal experience as described in Labov & Waletzky (1967) and Labov (1972), and chronicles of the border crossing, which were accounts of this event told in chronological order.

I focused on two aspects of identity: the representation and elaboration of social roles, and the presentation and negotiation of membership into communities. The first aspect was connected to agency, or the degree of initiative and responsibility attributed to the self in storytelling worlds and to the degree of orientation to others in both storytelling world and story world. Negotiation of membership into communities was studied through categorization of self and others as done by narrators again both in the story world and in negotiation with me as an interviewer.

Thus, the analysis of identity did not focus on the content of the stories, but on the strategies used by narrators to construct the self.

Results: Results indicated a prevalence of nonagentive constructions and a strong tendency of narrators to identify with different in-groups (the family, members of their nation of origin, members of the community of immigrants, etc.). Categorization processes were also shown to be strategic, in the sense that categories of affiliation were managed according to topics, stances and communicative objectives. I also found that different story-world experiences elicited different types of categories for membership.

Discussion and conclusions: My research illustrates many of the dilemmas, advantages and disadvantages of narrative research in general and of interactionist approaches in particular.

With respect to the dilemma between studying naturally occurring narratives or interview-generated narratives, my work illustrates how researchers do not always have a choice between these two kinds of foci. In the case of a population of undocumented immigrants like the ones I studied, it would have been extremely difficult to conduct a traditional ethnography – to tape-record and observe participants in their everyday environments – because of their reticence about being recorded. Thus, interviews offered the only tool to tap into processes of self and other construction by members of this group.

With respect to the choice and description of communities, my research illustrates that there is always a risk of creating a community where there is none. By choosing a group of people, the researcher may be artificially creating a group that does not exist in real life. That is why the analyst needs to look very carefully at the process through which both interviewer and interviewees negotiate identities. For example, in the case of categorization processes related to stories, the analyst needs to trace back first mentions of categories (for example ethnic categories), who introduced them and how they were negotiated before and after the story was told. If the analyst only studies for example how characters are categorized in story worlds, there is the risk of missing the role that interviewers may play in the way identities and experiences are presented through stories (on this point, see Dervin this volume, Chapter 9).

The choice of units of analysis is another important issue. Selecting the type of narratives that are going to be the object of study always implies looking at the data through particular lenses. In this case, the fact that I focused on narratives of personal experience and chronicles excluded other possible sources of interpretation such as habitual or hypothetical narratives, small stories, etc.

The interpretation and generalization of results is of course the central issue for qualitative research. In the case of my study, for example, certain tendencies shown by the interviewees, such as the trend towards un-agentivity and their orientation to a social view of the self, could, at a superficial level, be attributed to their "culture" as Mexicans. But, there are other possible sources of explanation for these tendencies. For example, the fact that interviewees were mostly undocumented seemed to play an important part in their development of a "defensive" discourse style in which they did not want to stress responsibility. And their dependence and reliance on others in the process of migration and settlement could explain their social orientation in stories. Thus, this study also shows how narrative discourse and identity constructions are embedded in different contexts at different levels and that interpretations must rely on ethnographic observation.

Finally, my study illustrates the labor-intensive nature of qualitative narrative analysis. In order to analyze stories within their interactional context the researcher needs to transcribe the whole interview and pay attention to all the details of interactional exchanges. Each transcription takes hours and the analysis is as elaborate. There is no coding that can substitute for this time-consuming effort.

However, the study also illustrates the virtues of a narrative approach to the study of experiences and identities. First, the insights on the ways identities are constructed come from the analysis of the data, not from some previously formed hypothesis, and therefore they provide authentic understandings of the issues that are being investigated. In my study I had no preconceived idea about the types of identities that would be put in play by Mexican undocumented workers before I studied the data. Secondly, narratives are a discourse genre that allows for the creation of emotional bonds between interviewers and interviewees. When interviewees tell stories they establish a much stronger connection with the interviewer because of the emotional import of narratives. Stories allow narrators to project themselves into worlds of experience without having to openly evaluate them and discuss them, but they also invite evaluation and participation by the researcher. Thus, they represent both an easy way to talk for interviewees and a significant source of data for the researchers. Thirdly, through the analysis of stories analysts have access to experiences that would not otherwise be accessible through more traditional and quantitative methods. Because qualitative interviews invite reflection on experience, they also usually lead to the telling of stories that convey them and such narratives, as shown, are rich sources of interpretation. In all these ways narrative analysis is an important tool for the study of communities, identities and experiences.

Further development will very likely open the field to the investigation of a wider set of contexts for storytelling, particularly those that pertain to mediated communication and to digital narratives. Qualitative analysis of narrative is also expanding to areas where it had not been a popular method in the past, such as the field of language teaching and learning and such trend will most likely continue.

Key Terms

Narrative Generic term referring to different kinds of noncanonical genres including habitual narratives, small stories, generic narratives and so forth.
Story A canonical narrative genre usually characterized by the presence of chronological ordering of events and causal links among them, a disruption and resolution, evaluation by the narrator.
Story world The world described and evoked by the narrator with its characters and events.
Storytelling world The interactional context in which the story is told, which includes narrators, audiences and their processes of communication.

References

Bailey, K.M. (1983). Competitiveness and anxiety in adult second language learning: Looking at and through the Diary Studies. In H.W. Seliger & M.H. Long (Eds.), *Classroom oriented research in second language acquisition* (pp. 67–103). Rowley, MA: Newbury House.
Bamberg, M. (Ed.) (1997). *Oral versions of personal experience: three decades of narrative analysis*. Special Issue of *Journal of Narrative and Life History*, 7.
Bamberg, M. (1997). Positioning between structure and performance. *Journal of Narrative and Life History* 7(1–4), 335–342.
Barkhuizen, G. (Ed.) (2013). *Narrative research in applied linguistics*. Cambridge: Cambridge University Press.
Barkhuizen, G. (2011). Narrative knowledging in TESOL. *TESOL Quarterly*, 8(1), 1–25.
Barkhuizen, G. (2015). Narrative knowledging in second language teaching and learning contexts. In A. De Fina & A. Georgakopoulou (Eds.), *Handbook of narrative analysis* (pp. 97–116). Oxford: Wiley-Blackwell.
Blum-Kulka, S. (1997). *Dinner talk: cultural patterns of sociability and socialization in family discourse*. Mahwah, NJ: Lawrence Erlbaum Associates.
Boydell, K., Goering, P., & Morrell-Bellai, T. (2000). Narratives of Identity: Re-presentation of self in people who are homeless. *Qualitative Health Research*, 10(1), 26–38.

Brice Heath, S. (1983). *Ways with words*. Cambridge: Cambridge University Press.
Bruner J. (1986). *Actual minds, possible worlds*. Cambridge, MA: Harvard University Press.
Canagarajah, A.S. (2012). Teacher development in a global profession: An autoethnography. *TESOL Quarterly*, 46(2), 258–279.
Casanave, C.P. (2012). Diary of a dabbler: Ecological influences on an EFL teacher's efforts to study Japanese informally. *TESOL Quarterly*, 46(4), 642–670.
Chafe, W. (ed.) (1980). *The Pear Stories: Cognitive, cultural, and linguistic aspects of narrative production*. Norwood, NJ: Ablex.
Coates, J. (2002). *Men talk: Stories in the making of masculinity*. Oxford: Blackwell.
De Fina, A. (2003). *Identity in narrative. A study of immigrant discourse*. Amsterdam: John Benjamins.
De Fina, A., & Georgakopoulou, A. (2008). Analysing narratives as practices. *Qualitative Research*, 8(3), 379–387.
De Fina, A., & Georgakopoulou, A. (2012). *Analyzing narrative: Discourse and sociolinguistic perspectives*. Cambridge. Cambridge University Press.
De Fina, A., & Georgakopoulou, A. (Eds.) (2015). *Handbook of narrative analysis*. Oxford: Wiley-Blackwell.
De Fina, A., & King, K. (2011). Language problem or language conflict? Narratives of immigrant women's experiences in the US. *Discourse Studies*, 13(2), 163–188.
De Fina, A., & Perrino, S. (Eds.). (2011). *Narratives in interviews, Interviews in narrative studies*. Special Issue *Language in Society, 40*.
De Fina, A., Schiffrin, D., & Bamberg, M. (Eds.) (2006). *Discourse and identity*. Cambridge: Cambridge University Press.
Depperman, A. (ed.). (2013). *Positioning in narrative interaction*. Special Issue *Narrative Inquiry, 23(1)*.
Dörnyei, Z., & Ushioda, E. (2011). *Teaching and researching motivation* (2nd ed.). Harlow: Pearson Education
Faerch, C., & Kasper, G. (1987). *Introspection in second language research*. Clevedon: Multilingual Matters.
Gee, J.P. (1986). Units in the production of narrative discourse. *Discourse Processes*, 9, 391–422.
Gee, J.P. (1989). Two styles of narrative construction and their linguistic and educational implications. *Discourse Processes*, 12, 287–307.
Georgakopoulou, A. (1997). *Narrative performances: A study of modern Greek storytelling*. Amsterdam: John Benjamins.
Georgakopoulou, A. (2007). *Small stories, interaction and identities*. Amsterdam: John Benjamins.
Gray, M. (2009). Negotiating identities/queering desires: Coming out online and the remediation of the coming-out story. *Journal of Computer-Mediated Communication*, 14(4), 1162–1189.
Gudykunst, William B. (2003). Intercultural communication theories. In W.B. Gudykunst (Ed.), *Cross-cultural and intercultural communication* (pp. 167–189). Thousand Oaks, CA: Sage.
Harkins, D.A., & Ray, S. (2004). An exploratory study of mother–child storytelling in east India and northeast United States. *Narrative Inquiry*, 14(2), 347–367.
Holmes, J. (2006). Workplace narratives, professional identity and relational practice. In A. De Fina, D. Schiffrin, & M. Bamberg (Eds.), *Discourse and identity* (pp. 166–187). Cambridge: Cambridge University Press.
Hymes, D. (1981). *"In vain I tried to tell you": Essays in Native American ethnopoetics*. Philadelphia: University of Pennsylvania Press.
Johnstone, B. (1990). *Stories, community and place: Narratives from middle America*. Bloomington: Indiana University Press.

Kiesling, S. (2006). Hegemonic identity-making in narrative. In A. De Fina, D. Schiffrin, & M. Bamberg (Eds.), *Discourse and identity* (pp. 261–287). Cambridge: Cambridge University Press.

Korhonen, T. (2014). Language narratives from adult upper secondary education: interrelating agency, autonomy and identity in foreign language learning. *Apples. Journal of Applied Language Studies*, 8(1), 65–87.

Koven, M. (2013). Speaking French in Portugal: An analysis of contested models of emigrant personhood in narratives about return migration and language use. *Journal of Sociolinguistics*, 17(3), 324–354.

Koven, M. (2015). Narrative and cultural identities: Performing and aligning with figures of personhood. In A. De Fina, & A. Georgakopoulou (Eds.), *Handbook of narrative analysis* (pp. 388–407). Oxford: Wiley Blackwell.

Labov, W. (1972). The transformation of experience in narrative syntax. In W. Labov (Ed.), *Language in the inner city: studies in the black English vernacular* (pp. 354–396). Philadelphia: University of Pennsylvania Press.

Labov, W., & Waletzky, J. (1967). Narrative analysis: oral versions of personal experience. In J. Helm (Ed.), *Essays on the verbal and visual arts* (pp. 12–44). Seattle: University of Washington Press.

Lave, J. & Wenger, E. (1991). *Situated learning: Legitimate peripheral participation*. Cambridge: Cambridge University Press.

Linde, C. (1993). *Life stories: The creation of coherence*. Oxford: Oxford University Press.

McAdams, D.P. (1993). *The stories we live by: Personal myths and the making of the self*. New York: William C. Morrow.

Maryns, K. (2005). Displacement and asylum seekers narratives. In M. Baynham, & A. De Fina (Eds.), *Dislocations/relocations: Narratives of displacement* (pp. 174–193). Manchester: St. Jerome Publishing.

Menard-Warwick, J. (2006). "The Thing About Work": Gendered Narratives of a transnational, trilingual Mexicano. *International Journal of Bilingual Education and Bilingualism*, 9, 359–415.

Michaels, S. (1981). "Sharing time": Children's narrative styles and differential access to literacy. *Language in Society*, 10(4), 423–442.

Miller, E.R. (2014). *The language of adult immigrants: Agency in the making*. Bristol: Multilingual Matters.

Miller, P.J., Wiley, A.R., Fung, H., & Liang, C.-H. (1997). Personal storytelling as a medium of socialization in Chinese and American families. *Child Development*, 68, 1557–1568.

Norton, B. (2000). *Identity and language learning: Gender, ethnicity, and educational change*. Harlow: Longman/Pearson.

Pavlenko, A. (2001). "In the world of the tradition I was unimagined": Negotiation of identities in cross-cultural autobiographies. *International Journal of Bilingualism*, 5(3), 317–344.

Piazza, R. (2014). "…might go to Birmingham, Leeds… up round there, Manchester … and then we always come back here …" The conceptualisation of place among a group of Irish women travellers. *Discourse & Society*, 25(2), 263–282.

Relaño Pastor, A. (2014). *Shame and pride in narrative: Mexican women's language experiences at the U.S.–Mexico Border*. Basingstoke: Palgrave McMillan.

Riessman, C.K. (1990). *Divorce talk. Women and men make sense of personal relationships*. New Brunswick, NJ: Rutgers University Press.

Rosaldo, R. (1993). *Meaning and truth: The remaking of social analysis*. Boston: Beacon Press.

Schiffrin, D. (1996). Narrative as self portrait: Sociolinguistic constructions of identity. *Language in society*, 25, 167–203.

Schumann, F.E., & Schumann, J.H. (1977). Diary of a language learner: An introspective study of second language learning. In H.D. Brown, R.H. Crymes, & C.A. Yorio (Eds.), *On*

TESOL '77: Teaching and Learning English as a Second Language: Trends in Research and Practice (pp. 241–249). Washington DC: TESOL.
Scollon, R., & Scollon, S. (1981). *Narrative, literacy, and face in interethnic communication.* Norwood, NJ: Ablex.
Scollon, R., Scollon, S., & Jones, R. (2012). *Intercultural communication: A discourse approach.* 3rd ed. Oxford: Wiley Blackwell.
White, J. (1987). *The content of the form: Narrative, discourse and historical representation.* Baltimore: Johns Hopkins University Press.

Further Reading and Resources

For an overview of main themes and approaches in narrative analysis see:
De Fina, A., & Georgakopoulou, A. (Eds.) (2015) *Handbook of narrative analysis.* Oxford: Wiley-Blackwell.
For a review of work on narrative in applied linguistics, see:
Barkhuizen, G. (Ed.). (2013). *Narrative Research in Applied Linguistics.* Cambridge: Cambridge University Press.
For a general discussion of William Labov's ground-breaking work on narrative see papers in:
Bamberg, M. (Ed.) (1997). Oral versions of personal experience: three decades of narrative analysis. Special Issue of *Journal of Narrative and Life History,* 7.

Index

access, 97–98, 155, 176, 185, 192
acquisition bias, 168
action research, 81
African American, 63, 330
African, 139
agency, 14–15, 42, 49, 50, 95, 144, 330, 337
American sign language, 64
American, 8, 10, 13, 54, 56, 57, 62, 63, 65, 226, 232, 240, 250, 304, 305, 317, 330
analytic observation, 304, 305, 306
Anglo, 65, 207
Anglo-Arab, 65
Anglo-centric, 89
Arab American, 57
Arabic, 65, 108, 109
Asante, Molefi Kete, 66
Asian, 108, 121, 139
Australian, 27, 105
autobiography of intercultural encounters, 130
auto-ethnography, 240, 244

Belgian, 226
Bergson, Henri, 136, 138
bias, 128, 129, 186, 198, 204, 206, 249, *see also* acquisition bias, insider bias
biography, 332, 333, *see also* auto-ethnography
bottom-up approach, 86, 262, 312, 314, 317, *see also* top-down approach
British English, 313
British, 40, 56, 99, 114, 141, 232, 288, 289, 290
Britishness, 290

Bulgarian, 94, 113
Byram, Michael, 121

categorization, 42, 44, 47, 50, 287, 288, 300, 304, 307, 320, 337, 338
category-bound activity, 300
Caucasian, 330
CCSARP project, 105, 212
census, 165, 170
Chinese, 14, 27, 104, 140, 215, 216, 232, 250, 304
co-construction, 28, 140, 141, 144, 229, 235, 335
coding, 84, 126, 153, 166, 191, 194, 233, 338
complimentarity, 177
computer-aided qualitative data analysis software (CAQDAS), 191, 193, 247
computer-mediated communication, 264
Confucianism, 23
constructionism, 12–13, 37, 38, 41–42, 50, 75
constructivism or constructivist, 6–12, 15, 17, 18, 23, 24, 25, 32, 33, 49, 75, 166, 177, 312
content analysis, 177, 178, 191, 233, 256
convenience sampling, 169
conversation analysis (CA), 25, 31, 41, 45, 47, 56, 57, 75, 256, 275, 297–310, 321
corpus linguistics, 310, 312, 319, 322, 323
corpus, 25, 274, 311–326, 333, 337
corpus-based intercultural studies, 313, 315
cosmopolitanism, 17, 24, 26, 28, 30, 33, 139

critical discourse analysis, 25, 27, 30, 32, 47, 57, 75, 106, 154, 281–296, 315
critical ethnography, 242–243
critical incident, 122, 223–238
critical paradigm, 3, 5, 6, 11–12, 15, 17
critical realism, 283, 285, 292
criticality, 136, 138, 142, 225, 235, 236
cross-cultural adaptation, 99, 225–226
cross-cultural comparison, 105, 227, 233, 330, 331
cross-cultural pragmatics, 89, 213
cross-cultural psychology, 4, 7
cross-linguistic difference, 215
cultural assimilator, 227
cultural
  keywords, 313, 315
  norm, 6, 7, 8, 15
  outsider, 107–112
  practice, 24, 29, 30, 31, 58, 104, 108, 239, 241, 304, 329, 331
  standard, 225, 229, 233
  values, 7, 17, 115, 223, 225, 233
  variation, 4

Danish, 330
data analysis, 156, 176–177, 191–192, 246–247
data display, 191
data generation, 95–97, 113
Deaf communities, 54, 57, 58, 59, 61–63, 64
demographic information, 167, 172, 178
dependent variable, 152
dialectic or dialectical, 282, 283–285, 286, 287, 288, 292
discourse analysis, 25, 27, 41, 54, 58–66, 106, 256, 281, 282, 291, 298, 312, 319, 321, 323
discourse prosody, 315–316, 323
discourse system, 54, 61
discourse, 12, 13, 15, 16, 53–71
discourse-centred online ethnography (DCOE), 262
Dutch, 226

ELAN, 275
elicited conversation, 221
elicited narrative, 332, 333, 335, 337
emic, 83, 155, 245, 246, 247–248, 299, 331
epistemological, 5, 6, 17, 41, 50, 76, 166, 168, 271, 283, 286, 291, 292, 298, 323
e-portfolio, 128
essentialism, 28, 38–40, 50, 287

ethics, 74, 83, 86, 89, 92, 95–98, 101, 114–117, 136, 191, 216, 275
ethnographic analysis, 272
ethnography of communication or ethnography of speaking, 9, 55
ethnography, 25, 75, 110, 154, 239–251, 272, 273, 328 *see also* virtual ethnography
ethnomethodology, 299, 307
etic perspective, 155, 247, 320
evaluation booklet, 198, 200–204, 209
experimental research, 25, 171
experimental stimuli, 167, 197, 198, 199–204, 209
external validity, 150, 154, 157, 159
extremism, 281, 286–291

facebook, 99, 259, 260–265
facilitation, 177
feminist ethnography, 243
field notes, 29, 110, 156, 191, 216, 245, 246, 248–251, 256, 259, 272, 274, 321
field, 259, 265, 271, 284, 285
fieldwork, 91, 93, 241, 243, 244, 245, 249, 251, 260, 262
Finnish, 137, 139, 141, 142
Flanagan, John, 223–224, 227–228, 231
focus group, 31, 75, 80, 96, 143, 151, 182, 194, 229, 244, 245–246, 261
format design, 171–175
French, 96, 141, 151, 184, 198, 207, 229, 292, 312
frequency, 182, 233, 263, 314, 315, 316, 317

Garfinkel, Harold, 299, 300, 307
generalizability, 39, 150, 169, 170, 171, 176, 179, 186, 235
German, 94, 106, 215, 225
Goffman, Erving, 45, 54, 55, 60, 61
Greek, 65, 240, 262, 330
grounded theory, 184, 189, 194, 245, 249, 256

habitus, 104, 284
Hall, Edward T., 8, 54
Halliday, Michael, 56
Hindu, 141
Hine, Christine, 256, 257, 258, 259, 264
HISTORY model, 53, 54, 62–63
holistic, 18, 45, 50, 80, 132, 153, 244, 247, 248, 258

Hong Kong, 151, 250, 251, 321
Hymes, Dell, 9, 53, 54, 55, 57, 58–60, 66, 242, 250, 270, 330
hyperethnography, 243
hypothesis, 74, 86, 152, 177, 182, 338

identity and culture, 12, 47–49, 144
identity, 37–52, 28, 138, 261, 262, 274, 290, 300, 303, 331–334, 335–337
  as brought about, 104
  as brought along, 104
  cultural, 13, 14, 15, 31, 37–52, 85, 183, 184, 312, 313, 319, 320, 321, 323
  ethnic identity, 14, 78, 331
  marker, 284, 287, 289
  national, 97, 331
  social, 44, 45, 50, 197, 261
  youth, 208
ideology, 17, 24, 25, 33, 39, 61, 62, 282–283, *see also* language ideology
INCA (Intercultural Competence Assessment), 130
independent variable, 152, 204, 302
Indian, 108, 226
inductive research, 298
insider bias, 107
interactional sociolinguistics, 4, 47, 56, 302
intercultural
  awareness, 27
  competence, 29, 31, 113, 120–133, 149, 170, 178, 182, 191, 230, 231, 242
  consciousness, 291
  dialogue, 57, 291
  differences, 12–13, 17, 64
  discourse, 53, 54, 57
  education, 4
  effectiveness, 85, 175
  ethics, 177
  interaction, 11, 217, 226–227
  learning, 120, 128, 151, 248
  miscommunication, 56, 316
  moments, 305, 306
  pragmatics, 4, 7
  reflection, 156
  responsibility, 113
  sensitivity, 149
  sensitizer, 227, 233
interculturality, 13, 136, 138, 140, 141, 142, 144, 298, 302, 303, 304–305, 306, 307
interdiscursivity, 285, 286, 287, 288, 292
intergroup relation, 321, 329
internal validity, 154, 159

interpretative paradigm, 3, 8–11, 15
interpreter, 64, 78, 89, 92, 95, 96, 101, 185
interpretivism, 5, 12
intersubjectivity, 298, 300, 301
interview, 25, 48, 55, 58, 95, 97, 116, 122, 126, 167, 170, 177, 178, 198, 206, 220, 221, 225, 228–229, 231, 232, 233, 234, 235, 244, 245, 246, 247, 248, 250, 256, 261, 262, 264, 272, 320, 321, 322, 323, 328, 332, 333, 335–339
Irish English, 313
Irish, 261, 262, 263, 313
Islamism or Islamist, 137, 141, 282, 286, 287, 288, 289, 290
Israeli, 142, 151, 250, 251, 321
Italian sign language, 64
Italian, 96, 99, 130
item sequence, 173
item type, 173

Japanese, 13, 65, 303, 304, 306, 316, 318, 321
Jewish, 63, 113, 316, 330

Keywords, 317, 324
Kress, Gunther, 269, 270, 271, 277, 278

Labov, William, 38, 53, 54, 56, 58, 60, 61, 66, 328, 336, 337
Lambert, Wallace, 198, 205–206, 208
language and identity, 38, 50
language attitude, 196, 197–198, 201, 204, 205, 206, 207, 208, 209
language ideology, 57
language policy, 208, 261, 262, 263
Laplantine, François, 136
Latin American, 86
learning contracts, 127
linguistic anthropology, 4, 53, 54, 57, 58, 66
linguistic landscape, 263
longitudinal study, 122, 153, 177, 248

Maffesoli, Michel, 141
Malaysian, 108
membership categorization analysis (MCA), 45, 287, 300, 307
methodological individualism, 141
methodological nationalism, 31, 138, 141, 144
mixed-method, 75, 76, 126, 149, 153, 156, 165, 168, 171, 177, 178, 255, 258, 268, 277

modal affordance, 270, 279
modality, 269–270
mode, 10, 269–272, 275, 276, 277, 278
model of discourse, 58–63, 66
multiculturalism, 137, 168, 281, 286–291
multilingualism, 4, 89, 94, 96, 262, 263
multimodality, 269–279, 311, 314, 318, 324
   ensemble, 271, 273, 276, 279
   transcription, 274–275
multiple methods, 232, 244, 246, 248

narrative analysis, 42, 54, 60–66, 154, 256, 327–339
narrative, 25, 29, 30, 32, 33, 41, 42, 54, 60–66, 113, 149, 156, 183, 193, 229, 246, 277, 286
nationalism, 27, 31
naturally occurring, 40, 41, 55, 212, 214, 215, 216, 221, 240, 305, 307, 328, 335, 337
neoracism, 32, 34
new media, 262, 268
New Zealand sign language, 64, 59, 61
New Zealand, 16, 54, 58, 59, 61, 62–65, 108, 335
Nishizaka, Aug, 303
non-probability sampling, 155, 169, 170

objectivist, 166
observation, 83, 92, 97, 122, 126, 148, 154, 155, 219, 228, 229, 231–232, 246, 248, 249, 250, 251, 261–262, 271, 300, 304, 321
online culture, 256, 261, 264
ontology, 5, 6, 17, 18, 38, 79, 166, 167, 168, 283, 312, 322, 323
oral DCT (Discourse Completion Task), 214, 215, 220, 221
order of discourse, 284, 285, 292
othering, 29, 108, 140, 141, 143, 144, 288, 280

Pakistani, 108, 141, 94
participant observation, 75, 105, 109–110, 244, 245, 248, 249, 250, 251, 261, 329
periphery, 28
phenomenology, 75, 184
Polish, 28
population, 150, 154, 155, 159, 166–167, 169–171, 179

poststructuralism, 282, 283, 286, 291, 292, 307
power differential, 186–187
pragmalinguistics, 212, 213, 217, 318
probability sampling, 169
prompt, 193, 229, 230–231, 234, *see also* situational prompt
positivism, 5, 6, 38–39, 49, 166
postpositivism, 5, 6
power, 6, 8, 11, 12, 14, 17, 18, 42, 44, 49, 50, 55, 57, 61, 63, 64, 66, 89, 106, 108, 139, 140, 141, 142, 143, 144, 171, 185, 201, 206, 216, 235, 242, 243, 278, 282, 283, 284, 287, 292, 299, 322
paradigm, 3–19, 23, 24, 26, 30, 32, 33, 37, 39, 40, 45, 132, 137, 138, 153, 165, 178, 198, 208, 209, 224, 302, 332
postmodernism, 5, 23, 24, 32, 33, 137, 292, 333

qualitative, 74, 126, 127, 150, 152, 153, 154, 155, 156, 166, 174, 177, 178, 182, 186, 187, 191, 193, 202, 219, 240, 245, 246, 247, 250, 256, 261, 312, 314, 319, 320, 321, 322, 323, 324, 328, 332, 338, 339
quantitative, 39, 54, 74, 75, 84, 86, 125, 126, 127, 150, 152, 153, 154, 155, 156, 166, 171, 173, 174, 176, 177, 178, 182, 187, 202, 219, 247, 248, 256, 311, 312, 314, 320, 321, 323, 332, 339
questionnaire administration, 175–176
questionnaire, 39, 84–85, 116, 154, 156, 158, 165–179, 182, 184, 187, 193, 194, 198, 206, 207, 208, 209, 213, 214, 215, 216, 220, 228, 229–230, 232, 235, 256, 262, 263, 302, 323
quota sampling, 169, 170

racism, 104, 136, 137, 287
record sheet, 228, 230, 234
reflective prompt, 91–100
reflexivity, 88, 93, 101, 110, 113, 135, 136, 138, 140, 142, 143, 144, 145, 244, 245, 247, 250, 298
rejoinder, 213, 216
replication, 151, 154
research design, 5, 6, 76, 90, 95, 104, 108, 111, 112, 138, 150, 153–154, 159, 171
research proposal, 147–160
researching multilingually, 88–101
retrospective questionnaire, 220

role play, 215, 220, 221
Russian, 137
Russian-American, 305

Sacks, Harvey, 41, 45, 229, 330
sample size, 150, 155, 166, 170–171, 176, 179, 187, 235
Sampling, 159, 185, 186, *also see* convenience sampling, probability sampling, non-probability sampling, snowball sampling
Scollon, Ron, 56, 61, 64, 106, 110, 287, 302, 330, 331
Scollon, Suzanne Wong, 56, 61, 106, 110, 287, 302, 330, 331
segmented-dialogue technique, 208
semiosis, 283, 284
semiotic mode, 270, 285, 288, 314
semi-structured interview, 177, 178, 182, 184, 194
Sen, Amartya, 136, 139, 140, 141
Sinclair, John, 315
Singapore, 85
Sino-British, 232
situational prompt, 213, 215, 216, 217
small culture, 24, 29, 30, 34
snowball sampling, 169
social action, 24, 31, 33, 106, 248, 273, 298, 307
social constructionism, 13, 38, 41, 42, 207
social identity theory, 44–45, 50
social network site (SNS), 261
social psychology of language, 197, 198, 206
social semiotics, 272
sociolinguistics, 4, 17, 37, 38, 39, 41, 42, 44, 47, 50, 54, 56, 197, 206, 242, 328, 335
solidarity, 16, 61, 62, 201, 202, 207
Somali, 137
Spanish, 94, 104, 105, 107, 111, 112, 313, 317
speaker evaluation paradigm, 198, 199, 208, 209
SPEAKING model, 53, 54, 58–60, 66
speech act, 105, 212, 215
speech perception experiment, 197, 198, 209

structure, 328, 329, 330, 331, 332, 336, 337, 339
Stubbs, Michael, 313, 315, 323
subjectivity, 12, 33, 144, 323, 328, 334, *see also* intersubjectivity
survey, 39, 122, 126, 127, 129, 132, 153, 154, 155, 156, 157, 166–179, 184, 248, 261, 323

Taiwan, 149
Thai, 62
theatre-audience technique, 208
thematic analysis, 232, 233, 334, 335
thick description, 8, 26, 33, 256
top-down approach, 302, 312, 314, 315, 317, *see also* bottom-up approach
transcription software, 156, 189, 191, 193
transcription, 189, 192, 215, 258, 274, 275, 276, 301, 304, 338
translation studies, 4, 89, 312, 318
translation, 5, 78, 96, 99–100, 168, 189, 197, 275
transnationalism, 17
triangulation, 156, 177, 206, 209, 246, 314
Turkish, 65, 97, 98, 106

unstructured interview, 182, 183, 187, 188, 246
Urdu, 91

verbal-guise technique, 208
video recording, 184, 188, 192, 232, 246, 268, 271, 272, 274–275, 299, 301, 305
virtual ethnography, 242, 243, 255–265
visual ethnography, 242, 243
variable, 7, 18, 25, 26, 150, 152, 154, 155, 159, 199, 194, 199, 202, 204, 205, 208, 209, 215, 224, 230, 249, 302
validity, 18, 26, 33, 39, 40, 49, 127, 133, 150, 154, 155, 157, 166, 168, 172, 179, 186, 213, 214, 216, 217, 220, 233, 235, 249, 250

Weber, Max, 141
white supremacism, 281, 287, 290

Printed and bound by CPI Group (UK) Ltd, Croydon, CR0 4YY
28/10/2021
03089410-0001